# COLIN COWDREY IN TEST CRICKET

# Colin Cowdrey
## IN TEST CRICKET

**Bernard Black**

**BB**
Waterlooville, Hants

Copyright © Bernard Black 2005

First published 2005

Published by BB, 22 Lynwood Avenue, Waterlooville, Hampshire PO8 8PZ.

ISBN 0 9549517 0 0

All rights reserved.
No part of this publication may be reproduced or transmitted in any form or by any means, electronic or mechanical, including photocopy, recording or any information storage and retrieval system, without permission in writing from the publisher.

*Cover photographs: Getty Images*

Book design and production for the publisher by
Bookprint Creative Services, P.O. Box 827, BN21 3YJ, England.
Printed in Great Britain.

*To*
# Bob

# CONTENTS

|     | Acknowledgements | 9 |
|---|---|---|
|     | Introduction | 11 |
| 1.  | Australia 1954/55 | 14 |
| 2.  | In New Zealand 1955 | 24 |
| 3.  | South Africa 1955 | 27 |
| 4.  | Australia 1956 | 34 |
| 5.  | South Africa 1956/57 | 43 |
| 6.  | West Indies 1957 | 50 |
| 7.  | New Zealand 1958 | 57 |
| 8.  | Australia 1958/59 | 64 |
| 9.  | In New Zealand 1959 | 72 |
| 10. | India 1959 | 75 |
| 11. | West Indies 1959/60 | 84 |
| 12. | South Africa 1960 | 92 |
| 13. | Australia 1961 | 102 |
| 14. | Pakistan | 110 |
| 15. | Australia 1962/63 | 117 |
| 16. | In New Zealand 1963 | 124 |
| 17. | West Indies 1963 | 129 |
| 18. | India 1963/64 | 136 |
| 19. | Australia 1964 | 143 |
| 20. | New Zealand 1965 | 152 |
| 21. | South Africa 1965 | 157 |
| 22. | Australia 1965/66 | 162 |
| 23. | In New Zealand 1966 | 169 |
| 24. | West Indies 1966 | 173 |

| | | |
|---|---|---|
| 25. | Pakistan 1967 | 181 |
| 26. | West Indies 1967/68 | 185 |
| 27. | Australia 1968 | 192 |
| 28. | Pakistan 1968/69 | 200 |
| 29. | Australia 1970/71 | 206 |
| 30. | In New Zealand 1971 | 214 |
| 31. | Pakistan 1971 | 217 |
| 32. | Australia 1974/75 | 221 |
| | Statistical Summary | 230 |
| | Epilogue | 234 |
| | Index | 236 |

# ACKNOWLEDGEMENTS

With thanks to Ian Crabtree and Stewart Whyte.

Test cricket scorecards in this book are reproduced from *The Wisden Book of Test Cricket 1876–77 to 1977–78*, Editor – Bill Frindall, by kind permission of Hodder Headline.

Every effort has been made to trace current copyright holders of photographs appearing in this book, and the publisher apologises where it has not been possible to trace all of them. Cover photographs and those appearing on pages 16, 51, 76, 145 and 193 are reproduced by permission of Getty Images; the photograph on page 18 is reproduced by permission of AP/Wide World Photos.

# INTRODUCTION

This book is about what it says it is – Colin Cowdrey in Test cricket.

Any reader who wants to read about that can proceed straight away to any chapter each of which is, chronologically, devoted to a Test series in which Cowdrey played. Any reader who wants to read about peripheral matters must look elsewhere. It is a view of a cricket-loving spectator. Inevitably there is more about those matches I was able to attend than the others. Much relies on television viewing. I must, however, acknowledge the reliance I have had on the recollections and records of others who had first hand knowledge, particularly of all the overseas series none of which I saw personally.

For the record Michael Colin Cowdrey was born on Christmas Eve 1932 in Bangalore, India. His father, who gave him the names with the initials very much in his mind, was in the locality.

In a very real sense therefore Colin Cowdrey in Test cricket started from the moment he was born. In another it began with an announcement over the 6 o'clock news in the late summer of 1954 of the party to tour Australia during the ensuing winter. In a note written to Colin when he heard this book was being written, a Professor at the Royal College of Music, captured the moment thus:

> As an old friend of the family, I was privileged to be present when Colin first heard that he was to play for England. I was sitting with Colin's father, Ernest, watching the closing overs of a Kent match[1] when, at six o'clock, Colin, who

---

1. Kent v. Surrey at Blackheath on July 27 1954. The match was drawn after the loss of the second day due to rain. Cowdrey made 19 of Kent's 202 in reply to Surrey's 387. His dismissal

was already out, joined us in the car, from which we were watching the game. We switched on the car radio for the six o'clock news, and, having listened to a lot of news, which must have been consequential at the time, we heard the announcer say "Cricket – here are the names of those chosen for the forthcoming tour of Australia". I cannot say what was in the minds of Ernest and Colin; in mine was a high degree of guarded hope. But I do know their reactions when the name M. C. Cowdrey was announced. Ernest's face lit up with very understandable paternal pride; for him, it was the fulfilment of an ambition which started when he chose the names Michael Colin for the new-born son, to give him the initials M.C.C. Colin's reaction was typical of him. In a voice which couldn't fail to show his excitement, albeit suppressed, he modestly said "But there are several others who deserve it before me". These characteristics of self-control and modesty set the seal on the whole of his Test career. When you know him as well as I do, you will know that, underneath that quiet, self-effacing exterior, there is always a mixture of burning enthusiasm and determination, which also mark his play. What else could account for that marathon partnership with Peter May against the West Indies at Edgbaston, which alas I was not able to see.

It is right and proper that a book is being written about Cowdrey's test career, for I am certain that it will read like a tense thriller, if for no other reason that it will contain moments of disappointment, among the peaks of happiness. But it will read also, as a reading of his character, for this man is one who lives his life according to the rule book – he not only "walks" when he knows he is out, but I can vouch for the fact that he walks away from things which, in his heart, do not measure to his standards.

In due course Cowdrey found himself on the boat to Australia recalling how his father had awoken him as a child in 1938 to watch another ship pass in the night, emphasising that Don Bradman was aboard that one, bringing the Australian touring team to England.

Cowdrey was sent home to England from India at the age of five. He went to Homefield Preparatory School, Sutton where Charles Walford was headmaster, before moving to Tonbridge, where he spent five years in the 1st XI.

---

Footnote 1 *continued*
c Lock b Laker, who took 3 for 56 and 7 for 83 respectively, rather emphasised his initial reaction to omissions in the touring party.

In the first of those he became the youngest – and probably the smallest – to play at Lord's scoring 75 and 44 against Clifton and taking eight wickets. In his last year at school he scored 1,033 at an average of 79.

As a freshman in Brasenose College, Oxford in 1952 he won a cricket blue and in 1953 scored 116 against Cambridge and finished 1954, the year in which he captained Oxford, by being chosen, when still only 21, to make the first of what became six tours of Australia. He had not made a championship century. It was a case of the selectors backing evident class. He was the youngest member of the touring party.

Sadly, when Colin landed in Australia in 1954, waiting for him, at the England team's hotel in Perth, was a cable telling him that his father had died. Ernest Cowdrey had heard the news of his son's undefeated 66 in the match en route to Australia in Colombo. Hurrying to make a note of the details he had a heart attack and died. Born in the same year as my own father he died aged 54.

Chapter 1
# AUSTRALIA 1954/55

Colin Cowdrey in Test cricket began at Brisbane in the 1954/55 series. It was anything but an encouraging start for England. Hutton had won the toss and put Australia in. England were still fielding as lunch was taken on the Monday. Cowdrey's main fear during his early days in the test match arena was of dropping a catch. In that respect he made a good start. He caught both the opening batsmen Morris and Favell. The first saw Favell swinging hard at a ball from Statham which rose shoulder high, touched it with his glove and Cowdrey at short fine leg took the catch near his boot tops. Ian Peebles wrote "Though in fact the ball travelled quite gently, it was a very good catch as the fieldsman in such cases is usually ducking, and not without very good reason." Unfortunately Arthur Morris had made 153[1] before he was out caught, flicking at one from Bailey, at first slip. Australia eventually declared at 601 for 8. Dropped catches were a feature of this long innings. When Cowdrey badly missed Ian Johnson in the gully, the chances missed reached double figures and more were missed before the declaration came.

The visitors only hope was a draw. It was a forlorn one. They were dismissed for 190 and 257 to lose by an innings and 154 runs. Australia had more than a day to spare. The tactic of fielding first with four fast bowlers had been an unmitigated disaster. Again Cowdrey made a good start scoring 40 in his first innings in Test cricket. In partnership with Bailey he had added 82. Sadly he only achieved every batsman's second target in his second.

In the second Test at Sydney Morris put England into bat. This time the

---

1. I was feeling rather proud in 1954 having made 153*. Although that was at the 'Bat & Ball' County Ground Gravesend (which Cowdrey described as "one of the fastest-scoring grounds in the world"), it was for their second XI against Wilmington.

*31 December 1954: Cowdrey drives Lindwall during his masterly maiden Test hundred. Head and position of feet show how he stayed sideways through the hitting area of the stroke.*

spearhead of England's fast attack, Tyson, was successful taking ten wickets for 130 in the match. Cowdrey made his first Test fifty scoring 54 in the second innings and a useful 23 in a low scoring match in the first. The partnership between May and Cowdrey in the second innings began eight minutes before lunch and was not broken until just after five o'clock. Between lunch and tea the pair added 71 runs. Then they carried the rally to 171 before Cowdrey, possibly disturbed by the fact that he had made only a single in half-an-hour, lofted Benaud to deep mid-off to be caught by Archer. This disappointing end did not alter the fact in retrospect that the stand had been one of the crucial factors in winning the series.

*Colin hooks Australian Ron Archer on his way to his first test century in the 3rd Test at Melbourne in 1954.*

The third Test at Melbourne produced what was to be regarded as the best innings of Cowdrey's career. England lost four wickets in reaching 41. Their total was only 191 of which Cowdrey made 102. I had recently acquired a portable wireless and was listening in bed in the early hours. In my excitement as Cowdrey ran three to reach his maiden test century, I knocked the radio out of the bed. By the time I had got it working again he was out to a freak ball from Ian Johnson. One of many recollections I have received about this innings came from W. J. "Bill" Edrich who wrote:

> My happiest memory is of Colin's great century during the third test at Melbourne during which he clearly showed that he was on the threshold of a great Test career. He really did play magnificently with all the artistry and perfect timing which were to become so much part of the English Test scene over the years to come. In spite of his great success he has always remained the quiet, softly spoken gentleman who has endeared himself to the cricket scene the world over, and it gives me great pleasure to pay this small tribute to a great Test cricketer and a wonderful man.

It was another success for Tyson too. Many thought that the initiative would rest with Appleyard and Wardle in Australia's second innings. In the event Tyson took 7 for 27. England who had been one down were one up.

The series was secured in the fourth test at Adelaide. Cowdrey made 79 in the first innings. During that innings Cowdrey attempted to increase the scoring rate with shots he had not previously attempted during a Test innings. Hutton used the old device of sending out Vic Wilson, the twelfth man, ostensibly with a change of bat. In fact it was to urge caution and offer bananas to meet Cowdrey's already famous appetite. He then had the misfortune to break his nose fielding close to Arthur Morris. England only required 94 to win the match in their second innings but although Cowdrey's eyes were black and almost closed, Hutton stipulated that he bat in his normal position. He was one of four failures before victory was assured.

It was about this time that I had written to Cowdrey to invite him to be Guest of Honour at the dinner of Northend CC[2]. I still have the typed letter indicating that he would like to do so but would have to do his National

---

2. A side comprising players from Northfleet and Gravesend.

*Colin's first tour. His pivotal hook off Benaud brings four runs at Adelaide in the fourth Test against Australia in 1955. He made 79.*

Service on his return. He indicated in the letter that they were going all out for a win in the final Test despite having already won the series. In fact torrential rain confined England to only one innings in a draw. Cowdrey's contribution was his first duck in Test cricket. Cowdrey was already known to be at his best when facing a challenge. When he came in the scoreboard was reading 188 for 2. It brought his average down to a misleading figure of 35 for the series.

|  | Matches | Innings | Not out | Runs | Highest score | Average | 100s | 50s | Caught |
|---|---|---|---|---|---|---|---|---|---|
| This series | 5 | 9 | 0 | 319 | 102 | 35.44 | 1 | 2 | 4 |

Test No. 391/164

# AUSTRALIA v ENGLAND 1954-55 (1st Test)

Played at Woolloongabba, Brisbane, on 26, 27, 29, 30 November, 1 December.
Toss: England. Result: AUSTRALIA won by an innings and 154 runs.
Debuts: Australia – L.E. Favell; England – K.V. Andrew, M.C. Cowdrey.

Hutton was the first England captain to put the opposition in to bat in Australia since J.W.H.T. Douglas (1911-12) and Australia's total was the highest in response to this action in a Test match. England took the field without a slow bowler for only the second time (also *Test No. 221*). Compton fractured a bone in his left hand on the fencing while fielding.

## AUSTRALIA

| | | |
|---|---|---|
| L.E. Favell | c Cowdrey b Statham | 23 |
| A.R. Morris | c Cowdrey b Bailey | 153 |
| K.R. Miller | b Bailey | 49 |
| R.N. Harvey | c Bailey b Bedser | 162 |
| G.B. Hole | run out | 57 |
| R. Benaud | c May b Tyson | 34 |
| R.G. Archer | c Bedser b Statham | 0 |
| R.R. Lindwall | not out | 64 |
| G.R.A. Langley† | b Bailey | 16 |
| I.W. Johnson* | not out | 24 |
| W.A. Johnston | did not bat | |
| Extras | (B 11, LB 7, NB 1) | 19 |
| **Total** | **(8 wickets declared)** | **601** |

## ENGLAND

| | | | | | |
|---|---|---|---|---|---|
| L. Hutton* | c Langley b Lindwall | 4 | lbw b Miller | | 13 |
| R.T. Simpson | b Miller | 2 | run out | | 9 |
| W.J Edrich | c Langley b Archer | 15 | b Johnston | | 88 |
| P.B.H May | b Lindwall | 1 | lbw b Lindwall | | 44 |
| M.C. Cowdrey | c Hole b Johnston | 40 | b Benaud | | 10 |
| T.E. Bailey | b Johnston | 88 | c Langley b Lindwall | | 23 |
| F.H. Tyson | b Johnson | 7 | not out | | 37 |
| A.V. Bedser | b Johnson | 5 | c Archer b Johnson | | 5 |
| K.V. Andrew† | b Lindwall | 6 | b Johnson | | 5 |
| J.B. Statham | b Johnson | 11 | (11) c Harvey b Benaud | | 14 |
| D.C.S. Compton | not out | 2 | (10) c Langley b Benaud | | 0 |
| Extras | (B 3, LB 6) | 9 | (B 7, LB 2) | | 9 |
| **Total** | | **190** | | | **257** |

| ENGLAND | O | M | R | W | O | M | R | W | | FALL OF WICKETS | | |
|---|---|---|---|---|---|---|---|---|---|---|---|---|
| | | | | | | | | | | A | E | E |
| Bedser | 37 | 4 | 131 | 1 | | | | | Wkt | 1st | 1st | 2nd |
| Statham | 34 | 2 | 123 | 2 | | | | | 1st | 51 | 4 | 22 |
| Tyson | 29 | 1 | 160 | 1 | | | | | 2nd | 123 | 10 | 23 |
| Bailey | 26 | 1 | 140 | 3 | | | | | 3rd | 325 | 11 | 147 |
| Edrich | 3 | 0 | 28 | 0 | | | | | 4th | 456 | 25 | 163 |
| AUSTRALIA | | | | | | | | | 5th | 463 | 107 | 181 |
| Lindwall | 14 | 4 | 27 | 3 | 17 | 3 | 50 | 2 | 6th | 464 | 132 | 220 |
| Miller | 11 | 5 | 19 | 1 | 12 | 2 | 30 | 1 | 7th | 545 | 141 | 231 |
| Archer | 4 | 1 | 14 | 1 | 15 | 4 | 28 | 0 | 8th | 572 | 156 | 242 |
| Johnson | 19 | 5 | 46 | 3 | 17 | 5 | 38 | 2 | 9th | – | 181 | 243 |
| Benaud | 12 | 5 | 28 | 0 | 8·1 | 1 | 43 | 3 | 10th | – | 190 | 257 |
| Johnston | 16·1 | 5 | 47 | 2 | 21 | 8 | 59 | 1 | | | | |

Umpires: M.J. McInnes and C. Hoy.

Test No. 392/165

# AUSTRALIA v ENGLAND 1954–55 (2nd Test)

Played at Sydney Cricket Ground on 17, 18, 20, 21, 22 December.
Toss: Australia. Result: ENGLAND won by 38 runs.
Debuts: Nil.

Tyson, having been knocked unconscious by a Lindwall bouncer, bowled with great speed and stamina to win a palpitating victory for England. He was only the fourth fast bowler this century to take ten wickets in an England v Australia Test – Larwood, Farnes and Voce being the others. Statham, bowling into a very strong wind, gave him splendid support.

### ENGLAND

| | | | | |
|---|---|---|---|---|
| L. Hutton* | c Davidson b Johnston | 30 | c Benaud b Johnston | 28 |
| T.E. Bailey | b Lindwall | 0 | c Langley b Archer | 6 |
| P.B.H. May | c Johnston b Archer | 5 | b Lindwall | 104 |
| T.W. Graveney | c Favell b Johnston | 21 | c Langley b Johnston | 0 |
| M.C. Cowdrey | c Langley b Davidson | 23 | c Archer b Benaud | 54 |
| W.J. Edrich | c Benaud b Archer | 10 | b Archer | 29 |
| F.H. Tyson | b Lindwall | 0 | b Lindwall | 9 |
| T.G. Evans† | c Langley b Archer | 3 | c Lindwall b Archer | 4 |
| J.H. Wardle | c Burke b Johnson | 35 | lbw b Lindwall | 8 |
| R. Appleyard | c Hole b Davidson | 8 | not out | 19 |
| J.B. Statham | not out | 14 | c Langley b Johnston | 25 |
| Extras | (LB 5) | 5 | (LB 6, NB 4) | 10 |
| **Total** | | **154** | | **296** |

### AUSTRALIA

| | | | | |
|---|---|---|---|---|
| L.E. Favell | c Graveney b Bailey | 26 | c Edrich b Tyson | 16 |
| A.R. Morris* | c Hutton b Bailey | 12 | lbw b Statham | 10 |
| J.W. Burke | c Graveney b Bailey | 44 | b Tyson | 14 |
| R.N. Harvey | c Cowdrey b Tyson | 12 | not out | 92 |
| G.B. Hole | b Tyson | 12 | b Tyson | 0 |
| R. Denaud | lbw b Statham | 20 | c Tyson b Appleyard | 12 |
| R.G. Archer | c Hutton b Tyson | 49 | b Tyson | 6 |
| A.K. Davidson | b Statham | 20 | c Evans b Statham | 5 |
| R.R. Lindwall | c Evans b Tyson | 19 | b Tyson | 8 |
| G.R.A. Langley† | b Bailey | 5 | b Statham | 0 |
| W.A. Johnston | not out | 0 | c Evans b Tyson | 11 |
| Extras | (B 5, LB 2, NB 2) | 9 | (LB 7, NB 3) | 10 |
| **Total** | | **228** | | **184** |

| AUSTRALIA | O | M | R | W | O | M | R | W |
|---|---|---|---|---|---|---|---|---|
| Lindwall | 17 | 3 | 47 | 2 | 31 | 10 | 69 | 3 |
| Archer | 12 | 7 | 12 | 3 | 22 | 9 | 53 | 3 |
| Davidson | 12 | 3 | 34 | 2 | 13 | 2 | 52 | 0 |
| Johnston | 13.3 | 1 | 56 | 3 | 19.3 | 2 | 70 | 3 |
| Benaud | | | | | 19 | 3 | 42 | 1 |
| AUSTRALIA | | | | | | | | |
| Statham | 18 | 1 | 83 | 2 | 19 | 6 | 45 | 3 |
| Bailey | 17.4 | 3 | 59 | 4 | 6 | 0 | 21 | 0 |
| Tyson | 13 | 2 | 45 | 4 | 18.4 | 1 | 85 | 6 |
| Appleyard | 7 | 1 | 32 | 0 | 6 | 1 | 12 | 1 |
| Wardle | | | | | 4 | 2 | 11 | 0 |

FALL OF WICKETS

| Wkt | E 1st | A 1st | E 2nd | A 2nd |
|---|---|---|---|---|
| 1st | 14 | 18 | 18 | 27 |
| 2nd | 19 | 65 | 55 | 34 |
| 3rd | 58 | 100 | 55 | 77 |
| 4th | 63 | 104 | 171 | 77 |
| 5th | 84 | 122 | 222 | 102 |
| 6th | 85 | 141 | 232 | 122 |
| 7th | 88 | 193 | 239 | 127 |
| 8th | 99 | 213 | 249 | 136 |
| 9th | 111 | 224 | 250 | 145 |
| 10th | 154 | 228 | 296 | 184 |

Umpires: M.J. McInnes and R. Wright.

Test No. 393/166

# AUSTRALIA v ENGLAND 1954-55 (3rd Test)

Played at Melbourne Cricket Ground on 31 December, 1, 3, 4, 5 January.
Toss: England.   Result: ENGLAND won by 128 runs.
Debuts: Australia – L.V. Maddocks.

Cowdrey, the fiftieth England batsman to score a hundred against Australia, made his runs out of the lowest total to contain a century in this series to share that record with Bradman (103* out of 191 in 1932-33 – *Test No. 221*). Australia's last eight second-innings wickets fell for 36 runs, Tyson taking 6 for 16 in 51 balls to finish with an exceptional analysis for a fast bowler in this long series.

## ENGLAND

| | | | | | |
|---|---|---|---|---|---|
| L. Hutton* | c Hole b Miller | 12 | lbw b Archer | | 42 |
| W.J. Edrich | c Lindwall b Miller | 4 | b Johnston | | 13 |
| P.B.H. May | c Benaud b Lindwall | 0 | b Johnston | | 91 |
| M.C. Cowdrey | b Johnson | 102 | b Benaud | | 7 |
| D.C.S. Compton | c Harvey b Miller | 14 | c Maddocks b Archer | | 23 |
| T.E. Bailey | c Maddocks b Johnston | 30 | not out | | 24 |
| T.G. Evans† | lbw b Archer | 20 | c Maddocks b Miller | | 22 |
| J.H. Wardle | b Archer | 0 | b Johnson | | 38 |
| F.H. Tyson | b Archer | 6 | c Harvey b Johnston | | 6 |
| J.B. Statham | b Archer | 3 | c Favell b Johnston | | 0 |
| R. Appleyard | not out | 1 | b Johnston | | 6 |
| Extras | (B 9) | 9 | (B 2, LB 4, W 1) | | 7 |
| **Total** | | **191** | | | **279** |

## AUSTRALIA

| | | | | | |
|---|---|---|---|---|---|
| L.E. Favell | lbw b Statham | 25 | b Appleyard | | 30 |
| A.R. Morris | lbw b Tyson | 3 | c Cowdrey b Tyson | | 4 |
| K.R. Miller | c Evans b Statham | 7 | (5) c Edrich b Tyson | | 6 |
| R.N. Harvey | b Appleyard | 31 | c Evans b Tyson | | 11 |
| G.B. Hole | b Tyson | 11 | (6) c Evans b Statham | | 5 |
| R. Benaud | c sub (J.V. Wilson) b Appleyard | 15 | (3) b Tyson | | 22 |
| R.G. Archer | b Wardle | 23 | b Statham | | 15 |
| L.V. Maddocks† | c Evans b Statham | 47 | b Tyson | | 0 |
| R.R. Lindwall | b Statham | 13 | lbw b Tyson | | 0 |
| I.W. Johnson* | not out | 33 | not out | | 4 |
| W.A. Johnston | b Statham | 11 | c Evans b Tyson | | 0 |
| Extras | (B 7, LB 3, NB 2) | 12 | (B 1, LB 13) | | 14 |
| **Total** | | **231** | | | **111** |

| AUSTRALIA | O | M | R | W | O | M | R | W | FALL OF WICKETS | | | | |
|---|---|---|---|---|---|---|---|---|---|---|---|---|---|
| Lindwall | 13 | 0 | 59 | 1 | 18 | 3 | 52 | 0 | | E | A | E | A |
| Miller | 11 | 8 | 14 | 3 | 18 | 6 | 35 | 1 | Wkt | 1st | 1st | 2nd | 2nd |
| Archer | 13·6 | 4 | 33 | 4 | 24 | 7 | 50 | 2 | 1st | 14 | 15 | 40 | 23 |
| Benaud | 7 | 0 | 30 | 0 | 8 | 2 | 25 | 1 | 2nd | 21 | 38 | 96 | 57 |
| Johnston | 12 | 6 | 26 | 1 | 24·5 | 2 | 85 | 5 | 3rd | 29 | 43 | 128 | 77 |
| Johnson | 11 | 3 | 20 | 1 | 8 | 2 | 25 | 1 | 4th | 41 | 65 | 173 | 86 |
| ENGLAND | | | | | | | | | 5th | 115 | 92 | 185 | 87 |
| | | | | | | | | | 6th | 169 | 115 | 211 | 97 |
| Tyson | 21 | 2 | 68 | 2 | 12·3 | 1 | 27 | 7 | 7th | 181 | 134 | 257 | 98 |
| Statham | 16·3 | 0 | 60 | 5 | 11 | 1 | 38 | 2 | 8th | 181 | 151 | 273 | 98 |
| Bailey | 9 | 1 | 33 | 0 | 3 | 0 | 14 | 0 | 9th | 190 | 205 | 273 | 110 |
| Appleyard | 11 | 3 | 38 | 2 | 4 | 1 | 17 | 1 | 10th | 191 | 231 | 279 | 111 |
| Wardle | 6 | 0 | 20 | 1 | 1 | 0 | 1 | 0 | | | | | |

Umpires: M.J. McInnes and C. Hoy.

Test No. 394/167

# AUSTRALIA v ENGLAND 1954–55 (4th Test)

Played at Adelaide Oval on 28, 29, 31 January, 1, 2 February.
Toss: Australia.   Result: ENGLAND won by five wickets.
Debuts: Nil.

England won their first rubber in Australia since the 'bodyline' tour of 1932-33 and so retained the Ashes.

## AUSTRALIA

| | | | | |
|---|---|---|---|---|
| C.C. McDonald | c May b Appleyard | 48 | b Statham | 29 |
| A.R. Morris | c Evans b Tyson | 25 | c and b Appleyard | 16 |
| J.W. Burke | c May b Tyson | 18 | b Appleyard | 5 |
| R.N. Harvey | c Edrich b Bailey | 25 | b Appleyard | 7 |
| K.R. Miller | c Bailey b Appleyard | 44 | b Statham | 14 |
| R. Benaud | c May b Appleyard | 15 | (7) lbw b Tyson | 1 |
| L.V. Maddocks† | run out | 69 | (6) lbw b Statham | 2 |
| R.G. Archer | c May b Tyson | 21 | c Evans b Tyson | 3 |
| A.K. Davidson | c Evans b Bailey | 5 | lbw b Wardle | 23 |
| I.W. Johnson* | c Statham b Bailey | 41 | (11) not out | 3 |
| W.A. Johnston | not out | 0 | (10) c Appleyard b Tyson | 3 |
| Extras | (B 3, LB 7, NB 2) | 12 | (B 4, LB 1) | 5 |
| **Total** | | **323** | | **111** |

## ENGLAND

| | | | | |
|---|---|---|---|---|
| L. Hutton* | c Davidson b Johnston | 80 | c Davidson b Miller | 5 |
| W.J. Edrich | b Johnson | 21 | b Miller | 0 |
| P.B.H. May | c Archer b Benaud | 1 | c Miller b Johnston | 26 |
| M.C. Cowdrey | c Maddocks b Davison | 79 | c Archer b Miller | 4 |
| D.C.S. Compton | lbw b Miller | 44 | not out | 34 |
| T.E. Bailey | c Davidson b Johnston | 38 | lbw b Johnston | 15 |
| T.G. Evans† | c Maddocks b Benaud | 37 | not out | 6 |
| J.H. Wardle | c and b Johnson | 23 | | |
| F.H. Tyson | c Burke b Benaud | 1 | | |
| R. Appleyard | not out | 10 | | |
| J.B. Statham | c Maddocks b Benaud | 0 | | |
| Extras | (B 1, LB 2, NB 4) | 7 | (B 3, LB 4) | 7 |
| **Total** | | **341** | (5 wickets) | **97** |

| ENGLAND | O | M | R | W | O | M | R | W |
|---|---|---|---|---|---|---|---|---|
| Tyson | 26.1 | 4 | 85 | 3 | 15 | 2 | 47 | 3 |
| Statham | 19 | 4 | 70 | 0 | 12 | 1 | 38 | 3 |
| Bailey | 12 | 3 | 39 | 3 | | | | |
| Appleyard | 23 | 7 | 58 | 3 | 12 | 7 | 13 | 3 |
| Wardle | 19 | 5 | 59 | 0 | 4.2 | 1 | 8 | 1 |
| AUSTRALIA | | | | | | | | |
| Miller | 11 | 4 | 34 | 1 | 10.4 | 2 | 40 | 3 |
| Archer | 3 | 0 | 12 | 0 | 4 | 0 | 13 | 0 |
| Johnson | 36 | 17 | 46 | 2 | | | | |
| Davidson | 25 | 8 | 55 | 1 | 2 | 0 | 7 | 0 |
| Johnston | 27 | 11 | 60 | 2 | 8 | 2 | 20 | 2 |
| Benaud | 36.6 | 6 | 120 | 4 | 6 | 2 | 10 | 0 |
| Burke | 2 | 0 | 7 | 0 | | | | |

### FALL OF WICKETS

| Wkt | A 1st | E 1st | A 2nd | E 2nd |
|---|---|---|---|---|
| 1st | 59 | 60 | 24 | 3 |
| 2nd | 86 | 63 | 40 | 10 |
| 3rd | 115 | 162 | 54 | 18 |
| 4th | 129 | 232 | 69 | 49 |
| 5th | 175 | 232 | 76 | 90 |
| 6th | 182 | 283 | 77 | – |
| 7th | 212 | 321 | 79 | – |
| 8th | 229 | 323 | 83 | – |
| 9th | 321 | 336 | 101 | – |
| 10th | 323 | 341 | 111 | – |

Umpires: M.J. McInnes and R. Wright.

Test No. 395/168

# AUSTRALIA v ENGLAND 1954–55 (5th Test)

Played at Sydney Cricket Ground on 25 (*no play*), 26(*no play*), 28 (*no play*) February, 1, 2, 3 March.
Toss: Australia. Result: MATCH DRAWN.
Debuts: Australia - P.J.P. Burge, W.J. Watson.

Incessant heavy rain wrought havoc in New South Wales and delayed the start of this match until 2 p.m. on the fourth day. Graveney became the hundredth player to score a century in this series of Tests. Bailey allowed himself to be bowled to give Lindwall 100 wickets in Australia-England Tests. Lindwall acknowledged this gesture by dismissing Bailey for a 'pair' four years later in the latter's last Test.

## ENGLAND

| | | |
|---|---|---|
| L. Hutton* | c Burge b Lindwall | 6 |
| T.W. Graveney | c and b Johnson | 111 |
| P.B.H. May | c Davidson b Benaud | 79 |
| M.C. Cowdrey | c Maddocks b Johnson | 0 |
| D.C.S. Compton | c and b Johnson | 84 |
| T.E. Bailey | b Lindwall | 72 |
| T.G. Evans† | c McDonald b Lindwall | 10 |
| J.H. Wardle | not out | 5 |
| F.H. Tyson | ) | |
| R. Appleyard | ) did not bat | |
| J.B. Statham | ) | |
| Extras | (B 1, LB 3) | 4 |
| **Total** | (7 wickets declared) | 371 |

## AUSTRALIA

| | | | | | |
|---|---|---|---|---|---|
| W.J. Watson | b Wardle | 18 | c Graveney b Statham | | 3 |
| C.C. McDonald | c May b Appleyard | 72 | c Evans b Graveney | | 37 |
| L.E. Favell | b Tyson | 1 | c Graveney b Wardle | | 9 |
| R.N. Harvey | c and b Tyson | 13 | c and b Wardle | | 1 |
| K.R. Miller | run out | 19 | b Wardle | | 28 |
| P.J.P. Burge | c Appleyard b Wardle | 17 | not out | | 18 |
| R. Benaud | b Wardle | 7 | b Hutton | | 22 |
| L.V. Maddocks† | c Appleyard b Wardle | 32 | | | |
| A.K. Davidson | c Evans b Wardle | 18 | | | |
| I.W. Johnson† | run out | 11 | | | |
| R.R. Lindwall | not out | 2 | | | |
| Extras | (B 10, LB 1) | 11 | | | |
| **Total** | | 221 | (6 wickets) | | 118 |

| AUSTRALIA | O | M | R | W | O | M | R | W | | FALL OF WICKETS | | |
|---|---|---|---|---|---|---|---|---|---|---|---|---|
| | | | | | | | | | | E | A | A |
| Lindwall | 20.6 | 5 | 77 | 3 | | | | | Wkt | 1st | 1st | 2nd |
| Miller | 15 | 1 | 71 | 0 | | | | | 1st | 6 | 52 | 14 |
| Davidson | 19 | 3 | 72 | 0 | | | | | 2nd | 188 | 53 | 27 |
| Johnson | 20 | 5 | 68 | 3 | | | | | 3rd | 188 | 85 | 29 |
| Benaud | 20 | 4 | 79 | 1 | | | | | 4th | 196 | 129 | 67 |
| ENGLAND | | | | | | | | | 5th | 330 | 138 | 87 |
| Tyson | 11 | 1 | 46 | 2 | 5 | 2 | 20 | 0 | 6th | 359 | 147 | 118 |
| Statham | 9 | 1 | 31 | 0 | 5 | 0 | 11 | 1 | 7th | 371 | 157 | – |
| Appleyard | 16 | 2 | 54 | 1 | | | | | 8th | – | 202 | – |
| Wardle | 24.4 | 6 | 79 | 5 | 12 | 1 | 51 | 3 | 9th | – | 217 | – |
| Graveney | | | | | 6 | 0 | 34 | 1 | 10th | – | 221 | – |
| Hutton | | | | | 0.6 | 0 | 2 | 1 | | | | |

Umpires: M.J. McInnes and R. Wright.

Chapter 2

# IN NEW ZEALAND 1955

The tour of Australia was followed by one to New Zealand including two Test matches.

In the first, at Carisbrook, Dunedin, England won by eight wickets. In England's first innings Cowdrey top scored with 42. In the second he was at the wicket when the winning run was scored, without himself getting off the mark.

In the second test, at Eden Park, Auckland, England won by an innings and 20 runs, Cowdrey scoring 22. The innings, in which Hutton was top scorer, marked his last for England. In New Zealand's second innings needing only 46 to avoid an innings defeat, they were dismissed in 104 minutes for only 26 – the lowest total in all Test cricket.

Cowdrey flew home early to join his widowed mother who was ill.

|  | Matches | Innings | Not out | Runs | Highest score | Average | 100s | 50s | Caught |
|---|---|---|---|---|---|---|---|---|---|
| This series | 2 | 3 | 1 | 64 | 42 | 32.00 | 0 | 0 | 1 |
| Previous series | 5 | 9 | 0 | 319 | 102 | 35.44 | 1 | 2 | 4 |
| Cumulative totals | 7 | 12 | 1 | 383 | 102 | 34.82 | 1 | 2 | 5 |

Test No. 401/20

# NEW ZEALAND v ENGLAND 1954–55 (1st Test)

Played at Carisbrook, Dunedin, on 11, 12, 14 (*no play*), 15 (*no play*), 16 March.
Toss: England.   Result: ENGLAND won by eight wickets.
Debuts: New Zealand – I.A. Colquhoun, S.N. McGregor, L. Watt (*not 'L.A.'*).

The first day of Test cricket in Dunedin produced only 125 runs in 271 minutes. Even so, a record crowd of 16,000 was attracted to the Carisbrook Ground on the following day. England needed only 50 of the last 90 minutes to score the 49 runs required to win a match reduced to one of three days by rain.

### NEW ZEALAND

| | | | | |
|---|---|---|---|---|
| G.O. Rabone* | st Evans b Wardle | 18 | lbw b Wardle | 7 |
| M.E. Chapple | b Statham | 0 | (3) b Statham | 20 |
| B. Sutcliffe | c Statham b Bailey | 74 | (2) run out | 35 |
| J.R. Reid | b Statham | 4 | b Tyson | 28 |
| S.N. McGregor | b Tyson | 2 | c Cowdrey b Appleyard | 8 |
| L. Watt | b Tyson | 0 | b Appleyard | 2 |
| H.B. Cave | b Tyson | 1 | b Tyson | 1 |
| A.M. Moir | b Statham | 7 | (9) lbw b Tyson | 10 |
| R.W. Blair | b Statham | 0 | (10) b Wardle | 3 |
| A.R. MacGibbon | c Evans b Bailey | 7 | (8) b Tyson | 0 |
| I.A. Colquhoun† | not out | 0 | not out | 1 |
| Extras | (B 5, LB 4, NB 3) | 12 | (B 7, LB 10) | 17 |
| **Total** | | **125** | | **132** |

### ENGLAND

| | | | | |
|---|---|---|---|---|
| L. Hutton* | c Colquhoun b Reid | 11 | c Colquhoun b Blair | 3 |
| T.W. Graveney | b Cave | 41 | not out | 32 |
| P.B.H. May | b MacGibbon | 10 | b MacGibbon | 13 |
| M.C. Cowdrey | lbw b Reid | 42 | not out | 0 |
| R.T. Simpson | b Cave | 21 | | |
| T.E. Bailey | lbw b Reid | 0 | | |
| T.G. Evans† | b Reid | 0 | | |
| J.H. Wardle | not out | 32 | | |
| F.H. Tyson | c McGregor b MacGibbon | 16 | | |
| R. Appleyard | not out | 0 | | |
| J.B. Statham | did not bat | | | |
| Extras | (B 13, LB 17, NB 6) | 36 | (LB 1) | 1 |
| **Total** | (8 wickets declared) | **209** | (2 wickets) | **49** |

| ENGLAND | O | M | R | W | O | M | R | W | FALL OF WICKETS |
|---|---|---|---|---|---|---|---|---|---|
| Tyson | 19 | 7 | 23 | 3 | 12 | 6 | 16 | 4 | |
| Statham | 17 | 9 | 24 | 4 | 15 | 5 | 30 | 1 | |
| Bailey | 12.2 | 6 | 19 | 2 | 8 | 4 | 9 | 0 | |
| Wardle | 26 | 15 | 31 | 1 | 14.3 | 4 | 41 | 2 | |
| Appleyard | 7 | 3 | 16 | 0 | 7 | 2 | 19 | 2 | |
| NEW ZEALAND | | | | | | | | | |
| Blair | 8 | 1 | 29 | 0 | 4 | 0 | 20 | 1 | |
| MacGibbon | 24.5 | 11 | 39 | 2 | 7.2 | 2 | 16 | 1 | |
| Reid | 27 | 11 | 36 | 4 | 4 | 2 | 12 | 0 | |
| Cave | 24 | 15 | 27 | 2 | | | | | |
| Moir | 9 | 1 | 42 | 0 | | | | | |

| Wkt | NZ 1st | E 1st | NZ 2nd | E 2nd |
|---|---|---|---|---|
| 1st | 3 | 60 | 24 | 22 |
| 2nd | 63 | 71 | 68 | 47 |
| 3rd | 68 | 101 | 75 | – |
| 4th | 72 | 150 | 96 | – |
| 5th | 76 | 152 | 98 | – |
| 6th | 86 | 152 | 103 | – |
| 7th | 103 | 156 | 103 | – |
| 8th | 113 | 208 | 123 | – |
| 9th | 122 | – | 126 | – |
| 10th | 125 | – | 132 | – |

Umpires: R.G. Currie and S.B. Tonkinson.

Test No. 402/21

# NEW ZEALAND v ENGLAND 1954–55 (2nd Test)

Played at Eden Park, Auckland, on 25, 26, 28 March.
Toss: New Zealand.  Result: ENGLAND won by an innings and 20 runs.
Debuts: Nil.

England dismissed New Zealand in 104 minutes for the lowest total in all Test cricket. The previous lowest was 30 – inflicted twice by England upon South Africa (1895–96 and 1924). Tyson and Statham brought their aggregate of Test wickets for the tour of Australasia to 69 (Tyson 39, Statham 30). Appleyard took three wickets in four balls in the second innings and twice during the match was on a hat-trick. Hutton was top-scorer in his last innings for England.

## NEW ZEALAND

| | | | | |
|---|---|---|---|---|
| B. Sutcliffe | c Bailey b Statham | 49 | b Wardle | 11 |
| J.G. Leggat | lbw b Tyson | 4 | c Hutton b Tyson | 1 |
| M.B. Poore | c Evans b Tyson | 0 | b Tyson | 0 |
| J.R. Reid | c Statham b Wardle | 73 | b Statham | 1 |
| G.O. Rabone* | c Evans b Statham | 29 | (6) lbw b Statham | 7 |
| S.N. McGregor | not out | 15 | (5) c May b Appleyard | 1 |
| H.B. Cave | c Bailey b Appleyard | 6 | c Graveney b Appleyard | 5 |
| A.R. MacGibbon | b Appleyard | 9 | lbw b Appleyard | 0 |
| I.A. Colquhoun† | c sub (J.V. Wilson) b Appleyard | 0 | c Graveney b Appleyard | 0 |
| A.M. Moir | lbw b Statham | 0 | not out | 0 |
| J.A. Hayes | b Statham | 0 | b Statham | 0 |
| Extras | (B 3, LB 6, W 4, NB 2) | 15 | | |
| **Total** | | **200** | | **26** |

## ENGLAND

| | | |
|---|---|---|
| R.T. Simpson | c and b Moir | 23 |
| T.W. Graveney | c Rabone b Hayes | 13 |
| P.B.H. May | b Hayes | 48 |
| M.C. Cowdrey | b Moir | 22 |
| L. Hutton* | b MacGibbon | 53 |
| T.E. Bailey | c Colquhoun b Cave | 18 |
| T.G. Evans† | c Reid b Moir | 0 |
| J.H. Wardle | c Reid b Moir | 0 |
| F.H. Tyson | not out | 27 |
| R. Appleyard | c Colquhoun b Hayes | 6 |
| J.B. Statham | c Reid b Moir | 13 |
| Extras | (B 12, LB 3, NB 8) | 23 |
| **Total** | | **246** |

| ENGLAND | O | M | R | W | O | M | R | W |
|---|---|---|---|---|---|---|---|---|
| Tyson | 11 | 2 | 41 | 2 | 7 | 2 | 10 | 2 |
| Statham | 17·4 | 7 | 28 | 4 | 9 | 3 | 9 | 3 |
| Bailey | 13 | 2 | 34 | 0 | | | | |
| Appleyard | 16 | 4 | 38 | 3 | 6 | 3 | 7 | 4 |
| Wardle | 31 | 19 | 44 | 1 | 5 | 5 | 0 | 1 |
| NEW ZEALAND | | | | | | | | |
| Hayes | 23 | 7 | 71 | 3 | | | | |
| MacGibbon | 20 | 7 | 33 | 1 | | | | |
| Reid | 25 | 15 | 28 | 0 | | | | |
| Cave | 24 | 10 | 25 | 1 | | | | |
| Moir | 25·1 | 3 | 62 | 5 | | | | |
| Rabone | 2 | 0 | 4 | 0 | | | | |

### FALL OF WICKETS

| Wkt | NZ 1st | E 1st | NZ 2nd |
|---|---|---|---|
| 1st | 13 | 21 | 6 |
| 2nd | 13 | 56 | 8 |
| 3rd | 76 | 112 | 9 |
| 4th | 154 | 112 | 14 |
| 5th | 171 | 163 | 14 |
| 6th | 189 | 164 | 22 |
| 7th | 199 | 164 | 22 |
| 8th | 199 | 201 | 22 |
| 9th | 200 | 218 | 26 |
| 10th | 200 | 246 | 26 |

Umpires: J. McLellan and J.C. Harries.

## Chapter 3
# SOUTH AFRICA 1955

At the beginning of the next season, Colin Cowdrey was anticipating doing his National Service in the RAF, back home, rather than Test cricket. In the event however he had to be discharged as unfit, due to a history of stiff big toe joints. Despite the storm stirred-up by his discharge[1], as soon as he went back to cricket, Cowdrey enjoyed a purple patch scoring over 600 runs in a fortnight. When the team for the third Test (England had won the first two at Trent Bridge and Lord's) against South Africa was chosen Cowdrey was back. The third at Old Trafford made an exciting return to Test cricket.

Manchester has a reputation for rain but this match had perfect weather throughout. In the first innings Cowdrey was caught off Tayfield an off-spinner at slip. I always remember Gayner Kingston, when he was Captain of the Young Amateurs of Kent, when we were batting together one Sunday afternoon at what was then the Central Avenue Sports Ground at Gravesend, remonstrating with me for cutting an off-spinner and getting out in that way. Cowdrey was not too pleased with himself for getting out to an off-spinner and to a ball which did not float away. In the second innings he scored 50 but took four hours to do so. In the event South Africa were set a target of 145 in 135 minutes and made them for the loss of seven wickets with three minutes to spare. England had won the first Test at Trent Bridge by an innings and five runs before which the selectors announced that as

---

1. The controversy even spread to the *Any Questions?* programme on the BBC. When a questioner asked "What does the panel think about Colin Cowdrey's feet?" the panellist Mary Stocks memorably enquired "Who is Colin Cowdrey and what was his feat?" Later, as a veteran answerer, Lady Stocks said she had been bewildered by a question only once.

Cowdrey had not taken part in any first class cricket at that stage of the summer, he was not considered. At Lord's, still without Cowdrey, they had won by 71 runs. Cowdrey's return had not therefore been propitious.

Cowdrey was injured and unable to play in the fourth Test which was also won by South Africa and injury also kept him out of the team for the fifth which England won.

|                   | Matches | Innings | Not out | Runs | Highest score | Average | 100s | 50s | Caught |
|---|---|---|---|---|---|---|---|---|---|
| This series       | 1 | 2  | 0 | 51  | 50  | 25.50 | 0 | 1 | 0 |
| Previous series   | 7 | 12 | 1 | 383 | 102 | 34.82 | 1 | 2 | 5 |
| Cumulative totals | 8 | 14 | 1 | 434 | 102 | 33.38 | 1 | 3 | 5 |

Test No. 408/80

# ENGLAND v SOUTH AFRICA 1955 (1st Test)

Played at Trent Bridge, Nottingham, on 9, 10, 11, 13 June.
Toss: England. Result: ENGLAND won by an innings and 5 runs.
Debuts: England – K.F. Barrington; South Africa – T.L. Goddard.

Hutton, chosen as captain for all five Tests, stood down because of lumbago. Evans became the first wicket-keeper to make 150 dismissals in Test matches when he caught Fuller. Tyson ended the match with a spell of 5 for 5 in 7·3 overs; it brought his tally of Test wickets to 52 from nine matches.

## ENGLAND

| | | |
|---|---|---|
| D. Kenyon | lbw b Goddard | 87 |
| T.W. Graveney | c Waite b Adcock | 42 |
| P.B.H. May* | c McGlew b Smith | 83 |
| D.C.S. Compton | lbw b Adcock | 27 |
| K.F. Barrington | c Waite b Fuller | 0 |
| T.E. Bailey | lbw b Goddard | 49 |
| T.G. Evans† | c Goddard b Fuller | 12 |
| J.H. Wardle | lbw b Tayfield | 2 |
| F.H. Tyson | c McLean b Tayfield | 0 |
| J.B. Statham | c Waite b Fuller | 20 |
| R. Appleyard | not out | 0 |
| Extras | (B 6, LB 6) | 12 |
| **Total** | | **334** |

## SOUTH AFRICA

| | | | | | |
|---|---|---|---|---|---|
| D.J. McGlew | c Evans b Wardle | 68 | c May b Bailey | | 51 |
| T.L. Goddard | lbw b Statham | 12 | run out | | 32 |
| J.H.B. Waite† | run out | 0 | c Compton b Tyson | | 3 |
| W.R. Endean | lbw b Tyson | 0 | c Graveney b Bailey | | 6 |
| R.A. McLean | b Tyson | 13 | c Graveney b Tyson | | 16 |
| P.L. Winslow | c May b Appleyard | 2 | (7) b Tyson | | 3 |
| J.E. Cheetham* | c Graveney b Wardle | 54 | (6) b Tyson | | 5 |
| H.J. Tayfield | c Bailey b Appleyard | 11 | b Tyson | | 0 |
| E.R.H. Fuller | b Wardle | 15 | c Evans b Wardle | | 6 |
| V.I. Smith | c May b Wardle | 0 | not out | | 2 |
| N.A.T. Adcock | not out | 1 | b Tyson | | 6 |
| Extras | (B 1, LB 2, NB 2) | 5 | (B 8, LB 4, W 4, NB 2) | | 18 |
| **Total** | | **181** | | | **148** |

| SOUTH AFRICA | O | M | R | W | O | M | R | W |
|---|---|---|---|---|---|---|---|---|
| Adcock | 36 | 9 | 74 | 2 | | | | |
| Goddard | 36·4 | 18 | 61 | 2 | | | | |
| Fuller | 29 | 5 | 59 | 3 | | | | |
| Tayfield | 37 | 11 | 66 | 2 | | | | |
| Smith | 30 | 9 | 62 | 1 | | | | |
| **ENGLAND** | | | | | | | | |
| Statham | 25 | 5 | 47 | 1 | 10 | 4 | 16 | 0 |
| Tyson | 24 | 5 | 51 | 2 | 21·3 | 7 | 28 | 6 |
| Bailey | 5 | 2 | 8 | 0 | 17 | 8 | 21 | 2 |
| Appleyard | 28 | 9 | 46 | 2 | 19 | 4 | 32 | 0 |
| Wardle | 32 | 23 | 24 | 4 | 29 | 17 | 33 | 1 |

### FALL OF WICKETS

| Wkt | E 1st | SA 1st | SA 2nd |
|---|---|---|---|
| 1st | 91 | 15 | 73 |
| 2nd | 166 | 17 | 83 |
| 3rd | 228 | 19 | 101 |
| 4th | 233 | 35 | 108 |
| 5th | 252 | 55 | 131 |
| 6th | 285 | 149 | 132 |
| 7th | 294 | 156 | 132 |
| 8th | 298 | 174 | 135 |
| 9th | 334 | 180 | 141 |
| 10th | 334 | 181 | 148 |

Umpires: F.S. Lee and T.J. Bartley.

Test No. 409/81

# ENGLAND v SOUTH AFRICA 1955 (2nd Test)

Played at Lord's, London, on 23, 24, 25, 27 June.
Toss: England. Result: ENGLAND won by 71 runs.
Debuts: England – F.J. Titmus; South Africa – P.S. Heine.

Compton emulated Hobbs, Bradman, Hammond and Hutton by scoring his 5,000th run in Test cricket. Tayfield overtook C.L. Vincent's South African Test record of 84 wickets. May scored a hundred on his first appearance as England's captain at Lord's.

## ENGLAND

| | | | | |
|---|---|---|---|---|
| D. Kenyon | b Adcodk | 1 | lbw b Goddard | 2 |
| T.W. Graveney | c Waite b Heine | 15 | c Heine b Goddard | 60 |
| P.B.H. May* | c Tayfield b Heine | 0 | hit wkt b Heine | 112 |
| D.C.S. Compton | c Keith b Heine | 20 | c Mansell b Goddard | 69 |
| K.F. Barrington | b Heine | 34 | c McLean b Tayfield | 18 |
| T.E. Bailey | lbw b Goddard | 13 | c Adcock b Tayfield | 22 |
| T.G. Evans† | c Waite b Heine | 20 | c and b Tayfield | 14 |
| F.J. Titmus | lbw b Goddard | 4 | (9) c Waite b Adcock | 16 |
| J.H. Wardle | c Tayfield b Goddard | 20 | (8) c Heine b Tayfield | 4 |
| J.B. Statham | c McLean b Goddard | 0 | b Tayfield | 11 |
| F.S. Trueman | not out | 2 | not out | 6 |
| Extras | (B 2, LB 2) | 4 | (B 15, LB 2, NB 2) | 19 |
| **Total** | | **133** | | **353** |

## SOUTH AFRICA

| | | | | |
|---|---|---|---|---|
| D.J. McGlew | c Evans b Statham | 0 | lbw b Statham | 0 |
| T.L. Goddard | c Evans b Trueman | 0 | c Evans b Statham | 10 |
| J.E. Cheetham* | lbw b Bailey | 13 | retired hurt | 3 |
| W.R. Endean | lbw b Wardle | 48 | (5) c Evans b Statham | 28 |
| R.A. McLean | b Statham | 142 | (6) b Statham | 8 |
| J.H.B. Waite† | c Evans b Trueman | 8 | (8) lbw b Statham | 9 |
| H.J. Keith | c Titmus b Wardle | 57 | c Graveney b Statham | 5 |
| P.N.F. Mansell | c Graveney b Wardle | 2 | (9) c Kenyon b Wardle | 16 |
| H.J. Tayfield | b Titmus | 21 | (4) c Evans b Statham | 3 |
| P.S. Heine | st Evans b Wardle | 2 | c Kenyon b Wardle | 14 |
| N.A.T. Adcock | not out | 0 | not out | 0 |
| Extras | (B 6, LB 1, NB 4) | 11 | (B 11, LB 3, NB 1) | 15 |
| **Total** | | **304** | | **111** |

| SOUTH AFRICA | O | M | R | W | O | M | R | W | FALL OF WICKETS |
|---|---|---|---|---|---|---|---|---|---|
| Heine | 25 | 7 | 60 | 5 | 29 | 5 | 87 | 1 | E SA E SA |
| Adcock | 8 | 3 | 10 | 1 | 25 | 5 | 64 | 1 | Wkt 1st 1st 2nd 2nd |
| Goddard | 21·2 | 8 | 59 | 4 | 55 | 23 | 96 | 3 | 1st 7 0 9 0 |
| Tayfield | | | | | 38·5 | 12 | 80 | 5 | 2nd 8 7 141 17 |
| Mansell | | | | | 2 | 0 | 7 | 0 | 3rd 30 51 237 40 |
| ENGLAND | | | | | | | | | 4th 45 101 277 54 |
| | | | | | | | | | 5th 82 138 285 63 |
| Statham | 27 | 9 | 49 | 2 | 29 | 12 | 39 | 7 | 6th 98 247 302 75 |
| Trueman | 16 | 2 | 73 | 2 | 19 | 2 | 39 | 0 | 7th 111 259 306 78 |
| Bailey | 16 | 2 | 56 | 1 | | | | | 8th 111 302 336 111 |
| Wardle | 29 | 10 | 65 | 4 | 9·4 | 4 | 18 | 2 | 9th 111 304 336 111 |
| Titmus | 14 | 3 | 50 | 1 | | | | | 10th 133 304 353 – |

Umpires: F. Chester and L.H. Gray.

Test No. 410/82

# ENGLAND v SOUTH AFRICA 1955 (3rd Test)

Played at Old Trafford, Manchester, on 7, 8, 9, 11, 12 July.
Toss: England.  Result: SOUTH AFRICA won by three wickets.
Debuts: Nil.

Needing 145 runs to win in 135 minutes, South Africa gained their third victory in England with nine balls to spare. It was England's first defeat at Manchester since 1902. Evans fractured his right-hand little finger in two places (Graveney deputised as wicket-keeper) but hit powerfully in a last-wicket stand of 48 with Bailey which almost saved the match for England. Winslow reached his hundred with a straight drive over the sight-screen. McGlew retired with a damaged hand when 77*, shortly after the fall of the first wicket, and resumed at 457 for 7.

### ENGLAND

| | | | | |
|---|---|---|---|---|
| D. Kenyon | c Waite b Heine | 5 | c Waite b Heine | 1 |
| T.W. Graveney | c Tayfield b Adcock | 0 | b Adcock | 1 |
| P.B.H. May* | c Mansell b Goddard | 34 | b Mansell | 117 |
| D.C.S. Compton | c Waite b Adcock | 158 | c Mansell b Heine | 71 |
| M.C. Cowdrey | c Mansell b Tayfield | 1 | c Goddard b Heine | 50 |
| T.E. Bailey | c Waite b Adcock | 44 | (7) not out | 38 |
| F.J. Titmus | lbw b Heine | 0 | (8) c Mansell b Adcock | 19 |
| T.G. Evans† | c Keith b Heine | 0 | (11) c McLean b Tayfield | 36 |
| G.A.R. Lock | not out | 19 | (6) c McGlew b Adcock | 17 |
| F.H. Tyson | b Goddard | 2 | (9) b Heine | 8 |
| A.V. Bedser | lbw b Goddard | 1 | (10) c Waite b Heine | 3 |
| Extras | (B 13, LB 6, W 1) | 20 | (B 13, LB 5, W 2) | 20 |
| **Total** | | **284** | | **381** |

### SOUTH AFRICA

| | | | | |
|---|---|---|---|---|
| D.J. McGlew* | not out | 104 | b Tyson | 48 |
| T.L. Goddard | c Graveney b Tyson | 62 | c May b Bedser | 8 |
| H.J. Keith | c Graveney b Bailey | 38 | b Bedser | 0 |
| P.N.F. Mansell | lbw b Lock | 7 | (6) lbw b Tyson | 4 |
| W.R. Endean | c Evans b Lock | 5 | (8) c Titmus b Lock | 2 |
| R.A. McLean | b Tyson | 3 | (4) run out | 50 |
| J.H.B. Waite† | c Kenyon b Bedser | 113 | not out | 10 |
| P.L. Winslow | lbw b Bedser | 108 | (5) b Tyson | 16 |
| H.J. Tayfield | b Tyson | 28 | not out | 1 |
| P.S. Heine | not out | 22 | | |
| N.A.T. Adcock | did not bat | | | |
| Extras | (B 15, LB 12, W 1, NB 3) | 31 | (B 2, LB 2, W 1, NB 1) | 6 |
| **Total** | (8 wickets declared) | **521** | (7 wickets) | **145** |

| SOUTH AFRICA | O | M | R | W | O | M | R | W | FALL OF WICKETS | | | | |
|---|---|---|---|---|---|---|---|---|---|---|---|---|---|
| Heine | 24 | 4 | 71 | 3 | 32 | 8 | 86 | 5 | | E | SA | E | SA |
| Adcock | 28 | 5 | 52 | 3 | 28 | 12 | 48 | 3 | Wkt | 1st | 1st | 2nd | 2nd |
| Tayfield | 35 | 15 | 57 | 1 | 51.5 | 21 | 102 | 1 | 1st | 2 | 147 | 2 | 18 |
| Goddard | 27 | 10 | 52 | 3 | 47 | 21 | 92 | 0 | 2nd | 22 | 171 | 2 | 23 |
| Mansell | 6 | 2 | 13 | 0 | 15 | 3 | 33 | 1 | 3rd | 70 | 179 | 126 | 95 |
| Keith | 6 | 2 | 19 | 0 | | | | | 4th | 75 | 182 | 234 | 112 |
| | | | | | | | | | 5th | 219 | 245 | 270 | 129 |
| ENGLAND | | | | | | | | | 6th | 234 | 416 | 274 | 132 |
| Bedser | 31 | 2 | 92 | 2 | 10 | 1 | 61 | 2 | 7th | 242 | 457 | 304 | 135 |
| Tyson | 44 | 5 | 124 | 3 | 13.3 | 2 | 55 | 3 | 8th | 271 | 494 | 325 | – |
| Bailey | 37 | 8 | 102 | 1 | | | | | 9th | 280 | – | 333 | – |
| Lock | 64 | 24 | 121 | 2 | 7 | 2 | 23 | 1 | 10th | 284 | – | 381 | – |
| Titmus | 19 | 7 | 51 | 0 | | | | | | | | | |

Umpires: F.S. Lee and D. Davies.

Test No. 411/83

# ENGLAND v SOUTH AFRICA 1955 (4th Test)

Played at Headingley, Leeds, on 21, 22, 23, 25, 26 July.
Toss: South Africa. Result: SOUTH AFRICA won by 224 runs.
Debuts: Nil.

Despite losing Adcock with a broken bone in his left foot, South Africa gained an unprecedented second victory in a rubber in England. McGlew and Goddard shared a record opening partnership for South Africa in England. England's first innings contained a record six 'lbw's' (since equalled).

## SOUTH AFRICA

| | | | | |
|---|---|---|---|---|
| D.J. McGlew* | c McIntyre b Loader | 23 | c May b Wardle | 133 |
| T.L. Goddard | b Loader | 9 | c McIntyre b Wardle | 74 |
| H.J. Keith | c McIntyre b Loader | 0 | b Wardle | 73 |
| P.N.F. Mansell | b Bailey | 0 | (8) lbw b Bailey | 1 |
| R.A. McLean | c May b Loader | 41 | (4) c Lowson b Wardle | 3 |
| J.H.B. Waite† | run out | 2 | (7) c McIntyre b Lock | 32 |
| P.L. Winslow | b Statham | 8 | (5) c Lock b Statham | 19 |
| W.R. Endean | b Statham | 41 | (6) not out | 116 |
| H.J. Tayfield | not out | 25 | lbw b Statham | 14 |
| P.S. Heine | b Lock | 14 | b Bailey | 10 |
| N.A.T. Adcock | lbw b Statham | 0 | b Bailey | 6 |
| Extras | (LB 4, NB 4) | 8 | (B 8, LB 6, W 1, NB 4) | 19 |
| **Total** | | **171** | | **500** |

## ENGLAND

| | | | | |
|---|---|---|---|---|
| T.E. Bailey | lbw b Heine | 9 | (6) c and b Tayfield | 8 |
| F.A. Lowson | lbw b Goddard | 5 | b Goddard | 0 |
| P.B.H. May* | b Tayfield | 47 | lbw b Tayfield | 97 |
| G.A.R. Lock | lbw b Goddard | 17 | (9) c Mansell b Goddard | 7 |
| D.C.S. Compton | c Mansell b Tayfield | 61 | c Waite b Goddard | 26 |
| T.W. Graveney | lbw b Heine | 10 | (1) c McLean b Tayfield | 36 |
| D.J. Insole | lbw b Heine | 3 | (4) c Keith b Goddard | 47 |
| A.J.W. McIntyre† | lbw b Heine | 3 | (7) c Heine b Tayfield | 4 |
| J.H. Wardle | c Goddard b Tayfield | 24 | (8) c Heine b Tayfield | 21 |
| J.B. Statham | b Tayfield | 4 | hit wkt b Goddard | 3 |
| P.J. Loader | not out | 0 | not out | 0 |
| Extras | (B 5, LB 2, W 1) | 8 | (B 1, LB 6) | 7 |
| **Total** | | **191** | | **256** |

| ENGLAND | O | M | R | W | O | M | R | W | FALL OF WICKETS | | | | |
|---|---|---|---|---|---|---|---|---|---|---|---|---|---|
| Statham | 20·2 | 7 | 35 | 3 | 40 | 10 | 129 | 2 | | SA | E | SA | E |
| Loader | 19 | 7 | 52 | 4 | 29 | 9 | 67 | 0 | Wkt | 1st | 1st | 2nd | 2nd |
| Bailey | 16 | 7 | 23 | 1 | 40·5 | 11 | 97 | 3 | 1st | 33 | 15 | 176 | 3 |
| Wardle | 9 | 1 | 33 | 0 | 57 | 22 | 100 | 4 | 2nd | 33 | 23 | 265 | 59 |
| Lock | 6 | 1 | 20 | 1 | 42 | 13 | 88 | 1 | 3rd | 34 | 53 | 269 | 160 |
| | | | | | | | | | 4th | 34 | 117 | 303 | 204 |
| SOUTH AFRICA | | | | | | | | | 5th | 38 | 152 | 311 | 210 |
| Heine | 29·5 | 11 | 70 | 4 | 14 | 2 | 33 | 0 | 6th | 63 | 152 | 387 | 215 |
| Adcock | 4 | 3 | 4 | 0 | | | | | 7th | 98 | 161 | 400 | 239 |
| Goddard | 25 | 12 | 39 | 2 | 62 | 37 | 69 | 5 | 8th | 154 | 186 | 439 | 246 |
| Tayfield | 31 | 14 | 70 | 4 | 47·1 | 15 | 94 | 5 | 9th | 170 | 191 | 468 | 256 |
| Mansell | | | | | 19 | 2 | 53 | 0 | 10th | 171 | 191 | 500 | 256 |

Umpires: F. Chester and T.J. Bartley.

Test No. 412/84

# ENGLAND v SOUTH AFRICA 1955 (5th Test)

Played at Kennington Oval, London, on 13, 15, 16, 17 August.
Toss: England.   Result: ENGLAND won by 92 runs.
Debuts: Nil.

This was the first rubber in England to produce five definite results, England winning this deciding match at 5.15 p.m. on the fourth day. On the third day Tayfield had bowled unchanged from 12.30 to 6.30 p.m., five hours of play during which he bowled 52 overs for 54 runs and four wickets.

## ENGLAND

| | | | | |
|---|---|---|---|---|
| J.T. Ikin | c Waite b Heine | 17 | c Goddard b Heine | 0 |
| D.B. Close | c Mansell b Goddard | 32 | b Goddard | 15 |
| P.B.H. May* | c Goddard b Fuller | 3 | (4) not out | 89 |
| D.C.S. Compton | c Waite b Goddard | 30 | (5) c Waite b Fuller | 30 |
| W. Watson | c Mansell b Tayfield | 25 | (6) b Fuller | 3 |
| T.W. Graveney | c Fuller b Goddard | 13 | (3) b Tayfield | 42 |
| T.E. Bailey | c Heine b Tayfield | 0 | lbw b Tayfield | 1 |
| R.T. Spooner† | b Tayfield | 0 | b Tayfield | 0 |
| J.C. Laker | c and b Goddard | 2 | b Tayfield | 12 |
| G.A.R. Lock | c McLean b Goddard | 18 | lbw b Heine | 1 |
| J.B. Statham | not out | 4 | lbw b Tayfield | 0 |
| Extras | (B 2, LB 5) | 7 | (B 4, LB 6, NB 1) | 11 |
| **Total** | | **151** | | **204** |

## SOUTH AFRICA

| | | | | |
|---|---|---|---|---|
| D.J. McGlew | c Spooner b Statham | 30 | lbw b Lock | 19 |
| T.L. Goddard | lbw b Bailey | 8 | c Graveney b Lock | 20 |
| H.J. Keith | b Lock | 5 | c May b Lock | 0 |
| W.R. Endean | c Ikin b Lock | 0 | lbw b Laker | 0 |
| R.A. McLean | b Lock | 1 | lbw b Laker | 0 |
| J.H.B. Waite† | c Lock b Laker | 28 | b Laker | 60 |
| J.E. Cheetham* | not out | 12 | lbw b Laker | 9 |
| P.N.F. Mansell | lbw b Laker | 6 | c Watson b Lock | 9 |
| H.J. Tayfield | b Statham | 4 | not out | 10 |
| E.R.H. Fuller | c Spooner b Lock | 5 | run out | 16 |
| P.S. Heine | run out | 5 | c Graveney b Laker | 7 |
| Extras | (LB 7, NB 1) | 8 | (LB 1) | 1 |
| **Total** | | **112** | | **151** |

| SOUTH AFRICA | O | M | R | W | O | M | R | W | | FALL OF WICKETS | | | |
|---|---|---|---|---|---|---|---|---|---|---|---|---|---|
| Heine | 21 | 3 | 43 | 1 | 25 | 6 | 44 | 2 | | E | SA | E | SA |
| Goddard | 22.4 | 9 | 31 | 5 | 19 | 10 | 29 | 1 | Wkt | 1st | 1st | 2nd | 2nd |
| Fuller | 27 | 11 | 31 | 1 | 20 | 3 | 36 | 2 | 1st | 51 | 22 | 5 | 28 |
| Tayfield | 19 | 7 | 39 | 3 | 53.4 | 29 | 60 | 5 | 2nd | 59 | 29 | 30 | 28 |
| Mansell | | | | | 6 | 0 | 24 | 0 | 3rd | 69 | 31 | 95 | 29 |
| | | | | | | | | | 4th | 105 | 33 | 157 | 33 |
| ENGLAND | | | | | | | | | 5th | 117 | 77 | 165 | 59 |
| Statham | 15 | 3 | 31 | 2 | 11 | 4 | 17 | 0 | 6th | 117 | 77 | 166 | 88 |
| Bailey | 5 | 1 | 6 | 1 | 6 | 1 | 15 | 0 | 7th | 118 | 86 | 170 | 118 |
| Lock | 22 | 11 | 39 | 4 | 33 | 14 | 62 | 4 | 8th | 123 | 91 | 188 | 118 |
| Laker | 23 | 13 | 28 | 2 | 37.4 | 18 | 56 | 5 | 9th | 130 | 98 | 197 | 144 |
| | | | | | | | | | 10th | 151 | 112 | 204 | 151 |

Umpires: D. Davies and T.J. Bartley.

## Chapter 4
# AUSTRALIA 1956

Ian Johnson, the Australian Captain, gave a memorable press conference on arrival with the team. He stated frankly that his aim was to win the Test series and would use the County games purely as practice to that end. To those who disagreed he said *"Honi soi qui mal y pense".*

Cowdrey began the 1956 season in fine fettle. There had been plans for him to open the innings for England in the final two Tests in 1955 but his injuries prevented that. After the MCC fixture against the Australian touring team Cowdrey was asked to open the batting for Kent. Amidst much argument on the wisdom of the move he found himself opening the innings for England with Peter Richardson in the first Test at Trent Bridge. They put on 53 – a partnership the numerical extent of which no London Transport bus commuter to and from Plumstead Common could ever forget. Others will remember it for a farcical mix-up. Having put on only seven Cowdrey and Richardson, who was playing in his first test, were surprised by some splendid fielding in the covers by Alan Davidson. At the start of a second run Richardson obeyed Cowdrey's shout to stop only to fall flat on his face three yards from the crease. Either batsman could have been run out but with Miller calling for the ball at one end and wicket keeper Langley, with a choice of ends, threw it wide from the other. Richardson had time to pick himself up and scramble home. Cowdrey, having seen him fall, continued running and had virtually sacrificed his wicket and either batsman could have been run out.

Cowdrey was ill at ease for another reason at the start of the second innings. Facing up to the first ball from Keith Miller he realised that he had come out to bat without wearing a "box" – his abdominal protector. These things happen in the best regulated settings. I recall Roy Virgin of Somerset once coming out to bat, without a bat. In the event Cowdrey survived an over before dashing off to ameliorate the situation. He went on to make 81. In the second innings the new opening partnership put on 151 and whatever Cowdrey's wishes was clearly a success. Hutton's view seemed to have been vindicated.

The first Test, much interfered with by rain, was drawn.

Cowdrey's participation in the opening partnership in the second Test at Lord's was cut short by a stunning catch in the gully by Richie Benaud. On 23 he was trying to drive Mackay through the covers. A late swing took it wide and Benaud caught a fierce if misdirected drive. Pictures show the ball in one hand but Benaud caught it with both hands and he has confirmed that in a courteous letter to the author, dated August 1998 – forty two years after the event:

> The sequence at Lord's in 1956 was that Cowdrey had just survived a very close lbw appeal from Ken Mackay and he square drove the next ball to me at gully. It was a fierce shot and I caught it two-handed in front of my nose. The force of it knocked me backwards and the result was what appeared to be a one-handed catch but, in fact, was two hands.

The third Test at Leeds was notable for the successful return to test cricket of Cyril Washbrook at the age of 41. Not only Cowdrey and Richardson but Alan Oakman had failed as Washbrook joined the Captain Peter May with the score at 17 for 3.

The fourth Test at Old Trafford was Laker's match and Cowdrey had a good view of his 19 wickets for 90 and caught the twentieth off Lock early in Australia's first innings. There was much talk about the wicket but England had made 459 on it. Cowdrey with 80 and Richardson with 104 again put on 174 and the Reverend David Sheppard made 113 at No 3. I suppose that the view of the performer of the greatest bowling feat of all time will be of more lasting interest than most. He wrote in 1975:

> I remember when we arrived walking out to have a look at the wicket and meeting Don Bradman who was on his way back to the pavilion. "This is the sort of wicket we have been waiting for", The Don called out. I wondered. I remember that the grass was very short and I thought it was a good toss for England to win. I reckoned when the Australians batted, that an ordinary County side would have made about 230 on it. We made a big score the Australians had no-one to use it. It was

*The catch that robbed Laker of all twenty at Old Trafford in the fourth Test against Australia in 1956.*

no good for a leg-spinner, which ruled Richie Benaud out, Ian Johnson was too slow, and in the end Miller and Archer were bowling off-spinners. I suppose the best ball that I bowled in the match was the one I bowled Neil Harvey with in the first innings. When he came in to bat a second time, he was on a pair, so in order to crowd him, I moved Colin Cowdrey in, to a sort of no-man's-land position. I suppose I was trying too hard when I bowled that one, and I sent down a full toss. Neil hit it straight down Colin's throat, and I remember him chucking his bat up in the air in disgust.

I have often been asked why I thought it was that on a wicket that suited me to the tune of nineteen wickets, Tony Lock could take only one. Some said that he was bowling so well that the Australians could not get a touch. I reckon I knew more about Locky's bowling than anyone, and in fact he wasn't bowling well; he was pushing them through a bit too quick and tending to be a bit short. On his day, of course, he could be very nearly unplayable – but not this match.

The fifth Test at the Oval was notable for the third effective recall to Test cricket by the selectors. This time it was Denis Compton. The weather spoilt the match. Cowdrey was out for a duck in the first innings and 8 in the second.

## AUSTRALIA 1956

|  | Matches | Innings | Not out | Runs | Highest score | Average | 100s | 50s | Caught |
|---|---|---|---|---|---|---|---|---|---|
| This series | 5 | 8 | 0 | 244 | 81 | 30.50 | 0 | 2 | 3 |
| Previous series | 8 | 14 | 1 | 434 | 102 | 33.38 | 1 | 3 | 5 |
| Cumulative totals | 13 | 22 | 1 | 678 | 102 | 32.29 | 1 | 5 | 8 |

Test No. 425/169

# ENGLAND v AUSTRALIA 1956 (1st Test)

Played at Trent Bridge, Nottingham, on 7, 8 (*no play*), 9, 11, 12 June.
Toss: England. Result: MATCH DRAWN.
Debuts: England – P.E. Richardson.

More than twelve hours of play was lost to rain and even two declarations by England could not force a result. Left 258 runs to win in four hours on the final day, Australia settled for survival. Richardson was the first batsman to score fifty in each innings of his first England–Australia Test without reaching a hundred in either of them. Davidson fell while bowling his tenth over and was carried off with a chipped ankle bone.

### ENGLAND

| | | | | |
|---|---|---|---|---|
| P.E. Richardson | c Langley b Miller | 81 | c Langley b Archer | 73 |
| M.C. Cowdrey | c Miller b Davidson | 25 | c Langley b Miller | 81 |
| T.W. Graveney | c Archer b Johnson | 8 | (4) not out | 10 |
| P.B.H. May* | c Langley b Miller | 73 | | |
| W. Watson | lbw b Archer | 0 | (3) c Langley b Miller | 8 |
| T.E. Bailey | c Miller b Archer | 14 | | |
| T.G. Evans† | c Langley b Miller | 0 | (5) not out | 8 |
| J.C. Laker | not out | 9 | | |
| G.A.R. Lock | lbw b Miller | 0 | | |
| R. Appleyard | not out | 1 | | |
| A.E. Moss | did not bat | | | |
| Extras | (B 5, LB 1) | 6 | (B 4, LB 1, W 2, NB 1) | 8 |
| **Total** | **(8 wickets declared)** | **217** | **(3 wickets declared)** | **188** |

### AUSTRALIA

| | | | | |
|---|---|---|---|---|
| C.C. McDonald | lbw b Lock | 1 | c Lock b Laker | 6 |
| J.W. Burke | c Lock b Laker | 11 | not out | 58 |
| R.N. Harvey | lbw b Lock | 64 | b Lock | 3 |
| P.J.P. Burge | c sub (J.M. Parks) b Lock | 7 | (5) not out | 35 |
| K.R. Miller | lbw b Laker | 0 | (4) lbw b Laker | 4 |
| R.G. Archer | c Lock b Appleyard | 33 | | |
| R. Benaud | b Appleyard | 17 | | |
| I.W. Johnson* | c Bailey b Laker | 12 | | |
| R.R. Lindwall | c Bailey b Laker | 0 | | |
| G.R.A. Langley† | not out | 0 | | |
| A.K. Davidson | absent hurt | – | | |
| Extras | (LB 3) | 3 | (B 10, LB 3, NB 1) | 14 |
| **Total** | | **148** | **(3 wickets)** | **120** |

| AUSTRALIA | O | M | R | W | O | M | R | W | | FALL OF WICKETS | | | |
|---|---|---|---|---|---|---|---|---|---|---|---|---|---|
| | | | | | | | | | | E | A | E | A |
| Lindwall | 15 | 4 | 43 | 0 | | | | | Wkt | 1st | 1st | 2nd | 2nd |
| Miller | 33 | 5 | 69 | 4 | 19 | 2 | 58 | 2 | 1st | 53 | 10 | 151 | 13 |
| Davidson | 9·4 | 1 | 22 | 1 | | | | | 2nd | 72 | 12 | 163 | 18 |
| Archer | 31 | 10 | 51 | 2 | 9 | 0 | 46 | 1 | 3rd | 180 | 33 | 178 | 41 |
| Johnson | 14 | 7 | 26 | 1 | 12 | 2 | 29 | 0 | 4th | 181 | 36 | – | – |
| Burke | 1 | 1 | 0 | 0 | 3 | 1 | 6 | 0 | 5th | 201 | 90 | – | – |
| Benaud | | | | | 18 | 4 | 41 | 0 | 6th | 203 | 110 | – | – |
| ENGLAND | | | | | | | | | 7th | 213 | 148 | – | – |
| Moss | 4 | 3 | 1 | 0 | | | | | 8th | 214 | 148 | – | – |
| Bailey | 3 | 1 | 8 | 0 | 9 | 3 | 16 | 0 | 9th | – | 148 | – | – |
| Laker | 29·1 | 11 | 58 | 4 | 30 | 19 | 29 | 2 | 10th | – | – | – | – |
| Lock | 36 | 16 | 61 | 3 | 22 | 11 | 23 | 1 | | | | | |
| Appleyard | 11 | 4 | 17 | 2 | 19 | 6 | 32 | 0 | | | | | |
| Graveney | | | | | 6 | 3 | 6 | 0 | | | | | |

Umpires: T.J. Bartley and J.S. Buller.

**Test No. 426/170**

# ENGLAND v AUSTRALIA 1956 (2nd Test)

Played at Lord's, London, on 21, 22, 23, 25, 26 June.
Toss: Australia.    Result: AUSTRALIA won by 185 runs.
Debuts: Australia – W.P.A. Crawford, K.D. Mackay.

Australia gained their first victory in England since 1948. McDonald and Burke's stand of 137 was the highest by Australia against England since 1930. Langley established a world Test record (which still stands) when he made his ninth dismissal of the match. Miller took ten wickets in the Test for the only time in his 55-match career. Crawford pulled a muscle behind his thigh and was unable to complete his first spell in Test cricket.

## AUSTRALIA

| | | | | |
|---|---|---|---|---|
| C.C. McDonald | c Trueman b Bailey | 78 | c Cowdrey b Bailey | 26 |
| J.W. Burke | st Evans b Laker | 65 | c Graveney b Trueman | 16 |
| R.N. Harvey | c Evans b Bailey | 0 | c Bailey b Trueman | 10 |
| P.J.P. Burge | b Statham | 21 | b Trueman | 14 |
| K.R. Miller | b Trueman | 28 | (7) c Evans b Trueman | 30 |
| K.D. Mackay | c Bailey b Laker | 38 | (5) c Evans b Statham | 31 |
| R.G. Archer | b Wardle | 28 | (6) c Evans b Bailey | 1 |
| R. Benaud | b Statham | 5 | c Evans b Trueman | 97 |
| I.W. Johnson* | c Evans b Trueman | 6 | lbw b Bailey | 17 |
| G.R.A. Langley† | c Bailey b Laker | 14 | not out | 7 |
| W.P.A. Crawford | not out | 0 | lbw b Bailey | 0 |
| Extras | (LB 2) | 2 | (B 2, LB 2, NB 4) | 8 |
| **Total** | | **285** | | **257** |

## ENGLAND

| | | | | |
|---|---|---|---|---|
| P.E. Richardson | c Langley b Miller | 9 | c Langley b Archer | 21 |
| M.C. Cowdrey | c Benaud b Mackay | 23 | lbw b Benaud | 27 |
| T.W. Graveney | b Miller | 5 | c Langley b Miller | 18 |
| P.B.H. May* | b Benaud | 63 | (5) c Langley b Miller | 53 |
| W. Watson | c Benaud b Miller | 6 | (4) b Miller | 18 |
| T.E. Bailey | b Miller | 32 | c Harvey b Archer | 18 |
| T.G. Evans† | st Langley b Benaud | 0 | c Langley b Miller | 20 |
| J.C. Laker | b Archer | 12 | c Langley b Archer | 4 |
| J.H. Wardle | c Langley b Archer | 0 | b Miller | 0 |
| F.S. Trueman | c Langley b Miller | 7 | b Archer | 2 |
| J.B. Statham | not out | 0 | not out | 0 |
| Extras | (LB 14) | 14 | (LB 5) | 5 |
| **Total** | | **171** | | **186** |

| ENGLAND | O | M | R | W | O | M | R | W |
|---|---|---|---|---|---|---|---|---|
| Statham | 35 | 9 | 70 | 2 | 26 | 5 | 59 | 1 |
| Trueman | 28 | 6 | 54 | 2 | 28 | 2 | 90 | 5 |
| Bailey | 34 | 12 | 72 | 2 | 24.5 | 8 | 64 | 4 |
| Laker | 29.1 | 10 | 47 | 3 | 7 | 3 | 17 | 0 |
| Wardle | 20 | 7 | 40 | 1 | 7 | 2 | 19 | 0 |
| AUSTRALIA | | | | | | | | |
| Miller | 34.1 | 9 | 72 | 5 | 36 | 12 | 80 | 5 |
| Crawford | 4.5 | 2 | 4 | 0 | | | | |
| Archer | 23 | 9 | 47 | 2 | 31.2 | 8 | 71 | 4 |
| Mackay | 11 | 3 | 15 | 1 | | | | |
| Benaud | 9 | 2 | 19 | 2 | 28 | 14 | 27 | 1 |
| Johnson | | | | | 4 | 2 | 3 | 0 |

### FALL OF WICKETS

| | A | E | A | E |
|---|---|---|---|---|
| Wkt | 1st | 1st | 2nd | 2nd |
| 1st | 137 | 22 | 36 | 35 |
| 2nd | 137 | 32 | 47 | 59 |
| 3rd | 151 | 60 | 69 | 89 |
| 4th | 185 | 87 | 70 | 91 |
| 5th | 196 | 128 | 79 | 142 |
| 6th | 249 | 128 | 112 | 175 |
| 7th | 255 | 161 | 229 | 180 |
| 8th | 265 | 161 | 243 | 184 |
| 9th | 285 | 170 | 257 | 184 |
| 10th | 285 | 171 | 257 | 186 |

Umpires: F.S. Lee and E. Davies.

Test No. 427/171

# ENGLAND v AUSTRALIA 1956 (3rd Test)

Played at Headingley, Leeds, on 12, 13, 14 (*no play*), 16, 17 July.
Toss: England. Result: ENGLAND won by an innings and 42 runs.
Debuts: England – A.S.M. Oakman.

Washbrook, who had not played Test cricket since the 1950-51 Australasian tour, was recalled to the England team at the age of 41 and whilst a selector. He joined May with the score 17 for 3 and their partnership of 187 in 287 minutes proved to be the turning point of the rubber. May became the first England batsman to score five consecutive fifties against Australia.

### ENGLAND

| | | |
|---|---|---:|
| P.E. Richardson | c Maddocks b Archer | 5 |
| M.C. Cowdrey | c Maddocks b Archer | 0 |
| A.S.M. Oakman | b Archer | 4 |
| P.B.H. May* | c Lindwall b Johnson | 101 |
| C. Washbrook | lbw b Benaud | 98 |
| G.A.R. Lock | c Miller b Benaud | 21 |
| D.J. Insole | c Mackay b Benaud | 5 |
| T.E. Bailey | not out | 33 |
| T.G. Evans† | b Lindwall | 40 |
| J.C. Laker | b Lindwall | 5 |
| F.S. Trueman | c and b Lindwall | 0 |
| Extras | (B 4, LB 9) | 13 |
| **Total** | | **325** |

### AUSTRALIA

| | | | | |
|---|---|---:|---|---:|
| C.C. McDonald | c Evans b Trueman | 2 | b Trueman | 6 |
| J.W. Burke | lbw b Lock | 41 | b Laker | 16 |
| R.N. Harvey | c Trueman b Lock | 11 | c and b Lock | 69 |
| P.J.P. Burge | lbw b Laker | 2 | (5) lbw b Laker | 5 |
| K.D. Mackay | c Bailey b Laker | 2 | (8) b Laker | 2 |
| K.R. Miller | b Laker | 41 | (4) c Trueman b Laker | 26 |
| R.G. Archer | b Laker | 4 | (9) c Washbrook b Lock | 1 |
| R. Benaud | c Oakman b Laker | 30 | (6) b Laker | 1 |
| L.V. Maddocks† | c Trueman b Lock | 0 | (10) lbw b Lock | 0 |
| I.W. Johnson* | c Richardson b Lock | 0 | (7) c Oakman b Laker | 3 |
| R.R. Lindwall | not out | 0 | not out | 0 |
| Extras | (B 4, LB 6) | 10 | (B 7, LB 4) | 11 |
| **Total** | | **143** | | **140** |

| AUSTRALIA | O | M | R | W | O | M | R | W |
|---|---|---|---|---|---|---|---|---|
| Lindwall | 33.4 | 11 | 67 | 3 | | | | |
| Archer | 50 | 24 | 68 | 3 | | | | |
| Mackay | 13 | 3 | 29 | 0 | | | | |
| Benaud | 42 | 9 | 89 | 3 | | | | |
| Johnson | 29 | 8 | 59 | 1 | | | | |
| ENGLAND | | | | | | | | |
| Trueman | 8 | 2 | 19 | 1 | 11 | 3 | 21 | 1 |
| Bailey | 7 | 2 | 15 | 0 | 7 | 2 | 13 | 0 |
| Laker | 29 | 10 | 58 | 5 | 41.3 | 21 | 55 | 6 |
| Lock | 27.1 | 11 | 41 | 4 | 40 | 23 | 40 | 3 |

### FALL OF WICKETS

| | E | A | A |
|---|---|---|---|
| Wkt | 1st | 1st | 2nd |
| 1st | 2 | 2 | 10 |
| 2nd | 8 | 40 | 45 |
| 3rd | 17 | 59 | 108 |
| 4th | 204 | 59 | 120 |
| 5th | 226 | 63 | 128 |
| 6th | 243 | 69 | 136 |
| 7th | 248 | 142 | 138 |
| 8th | 301 | 143 | 140 |
| 9th | 321 | 143 | 140 |
| 10th | 325 | 143 | 140 |

Umpires: J.S. Buller and D. Davies.

Test No. 428/172

# ENGLAND v AUSTRALIA 1956 (4th Test)

Played at Old Trafford, Manchester, on 26, 27, 28, 30, 31 July.
Toss: England. Result: ENGLAND won by an innings and 170 runs.
Debuts: Nil.

'Laker's Match', in which the Yorkshire-born Surrey offspinner broke several major bowling records with his match analysis of 19 for 90, all taken from the Stretford End: most wickets in any first-class match; only instance of ten wickets in a Test innings; only instance of ten wickets in a season twice – also 10 for 88 for Surrey v Australians; 39 wickets in the rubber equalling A.V. Bedser's record for England–Australia matches with a game to play. Not since 1905 had England twice beaten Australia in a home rubber, nor indeed finished a Test against them at Manchester.

### ENGLAND

| | | |
|---|---|---|
| P.E. Richardson | c Maddocks b Benaud | 104 |
| M.C. Cowdrey | c Maddocks b Lindwall | 80 |
| Rev.D.S. Sheppard | b Archer | 113 |
| P.B.H. May* | c Archer b Benaud | 43 |
| T.E. Bailey | b Johnson | 20 |
| C. Washbrook | lbw b Johnson | 6 |
| A.S.M. Oakman | c Archer b Johnson | 10 |
| T.G. Evans† | st Maddocks b Johnson | 47 |
| J.C. Laker | run out | 3 |
| G.A.R. Lock | not out | 25 |
| J.B. Statham | c Maddocks b Lindwall | 0 |
| Extras | (B 2, LB 5, W 1) | 8 |
| **Total** | | **459** |

### AUSTRALIA

| | | | | | |
|---|---|---|---|---|---|
| C.C. McDonald | c Lock b Laker | 32 | | c Oakman b Laker | 89 |
| J.W. Burke | c Cowdrey b Lock | 22 | | c Lock b Laker | 33 |
| R.N. Harvey | b Laker | 0 | | c Cowdrey b Laker | 0 |
| I.D. Craig | lbw b Laker | 8 | | lbw b Laker | 38 |
| K.R. Miller | c Oakman b Laker | 6 | (6) | b Laker | 0 |
| K.D. Mackay | c Oakman b Laker | 0 | (5) | c Oakman b Laker | 0 |
| R.G. Archer | st Evans b Laker | 6 | | c Oakman b Laker | 0 |
| R. Benaud | c Statham b Laker | 0 | | b Laker | 18 |
| R.R. Lindwall | not out | 6 | | c Lock b Laker | 8 |
| L.V. Maddocks† | b Laker | 4 | (11) | lbw b Laker | 2 |
| I.W. Johnson* | b Laker | 0 | (10) | not out | 1 |
| Extras | | 0 | | (B 12, LB 4) | 16 |
| **Total** | | **84** | | | **205** |

| AUSTRALIA | O | M | R | W | O | M | R | W | | FALL OF WICKETS | | |
|---|---|---|---|---|---|---|---|---|---|---|---|---|
| Lindwall | 21·3 | 6 | 63 | 2 | | | | | | E | A | A |
| Miller | 21 | 6 | 41 | 0 | | | | | Wkt | 1st | 1st | 2nd |
| Archer | 22 | 6 | 73 | 1 | | | | | 1st | 174 | 48 | 28 |
| Johnson | 47 | 10 | 151 | 4 | | | | | 2nd | 195 | 48 | 55 |
| Benaud | 47 | 17 | 123 | 2 | | | | | 3rd | 288 | 62 | 114 |
| | | | | | | | | | 4th | 321 | 62 | 124 |
| ENGLAND | | | | | | | | | 5th | 327 | 62 | 130 |
| Statham | 6 | 3 | 6 | 0 | 16 | 10 | 15 | 0 | 6th | 339 | 73 | 130 |
| Bailey | 4 | 3 | 4 | 0 | 20 | 8 | 31 | 0 | 7th | 401 | 73 | 181 |
| Laker | 16·4 | 4 | 37 | 9 | 51·2 | 23 | 53 | 10 | 8th | 417 | 78 | 198 |
| Lock | 14 | 3 | 37 | 1 | 55 | 30 | 69 | 0 | 9th | 458 | 84 | 203 |
| Oakman | | | | | 8 | 3 | 21 | 0 | 10th | 459 | 84 | 205 |

Umpires: F.S. Lee and E. Davies.

Test No. 429/173

# ENGLAND v AUSTRALIA 1956 (5th Test)

Played at Kennington Oval, London, on 23, 24, 25, 27 (*no play*), 28 August.
Toss: England.  Result: MATCH DRAWN.
Debuts: Nil.

Exactly the same amount of time, 12 hours 20 minutes, was lost to rain as in the 1st Test – with the same result. The selectors completed their hat-trick of successful recalls, Compton, minus his right knee-cap, top-scoring with 94 to follow the achievements of Washbrook and Sheppard in the previous two Tests. Laker extended his record haul to 46 wickets in the rubber. Harvey kept wicket when Langley retired to hospital after being struck on the forehead by a ball from Archer.

### ENGLAND

| | | | | |
|---|---|---|---|---|
| P.E. Richardson | c Langley b Miller | 37 | c Langley b Lindwall | 34 |
| M.C. Cowdrey | c Langley b Lindwall | 0 | c Benaud b Davidson | 8 |
| Rev.D.S. Sheppard | c Archer b Miller | 24 | c Archer b Miller | 62 |
| P.B.H. May* | not out | 83 | not out | 37 |
| D.C.S. Compton | c Davidson b Archer | 94 | not out | 35 |
| G.A.R. Lock | c Langley b Archer | 0 | | |
| C. Washbrook | lbw b Archer | 0 | | |
| T.G. Evans† | lbw b Miller | 0 | | |
| J.C. Laker | c Archer b Miller | 4 | | |
| F.H. Tyson | c Davidson b Archer | 3 | | |
| J.B. Statham | b Archer | 0 | | |
| Extras | (W2) | 2 | (B 3, LB 3) | 6 |
| Total | | 247 | (3 wickets declared) | 182 |

### AUSTRALIA

| | | | | |
|---|---|---|---|---|
| C.C. McDonald | c Lock b Tyson | 3 | lbw b Statham | 0 |
| J.W. Burke | b Laker | 8 | lbw b Laker | 1 |
| R.N. Harvey | c May b Lock | 39 | c May b Lock | 1 |
| I.D. Craig | c Statham b Lock | 2 | c Lock b Laker | 7 |
| I.W. Johnson* | b Laker | 12 | (6) c Lock b Laker | 10 |
| A.K. Davidson | c May b Laker | 8 | | |
| K.R. Miller | c Washbrook b Statham | 61 | (5) not out | 7 |
| R.G. Archer | c Tyson b Laker | 9 | | |
| R. Benaud | b Statham | 32 | (7) not out | 0 |
| R.R. Lindwall | not out | 22 | | |
| G.R.A. Langley† | lbw b Statham | 0 | | |
| Extras | (B 6) | 6 | (B 1) | 1 |
| Total | | 202 | (5 wickets) | 27 |

| AUSTRALIA | O | M | R | W | O | M | R | W | FALL OF WICKETS |
|---|---|---|---|---|---|---|---|---|---|
| | | | | | | | | | E A E A |
| Lindwall | 18 | 5 | 36 | 1 | 12 | 3 | 29 | 1 | Wkt 1st 1st 2nd 2nd |
| Miller | 40 | 7 | 91 | 4 | 22 | 3 | 56 | 1 | 1st 1 3 17 0 |
| Davidson | 5 | 1 | 16 | 0 | 5 | 0 | 18 | 1 | 2nd 53 17 100 1 |
| Archer | 28·2 | 7 | 53 | 5 | 13 | 3 | 42 | 0 | 3rd 66 20 108 5 |
| Johnson | 9 | 2 | 28 | 0 | 4 | 1 | 7 | 0 | 4th 222 35 – 10 |
| Benaud | 9 | 2 | 21 | 0 | 1 | 0 | 10 | 0 | 5th 222 47 – 27 |
| Burke | | | | | 4 | 2 | 14 | 0 | 6th 222 90 – – |
| ENGLAND | | | | | | | | | 7th 223 111 – – |
| Statham | 21 | 8 | 33 | 3 | 2 | 1 | 1 | 1 | 8th 231 154 – – |
| Tyson | 14 | 5 | 34 | 1 | | | | | 9th 243 202 – – |
| Laker | 32 | 12 | 80 | 4 | 18 | 14 | 8 | 3 | 10th 247 202 – – |
| Lock | 25 | 10 | 49 | 2 | 18·1 | 11 | 17 | 1 | |

Umpires: D. Davies and T.J. Bartley.

Chapter 5
# SOUTH AFRICA 1956/57

The winter of 1956/57 was the tour of South Africa. Cowdrey was chosen as an opener. In the event Trevor Bailey opened in all five tests and Cowdrey was able to revert to his preferred position but he had a moderate tour for a player of his capabilities. There were days when he looked in the highest class but on other occasions he found himself tied down completely by slow bowling, particularly that of Tayfield. Neither for the first nor the last time onlookers were saying that Cowdrey did not realise how good he was and if only he did and batted accordingly, he would take opposition attacks apart. I reflected that a batsman was only as good as he felt at the crease at the time. Be that as it may, because of his splendid anticipation Cowdrey developed into a first class slip fielder to the slow bowlers.

In the first Test at Johannesburg England won by 131 runs. The one effective partnership of the match was that between Richardson and Cowdrey after England were 48 for 3 on the first day. It soon ended the second day when Cowdrey was caught Goddard off Heine for 59. Cowdrey caught South Africa's No 2, 3 and 4, off Statham, Bailey and Laker respectively, in their first innings.

The second Test at Newlands, Cape Town was won by England by 312 runs. Cowdrey scored significantly in both innings. In the first Cowdrey joined Compton and they added 67. Cowdrey and Godfrey Evans put on 93 in 85 minutes of which Evans scored 62. Cowdrey needed 29 for his century when last man Statham joined him. Cowdrey himself was out one run after reaching it, having batted 6 hours and 10 minutes with one six and nine fours. In the second innings Cowdrey and Compton again shared a good stand. This time Cowdrey showed his wide range of strokes scoring 61 of the 87 added in 86 minutes. In South Africa's second innings Endean was given out "handled ball". Ironically he had been the wicket keeper when Hutton was given out "obstructing the field" at the Oval in 1951.

In the third, at Kingsmead, Durban, they had to fight for a draw. Cowdrey contributed only 6 and 24.

The fourth, at New Wanderers, Johannesburg, was lost by 17 runs. In the final innings England decided on a bold policy which nearly succeeded. Insole found good partners first with Richardson and then with Cowdrey who made a fine determined effort before being caught and bowled by Tayfield for 55. He was running out of partners having stayed 3 hours and twenty minutes.

In the fifth, at St George's Park, Port Elizabeth, England also lost, by 58 runs, so that the rubber was halved. It was a low scoring match – 164 110 134 130 – on a suspect pitch. Cowdrey made only 3 and 8. Endean's 70 in the first innings was the decisive innings.

|  | Matches | Innings | Not out | Runs | Highest score | Average | 100s | 50s | Caught |
|---|---|---|---|---|---|---|---|---|---|
| This series | 5 | 10 | 0 | 331 | 101 | 33.10 | 1 | 3 | 10 |
| Previous series | 13 | 22 | 1 | 678 | 102 | 32.29 | 1 | 5 | 8 |
| Cumulative totals | 18 | 32 | 1 | 1009 | 102 | 32.55 | 2 | 8 | 18 |

*1000 runs in test cricket*

Test No. 434/85

# SOUTH AFRICA v ENGLAND 1956–57 (1st Test)

Played at New Wanderers, Johannesburg, on 24, 26, 27, 28, 29 December.
Toss: England.   Result: ENGLAND won by 131 runs.
Debuts: South Africa – A.I. Taylor.

This was the first Test match to be played on the New Wanderers ground and it attracted the highest attendance (100,000) for any match in South Africa so far. Richardson took 488 minutes to reach what was then the slowest century in Test cricket. South Africa's total of 72 was their lowest in a home Test since 1898–99.

## ENGLAND

| | | | | |
|---|---|---|---|---|
| P.E. Richardson | lbw b Goddard | 117 | lbw b Adcock | 10 |
| T.E. Bailey | c Waite b Heine | 16 | c Endean b Heine | 10 |
| D.C.S. Compton | c Keith b Goddard | 5 | c and b Tayfield | 32 |
| P.B.H. May* | c Goddard b Adcock | 6 | (6) c Endean b Heine | 14 |
| M.C. Cowdrey | c Goddard b Heine | 59 | (7) c Goddard b Adcock | 6 |
| D.J. Insole | c Waite b Van Ryneveld | 1 | (5) c Waite b Goddard | 29 |
| T.G. Evans† | c Keith b Adcock | 20 | (8) c Heine b Tayfield | 30 |
| F.H. Tyson | b Adcock | 22 | (9) c Watkins b Adcock | 2 |
| J.H. Wardle | not out | 6 | (4) lbw b Heine | 0 |
| J.C. Laker | c Goddard b Adcock | 0 | not out | 3 |
| J.B. Statham | c Waite b Goddard | 0 | lbw b Tayfield | 2 |
| Extras | (B 4, LB 9, NB 3) | 16 | (B 8, LB 1, NB 3) | 12 |
| **Total** | | **268** | | **150** |

## SOUTH AFRICA

| | | | | |
|---|---|---|---|---|
| A.I. Taylor | st Evans b Wardle | 12 | c Insole b Bailey | 6 |
| T.L. Goddard | c Cowdrey b Statham | 49 | c Insole b Bailey | 5 |
| H.J. Keith | c Cowdrey b Bailey | 42 | c Evans b Bailey | 2 |
| W.R. Endean | c Cowdrey b Laker | 18 | (5) b Statham | 3 |
| R.A. McLean | lbw b Bailey | 0 | (6) c Insole b Bailey | 6 |
| J.C. Watkins | c Insole b Wardle | 9 | (7) b Laker | 8 |
| C.B. van Ryneveld* | c Bailey b Statham | 10 | (8) run out | 16 |
| J.H.B. Waite† | c Evans b Bailey | 17 | (4) b Statham | 0 |
| H.J. Tayfield | b Wardle | 24 | c Evans b Bailey | 2 |
| P.S. Heine | not out | 13 | run out | 17 |
| N.A.T. Adcock | b Statham | 17 | not out | 0 |
| Extras | (B 1, LB 3) | 4 | (B 2, LB 3, NB 2) | 7 |
| **Total** | | **215** | | **72** |

| SOUTH AFRICA | O | M | R | W | O | M | R | W | FALL OF WICKETS | | | | |
|---|---|---|---|---|---|---|---|---|---|---|---|---|---|
| Heine | 31 | 5 | 89 | 2 | 19 | 7 | 41 | 3 | | E | SA | E | SA |
| Adcock | 20 | 6 | 36 | 4 | 13 | 1 | 33 | 3 | Wkt | 1st | 1st | 2nd | 2nd |
| Goddard | 28·5 | 9 | 51 | 3 | 14 | 7 | 14 | 1 | 1st | 28 | 54 | 11 | 6 |
| Watkins | 11 | 3 | 23 | 0 | 3 | 0 | 10 | 0 | 2nd | 37 | 92 | 37 | 10 |
| Tayfield | 20 | 4 | 30 | 0 | 17·6 | 5 | 40 | 3 | 3rd | 48 | 112 | 37 | 11 |
| Van Ryneveld | 8 | 2 | 23 | 1 | | | | | 4th | 169 | 112 | 84 | 20 |
| ENGLAND | | | | | | | | | 5th | 170 | 126 | 100 | 25 |
| Statham | 24·1 | 4 | 71 | 3 | 13 | 4 | 22 | 2 | 6th | 205 | 141 | 107 | 36 |
| Tyson | 9 | 1 | 22 | 0 | | | | | 7th | 259 | 141 | 126 | 40 |
| Wardle | 20 | 4 | 52 | 3 | 3 | 0 | 18 | 0 | 8th | 263 | 176 | 145 | 44 |
| Laker | 21 | 10 | 33 | 1 | 2 | 1 | 5 | 1 | 9th | 263 | 194 | 147 | 71 |
| Bailey | 15 | 5 | 33 | 3 | 15·4 | 6 | 20 | 5 | 10th | 268 | 215 | 150 | 72 |

Umpires: W. Marais and J.H. McMenamin.

Test No. 435/86

# SOUTH AFRICA v ENGLAND 1956–57 (2nd Test)

Played at Newlands, Cape Town, on 1, 2, 3, 4, 5 January.
Toss: England.   Result: ENGLAND won by 312 runs.
Debuts: Nil.

The only 'handled ball' dismissal in Test cricket occurred on the fifth day; Endean padded away a ball from Laker pitched outside the off stump and, as it deflected upwards and towards the stumps, he diverted it with his hand. Endean was involved in Test cricket's other unique dismissal when Hutton was given out 'obstructing the field' in 1951 (*Test No. 338*).

### ENGLAND

| | | | | |
|---|---|---|---|---|
| P.E. Richardson | lbw b Heine | 45 | c Endean b Goddard | 44 |
| T.E. Bailey | c Waite b Tayfield | 34 | b Heine | 28 |
| D.C.S. Compton | c McLean b Tayfield | 58 | c and b Goddard | 64 |
| P.B.H. May* | c Waite b Tayfield | 8 | c Waite b Heine | 15 |
| M.C. Cowdrey | lbw b Adcock | 101 | c Waite b Tayfield | 61 |
| D.J. Insole | c Goddard b Adcock | 29 | (7) not out | 3 |
| T.G. Evans† | c McGlew b Goddard | 62 | (6) c Endean b Goddard | 1 |
| J.H. Wardle | st Waite b Tayfield | 3 | | |
| J.C. Laker | b Adcock | 0 | | |
| P.J. Loader | c Keith b Tayfield | 10 | | |
| J.B. Statham | not out | 2 | | |
| Extras | (B 6, LB 6, NB 5) | 17 | (LB 2, NB 2) | 4 |
| Total | | 369 | (6 wickets declared) | 220 |

### SOUTH AFRICA

| | | | | |
|---|---|---|---|---|
| D.J. McGlew | c Cowdrey b Laker | 14 | b Wardle | 7 |
| T.L. Goddard | c Evans b Loader | 18 | c Bailey b Wardle | 26 |
| H.J. Keith | c Evans b Loader | 14 | c May b Wardle | 4 |
| C.B. van Ryneveld* | b Wardle | 25 | (7) not out | 0 |
| H.J. Tayfield | run out | 5 | (10) c Evans b Wardle | 4 |
| R.A. McLean | c May b Statham | 42 | (5) lbw b Laker | 22 |
| J.H.B. Waite† | c Evans b Wardle | 49 | (6) c Cowdrey b Wardle | 2 |
| W.R. Endean | b Wardle | 17 | (4) handled ball | 3 |
| J.C. Watkins | not out | 7 | (8) c and b Wardle | 0 |
| P.S. Heine | b Wardle | 0 | (9) b Wardle | 0 |
| N.A.T. Adcock | c Evans b Wardle | 11 | b Laker | 1 |
| Extras | (B 1, LB 1, NB 1) | 3 | (LB 2, NB 1) | 3 |
| Total | | 205 | | 72 |

| SOUTH AFRICA | O | M | R | W | O | M | R | W | FALL OF WICKETS | | | | |
|---|---|---|---|---|---|---|---|---|---|---|---|---|---|
| Heine | 19 | 0 | 78 | 1 | 21 | 1 | 67 | 2 | | E | SA | E | SA |
| Adcock | 22·2 | 2 | 54 | 3 | 3 | 0 | 8 | 0 | Wkt | 1st | 1st | 2nd | 2nd |
| Tayfield | 53 | 21 | 130 | 5 | 12 | 4 | 33 | 1 | 1st | 76 | 23 | 74 | 21 |
| Goddard | 38 | 12 | 74 | 1 | 17·5 | 1 | 62 | 3 | 2nd | 88 | 39 | 74 | 28 |
| Van Ryneveld | 3 | 0 | 16 | 0 | | | | | 3rd | 116 | 48 | 109 | 42 |
| Watkins | | | | | 10 | 2 | 46 | 0 | 4th | 183 | 63 | 196 | 56 |
| ENGLAND | | | | | | | | | 5th | 233 | 110 | 208 | 67 |
| Statham | 16 | 0 | 38 | 1 | 8 | 2 | 12 | 0 | 6th | 326 | 126 | 220 | 67 |
| Loader | 21 | 5 | 33 | 2 | 7 | 2 | 11 | 0 | 7th | 334 | 178 | – | 67 |
| Laker | 28 | 8 | 65 | 1 | 14·1 | 9 | 7 | 2 | 8th | 335 | 191 | – | 67 |
| Bailey | 11 | 5 | 13 | 0 | | | | | 9th | 346 | 191 | – | 71 |
| Wardle | 23·6 | 9 | 53 | 5 | 19 | 3 | 36 | 7 | 10th | 369 | 205 | – | 72 |
| Compton | | | | | 2 | 1 | 3 | 0 | | | | | |

Umpires: D. Collins and V. Costello.

Test No. 436/87

# SOUTH AFRICA v ENGLAND 1956–57 (3rd Test)

Played at Kingsmead, Durban, on 25, 26, 28, 29, 30 January.
Toss: England.   Result: MATCH DRAWN.
Debuts: South Africa – A.J. Pithey.

In the second innings, Bailey retired hurt at 48 for 1, a bone in his right hand fractured by a short ball from Heine. He resumed at 167 for 5 with his hand in plaster and scored three more runs in 55 minutes. Tayfield's analysis of 8 for 69 was the best by a South African bowler in Tests and his spell of 137 balls without conceding a run remains a record for all first-class cricket.

## ENGLAND

| | | | | | |
|---|---|---|---|---|---|
| P.E. Richardson | lbw b Adcock | 68 | b Van Ryneveld | | 32 |
| T.E. Bailey | c Keith b Adcock | 80 | c Van Ryneveld b Tayfield | | 18 |
| D.C.S. Compton | b Heine | 16 | c Keith b Tayfield | | 19 |
| P.B.H. May* | c Goddard b Tayfield | 2 | (5) lbw b Tayfield | | 2 |
| M.C. Cowdrey | lbw b Goddard | 6 | (6) lbw b Heine | | 24 |
| D.J. Insole | b Van Ryneveld | 13 | (4) not out | | 110 |
| T.G. Evans† | st Waite b Van Ryneveld | 0 | c Waite b Tayfield | | 10 |
| J.H. Wardle | b Heine | 13 | c Waite b Tayfield | | 8 |
| J.C. Laker | not out | 0 | c Goddard b Tayfield | | 6 |
| P.J. Loader | c Waite b Adcock | 1 | lbw b Tayfield | | 3 |
| J.B. Statham | b Adcock | 6 | c Van Ryneveld b Tayfield | | 9 |
| Extras | (B 2, LB 4, W 5, NB 2) | 13 | (B 8, LB 4, NB 1) | | 13 |
| **Total** | | **218** | | | **254** |

## SOUTH AFRICA

| | | | | | |
|---|---|---|---|---|---|
| A.J. Pithey | st Evans b Wardle | 25 | b Statham | | 0 |
| T.L. Goddard | lbw b Statham | 69 | c Cowdrey b Wardle | | 18 |
| H.J. Keith | c Evans b Loader | 6 | c sub (G.A.R. Lock) b Laker | | 22 |
| W.R. Endean | c sub (G.A.R. Lock) b Wardle | 5 | c and b Laker | | 26 |
| R.A. McLean | c Insole b Bailey | 100 | b Wardle | | 4 |
| K.J. Funston | b Wardle | 19 | b Loader | | 44 |
| J.H.B. Waite† | b Statham | 12 | (8) not out | | 1 |
| C.B. van Ryneveld* | c Cowdrey b Loader | 16 | (7) not out | | 14 |
| H.J. Tayfield | not out | 20 | | | |
| P.S. Heine | b Wardle | 6 | | | |
| N.A.T. Adcock | lbw b Wardle | 3 | | | |
| Extras | (LB 2) | 2 | (B 5, LB 6, NB 2) | | 13 |
| **Total** | | **283** | (6 wickets) | | **142** |

| SOUTH AFRICA | O | M | R | W | O | M | R | W | | FALL OF WICKETS | | | |
|---|---|---|---|---|---|---|---|---|---|---|---|---|---|
| Heine | 16 | 2 | 65 | 2 | 22 | 3 | 58 | 1 | | E | SA | E | SA |
| Adcock | 15.3 | 3 | 39 | 4 | 21 | 8 | 39 | 0 | Wkt | 1st | 1st | 2nd | 2nd |
| Goddard | 25 | 11 | 42 | 1 | 13 | 5 | 26 | 0 | 1st | 115 | 65 | 45 | 0 |
| Tayfield | 24 | 17 | 21 | 1 | 37.7 | 14 | 69 | 8 | 2nd | 148 | 76 | 77 | 39 |
| Van Ryneveld | 14 | 4 | 38 | 2 | 14 | 2 | 49 | 1 | 3rd | 151 | 81 | 79 | 45 |
| ENGLAND | | | | | | | | | 4th | 163 | 145 | 144 | 49 |
| Statham | 22 | 4 | 56 | 2 | 11 | 0 | 32 | 1 | 5th | 186 | 199 | 167 | 124 |
| Loader | 25 | 6 | 79 | 2 | 8 | 2 | 21 | 1 | 6th | 186 | 225 | 192 | 124 |
| Bailey | 17 | 4 | 38 | 1 | | | | | 7th | 202 | 241 | 203 | – |
| Wardle | 20.2 | 6 | 61 | 5 | 20 | 7 | 42 | 2 | 8th | 210 | 264 | 220 | – |
| Laker | 12 | 1 | 47 | 0 | 18 | 7 | 29 | 2 | 9th | 212 | 279 | 230 | – |
| Compton | | | | | 1 | 0 | 5 | 0 | 10th | 218 | 283 | 254 | – |

Umpires: W. Marais and B.V. Malan.

Test No. 437/88

# SOUTH AFRICA v ENGLAND 1956-57 (4th Test)

Played at New Wanderers, Johannesburg, on 15, 16, 18, 19, 20 February.
Toss: South Africa.  Result: SOUTH AFRICA won by 17 runs.
Debuts: South Africa – C.A.R. Duckworth.

South Africa gained their first win against England at home since 1930-31; it was their first home win on a turf pitch in this series. Tayfield remains the only South African to take nine wickets in a Test innings, or 13 in a match. He bowled throughout the last day, sending down 35 eight-ball overs in 4 hours 50 minutes, and had Loader caught by his brother, Arthur, who was substituting for Funston.

### SOUTH AFRICA

| | | | | |
|---|---|---|---|---|
| A.J. Pithey | c Wardle b Bailey | 10 | b Laker | 18 |
| T.L. Goddard | b Bailey | 67 | c Evans b Bailey | 49 |
| J.H.B. Waite† | c Evans b Statham | 61 | (7) c Cowdrey b Statham | 17 |
| K.J. Funston | c Evans b Bailey | 20 | (3) run out | 23 |
| R.A. McLean | run out | 93 | (4) c Cowdrey b Statham | 0 |
| C.A.R. Duckworth | c Wardle b Loader | 13 | b Wardle | 3 |
| W.R. Endean | b Statham | 13 | (5) c Insole b Bailey | 2 |
| C.B. van Ryneveld* | c Cowdrey b Laker | 36 | c and b Statham | 12 |
| H.J. Tayfield | c Bailey b Wardle | 10 | not out | 12 |
| P.S. Heine | not out | 1 | c Insole b Wardle | 0 |
| N.A.T. Adcock | lbw b Wardle | 6 | run out | 1 |
| Extras | (LB 8, W 1, NB 1) | 10 | (B 4, LB 1) | 5 |
| **Total** | | **340** | | **142** |

### ENGLAND

| | | | | |
|---|---|---|---|---|
| P.E. Richardson | c Tayfield b Heine | 11 | b Tayfield | 39 |
| T.E. Bailey | c Waite b Adcock | 13 | c Endean b Tayfield | 1 |
| D.J. Insole | run out | 47 | c Tayfield b Goddard | 68 |
| P.B.H. May* | b Adcock | 61 | (5) c Endean b Tayfield | 0 |
| D.C.S. Compton | c Pithey b Heine | 42 | (6) c Goddard b Tayfield | 1 |
| M.C. Cowdrey | c Goddard b Tayfield | 8 | (4) c and b Tayfield | 55 |
| T.G. Evans† | c Endean b Tayfield | 7 | (8) b Tayfield | 8 |
| J.H. Wardle | c Goddard b Tayfield | 16 | (7) c Waite b Tayfield | 22 |
| J.C. Laker | lbw b Tayfield | 17 | c Duckworth b Tayfield | 5 |
| P.J. Loader | c Endean b Goddard | 13 | c sub (A. Tayfield) b Tayfield | 7 |
| J.B. Statham | not out | 12 | not out | 4 |
| Extras | (LB 1, NB 3) | 4 | (B 1, LB 3) | 4 |
| **Total** | | **251** | | **214** |

| ENGLAND | O | M | R | W | O | M | R | W | FALL OF WICKETS | | | |
|---|---|---|---|---|---|---|---|---|---|---|---|---|
| Statham | 23 | 5 | 81 | 2 | 13 | 1 | 37 | 3 | | SA | E | SA | E |
| Loader | 23 | 3 | 78 | 1 | 13 | 3 | 33 | 0 | Wkt | 1st | 1st | 2nd | 2nd |
| Bailey | 21 | 3 | 54 | 3 | 13 | 4 | 12 | 2 | 1st | 22 | 25 | 62 | 10 |
| Wardle | 19·6 | 4 | 68 | 2 | 14 | 4 | 29 | 2 | 2nd | 134 | 40 | 91 | 65 |
| Laker | 15 | 3 | 49 | 1 | 7 | 1 | 26 | 1 | 3rd | 151 | 131 | 94 | 147 |
| SOUTH AFRICA | | | | | | | | | 4th | 172 | 135 | 95 | 148 |
| Adcock | 21 | 5 | 52 | 2 | 8 | 1 | 22 | 0 | 5th | 238 | 152 | 97 | 156 |
| Heine | 23 | 6 | 54 | 2 | 8 | 1 | 21 | 0 | 6th | 251 | 160 | 104 | 186 |
| Goddard | 25·2 | 15 | 22 | 1 | 25 | 5 | 54 | 1 | 7th | 309 | 176 | 129 | 196 |
| Tayfield | 37 | 15 | 79 | 4 | 37 | 11 | 113 | 9 | 8th | 328 | 213 | 130 | 199 |
| Van Ryneveld | 8 | 0 | 40 | 0 | | | | | 9th | 333 | 227 | 131 | 208 |
| | | | | | | | | | 10th | 340 | 251 | 142 | 214 |

Umpires: B.V. Malan and J.H. McMenamin.

Test No. 438/89

# SOUTH AFRICA v ENGLAND 1956-57 (5th Test)

Played at St. George's Park, Port Elizabeth, on 1, 2, 4, 5 March.
Toss: South Africa.   Result: SOUTH AFRICA won by 58 runs.
Debuts: Nil.

Evans conceded only one bye on a recently relaid pitch where the ball frequently kept low or 'shot'. Waite tore fibres in his shoulder diving to stop a 'shooter' towards the end of the first innings and Endean took over as wicket-keeper after the first few overs of the second innings. Tayfield's 37 wickets in this rubber still stands as the South African record against any country.

## SOUTH AFRICA

| | | | | |
|---|---|---|---|---|
| A.J. Pithey | c Evans b Bailey | 15 | b Laker | 6 |
| T.L. Goddard | lbw b Bailey | 2 | c Evans b Tyson | 30 |
| J.H.B. Waite† | c Evans b Loader | 3 | (9) not out | 7 |
| K.J. Funston | b Bailey | 3 | b Lock | 24 |
| W.R. Endean | lbw b Tyson | 70 | (3) b Tyson | 1 |
| R.A. McLean | c Evans b Lock | 23 | b Bailey | 19 |
| C.B. van Ryneveld* | c Tyson b Loader | 24 | (5) lbw b Tyson | 13 |
| C.A.R. Duckworth | lbw b Laker | 6 | (7) b Tyson | 6 |
| H.J. Tayfield | b Loader | 4 | (8) c Evans b Tyson | 10 |
| P.S. Heine | b Tyson | 4 | c Evans b Tyson | 4 |
| N.A.T. Adcock | not out | 0 | b Bailey | 3 |
| Extras | (LB 1, NB 9) | 10 | (B 1, LB 7, NB 3) | 11 |
| **Total** | | **164** | | **134** |

## ENGLAND

| | | | | |
|---|---|---|---|---|
| P.E. Richardson | lbw b Adcock | 0 | b Adcock | 3 |
| T.E. Bailey | b Heine | 41 | c McLean b Tayfield | 18 |
| D.C.S. Compton | b Adcock | 0 | (6) c Endean b Tayfield | 5 |
| P.B.H. May* | c Duckworth b Goddard | 24 | (3) lbw b Goddard | 21 |
| D.J. Insole | lbw b Heine | 4 | c Duckworth b Tayfield | 8 |
| M.C. Cowdrey | c Waite b Adcock | 3 | (4) c Van Ryneveld b Tayfield | 8 |
| T.G. Evans† | b Heine | 5 | c Endean b Heine | 21 |
| G.A.R. Lock | b Adcock | 14 | c Goddard b Tayfield | 12 |
| F.H. Tyson | c and b Heine | 1 | c Tayfield b Goddard | 23 |
| J.C. Laker | b Goddard | 6 | not out | 3 |
| P.J. Loader | not out | 0 | c McLean b Tayfield | 0 |
| Extras | (B 8, LB 4) | 12 | (B 5, LB 3) | 8 |
| **Total** | | **110** | | **130** |

| ENGLAND | O | M | R | W | O | M | R | W | FALL OF WICKETS | | | | |
|---|---|---|---|---|---|---|---|---|---|---|---|---|---|
| Loader | 20 | 3 | 35 | 3 | 4 | 3 | 1 | 0 | | SA | E | SA | E |
| Bailey | 25 | 12 | 23 | 3 | 24.7 | 5 | 39 | 2 | Wkt | 1st | 1st | 2nd | 2nd |
| Tyson | 17 | 6 | 38 | 2 | 23 | 7 | 40 | 6 | 1st | 4 | 1 | 20 | 15 |
| Laker | 14 | 1 | 37 | 1 | 14 | 5 | 26 | 1 | 2nd | 15 | 1 | 21 | 41 |
| Lock | 11 | 5 | 21 | 1 | 15 | 6 | 17 | 1 | 3rd | 21 | 55 | 65 | 53 |
| | | | | | | | | | 4th | 41 | 77 | 98 | 57 |
| SOUTH AFRICA | | | | | | | | | 5th | 78 | 78 | 99 | 71 |
| Heine | 15 | 6 | 22 | 4 | 11 | 3 | 22 | 1 | 6th | 143 | 86 | 105 | 72 |
| Adcock | 11.3 | 4 | 20 | 4 | 7 | 2 | 10 | 1 | 7th | 155 | 89 | 111 | 99 |
| Tayfield | 22 | 8 | 43 | 0 | 24.3 | 6 | 78 | 6 | 8th | 155 | 97 | 123 | 127 |
| Goddard | 13 | 8 | 13 | 2 | 16 | 8 | 12 | 2 | 9th | 163 | 110 | 129 | 129 |
| | | | | | | | | | 10th | 164 | 110 | 134 | 130 |

Umpires: W. Marais and V. Costello.

## Chapter 6
# WEST INDIES 1957

The first Test against the West Indians in 1957 – the year in which Schweppes introduced "Bitter Lemon" – was one of the most memorable of Cowdrey's Test career. It was at Edgbaston Birmingham. It began with Ramadhin demoralising the England batsmen. He took seven for 49. England struggled to 186. West Indies replied with 474 and England were 120 for 3 when Cowdrey joined May early on Monday morning in their second innings. At stumps they were still together May having made 193 and Cowdrey 78. They were 90 runs ahead.

They continued on Tuesday until at 5.24 when they had put on 411 Cowdrey was out for 154 caught on the long on boundary, going for a six, by substitute N R Asgarali. The stand lasted 8 hours 20 minutes. It was Cowdrey's first Test century in England. Evans came in and scored 29 before May, having scored 285, declared. The match was drawn.

The second Test at Lord's brought more success. Cowdrey scored 152 in the first innings and in partnership with Evans put on 174 in 115 minutes. England won on Saturday evening by an innings and 36 runs.

The third Test at Trent Bridge was dominated by batsmen. England amassed 619 for six. Cowdrey's 55 paled into insignificance as Graveney scored 258 and Richardson and May both made centuries. West Indies twice batted well. Collie Smith making a particularly good 168 in the second innings to earn a draw.

The fourth Test at Leeds was won by an innings and 5 runs. Laker for the third time in the series deceived Walcott, Cowdrey holding a sharp slip catch. In reply to 142 in the first innings of West Indies, England made 279. A May and Cowdrey stand produced 94 and one with Sheppard followed of 91. When West Indies batted again Cowdrey disposed of Worrell with an excellent right handed slip catch. He later caught Weekes again off Trueman.

*For a bulky man Colin had quick reaction: foiling Sobers at the Oval in 1957.*

In the fifth at The Oval England scored 412 with centuries from Richardson and Graveney. May made 1 and Cowdrey was bowled by Ramadhin for 2 who might have had the last laugh. West Indies, however, were dismissed for 89 and 86 leaving England winners by an innings and 237 runs. West Indies had been beaten in three days for the third time in the rubber.

|  | Matches | Innings | Not out | Runs | Highest score | Average | 100s | 50s | Caught |
|---|---|---|---|---|---|---|---|---|---|
| This series | 5 | 6 | 0 | 435 | 154 | 72.50 | 2 | 2 | 8 |
| Previous series | 18 | 32 | 1 | 1009 | 102 | 32.55 | 2 | 8 | 18 |
| Cumulative totals | 23 | 38 | 1 | 1444 | 154 | 39.01 | 4 | 10 | 26 |

Test No. 439/31

# ENGLAND v WEST INDIES 1957 (1st Test)

Played at Edgbaston, Birmingham, on 30, 31 May, 1, 3, 4 June.
Toss: England.   Result: MATCH DRAWN.
Debuts: West Indies – R. Gilchrist, R.B. Kanhai.

Birmingham's first Test for 28 years brought a host of records. May's 285* remains the highest score by an England captain and the highest in any Edgbaston Test. His stand of 411 is still England's highest for any wicket and the Test record for the fourth wicket. Ramadhin bowled most balls (588) in any first-class innings and the most in any Test match (774); both records still stand. Smith scored a hundred in his first Test against England.

## ENGLAND

| | | | | | |
|---|---|---|---|---|---|
| P.E. Richardson | c Walcott b Ramadhin | 47 | c sub (N.R. Asgarali) b Ramadhin | | 34 |
| D.B. Close | c Kanhai b Gilchrist | 15 | c Weekes b Gilchrist | | 42 |
| D.J. Insole | b Ramadhin | 20 | b Ramadhin | | 0 |
| P.B.H. May* | c Weekes b Ramadhin | 30 | not out | | 285 |
| M.C. Cowdrey | c Gilchrist b Ramadhin | 4 | c sub (N.R. Asgarali) b Smith | | 154 |
| T.E. Bailey | b Ramadhin | 1 | | | |
| G.A.R. Lock | b Ramadhin | 0 | | | |
| T.G. Evans† | b Gilchrist | 14 | (6) not out | | 29 |
| J.C. Laker | b Ramadhin | 7 | | | |
| F.S. Trueman | not out | 29 | | | |
| J.B. Statham | b Atkinson | 13 | | | |
| Extras | (B 3, LB 3) | 6 | (B 23, LB 16) | | 39 |
| **Total** | | **186** | (4 wickets declared) | | **583** |

## WEST INDIES

| | | | | | |
|---|---|---|---|---|---|
| B.H. Pairaudeau | b Trueman | 1 | b Trueman | | 7 |
| R.B. Kanhai† | lbw b Statham | 42 | c Close b Trueman | | 1 |
| C.L. Walcott | c Evans b Laker | 90 | (6) c Lock b Laker | | 1 |
| E. de C. Weekes | b Trueman | 9 | c Trueman b Lock | | 33 |
| G. St A. Sobers | c Bailey b Statham | 53 | (3) c Cowdrey b Lock | | 14 |
| O.G. Smith | lbw b Laker | 161 | (7) lbw b Laker | | 5 |
| F.M.M. Worrell | b Statham | 81 | (5) c May b Lock | | 0 |
| J.D.C. Goddard* | c Lock b Laker | 24 | not out | | 0 |
| D. St E. Atkinson | c Statham b Laker | 1 | not out | | 4 |
| S. Ramadhin | not out | 5 | | | |
| R. Gilchrist | run out | 0 | | | |
| Extras | (B 1, LB 6) | 7 | (B 7) | | 7 |
| **Total** | | **474** | (7 wickets) | | **72** |

| WEST INDIES | O | M | R | W | O | M | R | W | FALL OF WICKETS |
|---|---|---|---|---|---|---|---|---|---|
| Worrell | 9 | 1 | 27 | 0 | | | | | | | | |
| Gilchrist | 27 | 4 | 74 | 2 | 26 | 2 | 67 | 1 | |
| Ramadhin | 31 | 16 | 49 | 7 | 98 | 35 | 179 | 2 | |
| Atkinson | 12.4 | 3 | 30 | 1 | 72 | 29 | 137 | 0 | |
| Sobers | | | | | 30 | 4 | 77 | 0 | |
| Smith | | | | | 26 | 4 | 72 | 1 | |
| Goddard | | | | | 6 | 2 | 12 | 0 | |

| | E | WI | E | WI |
|---|---|---|---|---|
| Wkt | 1st | 1st | 2nd | 2nd |
| 1st | 32 | 4 | 63 | 1 |
| 2nd | 61 | 83 | 65 | 9 |
| 3rd | 104 | 120 | 113 | 25 |
| 4th | 115 | 183 | 524 | 27 |
| 5th | 116 | 197 | – | 43 |
| 6th | 118 | 387 | – | 66 |
| 7th | 121 | 466 | – | 68 |
| 8th | 130 | 469 | – | – |
| 9th | 150 | 474 | – | – |
| 10th | 186 | 474 | – | – |

| ENGLAND | O | M | R | W | O | M | R | W |
|---|---|---|---|---|---|---|---|---|
| Statham | 39 | 4 | 114 | 3 | 2 | 0 | 6 | 0 |
| Trueman | 30 | 4 | 99 | 2 | 5 | 3 | 7 | 2 |
| Bailey | 34 | 11 | 80 | 0 | | | | |
| Laker | 54 | 17 | 119 | 4 | 24 | 20 | 13 | 2 |
| Lock | 34.4 | 15 | 55 | 0 | 27 | 19 | 31 | 3 |
| Close | | | | | 2 | 1 | 8 | 0 |

Umpires: C.S. Elliott and E. Davies.

Test No. 440/32

# ENGLAND v WEST INDIES 1957 (2nd Test)

Played at Lord's, London, on 20, 21, 22 June.
Toss: West Indies.  Result: ENGLAND won by an innings and 36 runs.
Debuts: England – D.V. Smith; West Indies – N.R. Asgarali.

Bailey's analysis of 7 for 44, returned in his 50th Test match, was the best for England in a home Test against West Indies (equalled by F.S. Trueman in 1963). Bailey's eleven wickets equalled England's match record for any West Indies Test.

### WEST INDIES

| | | | | | |
|---|---|---|---|---|---|
| N.R. Asgarali | lbw b Trueman | 0 | (4) c Trueman b Wardle | 26 |
| R.B. Kanhai† | c Cowdrey b Bailey | 34 | (1) c Bailey b Statham | 0 |
| C.L. Walcott | lbw b Bailey | 14 | c Trueman b Bailey | 21 |
| G. St A. Sobers | c May b Statham | 17 | (5) c May b Bailey | 66 |
| E. de C. Weekes | c Evans b Bailey | 13 | (6) c Evans b Bailey | 90 |
| F.M.M. Worrell | c Close b Bailey | 12 | (7) c Evans b Trueman | 10 |
| O.G. Smith | c Graveney b Bailey | 25 | (2) lbw b Statham | 5 |
| J.D.C. Goddard* | c Cowdrey b Bailey | 1 | c Evans b Trueman | 21 |
| S. Ramadhin | b Trueman | 0 | c Statham b Bailey | 0 |
| R. Gilchrist | c and b Bailey | 4 | not out | 11 |
| A.L. Valentine | not out | 0 | b Statham | 1 |
| Extras | (B 2, LB 1, W 4) | 7 | (B 4, LB 6) | 10 |
| **Total** | | **127** | | **261** |

### ENGLAND

| | | |
|---|---|---|
| P.E. Richardson | b Gilchrist | 76 |
| D.V. Smith | lbw b Worrell | 8 |
| T.W. Graveney | lbw b Gilchrist | 0 |
| P.B.H. May* | c Kanhai b Gilchrist | 0 |
| M.C. Cowdrey | c Walcott b Sobers | 152 |
| T.E. Bailey | b Worrell | 1 |
| D.B. Close | c Kanhai b Goddard | 32 |
| T.G. Evans† | b Sobers | 82 |
| J.H. Wardle | c Sobers b Ramadhin | 11 |
| F.S. Trueman | not out | 36 |
| J.B. Statham | b Gilchrist | 7 |
| Extras | (B 7, LB 11, W 1) | 19 |
| **Total** | | **424** |

| ENGLAND | O | M | R | W | O | M | R | W | FALL OF WICKETS | | | |
|---|---|---|---|---|---|---|---|---|---|---|---|---|
| Statham | 18 | 3 | 46 | 1 | 29.1 | 9 | 71 | 3 | | WI | E | WI |
| Trueman | 12.3 | 2 | 30 | 2 | 23 | 5 | 73 | 2 | Wkt | 1st | 1st | 2nd |
| Bailey | 21 | 8 | 44 | 7 | 22 | 6 | 54 | 4 | 1st | 7 | 25 | 0 |
| Wardle | | | | | 22 | 5 | 53 | 1 | 2nd | 34 | 34 | 17 |
| WEST INDIES | | | | | | | | | 3rd | 55 | 34 | 32 |
| Worrell | 42 | 7 | 114 | 2 | | | | | 4th | 79 | 129 | 80 |
| Gilchrist | 36.3 | 7 | 115 | 4 | | | | | 5th | 85 | 134 | 180 |
| Ramadhin | 22 | 5 | 83 | 1 | | | | | 6th | 118 | 192 | 203 |
| Valentine | 3 | 0 | 20 | 0 | | | | | 7th | 120 | 366 | 233 |
| Goddard | 13 | 1 | 45 | 1 | | | | | 8th | 123 | 379 | 241 |
| Sobers | 7 | 0 | 28 | 2 | | | | | 9th | 127 | 387 | 256 |
| | | | | | | | | | 10th | 127 | 424 | 261 |

Umpires: C.S. Elliott and E. Davies.

Test No. 441/33

# ENGLAND v WEST INDIES 1957 (3rd Test)

Played at Trent Bridge, Nottingham, on 4, 5, 6, 8, 9 July.
Toss: England.   Result: MATCH DRAWN.
Debuts: England – D.W. Richardson.

England's partnership of 266 between Richardson and Graveney, whose highest first-class score took 475 minutes and included 30 fours, remains their highest for the second wicket against West Indies. Worrell was the first to carry his bat through a completed West Indies innings and his stand of 55 with Ramadhin, who batted with a runner, is still the West Indies tenth-wicket record against England. Worrell was on the field for the first 20½ hours of the match.

### ENGLAND

| | | | | |
|---|---|---|---|---|
| P.E. Richardson | c Walcott b Atkinson | 126 | c Kanhai b Gilchrist | 11 |
| D.V. Smith | c Kanhai b Worrell | 1 | not out | 16 |
| T.W. Graveney | b Smith | 258 | not out | 28 |
| P.B.H. May* | lbw b Smith | 104 | | |
| M.C. Cowdrey | run out | 55 | | |
| D.W. Richardson | b Sobers | 33 | | |
| T.G. Evans† | not out | 26 | | |
| T.E. Bailey | not out | 3 | | |
| J.C. Laker | ) | | | |
| F.S. Trueman | ) did not bat | | | |
| J.B. Statham | ) | | | |
| Extras | (B 1, LB 10, W 1, NB 1) | 13 | (B 7, LB 2) | 9 |
| Total | (6 wickets declared) | 619 | (1 wicket) | 64 |

### WEST INDIES

| | | | | |
|---|---|---|---|---|
| F.M.M. Worrell | not out | 191 | b Statham | 16 |
| G. St A. Sobers | b Laker | 47 | lbw b Trueman | 9 |
| C.L. Walcott | c and b Laker | 17 | c Evans b Laker | 7 |
| R.B. Kanhai† | c Evans b Bailey | 42 | c Evans b Trueman | 28 |
| E. de C.Weekes | b Trueman | 33 | b Statham | 3 |
| O.G. Smith | c Evans b Trueman | 2 | b Trueman | 168 |
| D. St E. Atkinson | c Evans b Trueman | 4 | c Evans b Statham | 46 |
| J.D.C. Goddard* | c May b Trueman | 0 | c Evans b Statham | 61 |
| R. Gilchrist | c D.W. Richardson b Laker | 1 | (10) b Statham | 0 |
| A.L. Valentine | b Trueman | 1 | (11) not out | 2 |
| S. Ramadhin | b Statham | 19 | (9) b Trueman | 15 |
| Extras | (B 5, LB 10) | 15 | (B 2, LB 10) | 12 |
| Total | | 372 | | 367 |

| WEST INDIES | O | M | R | W | O | M | R | W | FALL OF WICKETS | | | |
|---|---|---|---|---|---|---|---|---|---|---|---|---|
| Worrell | 21 | 4 | 79 | 1 | 7 | 1 | 27 | 0 | | E | WI | WI | E |
| Gilchrist | 29 | 3 | 118 | 0 | 7 | 0 | 21 | 1 | Wkt | 1st | 1st | 2nd | 2nd |
| Atkinson | 40 | 7 | 99 | 1 | 1 | 0 | 1 | 0 | 1st | 14 | 87 | 22 | 13 |
| Ramadhin | 38 | 5 | 95 | 0 | | | | | 2nd | 280 | 120 | 30 | – |
| Valentine | 23 | 4 | 68 | 0 | | | | | 3rd | 487 | 229 | 39 | – |
| Sobers | 21 | 6 | 60 | 1 | | | | | 4th | 510 | 295 | 56 | – |
| Goddard | 15 | 5 | 26 | 0 | 1 | 0 | 2 | 0 | 5th | 573 | 297 | 89 | – |
| Smith | 25 | 5 | 61 | 2 | | | | | 6th | 609 | 305 | 194 | – |
| Walcott | | | | | 1 | 0 | 4 | 0 | 7th | – | 305 | 348 | – |
| ENGLAND | | | | | | | | | 8th | – | 314 | 352 | – |
| Statham | 28·4 | 9 | 78 | 1 | 41·2 | 12 | 118 | 5 | 9th | – | 317 | 365 | – |
| Trueman | 30 | 8 | 63 | 5 | 35 | 5 | 80 | 4 | 10th | – | 372 | 367 | – |
| Laker | 62 | 27 | 101 | 3 | 43 | 14 | 98 | 1 | | | | | |
| Bailey | 28 | 9 | 77 | 1 | 12 | 3 | 22 | 0 | | | | | |
| Smith | 12 | 1 | 38 | 0 | 12 | 5 | 23 | 0 | | | | | |
| Graveney | | | | | 5 | 2 | 14 | 0 | | | | | |

Umpires: F.S. Lee and J.S. Buller.

Test No. 442/34

# ENGLAND v WEST INDIES 1957 (4th Test)

Played at Headingley, Leeds, on 25, 26, 27 July.
Toss: West Indies.   Result: ENGLAND won by an innings and 5 runs.
Debuts: West Indies – F.C.M. Alexander.

West Indies last four first-innings wickets fell in consecutive balls, Trueman bowling Smith with the last ball of an over before Loader dismissed Goddard, Ramadhin and Gilchrist to complete the first hat-trick for England in a home Test since 1899. Evans became the first wicket-keeper to make 200 dismissals in Tests when he caught Smith.

## WEST INDIES

| | | | | | |
|---|---|---|---|---|---|
| F.M.M. Worrell | b Loader | 29 | c Cowdrey b Trueman | 7 |
| G. St A. Sobers | c Lock b Loader | 4 | run out | 29 |
| R.B. Kanhai | lbw b Laker | 47 | lbw b Loader | 0 |
| E. de C. Weekes | b Loader | 0 | c Cowdrey b Trueman | 14 |
| C.L. Walcott | c Cowdrey b Laker | 38 | c Sheppard b Loader | 35 |
| O.G. Smith | b Trueman | 15 | c Evans b Smith | 8 |
| B.H. Pairaudeau | b Trueman | 6 | c Trueman b Loader | 6 |
| J.D.C. Goddard* | b Loader | 1 | c Loader b Lock | 4 |
| F.C.M. Alexander† | not out | 0 | b Laker | 11 |
| S. Ramadhin | c Trueman b Loader | 0 | run out | 6 |
| R. Gilchrist | b Loader | 0 | not out | 6 |
| Extras | (LB 2) | 2 | (LB 5, NB 1) | 6 |
| **Total** | | **142** | | **132** |

## ENGLAND

| | | |
|---|---|---|
| P.E. Richardson | c Alexander b Worrell | 10 |
| D.V. Smith | b Worrell | 0 |
| T.W. Graveney | b Gilchrist | 22 |
| P.B.H. May* | c Alexander b Sobers | 69 |
| M.C. Cowdrey | c Weekes b Worrell | 68 |
| Rev. D.S. Sheppard | c Walcott b Worrell | 68 |
| T.G. Evans† | b Worrell | 10 |
| G.A.R. Lock | b Gilchrist | 20 |
| J.C. Laker | c Alexander b Worrell | 1 |
| F.S. Trueman | not out | 2 |
| P.J. Loader | c Pairaudeau b Worrell | 1 |
| Extras | (B 2, LB 5, W 1) | 8 |
| **Total** | | **279** |

| ENGLAND | O | M | R | W | O | M | R | W | | FALL OF WICKETS | | |
|---|---|---|---|---|---|---|---|---|---|---|---|---|
| | | | | | | | | | | WI | E | WI |
| Trueman | 17 | 4 | 33 | 2 | 11 | 0 | 42 | 2 | Wkt | 1st | 1st | 2nd |
| Loader | 20.3 | 9 | 36 | 6 | 14 | 2 | 50 | 3 | 1st | 16 | 1 | 40 |
| Smith | 17 | 6 | 24 | 0 | 4 | 1 | 12 | 1 | 2nd | 42 | 12 | 40 |
| Laker | 17 | 4 | 24 | 2 | 6.2 | 1 | 16 | 1 | 3rd | 42 | 42 | 49 |
| Lock | 14 | 6 | 23 | 0 | 1 | 0 | 6 | 1 | 4th | 112 | 136 | 56 |
| WEST INDIES | | | | | | | | | 5th | 125 | 227 | 71 |
| Worrell | 38.2 | 9 | 70 | 7 | | | | | 6th | 139 | 239 | 92 |
| Gilchrist | 27 | 3 | 71 | 2 | | | | | 7th | 142 | 264 | 103 |
| Sobers | 32 | 9 | 79 | 1 | | | | | 8th | 142 | 272 | 113 |
| Ramadhin | 19 | 5 | 34 | 0 | | | | | 9th | 142 | 278 | 123 |
| Smith | 8 | 1 | 17 | 0 | | | | | 10th | 142 | 279 | 132 |

Umpires: J.S. Buller and D. Davies.

Test No. 443/35

# ENGLAND v WEST INDIES 1957 (5th Test)

Played at Kennington Oval, London, on 22, 23, 24 August.
Toss: England. Result: ENGLAND won by an innings and 237 runs.
Debuts: Nil.

Dismissed for what are still their two lowest totals against England, West Indies were beaten in three days for the third time in this rubber, the match ending at 2.30 p.m. Walcott took over the captaincy when Goddard was taken ill with influenza at the end of the first day.

## ENGLAND

| | | |
|---|---|---|
| P.E. Richardson | b Smith | 107 |
| Rev.D.S. Sheppard | c and b Goddard | 40 |
| T.W. Graveney | b Ramadhin | 164 |
| P.B.H. May* | c Worrell b Smith | 1 |
| M.C. Cowdrey | b Ramadhin | 2 |
| T.E. Bailey | run out | 0 |
| T.G. Evans† | c Weekes b Dewdney | 40 |
| G.A.R. Lock | c Alexander b Sobers | 17 |
| F.S. Trueman | b Ramadhin | 22 |
| J.C. Laker | not out | 10 |
| P.J. Loader | lbw b Ramadhin | 0 |
| Extras | (B 1, LB 8) | 9 |
| **Total** | | **412** |

## WEST INDIES

| | | | | | |
|---|---|---|---|---|---|
| F.M.M. Worrell | c Lock b Loader | 4 | (4) c Cowdrey b Lock | | 0 |
| N.R. Asgarali | c Cowdrey b Lock | 29 | b Lock | | 7 |
| G. St A. Sobers | b Lock | 39 | b Lock | | 42 |
| C.L. Walcott | b Laker | 5 | (5) not out | | 19 |
| E. de C. Weekes | c Trueman b Laker | 0 | (6) b Lock | | 0 |
| O.G. Smith | c May b Laker | 7 | (7) c Sheppard b Lock | | 0 |
| R.B. Kanhai | not out | 4 | (1) c Evans b Trueman | | 8 |
| F.C.M. Alexander† | b Lock | 0 | b Laker | | 0 |
| D.T. Dewdney | b Lock | 0 | st Evans b Lock | | 1 |
| S. Ramadhin | c Trueman b Lock | 0 | b Laker | | 2 |
| J.D.C. Goddard* | absent ill | – | absent ill | | – |
| Extras | (NB 1) | 1 | (B 4, LB 2, NB 1) | | 7 |
| **Total** | | **89** | | | **86** |

| WEST INDIES | O | M | R | W | O | M | R | W |
|---|---|---|---|---|---|---|---|---|
| Worrell | 11 | 3 | 26 | 0 | | | | |
| Dewdney | 15 | 2 | 43 | 1 | | | | |
| Ramadhin | 53.3 | 12 | 107 | 4 | | | | |
| Sobers | 44 | 6 | 111 | 1 | | | | |
| Goddard | 23 | 10 | 43 | 1 | | | | |
| Smith | 30 | 4 | 73 | 2 | | | | |
| ENGLAND | | | | | | | | |
| Trueman | 5 | 1 | 9 | 0 | 5 | 2 | 19 | 1 |
| Loader | 7 | 4 | 12 | 1 | 3 | 2 | 2 | 0 |
| Laker | 23 | 12 | 39 | 3 | 17 | 4 | 38 | 2 |
| Lock | 21.4 | 12 | 28 | 5 | 16 | 7 | 20 | 6 |

### FALL OF WICKETS

| Wkt | E 1st | WI 1st | WI 2nd |
|---|---|---|---|
| 1st | 92 | 7 | 10 |
| 2nd | 238 | 68 | 39 |
| 3rd | 242 | 73 | 43 |
| 4th | 255 | 73 | 69 |
| 5th | 256 | 85 | 69 |
| 6th | 322 | 89 | 69 |
| 7th | 366 | 89 | 70 |
| 8th | 399 | 89 | 75 |
| 9th | 412 | 89 | 86 |
| 10th | 412 | – | – |

Umpires: E. Davies and F.S. Lee.

Chapter 7

# NEW ZEALAND 1958

The 1958 series against New Zealand did not begin very well for England who lost three wickets for a paltry 29 but another partnership by May and Cowdrey at Edgbaston put on 121. May and Cowdrey were by now established as two class batsmen together as well as good friends with a high regard for the ability of the other. Their first innings partnership was the most vital factor of a low scoring match. Cowdrey, 81, was eighth out, excelled in driving, hitting ten fours. England were all out for 221 but New Zealand only managed 94. In the second innings New Zealand were again checked by Cowdrey who had one six and nine fours in his 70 largely in partnership with Richardson who scored 100. England declared at 215 for 6 and had New Zealand out for 137 to win by 205 runs.

Thereafter the home side had little difficulty. In the second Test at Lord's England won by an innings and 148 runs. In England's 269 it was sheer joy to see Cowdrey pierce the field with dazzling cover drives and powerful on-side strokes, making 65 in two hours and ten minutes, hitting nine fours in the process. New Zealand were dismissed for 47 and 74.

In the third Test at Headingley England again won inside three days. New Zealand having been put out for 67 England made 267 for 2 declared with opener Arthur Milton and Peter May both scoring undefeated centuries. Cowdrey did not bat. Then New Zealand were again put out for 129. England's victory was by an innings and 71 runs.

So one-sided had the matches become that Cowdrey was left out of the team for the fourth test at Old Trafford and England won again by an innings and 1 run. I was not alone in my disgust. The England cap should be hard to come by and the team selected should be the best fit and able eleven at the time. Cowdrey wrote that "it was never a matter about which I was in the least concerned". He went on to say that the wet wickets and weak opposition that year were entirely abnormal and he was sure that the selectors' decision was sensible and justified. Godfrey Evans in his book *The Gloves Are Off* asserts that Cowdrey was upset at being rested against weak test opposition.

Cowdrey was back for the Oval Test which was a Draw rain having frustrated England's hopes of winning all five Tests of a rubber for the first time. New Zealand were put out for 161 and England declared at 219 for 9 of which Cowdrey scored 25. Trueman top scored with an undefeated 39. New Zealand had reached 91 for 3 when the twelve hours of play that were possible came to an end.

|  | Matches | Innings | Not out | Runs | Highest score | Average | 100s | 50s | Caught |
|---|---|---|---|---|---|---|---|---|---|
| This series | 4 | 4 | 0 | 241 | 81 | 60.25 | 0 | 3 | 7 |
| Previous series | 23 | 38 | 1 | 1444 | 154 | 39.01 | 4 | 10 | 26 |
| Cumulative totals | 27 | 42 | 1 | 1685 | 154 | 41.10 | 4 | 13 | 33 |

*Overall Average tops 40*

Test No. 454/22

# ENGLAND v NEW ZEALAND 1958 (1st Test)

Played at Edgbaston, Birmingham, on 5, 6, 7, 9 June.
Toss: England.    Result: ENGLAND won by 205 runs.
Debuts: England – M.J.K. Smith; New Zealand – J.W. D'Arcy, T. Meale, W.R. Playle.

England won at 2.48 p.m. on the fourth day. Harford was struck in the face by a lifting ball from Trueman in the second innings and retired hurt for a time.

### ENGLAND

| | | | | | |
|---|---|---|---|---|---|
| P.E. Richardson | lbw b MacGibbon | 4 | c Cave b MacGibbon | | 100 |
| M.J.K. Smith | lbw b MacGibbon | 0 | c Petrie b MacGibbon | | 7 |
| T.W. Graveney | c Alabaster b Hayes | 7 | c Petrie b Cave | | 19 |
| P.B.H. May* | c Petrie b MacGibbon | 84 | c Petrie b MacGibbon | | 11 |
| M.C. Cowdrey | b MacGibbon | 81 | c Reid b Hayes | | 70 |
| T.E. Bailey | c Petrie b Alabaster | 2 | not out | | 6 |
| T.G. Evans† | c Petrie b MacGibbon | 2 | c Reid b Cave | | 0 |
| G.A.R. Lock | lbw b Alabaster | 4 | | | |
| F.S. Trueman | b Alabaster | 0 | | | |
| J.C. Laker | not out | 11 | | | |
| P.J. Loader | b Alabaster | 17 | | | |
| Extras | (LB 3, W 4, NB 2) | 9 | (B 1, LB 1) | | 2 |
| Total | | 221 | (6 wickets declared) | | 215 |

### NEW ZEALAND

| | | | | | |
|---|---|---|---|---|---|
| L.S.M. Miller | lbw b Trueman | 7 | b Trueman | | 8 |
| J.W. D'Arcy | c Evans b Trueman | 19 | c Trueman b Loader | | 25 |
| N.S. Harford | b Bailey | 9 | (4) c Graveney b Loader | | 23 |
| J.R. Reid* | b Bailey | 7 | (6) b Bailey | | 13 |
| W.R. Playle | b Trueman | 4 | (3) c Bailey b Loader | | 8 |
| T. Meale | lbw b Trueman | 7 | (5) c Smith b Lock | | 10 |
| A.R. MacGibbon | c Evans b Laker | 5 | (8) c Cowdrey b Laker | | 26 |
| E.C. Petrie† | lbw b Loader | 1 | (10) not out | | 5 |
| J.C. Alabaster | b Trueman | 9 | c Laker b Lock | | 11 |
| H.B. Cave | not out | 12 | (7) b Bailey | | 1 |
| J.A. Hayes | run out | 14 | c Bailey b Lock | | 5 |
| Extras | | | (LB 1, W 1) | | 2 |
| Total | | 94 | | | 137 |

| NEW ZEALAND | O | M | R | W | O | M | R | W | FALL OF WICKETS | | | | |
|---|---|---|---|---|---|---|---|---|---|---|---|---|---|
| | | | | | | | | | | E | NZ | E | NZ |
| Hayes | 15 | 2 | 57 | 1 | 20 | 3 | 51 | 1 | | | | | |
| MacGibbon | 27 | 11 | 64 | 5 | 24 | 8 | 41 | 3 | Wkt | 1st | 1st | 2nd | 2nd |
| Cave | 12 | 2 | 29 | 0 | 28.2 | 9 | 70 | 2 | 1st | 4 | 12 | 24 | 19 |
| Reid | 6 | 3 | 16 | 0 | 9 | 2 | 18 | 0 | 2nd | 11 | 21 | 71 | 42 |
| Alabaster | 15.5 | 4 | 46 | 4 | 15 | 7 | 33 | 0 | 3rd | 29 | 39 | 94 | 49 |
| | | | | | | | | | 4th | 150 | 43 | 198 | 64 |
| ENGLAND | | | | | | | | | 5th | 153 | 46 | 214 | 93 |
| Trueman | 21 | 8 | 31 | 5 | 17 | 5 | 33 | 1 | 6th | 172 | 54 | 215 | 94 |
| Loader | 21.3 | 6 | 37 | 1 | 23 | 11 | 40 | 3 | 7th | 185 | 59 | – | 95 |
| Bailey | 20 | 9 | 17 | 2 | 20 | 9 | 23 | 2 | 8th | 191 | 67 | – | 123 |
| Lock | 2 | 2 | 0 | 0 | 8.3 | 3 | 25 | 3 | 9th | 191 | 68 | – | 131 |
| Laker | 5 | 2 | 9 | 1 | 9 | 4 | 14 | 1 | 10th | 221 | 94 | – | 137 |

Umpires: J.S. Buller and C.S. Elliott.

Test No. 455/23

# ENGLAND v NEW ZEALAND 1958 (2nd Test)

Played at Lord's, London, on 19, 20, 21 June.
Toss: England.   Result: ENGLAND won by an innings and 148 runs.
Debuts: Nil.

New Zealand, trapped on a pitch affected by rain after England's innings, were dismissed for the then lowest total in a Lord's Test and beaten by 3.30 p.m. on the third day. Flags were flown at half-mast on the first day in tribute to the memory of D.R. Jardine who had died in Switzerland.

### ENGLAND

| | | |
|---|---|---|
| P.E. Richardson | c Petrie b Hayes | 36 |
| M.J.K. Smith | c Petrie b Hayes | 47 |
| T.W. Graveney | c Petrie b Alabaster | 37 |
| P.B.H. May* | c Alabaster b MacGibbon | 19 |
| M.C. Cowdrey | b Hayes | 65 |
| T.E. Bailey | c Petrie b Reid | 17 |
| T.G. Evans† | c Hayes b MacGibbon | 11 |
| G.A.R. Lock | not out | 23 |
| F.S. Trueman | b Hayes | 8 |
| J.C. Laker | c Blair b MacGibbon | 1 |
| P.J. Loader | c Playle b MacGibbon | 4 |
| Extras | (LB 1) | 1 |
| **Total** | | **269** |

### NEW ZEALAND

| | | | | | |
|---|---|---|---|---|---|
| L.S.M. Miller | lbw b Trueman | 4 | c Trueman b Loader | 0 |
| J.W. D'Arcy | c Trueman b Laker | 14 | c Bailey b Trueman | 33 |
| W.R. Playle | c Graveney b Laker | 1 | b Loader | 3 |
| N.S. Harford | c and b Laker | 0 | c May b Lock | 3 |
| J.R. Reid* | c Loader b Lock | 6 | c Cowdrey b Trueman | 5 |
| B. Sutcliffe | b Lock | 18 | b Bailey | 0 |
| A.R. MacGibbon | c May b Lock | 2 | c May b Lock | 7 |
| J.C. Alabaster | c and b Lock | 0 | b Laker | 5 |
| E.C. Petrie† | c Trueman b Laker | 0 | not out | 4 |
| R.W. Blair | not out | 0 | b Lock | 0 |
| J.A. Hayes | c Cowdrey b Lock | 1 | c and b Lock | 14 |
| Extras | (LB 1) | 1 | | |
| **Total** | | **47** | | **74** |

| NEW ZEALAND | O | M | R | W | O | M | R | W |
|---|---|---|---|---|---|---|---|---|
| Hayes | 22 | 5 | 36 | 4 | | | | |
| MacGibbon | 36.4 | 11 | 86 | 4 | | | | |
| Blair | 25 | 6 | 57 | 0 | | | | |
| Reid | 24 | 12 | 41 | 1 | | | | |
| Alabaster | 16 | 6 | 48 | 1 | | | | |
| ENGLAND | | | | | | | | |
| Trueman | 4 | 1 | 6 | 1 | 11 | 6 | 24 | 2 |
| Loader | 4 | 2 | 6 | 0 | 9 | 6 | 7 | 2 |
| Laker | 12 | 6 | 13 | 4 | 13 | 8 | 24 | 1 |
| Lock | 11.3 | 7 | 17 | 5 | 12.3 | 8 | 12 | 4 |
| Bailey | 1 | 0 | 4 | 0 | 5 | 1 | 7 | 1 |

### FALL OF WICKETS

| | E | NZ | NZ |
|---|---|---|---|
| Wkt | 1st | 1st | 2nd |
| 1st | 54 | 4 | 11 |
| 2nd | 113 | 12 | 21 |
| 3rd | 139 | 12 | 34 |
| 4th | 141 | 19 | 41 |
| 5th | 201 | 25 | 44 |
| 6th | 222 | 31 | 44 |
| 7th | 237 | 34 | 56 |
| 8th | 259 | 46 | 56 |
| 9th | 260 | 46 | 56 |
| 10th | 269 | 47 | 74 |

Umpires: C.S. Elliott and D. Davies.

**Test No. 456/24**

# ENGLAND v NEW ZEALAND 1958 (3rd Test)

Played at Headingley, Leeds, on 3 (*no play*), 4 (*no play*), 5, 7, 8 July.
Toss: New Zealand.  Result: ENGLAND won by an innings and 71 runs.
Debuts: England – C.A. Milton; New Zealand – J.T. Sparling.

England again won inside three days, there being no play on the first two. They omitted Richardson to try out possible opening partners for him on the forthcoming tour to Australia. Milton (Association Football) opened with his fellow double-international Smith (Rugby Union) and became the first Gloucestershire player since W.G. Grace in 1880 to score a hundred for England in his first Test. He was the first England player to be on the field throughout a Test match.

## NEW ZEALAND

| | | | | |
|---|---|---|---|---|
| L.S.M. Miller | c Smith b Laker | 26 | lbw b Lock | 18 |
| J.W. D'Arcy | c Smith b Trueman | 11 | b Lock | 6 |
| N.S. Harford | c Cowdrey b Laker | 0 | lbw b Lock | 0 |
| B. Sutcliffe | b Laker | 6 | lbw b Lock | 0 |
| J.R. Reid* | b Lock | 3 | c Trueman b Laker | 13 |
| W.R. Playle | c Milton b Lock | 0 | b Laker | 18 |
| A.R. MacGibbon | b Laker | 3 | lbw b Lock | 39 |
| J.T. Sparling | not out | 9 | c May b Lock | 18 |
| E.C. Petrie† | c Cowdrey b Lock | 5 | b Lock | 3 |
| H.B. Cave | c Milton b Laker | 2 | c Cowdrey b Laker | 2 |
| J.A. Hayes | c Evans b Lock | 1 | not out | 0 |
| Extras | (LB 1) | 1 | (B 6, LB 6) | 12 |
| **Total** | | **67** | | **129** |

## ENGLAND

| | | |
|---|---|---|
| M.J.K. Smith | c Reid b MacGibbon | 3 |
| C.A. Milton | not out | 104 |
| T.W. Graveney | c and b Sparling | 31 |
| P.B.H. May* | not out | 113 |
| M.C. Cowdrey | ) | |
| T.E. Bailey | ) | |
| T.G. Evans† | ) | |
| G.A.R. Lock | ) did not bat | |
| F.S. Trueman | ) | |
| J.C. Laker | ) | |
| P.J. Loader | ) | |
| Extras | (B 5, LB 8, W 1, NB 2) | 16 |
| **Total** | (2 wickets declared) | **267** |

| ENGLAND | O | M | R | W | O | M | R | W | | FALL OF WICKETS | | |
|---|---|---|---|---|---|---|---|---|---|---|---|---|
| Trueman | 11 | 5 | 18 | 1 | 14 | 6 | 22 | 0 | | NZ | E | NZ |
| Loader | 5 | 2 | 10 | 0 | 13 | 7 | 14 | 0 | Wkt | *1st* | *1st* | *2nd* |
| Bailey | 3 | 0 | 7 | 0 | 3 | 2 | 3 | 0 | 1st | 37 | 7 | 23 |
| Laker | 22 | 11 | 17 | 5 | 36 | 23 | 27 | 3 | 2nd | 37 | 73 | 23 |
| Lock | 18.1 | 13 | 14 | 4 | 35.2 | 20 | 51 | 7 | 3rd | 37 | – | 24 |
| NEW ZEALAND | | | | | | | | | 4th | 40 | – | 32 |
| Hayes | 13 | 4 | 30 | 0 | | | | | 5th | 46 | – | 42 |
| MacGibbon | 27 | 8 | 47 | 1 | | | | | 6th | 46 | – | 88 |
| Reid | 26 | 7 | 54 | 0 | | | | | 7th | 49 | – | 121 |
| Sparling | 23 | 2 | 78 | 1 | | | | | 8th | 59 | – | 124 |
| Cave | 13 | 4 | 42 | 0 | | | | | 9th | 66 | – | 129 |
| | | | | | | | | | 10th | 67 | – | 129 |

Umpires: F.S. Lee and J.S. Buller.

Test No. 457/25

# ENGLAND v NEW ZEALAND 1958 (4th Test)

Played at Old Trafford, Manchester, on 24, 25, 26, 28, 29 July.
Toss: New Zealand.   Result: ENGLAND won by an innings and 13 runs.
Debuts: England – E.R. Dexter, R. Illingworth, R. Subba Row.

England became the first team to win the first four Tests of a rubber in England – in spite of the loss of over eight hours to rain on the third and fourth days. Reid kept wicket on Friday and Saturday after Petrie had edged a hook on to his left ear while batting against Trueman. Lock's 29th wicket of this rubber was his hundredth in Tests.

### NEW ZEALAND

| | | | | | |
|---|---|---|---|---|---|
| B. Sutcliffe | b Statham | 41 | b Statham | | 28 |
| J.W. D'Arcy | lbw b Trueman | 1 | c Subba Row b Lock | | 8 |
| N.S. Harford | lbw b Statham | 2 | b Illingworth | | 4 |
| J.R. Reid* | c Trueman b Lock | 14 | c Watson b Lock | | 8 |
| W.R. Playle | lbw b Illingworth | 15 | lbw b Lock | | 1 |
| A.R. MacGibbon | c Evans b Statham | 66 | lbw b Lock | | 1 |
| J.T. Sparling | c Evans b Statham | 50 | c and b Lock | | 2 |
| E.C. Petrie† | retired hurt | 45 | c Statham b Illingworth | | 9 |
| A.M. Moir | not out | 21 | c Evans b Lock | | 12 |
| J.A. Hayes | b Trueman | 4 | not out | | 5 |
| R.W. Blair | b Trueman | 2 | b Lock | | 0 |
| Extras | (B 4, LB 2) | 6 | (B 5, LB 2) | | 7 |
| **Total** | | **267** | | | **85** |

### ENGLAND

| | | |
|---|---|---|
| P.E. Richardson | st Reid b Sparling | 74 |
| W. Watson | c MacGibbon b Moir | 66 |
| T.W. Graveney | c sub (J.C. Alabaster) b MacGibbon | 25 |
| P.B.H. May* | c Playle b MacGibbon | 101 |
| R. Subba Row | c Petrie b Blair | 9 |
| E.R. Dexter | lbw b Reid | 52 |
| T.G. Evans† | c Blair b Reid | 3 |
| R. Illingworth | not out | 3 |
| G.A.R. Lock | lbw b MacGibbon | 7 |
| F.S. Trueman | b Reid | 5 |
| J.B. Statham | did not bat | |
| Extras | (B 13, LB 4, W 1, NB 2) | 20 |
| **Total** | (9 wickets declared) | **365** |

| ENGLAND | O | M | R | W | O | M | R | W | FALL OF WICKETS |
|---|---|---|---|---|---|---|---|---|---|
| Trueman | 29·5 | 4 | 67 | 3 | 2 | 1 | 11 | 0 | |
| Statham | 33 | 10 | 71 | 4 | 9 | 4 | 12 | 1 | |
| Dexter | 5 | 0 | 23 | 0 | | | | | |
| Lock | 33 | 12 | 61 | 1 | 24 | 11 | 35 | 7 | |
| Illingworth | 28 | 9 | 39 | 1 | 17 | 9 | 20 | 2 | |

| | | | | | |
|---|---|---|---|---|---|
| | | | | NZ | E | NZ |
| | | | Wkt | 1st | 1st | 2nd |
| | | | 1st | 15 | 126 | 36 |
| | | | 2nd | 22 | 180 | 36 |
| | | | 3rd | 62 | 193 | 46 |
| | | | 4th | 62 | 248 | 49 |
| | | | 5th | 117 | 330 | 49 |
| | | | 6th | 166 | 337 | 51 |
| | | | 7th | 227 | 351 | 60 |
| | | | 8th | 257 | 360 | 78 |
| | | | 9th | 267 | 365 | 80 |
| | | | 10th | – | – | 85 |

| NEW ZEALAND | O | M | R | W |
|---|---|---|---|---|
| Hayes | 19 | 4 | 51 | 0 |
| MacGibbon | 34 | 8 | 86 | 3 |
| Blair | 27 | 5 | 68 | 1 |
| Moir | 17 | 3 | 47 | 1 |
| Sparling | 21 | 7 | 46 | 1 |
| Reid | 11·3 | 2 | 47 | 3 |

Umpires: E. Davies and W.E. Phillipson.

Test No. 458/26

# ENGLAND v NEW ZEALAND 1958 (5th Test)

Played at Kennington Oval, London, on 21, 22, 23 (*no play*), 25 (*no play*), 26 August.
Toss: New Zealand.   Result: MATCH DRAWN.
Debuts: Nil.

Rain frustrated England's attempt to win all five Tests of a rubber in England for the first time – only twelve hours of play was possible over the five days. Sparling ducked into a short-pitched ball from Trueman which bounced lower than he expected and he took no further part in the match. Lock's figures of 34 wickets at 7.47 runs each for the rubber are easily the record for this series.

## NEW ZEALAND

| | | | | |
|---|---|---|---|---|
| L.S.M. Miller | c Lock b Laker | 25 | c Evans b Statham | 4 |
| J.W. D'Arcy | c Milton b Bailey | 9 | c and b Lock | 10 |
| T. Meale | c Lock b Trueman | 1 | c Cowdrey b Laker | 3 |
| B. Sutcliffe | c Watson b Trueman | 11 | not out | 18 |
| J.R. Reid* | b Lock | 27 | not out | 51 |
| W.R. Playle | b Statham | 6 | | |
| A.R. MacGibbon | b Bailey | 26 | | |
| J.T. Sparling | retired hurt | 0 | | |
| E.C. Petrie† | c Milton b Lock | 8 | | |
| A.M. Moir | not out | 41 | | |
| R.W. Blair | run out | 3 | | |
| Extras | (LB 4) | 4 | (B 2, LB 3) | 5 |
| **Total** | | **161** | (3 wickets) | **91** |

## ENGLAND

| | | |
|---|---|---|
| P.E. Richardson | b Blair | 28 |
| C.A. Milton | lbw b MacGibbon | 36 |
| W. Watson | b MacGibbon | 10 |
| P.B.H. May* | c Petrie b Blair | 9 |
| M.C. Cowdrey | c Playle b Reid | 25 |
| T.E. Bailey | c Petrie b MacGibbon | 14 |
| T.G. Evans† | c Petrie b MacGibbon | 12 |
| G.A.R. Lock | c Reid b Moir | 25 |
| J.C. Laker | c Blair b Reid | 15 |
| F.S. Trueman | not out | 39 |
| J.B. Statham | did not bat | |
| Extras | (B 2, LB 4) | 6 |
| **Total** | (9 wickets declared) | **219** |

| ENGLAND | O | M | R | W | O | M | R | W |
|---|---|---|---|---|---|---|---|---|
| Trueman | 16 | 3 | 41 | 2 | 6 | 5 | 3 | 0 |
| Statham | 18 | 6 | 21 | 1 | 7 | 0 | 26 | 1 |
| Bailey | 14 | 3 | 32 | 2 | | | | |
| Laker | 14 | 3 | 44 | 1 | 20 | 10 | 25 | 1 |
| Lock | 13 | 6 | 19 | 2 | 18 | 11 | 20 | 1 |
| Milton | | | | | 4 | 2 | 12 | 0 |
| NEW ZEALAND | | | | | | | | |
| Blair | 26 | 5 | 85 | 2 | | | | |
| MacGibbon | 27 | 4 | 65 | 4 | | | | |
| Reid | 7.5 | 2 | 11 | 2 | | | | |
| Moir | 8 | 1 | 52 | 1 | | | | |

FALL OF WICKETS

| Wkt | NZ 1st | E 1st | NZ 2nd |
|---|---|---|---|
| 1st | 19 | 39 | 9 |
| 2nd | 24 | 62 | 17 |
| 3rd | 40 | 85 | 21 |
| 4th | 46 | 87 | – |
| 5th | 55 | 109 | – |
| 6th | 93 | 125 | – |
| 7th | 105 | 162 | – |
| 8th | 132 | 162 | – |
| 9th | 161 | 219 | – |
| 10th | – | – | – |

Umpires: F.S. Lee and E. Davies.

Chapter 8
# AUSTRALIA 1958/59

The 1958/59 tour of Australia, Cowdrey's second and first as Vice-Captain, began in high hopes but when the first Test at Brisbane began on an ostensibly beautiful wicket England were all out for 134. Cowdrey contributed 13. However the England bowlers did wonders and they began their second innings only 52 behind. There was some more bad batting. Even the success, Trevor Bailey, coming in at No 3, took seven and a half hours over his 68. Cowdrey was out for 28 to a controversial catch by Kline. England were one down and the high hopes evaporated. Australia made light of getting 147 for 2 to win the match.

The second Test at Melbourne began by England losing three quick wickets. A May and Cowdrey stand helped retrieve the situation but when May went, the innings collapsed for 259. Again the bowlers fought back well and Australia had much to thank Harvey's brilliant 167 for their total of 308. Then, in three hours, England were bowled out for 87. For the second match Australia won by eight wickets.

In the third Test at Sydney Cowdrey showed, in the first innings, by far his best form of the tour. Realising the necessity for aggression he hit boldly in company with wicket keeper Swetman but was out for 34 and England were all out for 219. Australia replied with 357 but May and Cowdrey had another long partnership of 182 in the second innings and before the declaration Cowdrey reached his second century against Australia. The match was drawn but with three gone and two to play, Australia were two up.

In the fourth Test at Adelaide, having been put in, Australia made 476. In England's first innings Cowdrey top scored again with 84 before playing on to Rorke. This was the second of two controversial fast bowlers that Australia fielded in this series. As Cowdrey himself put it "Rorke was

*A narrow escape for Lindsay Kline as Cowdrey pulls a ball over his head to take a four off Benaud at Melbourne in 1959.*

another fast bowler who was none too easy to see, especially from a distance of nineteen yards." Cowdrey added that he had never seen any one drag as much as Rorke did. England were all out for 240 and following on in the second innings he was bowled by Lindwall for 8. Perhaps confrontation again by a classic action came as too much of a surprise. Australia's victory by 10 wickets meant that they had regained the Ashes – a triumph for their new Captain Benaud.

Having lost the Ashes by 3–0 after four Tests, the prospect of the fifth, at Melbourne, with a side depleted by injuries, not all incurred on the field, was not something to which to look forward. Statham was hurt in a car accident with Loader. Rather twisting the knife Benaud put England in and out for 205 himself bowling seventeen overs and taking four wickets. Cowdrey made

22. In the second innings Cowdrey, going after Davidson, hit seven fours with perfectly timed strokes and had made 46 before being run out by a whisker, in partnership with Peter Richardson. All out for 214 after Australia had made 351, they went down again this time by nine wickets.

|  | Matches | Innings | Not out | Runs | Highest score | Average | 100s | 50s | Caught |
|---|---|---|---|---|---|---|---|---|---|
| This series | 5 | 10 | 1 | 391 | 100* | 43.44 | 1 | 1 | 6 |
| Previous series | 27 | 42 | 1 | 1685 | 154 | 41.10 | 4 | 13 | 33 |
| Cumulative totals | 32 | 52 | 2 | 2076 | 154 | 41.52 | 5 | 14 | 39 |

*2000 runs in test cricket*

Test No. 464/174

# AUSTRALIA v ENGLAND 1958-59 (1st Test)

Played at Woolloongabba, Brisbane, on 5, 6, 8, 9, 10 December.
Toss: England.   Result: AUSTRALIA won by eight wickets.
Debuts: Australia – N.C. O'Neill.

Bailey batted 357 minutes before reaching his fifty and this remains the slowest recorded half-century in all first-class cricket. His innings of 68 endured for 458 minutes at an average of slightly less than nine runs per hour. Out of 425 balls bowled to him, Bailey scored off 40: 4 fours, 3 threes, 10 twos and 23 singles.

### ENGLAND

| | | | | |
|---|---|---|---|---|
| P.E. Richardson | c Mackay b Davidson | 11 | c and b Benaud | 8 |
| C.A. Milton | b Meckiff | 5 | c Grout b Davidson | 17 |
| T.W. Graveney | c Grout b Davidson | 19 | (4) run out | 36 |
| P.B.H. May* | c Grout b Meckiff | 26 | (5) lbw b Benaud | 4 |
| M.C. Cowdrey | c Kline b Meckiff | 13 | (6) c Kline b Meckiff | 28 |
| T.E. Bailey | st Grout b Benaud | 27 | (3) b Mackay | 68 |
| T.G. Evans† | c Burge b Davidson | 4 | lbw b Davidson | 4 |
| G.A.R. Lock | c Davidson b Benaud | 5 | b Meckiff | 1 |
| J.C. Laker | c Burke b Benaud | 13 | b Benaud | 15 |
| J.B. Statham | c Grout b Mackay | 2 | c McDonald b Benaud | 3 |
| P.J. Loader | not out | 6 | not out | 0 |
| Extras | (LB 1, W 1, NB 1) | 3 | (B 10, LB 4) | 14 |
| **Total** | | **134** | | **198** |

### AUSTRALIA

| | | | | |
|---|---|---|---|---|
| C.C. McDonald | c Graveney b Bailey | 42 | c Statham b Laker | 15 |
| J.W. Burke | c Evans b Loader | 20 | not out | 28 |
| R.N. Harvey | lbw b Loader | 14 | c Milton b Lock | 23 |
| N.C. O'Neill | c Graveney b Bailey | 34 | not out | 71 |
| P.J.P. Burge | c Cowdrey b Bailey | 2 | | |
| K.D. Mackay | c Evans b Laker | 16 | | |
| R. Benaud* | lbw b Loader | 16 | | |
| A.K. Davidson | lbw b Laker | 25 | | |
| A.T.W. Grout† | b Statham | 2 | | |
| I. Meckiff | b Loader | 5 | | |
| L.F. Kline | not out | 4 | | |
| Extras | (B 4, LB 1, NB 1) | 6 | (B 2, LB 3, NB 5) | 10 |
| **Total** | | **186** | (2 wickets) | **147** |

| AUSTRALIA | O | M | R | W | O | M | R | W | FALL OF WICKETS |
|---|---|---|---|---|---|---|---|---|---|
| Davidson | 16 | 4 | 36 | 3 | 28 | 12 | 30 | 2 | |
| Meckiff | 17 | 5 | 33 | 3 | 19 | 7 | 30 | 2 | |
| Mackay | 8 | 1 | 16 | 1 | 9 | 6 | 7 | 1 | |
| Benaud | 18.4 | 9 | 46 | 3 | 39.2 | 10 | 66 | 4 | |
| Kline | | | | | 14 | 4 | 34 | 0 | |
| Burke | | | | | 10 | 5 | 17 | 0 | |
| ENGLAND | | | | | | | | | |
| Statham | 20 | 2 | 57 | 1 | 6 | 1 | 13 | 0 | |
| Loader | 19 | 4 | 56 | 4 | 9 | 1 | 27 | 0 | |
| Bailey | 13 | 2 | 35 | 3 | 5 | 1 | 21 | 0 | |
| Laker | 10.1 | 2 | 15 | 2 | 17 | 3 | 39 | 1 | |
| Lock | 10 | 4 | 17 | 0 | 14.7 | 5 | 37 | 1 | |

| | E | A | E | A |
|---|---|---|---|---|
| Wkt | 1st | 1st | 2nd | 2nd |
| 1st | 16 | 55 | 28 | 20 |
| 2nd | 16 | 65 | 34 | 58 |
| 3rd | 62 | 88 | 96 | – |
| 4th | 75 | 94 | 102 | – |
| 5th | 79 | 122 | 153 | – |
| 6th | 83 | 136 | 161 | – |
| 7th | 92 | 162 | 169 | – |
| 8th | 112 | 165 | 190 | – |
| 9th | 116 | 178 | 198 | – |
| 10th | 134 | 186 | 198 | – |

Umpires: M.J. McInnes and C. Hoy.

Test No. 465/175

# AUSTRALIA v ENGLAND 1958-59 (2nd Test)

Played at Melbourne Cricket Ground on 31 December, 1, 2, 3, 5 January.
Toss: England.  Result: AUSTRALIA won by eight wickets.
Debuts: Nil.

Davidson took the wickets of Richardson, Watson and Graveney with the first, fourth and fifth balls of his second over. May scored the first hundred by an England captain in Australia since A.C. MacLaren in 1901-02, and Harvey scored Australia's first hundred against England for eleven Tests. England's total of 87 was their lowest in Australia since 1903-04.

### ENGLAND

| | | | | |
|---|---|---|---|---|
| P.E. Richardson | c Grout b Davidson | 3 | c Harvey b Meckiff | 2 |
| T.E. Bailey | c Benaud b Meckiff | 48 | c Burke b Meckiff | 14 |
| W. Watson | b Davidson | 0 | c Davidson | 7 |
| T.W. Graveney | lbw b Davidson | 0 | c Davidson b Meckiff | 3 |
| P.B.H. May* | b Meckiff | 113 | c Davidson b Meckiff | 17 |
| M.C. Cowdrey | c Grout b Davidson | 44 | c Grout b Meckiff | 12 |
| T.G. Evans† | c Davidson b Meckiff | 4 | run out | 11 |
| G.A.R. Lock | st Grout b Benaud | 5 | c and b Davidson | 6 |
| J.C. Laker | not out | 22 | c Harvey b Davidson | 3 |
| J.B. Statham | b Davidson | 13 | not out | 8 |
| P.J. Loader | b Davidson | 1 | b Meckiff | 0 |
| Extras | (B 1, LB 2, W 3) | 6 | (B 1, LB 1, NB 2) | 4 |
| **Total** | | **259** | | **87** |

### AUSTRALIA

| | | | | |
|---|---|---|---|---|
| C.C. McDonald | c Graveney b Statham | 47 | lbw b Statham | 5 |
| J.W. Burke | b Statham | 3 | not out | 18 |
| R.N. Harvey | b Loader | 167 | (4) not out | 7 |
| N.C. O'Neill | c Evans b Statham | 37 | | |
| K.D. Mackay | c Evans b Statham | 18 | | |
| R.B. Simpson | lbw b Loader | 0 | | |
| R. Benaud* | lbw b Statham | 0 | | |
| A.K. Davidson | b Statham | 24 | | |
| A.T.W. Grout† | c May b Loader | 8 | (3) st Evans b Laker | 12 |
| I. Meckiff | b Statham | 0 | | |
| L.F. Kline | not out | 1 | | |
| Extras | (LB 3) | 3 | | |
| **Total** | | **308** | (2 wickets) | **42** |

| AUSTRALIA | O | M | R | W | O | M | R | W | | FALL OF WICKETS | | | |
|---|---|---|---|---|---|---|---|---|---|---|---|---|---|
| | | | | | | | | | | E | A | E | A |
| Davidson | 25.5 | 7 | 64 | 6 | 15 | 2 | 41 | 3 | Wkt | 1st | 1st | 2nd | 2nd |
| Meckiff | 24 | 4 | 69 | 3 | 15.2 | 3 | 38 | 6 | 1st | 7 | 11 | 3 | 6 |
| Mackay | 9 | 2 | 16 | 0 | | | | | 2nd | 7 | 137 | 14 | 26 |
| Benaud | 29 | 7 | 61 | 1 | 1 | 0 | 4 | 0 | 3rd | 7 | 255 | 21 | – |
| Kline | 11 | 2 | 43 | 0 | | | | | 4th | 92 | 257 | 27 | – |
| ENGLAND | | | | | | | | | 5th | 210 | 261 | 44 | – |
| Statham | 28 | 6 | 57 | 7 | 5 | 1 | 11 | 1 | 6th | 218 | 262 | 57 | – |
| Loader | 27.2 | 4 | 97 | 3 | 5 | 1 | 13 | 0 | 7th | 218 | 295 | 71 | – |
| Bailey | 16 | 0 | 50 | 0 | | | | | 8th | 233 | 300 | 75 | – |
| Laker | 12 | 1 | 47 | 0 | 4 | 1 | 7 | 1 | 9th | 253 | 300 | 80 | – |
| Lock | 17 | 2 | 54 | 0 | 3.1 | 1 | 11 | 0 | 10th | 259 | 308 | 87 | – |

Umpires: M.J. McInnes and R. Wright.

Test No. 466/176

# AUSTRALIA v ENGLAND 1958-59 (3rd Test)

Played at Sydney Cricket Ground on 9, 10, 12, 13, 14, 15 January.
Toss: England.   Result: MATCH DRAWN.
Debuts: Australia – K.N. Slater; England – R. Swetman.

Set to score 150 runs in 110 minutes on a wearing pitch, Australia were content to draw. Cowdrey's hundred took 362 minutes and was the slowest for either country in Australia-England Tests until R.A. Woolmer took 394 minutes to reach his century at The Oval in 1975 (*Test No. 763*). Rain delayed the start of play on the second day until 4.15 p.m.

## ENGLAND

| | | | | |
|---|---|---|---|---|
| T.E. Bailey | lbw b Meckiff | 8 | c sub (R.B. Simpson) b Benaud | 25 |
| C.A. Milton | c Meckiff b Davidson | 8 | c Davidson b Benaud | 8 |
| T.W. Graveney | c Harvey b Benaud | 33 | lbw b Davidson | 22 |
| P.B.H. May* | c Mackay b Slater | 42 | b Burke | 92 |
| M.C. Cowdrey | c Harvey b Benaud | 34 | not out | 100 |
| E.R. Dexter | lbw b Slater | 1 | c Grout b Benaud | 11 |
| R. Swetman† | c Mackay b Benaud | 41 | lbw b Burke | 5 |
| G.A.R. Lock | lbw b Mackay | 21 | (9) not out | 11 |
| F.S. Trueman | c Burke b Benaud | 18 | (8) st Grout b Benaud | 0 |
| J.C. Laker | c Harvey b Benaud | 2 | | |
| J.B. Statham | not out | 0 | | |
| Extras | (B 4, LB 5, W 2) | 11 | (B 11, LB 1, W 1) | 13 |
| **Total** | | **219** | (7 wickets declared) | **287** |

## AUSTRALIA

| | | | | |
|---|---|---|---|---|
| C.C. McDonald | c Graveney b Lock | 40 | b Laker | 16 |
| J.W. Burke | c Lock b Laker | 12 | b Laker | 7 |
| R.N. Harvey | b Laker | 7 | not out | 18 |
| N.C. O'Neill | c Swetman b Laker | 77 | not out | 7 |
| L.E. Favell | c Cowdrey b Lock | 54 | | |
| K.D. Mackay | b Trueman | 57 | | |
| R. Benaud* | b Laker | 6 | | |
| A.K. Davidson | lbw b Lock | 71 | | |
| A.T.W. Grout† | c Statham b Laker | 14 | | |
| K.N. Slater | not out | 1 | | |
| I. Meckiff | b Lock | 2 | | |
| Extras | (B 5, LB 10, NB 1) | 16 | (B 6) | 6 |
| **Total** | | **357** | (2 wickets) | **54** |

| AUSTRALIA | O | M | R | W | O | M | R | W | FALL OF WICKETS |
|---|---|---|---|---|---|---|---|---|---|
| Davidson | 12 | 3 | 21 | 1 | 33 | 11 | 65 | 1 | |
| Meckiff | 15 | 2 | 45 | 1 | 3 | 1 | 7 | 0 | |
| Benaud | 33.4 | 10 | 83 | 5 | 33 | 7 | 94 | 4 | |
| Slater | 14 | 4 | 40 | 2 | 18 | 5 | 61 | 0 | |
| Mackay | 8 | 3 | 19 | 1 | 11 | 2 | 21 | 0 | |
| Burke | | | | | 11 | 3 | 26 | 2 | |
| ENGLAND | | | | | | | | | |
| Statham | 16 | 2 | 48 | 0 | 2 | 0 | 6 | 0 | |
| Trueman | 18 | 3 | 37 | 1 | 4 | 1 | 9 | 0 | |
| Lock | 43.2 | 9 | 130 | 4 | 11 | 4 | 23 | 0 | |
| Laker | 46 | 9 | 107 | 5 | 8 | 3 | 10 | 2 | |
| Bailey | 5 | 0 | 19 | 0 | | | | | |

| Wkt | E 1st | A 1st | E 2nd | A 2nd |
|---|---|---|---|---|
| 1st | 19 | 26 | 30 | 22 |
| 2nd | 23 | 52 | 37 | 33 |
| 3rd | 91 | 87 | 64 | – |
| 4th | 97 | 197 | 246 | – |
| 5th | 98 | 199 | 262 | – |
| 6th | 155 | 208 | 269 | – |
| 7th | 194 | 323 | 270 | – |
| 8th | 200 | 353 | – | – |
| 9th | 202 | 355 | – | – |
| 10th | 219 | 357 | – | – |

Umpires: M.J. McInnes and C. Hoy.

Test No. 467/177

# AUSTRALIA v ENGLAND 1958-59 (4th Test)

Played at Adelaide Oval on 30, 31 January, 2, 3, 4, 5 February.
Toss: England.   Result: AUSTRALIA won by ten wickets.
Debuts: Australia – G.F. Rorke.

McDonald, almost bowled first ball of the match by Statham, became the fiftieth Australian to score a hundred against England. He pulled a thigh muscle when 137*, retired hurt 149* at lunch with Australia 268 for 1, and resumed his innings with a runner at 407 for 7. Evans re-fractured a little finger and, after continuing to keep wicket throughout the first day, handed over to Graveney for the rest of the match. Australia regained the Ashes after a period of five years 170 days.

## AUSTRALIA

| | | | | |
|---|---|---|---|---|
| C.C. McDonald | b Trueman | 170 | | |
| J.W. Burke | c Cowdrey b Bailey | 66 | not out | 16 |
| R.N. Harvey | run out | 41 | | |
| N.C. O'Neill | b Statham | 56 | | |
| L.E. Favell | b Statham | 4 | (1) not out | 15 |
| K.D. Mackay | c Evans b Statham | 4 | | |
| R. Benaud* | b Trueman | 46 | | |
| A.K. Davidson | c Bailey b Tyson | 43 | | |
| A.T.W. Grout† | lbw b Trueman | 9 | | |
| R.R. Lindwall | b Trueman | 19 | | |
| G.F. Rorke | not out | 2 | | |
| Extras | (B 2, LB 8, W 4, NB 2) | 16 | (B 4, LB 1) | 5 |
| **Total** | | **476** | (0 wickets) | **36** |

## ENGLAND

| | | | | |
|---|---|---|---|---|
| P.E. Richardson | lbw b Lindwall | 4 | lbw b Benaud | 43 |
| T.E. Bailey | b Davidson | 4 | (6) c Grout b Lindwall | 6 |
| P.B.H. May* | b Benaud | 37 | lbw b Rorke | 59 |
| M.C. Cowdrey | b Rorke | 84 | b Lindwall | 8 |
| T.W. Graveney | c Benaud b Rorke | 41 | not out | 53 |
| W. Watson | b Rorke | 25 | (2) c Favell b Benaud | 40 |
| F.S. Trueman | c Grout b Benaud | 0 | c Grout b Davidson | 0 |
| G.A.R. Lock | c Grout b Benaud | 2 | b Rorke | 9 |
| F.H. Tyson | c and b Benaud | 0 | c Grout b Benaud | 33 |
| T.G. Evans† | c Burke b Benaud | 4 | (11) c Benaud b Davidson | 0 |
| J.B. Statham | not out | 36 | (10) c O'Neill b Benaud | 2 |
| Extras | (LB 2, NB 1) | 3 | (B 5, LB 5, W 3, NB 4) | 17 |
| **Total** | | **240** | | **270** |

| ENGLAND | O | M | R | W | O | M | R | W | FALL OF WICKETS |
|---|---|---|---|---|---|---|---|---|---|
| Statham | 23 | 0 | 83 | 3 | 4 | 0 | 11 | 0 | | A | E | E | A |
| Trueman | 30.1 | 6 | 90 | 4 | 3 | 1 | 3 | 0 | Wkt | 1st | 1st | 2nd | 2nd |
| Tyson | 28 | 1 | 100 | 1 | | | | | 1st | 171 | 7 | 89 | – |
| Bailey | 22 | 2 | 91 | 1 | | | | | 2nd | 276 | 11 | 110 | – |
| Lock | 25 | 0 | 96 | 0 | 2 | 0 | 8 | 0 | 3rd | 286 | 74 | 125 | – |
| Cowdrey | | | | | 1.3 | 0 | 9 | 0 | 4th | 294 | 170 | 177 | – |
| | | | | | | | | | 5th | 369 | 173 | 198 | – |
| AUSTRALIA | | | | | | | | | 6th | 388 | 180 | 199 | – |
| Davidson | 12 | 0 | 49 | 1 | 8.3 | 3 | 17 | 2 | 7th | 407 | 184 | 222 | – |
| Lindwall | 15 | 0 | 66 | 1 | 26 | 6 | 70 | 2 | 8th | 445 | 184 | 268 | – |
| Rorke | 18.1 | 7 | 23 | 3 | 34 | 7 | 78 | 2 | 9th | 473 | 188 | 270 | – |
| Benaud | 27 | 6 | 91 | 5 | 29 | 10 | 82 | 4 | 10th | 476 | 240 | 270 | – |
| O'Neill | 2 | 1 | 8 | 0 | | | | | | | | | |
| Burke | | | | | 4 | 2 | 6 | 0 | | | | | |

Umpires: M.J. McInnes and R. Wright.

Test No. 468/178

# AUSTRALIA v ENGLAND 1958-59 (5th Test)

Played at Melbourne Cricket Ground on 13, 14, 16, 17, 18 February.
Toss: Australia.   Result: AUSTRALIA won by nine wickets.
Debuts: England – J.B. Mortimore.

McDonald scored his second consecutive hundred after being given not out when 12 after a bail had been dislodged as he glanced Trueman to the boundary. Bailey, playing in his final Test match, was dismissed for a 'pair' by the bowler to whom he had sacrificed his wicket (Lindwall's 100th against England) four years earlier (*Test No. 395*). During this match Lindwall broke C.V. Grimmett's Australian record of 216 Test wickets.

### ENGLAND

| | | | | |
|---|---|---|---|---|
| P.E. Richardson | c and b Benaud | 68 | lbw b Benaud | 23 |
| T.E. Bailey | c Davidson b Lindwall | 0 | b Lindwall | 0 |
| P.B.H. May* | c Benaud b Meckiff | 11 | c Harvey b Lindwall | 4 |
| M.C. Cowdrey | c Lindwall b Davidson | 22 | run out | 46 |
| T.W. Graveney | c McDonald b Benaud | 19 | c Harvey b Davidson | 54 |
| E.R. Dexter | c Lindwall b Meckiff | 0 | c Grout b Davidson | 6 |
| R. Swetman† | c Grout b Davidson | 1 | lbw b Lindwall | 9 |
| J.B. Mortimore | not out | 44 | b Rorke | 11 |
| F.S Trueman | c and b Benaud | 21 | b Rorke | 36 |
| F.H. Tyson | c Grout b Benaud | 9 | c Grout b Rorke | 6 |
| J.C. Laker | c Harvey b Davidson | 2 | not out | 5 |
| Extras | (B 4, W 4) | 8 | (B 9, LB 3, W 2) | 14 |
| **Total** | | **205** | | **214** |

### AUSTRALIA

| | | | | |
|---|---|---|---|---|
| C.C. McDonald | c Cowdrey b Laker | 133 | not out | 51 |
| J.W. Burke | c Trueman b Tyson | 16 | lbw b Tyson | 13 |
| R.N. Harvey | c Swetman b Trueman | 13 | not out | 1 |
| N.C. O'Neill | c Cowdrey b Trueman | 0 | | |
| K.D. Mackay | c Graveney b Laker | 23 | | |
| A.K. Davidson | b Mortimore | 17 | | |
| R. Benaud* | c Swetman b Laker | 64 | | |
| A.T.W. Grout† | c Trueman b Laker | 74 | | |
| R.R. Lindwall | c Cowdrey b Trueman | 0 | | |
| I. Meckiff | c and b Trueman | 2 | | |
| G.F. Rorke | not out | 0 | | |
| Extras | (B 5, LB 4) | 9 | (LB 4) | 4 |
| **Total** | | **351** | (1 wicket) | **69** |

| AUSTRALIA | O | M | R | W | O | M | R | W | FALL OF WICKETS | | | | |
|---|---|---|---|---|---|---|---|---|---|---|---|---|---|
| Davidson | 12·5 | 2 | 38 | 3 | 21 | 1 | 95 | 2 | | E | A | E | A |
| Lindwall | 14 | 2 | 36 | 1 | 11 | 2 | 37 | 3 | Wkt | 1st | 1st | 2nd | 2nd |
| Meckiff | 15 | 2 | 57 | 2 | 4 | 0 | 13 | 0 | 1st | 0 | 41 | 0 | 66 |
| Rorke | 6 | 1 | 23 | 0 | 12·4 | 2 | 41 | 3 | 2nd | 13 | 83 | 12 | – |
| Benaud | 17 | 5 | 43 | 4 | 6 | 1 | 14 | 1 | 3rd | 61 | 83 | 78 | – |
| | | | | | | | | | 4th | 109 | 154 | 105 | – |
| ENGLAND | | | | | | | | | 5th | 112 | 207 | 131 | – |
| Trueman | 25 | 0 | 92 | 4 | 6·7 | 0 | 45 | 0 | 6th | 124 | 209 | 142 | – |
| Tyson | 20 | 1 | 73 | 1 | 6 | 0 | 20 | 1 | 7th | 128 | 324 | 158 | – |
| Bailey | 14 | 2 | 43 | 0 | | | | | 8th | 191 | 327 | 172 | – |
| Laker | 30·5 | 4 | 93 | 4 | | | | | 9th | 203 | 329 | 182 | – |
| Mortimore | 11 | 1 | 41 | 1 | | | | | 10th | 205 | 351 | 214 | – |

Umpires: R. Wright and L. Townsend.

## Chapter 9
# IN NEW ZEALAND 1959

In 1959 Cowdrey enjoyed this second tour of New Zealand more than his first. His enjoyment owed nothing to personal success in the Test cricket.

They won the first Test at Lancaster Park, Christchurch by an innings and 99 runs. Ted Dexter made 141. Cowdrey only managed 15. The New Zealand wicket keeper, Petrie, had the misfortune to be struck near his eye by a ball bowled by Moir and had to retire for some time, whilst Reid the New Zealand captain kept wicket. Petrie returned only to be Trueman's one hundredth Test wicket. Lock with 5 for 31 and 6 for 53 was the outstanding bowler.

In the second, at Eden Park, Auckland, Peter May made 124 of England's 311 for 7 declared in reply to New Zealand's 181. He was certainly in great form and apparently in good health. Four months later he was struck down. Cowdrey this time managed only 5. The match was ruined by the weather and was drawn.

|  | Matches | Innings | Not out | Runs | Highest score | Average | 100s | 50s | Caught |
| --- | --- | --- | --- | --- | --- | --- | --- | --- | --- |
| This series | 2 | 2 | 0 | 20 | 15 | 10.00 | 0 | 0 | 2 |
| Previous series | 32 | 52 | 2 | 2076 | 154 | 41.52 | 5 | 14 | 39 |
| Cumulative totals | 34 | 54 | 2 | 2096 | 154 | 40.31 | 5 | 14 | 41 |

Test No. 472/27

# NEW ZEALAND v ENGLAND 1958–59 (1st Test)

Played at Lancaster Park, Christchurch, on 27, 28 February, 2 March.
Toss: England.   Result: ENGLAND won by an innings and 99 runs.
Debuts: New Zealand – B.A. Bolton, R.M. Harris, K.W. Hough.

Petrie, struck near his eye by a ball from Moir, retired for a time and Reid kept wicket. Later Petrie became Trueman's hundredth Test wicket. A record ground attendance of 20,000 watched the second day.

### ENGLAND

| | | |
|---|---|---|
| P.E. Richardson | c Petrie b Blair | 8 |
| W. Watson | c Petrie b Blair | 10 |
| T.W. Graveney | lbw b Hough | 42 |
| P.B.H. May* | c Hough b Moir | 71 |
| M.C. Cowdrey | b Hough | 15 |
| E.R. Dexter | b Reid | 141 |
| J.B. Mortimore | c and b Moir | 11 |
| R. Swetman† | b Hough | 9 |
| F.S. Trueman | lbw b Reid | 21 |
| G.A.R. Lock | b Reid | 15 |
| F.H. Tyson | not out | 6 |
| Extras | (B 12, LB 13) | 25 |
| **Total** | | **374** |

### NEW ZEALAND

| | | | | | |
|---|---|---|---|---|---|
| R.M. Harris | c Lock b Tyson | 6 | b Trueman | | 13 |
| B.A. Bolton | c Swetman b Lock | 33 | c May b Mortimore | | 26 |
| J.W. Guy | c Trueman b Lock | 3 | c Lock b Tyson | | 56 |
| J.R. Reid* | b Tyson | 40 | c Cowdrey b Lock | | 1 |
| B. Sutcliffe | c Lock b Tyson | 0 | c Trueman b Lock | | 12 |
| S.N. McGregor | c Lock b Mortimore | 0 | lbw b Lock | | 6 |
| J.T. Sparling | st Swetman b Lock | 12 | b Tyson | | 0 |
| A.M. Moir | c Graveney b Lock | 0 | c Swetman b Lock | | 1 |
| E.C. Petrie† | lbw b Trueman | 8 | not out | | 2 |
| R.W. Blair | lbw b Lock | 0 | c Trueman b Lock | | 2 |
| K.W. Hough | not out | 31 | b Lock | | 7 |
| Extras | (B 5, LB 4) | 9 | (B 1, LB 5, NB 1) | | 7 |
| **Total** | | **142** | | | **133** |

| NEW ZEALAND | O | M | R | W | O | M | R | W |
|---|---|---|---|---|---|---|---|---|
| Blair | 31 | 5 | 89 | 2 | | | | |
| Hough | 39 | 11 | 96 | 3 | | | | |
| Moir | 36 | 9 | 83 | 2 | | | | |
| Reid | 18.1 | 9 | 34 | 3 | | | | |
| Sparling | 16 | 7 | 38 | 0 | | | | |
| Sutcliffe | 2 | 0 | 9 | 0 | | | | |
| ENGLAND | | | | | | | | |
| Trueman | 10.5 | 3 | 39 | 1 | 8 | 2 | 20 | 1 |
| Tyson | 14 | 4 | 23 | 3 | 14 | 6 | 23 | 2 |
| Lock | 26 | 15 | 31 | 5 | 28.2 | 13 | 53 | 6 |
| Mortimore | 22 | 8 | 40 | 1 | 21 | 10 | 27 | 1 |
| Dexter | | | | | 1 | 0 | 3 | 0 |

### FALL OF WICKETS

| | E | NZ | NZ |
|---|---|---|---|
| Wkt | 1st | 1st | 2nd |
| 1st | 13 | 22 | 37 |
| 2nd | 30 | 33 | 68 |
| 3rd | 98 | 83 | 79 |
| 4th | 126 | 83 | 101 |
| 5th | 171 | 86 | 117 |
| 6th | 197 | 101 | 119 |
| 7th | 224 | 101 | 120 |
| 8th | 305 | 102 | 121 |
| 9th | 367 | 102 | 123 |
| 10th | 374 | 142 | 133 |

Umpires: J. Cowie and E.W.T. Tindill.

Test No. 473/28

# NEW ZEALAND v ENGLAND 1958–59 (2nd Test)

Played at Eden Park, Auckland, on 14, 16, 17 (*no play*), 18 (*no play*) March.
Toss: England.   Result: MATCH DRAWN.
Debuts: Nil.

The first two days were played in blustery conditions with the bails frequently being blown off, and the last two were completely ruined by rain.

## NEW ZEALAND

| | | |
|---|---|---|
| B.A. Bolton | run out | 0 |
| R.M. Harris | c Swetman b Dexter | 12 |
| S.N. McGregor | hit wkt b Trueman | 1 |
| J.W. Guy | b Dexter | 1 |
| B. Sutcliffe | b Lock | 61 |
| J.R. Reid* | b Dexter | 3 |
| J.T. Sparling | c Swetman b Trueman | 25 |
| A.M. Moir | c Graveney b Trueman | 10 |
| E.C. Petrie† | c Trueman b Lock | 13 |
| R.W. Blair | c Cowdrey b Tyson | 22 |
| K.W. Hough | not out | 24 |
| Extras | (B 7, LB 1, NB 1) | 9 |
| **Total** | | **181** |

## ENGLAND

| | | |
|---|---|---|
| P.E. Richardson | c Bolton b Moir | 67 |
| W. Watson | b Hough | 11 |
| T.W. Graveney | b Moir | 46 |
| P.B.H. May* | not out | 124 |
| M.C. Cowdrey | b Hough | 5 |
| E.R. Dexter | c Petrie b Moir | 1 |
| J.B. Mortimore | b Hough | 9 |
| R. Swetman† | run out | 17 |
| F.S. Trueman | not out | 21 |
| G.A.R. Lock | } did not bat | |
| F.H. Tyson | } | |
| Extras | (B 4, LB 6) | 10 |
| **Total** | (7 wickets) | **311** |

| ENGLAND | O | M | R | W |
|---|---|---|---|---|
| Trueman | 26 | 12 | 46 | 3 |
| Tyson | 20 | 9 | 50 | 1 |
| Dexter | 19 | 8 | 23 | 3 |
| Lock | 20.3 | 12 | 29 | 2 |
| Mortimore | 4 | 1 | 24 | 0 |
| NEW ZEALAND | | | | |
| Blair | 27 | 6 | 69 | 0 |
| Hough | 38 | 12 | 79 | 3 |
| Reid | 4 | 1 | 19 | 0 |
| Sparling | 20 | 6 | 48 | 0 |
| Moir | 27 | 14 | 84 | 3 |
| Sutcliffe | 1 | 0 | 2 | 0 |

### FALL OF WICKETS

| Wkt | NZ 1st | E 1st |
|---|---|---|
| 1st | 3 | 26 |
| 2nd | 6 | 94 |
| 3rd | 11 | 165 |
| 4th | 16 | 182 |
| 5th | 41 | 183 |
| 6th | 98 | 223 |
| 7th | 116 | 261 |
| 8th | 125 | – |
| 9th | 157 | – |
| 10th | 181 | – |

Umpires: J. Cowie and R.W.R. Shortt.

Chapter 10
# INDIA 1959

The Indians were the visiting side in 1959. I was managing an employment agency for accountants round the corner from the Guildhall in London at the time. A local authority inspector would call occasionally to ensure that the business was being conducted properly. At no time was any exception taken to City of London Chartered Accountants stipulating that they wanted 'NO Coloureds'. Perhaps it is apt that this is Chapter 10 as this was the year that Harold Macmillan received a majority of 100 in the first and only general election he faced as prime minister. He was able to address the South African Parliament in Cape Town in a famous speech that included the phrase "wind of change".

To those who ask what has this to do with Colin Cowdrey in Test cricket, the answer will become apparent later in this record of his contribution to test cricket which went deeper than playing.

At any rate in 1959 I listened to the opening overs of the first Test at Trent Bridge from my office in Gresham Street and was appalled to hear that Cowdrey was coming in No 3. For the life of me I could not understand why others continued to juggle someone in the batting order who had established himself as a No 4. Sure enough he was one of the first three out with the score no higher than 60. Then May, who should have been at No 3, came in at No 5 and made a century. Bradman secured much of his success by changing the batting order but it was by dropping down the order not going up from No 3 to open the innings. India following on soon lost Contractor to a smart low slip catch by Cowdrey to give Statham the first of his five wickets for 31. England won by an innings and 59 runs.

At Lord's they won by eight wickets. Cowdrey made 63 not out of a partnership with May which secured victory with 108 for 2. This Test marked the

*1959: Colin in action batting for England against India on the first day of the fourth Test in Manchester.*

end of 91 appearances by T G Evans who took his record to 219 including 46 stumpings – the last being Gupte off Greenhough.

In the third Test at Leeds India made only 161 and then Cowdrey showed his class from the start, driving and stroking the ball with effortless ease. He made 160 which was his highest test score to date and he thought it one of his best innings. He felt he had perfected the lofted straight drive and hit four sixes mostly off the leg spin of Gupte. May declared at 483 for 8 and India were all out for 149.

With the rubber already decided Cowdrey was among those the selectors decided to rest but between this match and the fourth Test at Old Trafford Peter May was taken ill and thus the captaincy fell to Cowdrey for the first time. He was soon involved on a controversial note. England were already three up in the series after three matches. Cowdrey won the toss and England scored nearly 500. By the Friday evening India had lost six wickets for 127. Cowdrey had a mixture of concern partly about the lack of interest in the match and partly to consequential discourtesy to the visitors. Envisaging that all to which the Saturday attendance and the television viewers had to look forward was a follow-on and a hard grind by India to save an innings defeat, Cowdrey mentioned the idea of not enforcing the follow-on to Gubby Allen, the Chairman of Selectors, and Geoffrey Howard, the Secretary of the Lancashire CC. They agreed that it might be a good idea but highlighted the necessity of letting everyone know that there would be a full day's cricket beforehand. Thus Cowdrey duly announced that, in view of the settled weather and Manchester holiday week in prospect, he would not enforce the follow-on. In the event that only added salt to the wound. The England batting in their second innings did nothing to provide bright cricket. The Indians recovered to make 376 in the last innings which ended after lunch on the Tuesday. I felt then as I do now that the first task of a test captain is to win the game as quickly as possible. Cowdrey began his Test captaincy unsatisfactorily. There was, however, much to admire in Barrington's leg spin. Seldom used by May, his Surrey and England captain, he was given plenty of scope by Cowdrey and off 14 overs in the first innings he took 3 for 36 and off 27 in the second took 2 for 75. England won by 171 runs.

In the last Test at The Oval England won by an innings and 27 runs. They thus became the first side to win a Test series in England 5–0. Cowdrey wrote of it being "rather unwanted". England would have welcomed such an outcome over many of the years since.

|  | Matches | Innings | Not out | Runs | Highest score | Average | 100s | 50s | Caught |
|---|---|---|---|---|---|---|---|---|---|
| This series | 5 | 7 | 1 | 344 | 160 | 57.33 | 1 | 2 | 7 |
| Previous series | 34 | 54 | 2 | 2096 | 154 | 40.31 | 5 | 14 | 41 |
| Cumulative totals | 39 | 61 | 3 | 2440 | 160 | 42.07 | 6 | 16 | 48 |

Test No. 474/20

# ENGLAND v INDIA 1959 (1st Test)

Played at Trent Bridge, Nottingham, on 4, 5, 6, 8 June.
Toss: England. Result: ENGLAND won by an innings and 59 runs.
Debuts: England – T. Greenhough, M.J. Horton, K. Taylor.

Borde's left-hand little finger was fractured by a ball from Trueman. England won at 3.30 p.m. on the fourth day. Nadkarni was unable to complete his 29th over after a drive from Statham had severely bruised his left hand. May gave no chances in scoring the last of his 13 Test hundreds.

### ENGLAND

| | | |
|---|---|---|
| C.A. Milton | b Surendranath | 9 |
| K. Taylor | lbw b Gupte | 24 |
| M.C. Cowdrey | c Borde b Surendranath | 5 |
| P.B.H. May* | c Joshi b Gupte | 106 |
| K.F. Barrington | b Nadkarni | 56 |
| M.J. Horton | c Nadkarni b Desai | 58 |
| T.G. Evans† | c Umrigar b Nadkarni | 73 |
| F.S. Trueman | b Borde | 28 |
| J.B. Statham | not out | 29 |
| T. Greenhough | c Gaekwad b Gupte | 0 |
| A.E. Moss | c Roy b Gupte | 11 |
| Extras | (B 15, LB 7, W 1) | 23 |
| **Total** | | **422** |

### INDIA

| | | | | |
|---|---|---|---|---|
| P. Roy | b Trueman | 54 | c Trueman b Greenhough | 49 |
| N.J. Contractor | c Barrington b Greenhough | 15 | c Cowdrey b Statham | 0 |
| P.R. Umrigar | b Trueman | 21 | b Statham | 20 |
| V.L. Manjrekar | lbw b Trueman | 17 | lbw b Greenhough | 44 |
| C.G. Borde | retired hurt | 15 | absent hurt | – |
| D.K. Gaekwad* | c Evans b Statham | 33 | (5) c Horton b Statham | 31 |
| R.G. Nadkarni | lbw b Trueman | 15 | (6) b Statham | 1 |
| P.G. Joshi† | lbw b Moss | 21 | (7) lbw b Trueman | 1 |
| S.P. Gupte | c Taylor b Moss | 2 | (8) c May b Statham | 8 |
| R. Surendranath | not out | 4 | (9) not out | 1 |
| R.B. Desai | b Statham | 0 | (10) c May b Trueman | 1 |
| Extras | (B 5, NB 4) | 9 | (NB 1) | 1 |
| **Total** | | **206** | | **157** |

| INDIA | O | M | R | W | O | M | R | W |
|---|---|---|---|---|---|---|---|---|
| Desai | 33 | 7 | 127 | 1 | | | | |
| Surendranath | 24 | 8 | 59 | 2 | | | | |
| Gupte | 38.1 | 11 | 102 | 4 | | | | |
| Nadkarni | 28.1 | 15 | 48 | 2 | | | | |
| Borde | 20 | 4 | 63 | 1 | | | | |
| ENGLAND | | | | | | | | |
| Statham | 23.5 | 11 | 46 | 2 | 21 | 10 | 31 | 5 |
| Trueman | 24 | 9 | 45 | 4 | 22.3 | 10 | 44 | 2 |
| Moss | 24 | 11 | 33 | 2 | 12 | 7 | 13 | 0 |
| Greenhough | 26 | 7 | 58 | 1 | 23 | 5 | 48 | 2 |
| Horton | 5 | 0 | 15 | 0 | 19 | 11 | 20 | 0 |

### FALL OF WICKETS

| Wkt | E 1st | I 1st | I 2nd |
|---|---|---|---|
| 1st | 17 | 34 | 8 |
| 2nd | 29 | 85 | 52 |
| 3rd | 60 | 95 | 85 |
| 4th | 185 | 126 | 124 |
| 5th | 221 | 158 | 140 |
| 6th | 327 | 190 | 143 |
| 7th | 358 | 198 | 147 |
| 8th | 389 | 206 | 156 |
| 9th | 390 | 206 | 157 |
| 10th | 422 | – | – |

Umpires: J.S. Buller and W.E. Phillipson.

Test No. 475/21

# ENGLAND v INDIA 1959 (2nd Test)

Played at Lord's, London, on 18, 19, 20 June.
Toss: India.   Result: ENGLAND won by eight wickets.
Debuts: India – M.L. Jaisimha.

England won shortly after tea on the third day. Contractor played the highest innings of the match, batting part of the time with a runner after a ball from Statham had fractured one of his ribs. Roy, captain in the absence of Gaekwad through bronchitis, became Statham's 150th Test wicket. In the last of his 91 Test appearances, Evans took his record total of Test dismissals to 219, including 46 stumpings.

### INDIA

| | | | | |
|---|---|---|---|---|
| P. Roy* | c Evans b Statham | 15 | c May b Trueman | 0 |
| N.J. Contractor | b Greenhough | 81 | (8) not out | 11 |
| P.R. Umrigar | b Statham | 1 | c Horton b Trueman | 0 |
| V.L. Manjrekar | lbw b Trueman | 12 | (5) lbw b Statham | 61 |
| J.M. Ghorpade | lbw b Greenhough | 41 | (4) c Evans b Statham | 22 |
| A.G. Kripal Singh | b Greenhough | 0 | b Statham | 41 |
| M.L. Jaisimha | lbw b Greenhough | 1 | (2) lbw b Moss | 8 |
| P.G. Joshi† | b Horton | 4 | (7) b Moss | 6 |
| R. Surendranath | b Greenhough | 0 | run out | 0 |
| S.P. Gupte | c May b Horton | 0 | st Evans b Greenhough | 7 |
| R.B. Desai | not out | 2 | b Greenhough | 5 |
| Extras | (LB 11) | 11 | (LB 4) | 4 |
| **Total** | | **168** | | **165** |

### ENGLAND

| | | | | |
|---|---|---|---|---|
| C.A. Milton | c Surendranath b Desai | 14 | c Joshi b Desai | 3 |
| K. Taylor | c Gupte b Desai | 6 | lbw b Surendranath | 3 |
| M.C. Cowdrey | c Joshi b Desai | 34 | not out | 63 |
| P.B.H. May* | b Surendranath | 9 | not out | 33 |
| K.F. Barrington | c sub (V.M. Muddiah) b Desai | 80 | | |
| M.J. Horton | b Desai | 2 | | |
| T.G. Evans† | b Surendranath | 0 | | |
| F.S. Trueman | lbw b Gupte | 7 | | |
| J.B. Statham | c Surendranath b Gupte | 38 | | |
| A.E. Moss | b Surendranath | 26 | | |
| T. Greenhough | not out | 0 | | |
| Extras | (B 5, LB 4, W 1) | 10 | (B 5, LB 1) | 6 |
| **Total** | | **226** | (2 wickets) | **108** |

| ENGLAND | O | M | R | W | O | M | R | W |
|---|---|---|---|---|---|---|---|---|
| Trueman | 16 | 4 | 40 | 1 | 21 | 3 | 55 | 2 |
| Statham | 16 | 6 | 27 | 2 | 17 | 7 | 45 | 3 |
| Moss | 14 | 5 | 31 | 0 | 23 | 10 | 30 | 2 |
| Greenhough | 16 | 4 | 35 | 5 | 18.1 | 8 | 31 | 2 |
| Horton | 15.4 | 7 | 24 | 2 | | | | |
| INDIA | | | | | | | | |
| Desai | 31.4 | 8 | 89 | 5 | 7 | 1 | 29 | 1 |
| Surendranath | 30 | 17 | 46 | 3 | 11 | 2 | 32 | 1 |
| Umrigar | 1 | 1 | 0 | 0 | 1 | 0 | 8 | 0 |
| Gupte | 19 | 2 | 62 | 2 | 6 | 2 | 21 | 0 |
| Kripal Singh | 3 | 0 | 19 | 0 | 1 | 1 | 0 | 0 |
| Jaisimha | | | | | 1 | 0 | 8 | 0 |
| Roy | | | | | 0.2 | 0 | 4 | 0 |

### FALL OF WICKETS

| | I | E | I | E |
|---|---|---|---|---|
| Wkt | 1st | 1st | 2nd | 2nd |
| 1st | 32 | 9 | 0 | 8 |
| 2nd | 40 | 26 | 0 | 12 |
| 3rd | 61 | 35 | 22 | – |
| 4th | 144 | 69 | 42 | – |
| 5th | 152 | 79 | 131 | – |
| 6th | 158 | 80 | 140 | – |
| 7th | 163 | 100 | 147 | – |
| 8th | 163 | 184 | 147 | – |
| 9th | 164 | 226 | 159 | – |
| 10th | 168 | 226 | 165 | – |

Umpires: E. Davies and C.S. Elliott.

**Test No. 476/22**

# ENGLAND v INDIA 1959 (3rd Test)

Played at Headingley, Leeds, on 2, 3, 4 July.
Toss: India. Result: ENGLAND won by an innings and 173 runs.
Debuts: England – G. Pullar, H.J. Rhodes; India – A.L. Apte.

May, who missed the next match, equalled F.E. Woolley's world record of 52 consecutive Test appearances. Rhodes dismissed Roy and Borde with his fourth and twelfth balls in Test cricket. The opening partnership of 146 between Parkhouse and Pullar set a new England record against India. England won the rubber shortly before 5 p.m. on the third day.

### INDIA

| | | | | |
|---|---|---|---|---|
| P. Roy | c Swetman b Rhodes | 2 | c Swetman b Trueman | 20 |
| A.L. Apte | b Moss | 8 | c Close b Moss | 7 |
| J.M. Ghorpade | c Swetman b Trueman | 8 | lbw b Trueman | 0 |
| C.G. Borde | c Swetman b Rhodes | 0 | c May b Close | 41 |
| P.R. Umrigar | c Trueman b Moss | 29 | c Trueman b Mortimore | 39 |
| D.K. Gaekwad* | c Cowdrey b Rhodes | 25 | c and b Close | 8 |
| R.G. Nadkarni | c Parkhouse b Rhodes | 27 | c Barrington b Close | 11 |
| N.S. Tamhane† | c Moss b Trueman | 20 | not out | 9 |
| R. Surendranath | c Close b Trueman | 5 | c Cowdrey b Mortimore | 1 |
| S.P. Gupte | c Swetman b Close | 21 | c and b Close | 1 |
| R.B. Desai | not out | 7 | c Cowdrey b Mortimore | 8 |
| Extras | (LB 4, NB 5) | 9 | (LB 4) | 4 |
| **Total** | | **161** | | **149** |

### ENGLAND

| | | |
|---|---|---|
| W.G.A. Parkhouse | c Tamhane b Desai | 78 |
| G. Pullar | c Borde b Nadkarni | 75 |
| M.C. Cowdrey | c Ghorpade b Gupte | 160 |
| P.B.H. May* | b Desai | 2 |
| K.F. Barrington | c Tamhane b Nadkarni | 80 |
| D.B. Close | b Gupte | 27 |
| J.B. Mortimore | b Gupte | 7 |
| R. Swetman† | not out | 19 |
| F.S. Trueman | c Desai b Gupte | 17 |
| A.E. Moss | ) did not bat | |
| H.J. Rhodes | ) | |
| Extras | (B 13, LB 5) | 18 |
| **Total** | (8 wickets declared) | **483** |

| ENGLAND | O | M | R | W | O | M | R | W | FALL OF WICKETS |
|---|---|---|---|---|---|---|---|---|---|
| Trueman | 15 | 6 | 30 | 3 | 10 | 1 | 29 | 2 | |
| Moss | 22 | 11 | 30 | 2 | 6 | 3 | 10 | 1 | |
| Rhodes | 18·5 | 3 | 50 | 4 | 10 | 2 | 35 | 0 | |
| Mortimore | 8 | 3 | 24 | 0 | 18·4 | 6 | 36 | 3 | |
| Close | 5 | 1 | 18 | 1 | 11 | 0 | 35 | 4 | |

| | I | E | I |
|---|---|---|---|
| Wkt | 1st | 1st | 2nd |
| 1st | 10 | 146 | 16 |
| 2nd | 10 | 180 | 19 |
| 3rd | 11 | 186 | 38 |
| 4th | 23 | 379 | 107 |
| 5th | 75 | 432 | 115 |
| 6th | 75 | 439 | 121 |
| 7th | 103 | 453 | 138 |
| 8th | 112 | 483 | 139 |
| 9th | 141 | – | 140 |
| 10th | 161 | – | 149 |

| INDIA | O | M | R | W |
|---|---|---|---|---|
| Desai | 38 | 10 | 111 | 2 |
| Surendranath | 32 | 11 | 84 | 0 |
| Gupte | 44·3 | 13 | 111 | 4 |
| Umrigar | 24 | 8 | 44 | 0 |
| Borde | 14 | 1 | 51 | 0 |
| Nadkarni | 22 | 2 | 64 | 2 |

Umpires: F.S. Lee and W.E. Phillipson.

Test No. 477/23

# ENGLAND v INDIA 1959 (4th Test)

Played at Old Trafford, Manchester, on 23, 24, 25, 27, 28 July.
Toss: England. Result: ENGLAND won by 171 runs.
Debuts: India – Abbas Ali Baig.

Baig, an Oxford University Freshman who had scored a hundred against Middlesex on his first appearance for the tourists in their previous match, remains the only Indian to score a hundred in his first Test, that match being in England. At 20 years 131 days he is still the youngest to score a hundred for India. Pullar was the first Lancashire player to score a hundred for England at Old Trafford.

## ENGLAND

| | | | | |
|---|---|---|---|---|
| W.G.A. Parkhouse | c Roy b Surendranath | 17 | c Contractor b Nadkarni | 49 |
| G. Pullar | c Joshi b Surendranath | 131 | c Joshi b Gupte | 14 |
| M.C. Cowdrey* | c Joshi b Nadkarni | 67 | (5) c Borde b Gupte | 9 |
| M.J.K. Smith | c Desai b Borde | 100 | c Desai b Gupte | 9 |
| K.F. Barrington | lbw b Surendranath | 87 | (6) lbw b Nadkarni | 46 |
| E.R. Dexter | c Roy b Surendranath | 13 | (3) c Umrigar b Gupte | 45 |
| R. Illingworth | c Gaekwad b Desai | 21 | not out | 47 |
| J.B. Mortimore | c Contractor b Gupte | 29 | (9) c Nadkarni b Borde | 7 |
| R. Swetman† | c Joshi b Gupte | 9 | (10) not out | 21 |
| F.S. Trueman | b Surendranath | 0 | (8) c Baig b Borde | 8 |
| H.J. Rhodes | not out | 0 | | |
| Extras | (B 7, LB 7, W 2) | 16 | (B 9, LB 1) | 10 |
| Total | | 490 | (8 wickets declared) | 265 |

## INDIA

| | | | | |
|---|---|---|---|---|
| P. Roy | c Smith b Rhodes | 15 | c Illingworth b Dexter | 21 |
| N.J. Contractor | c Swetman b Rhodes | 23 | c Barrington b Rhodes | 56 |
| A.A. Baig | c Cowdrey b Illingworth | 26 | run out | 112 |
| D.K. Gaekwad* | lbw b Trueman | 5 | c Illingworth b Rhodes | 0 |
| P.R. Umrigar | b Rhodes | 2 | c Illingworth b Barrington | 118 |
| C.G. Borde | c and b Barrington | 75 | c Swetman b Mortimore | 3 |
| R.G. Nadkarni | b Barrington | 31 | lbw b Trueman | 28 |
| P.G. Joshi† | run out | 5 | b Illingworth | 5 |
| R. Surendranath | b Illingworth | 11 | c Trueman b Barrington | 4 |
| S.P. Gupte | not out | 4 | b Trueman | 8 |
| R.B. Desai | b Barrington | 5 | not out | 7 |
| Extras | (LB 1, W 4, NB 1) | 6 | (B 8, LB 5, NB 1) | 14 |
| Total | | 208 | | 376 |

| INDIA | O | M | R | W | O | M | R | W |
|---|---|---|---|---|---|---|---|---|
| Desai | 39 | 7 | 129 | 1 | 8 | 2 | 14 | 0 |
| Surendranath | 47.1 | 17 | 115 | 5 | 8 | 5 | 15 | 0 |
| Umrigar | 19 | 3 | 47 | 0 | 7 | 3 | 4 | 0 |
| Gupte | 28 | 8 | 98 | 2 | 26 | 6 | 76 | 4 |
| Nadkarni | 28 | 14 | 47 | 1 | 30 | 6 | 93 | 2 |
| Borde | 13 | 1 | 38 | 1 | 11 | 1 | 53 | 2 |
| ENGLAND | | | | | | | | |
| Trueman | 15 | 4 | 29 | 1 | 23.1 | 6 | 75 | 2 |
| Rhodes | 18 | 3 | 72 | 3 | 28 | 2 | 87 | 2 |
| Dexter | 3 | 0 | 3 | 0 | 12 | 2 | 33 | 1 |
| Illingworth | 16 | 10 | 16 | 2 | 39 | 13 | 63 | 1 |
| Mortimore | 13 | 6 | 46 | 0 | 16 | 6 | 29 | 1 |
| Barrington | 14 | 3 | 36 | 3 | 27 | 4 | 75 | 2 |

### FALL OF WICKETS

| Wkt | E 1st | I 1st | E 2nd | I 2nd |
|---|---|---|---|---|
| 1st | 33 | 23 | 44 | 35 |
| 2nd | 164 | 54 | 100 | 144 |
| 3rd | 262 | 70 | 117 | 146 |
| 4th | 371 | 72 | 132 | 180 |
| 5th | 417 | 78 | 136 | 243 |
| 6th | 440 | 124 | 196 | 321 |
| 7th | 454 | 154 | 209 | 334 |
| 8th | 490 | 199 | 219 | 358 |
| 9th | 490 | 199 | – | 361 |
| 10th | 490 | 208 | – | 376 |

Umpires: J.S. Buller and C.S. Elliott.

**Test No. 478/24**

# ENGLAND v INDIA 1959 (5th Test)

Played at Kennington Oval, London, on 20, 21, 22, 24 August.
Toss: India. Result: ENGLAND won by an innings and 27 runs.
Debuts: Nil.

England won before lunch on the fourth day and for the first time gained five victories in a series. It was also the first time that this had been achieved in England, the only other instances so far being by Australia at home – against England in 1920-21 and against South Africa in 1931-32. The partnership of 169 between Subba Row and Smith remains England's highest for the third wicket against India.

## INDIA

| | | | | | |
|---|---|---:|---|---|---:|
| P. Roy | b Statham | 3 | lbw b Statham | | 0 |
| N.J. Contractor | c Illingworth b Dexter | 22 | c Trueman b Statham | | 25 |
| A.A. Baig | c Cowdrey b Trueman | 23 | c Cowdrey b Statham | | 4 |
| R.G. Nadkarni | c Swetman b Trueman | 6 | lbw b Illingworth | | 76 |
| C.G. Borde | b Greenhough | 0 | run out | | 6 |
| D.K. Gaekwad* | c Barrington b Dexter | 11 | c Swetman b Greenhough | | 15 |
| J.M. Ghorpade | b Greenhough | 5 | b Greenhough | | 24 |
| N.S. Tamhane† | c Swetman b Statham | 32 | b Trueman | | 9 |
| R. Surendranath | c Illingworth b Trueman | 27 | not out | | 17 |
| S.P. Gupte | b Trueman | 2 | c Greenhough b Trueman | | 5 |
| R.B. Desai | not out | 3 | c Swetman b Trueman | | 0 |
| Extras | (B 1, LB 4, NB 1) | 6 | (B 4, LB 6, NB 3) | | 13 |
| **Total** | | **140** | | | **194** |

## ENGLAND

| | | |
|---|---|---:|
| G. Pullar | c Tamhane b Surendranath | 22 |
| R. Subba Row | c Tamhane b Desai | 94 |
| M.C. Cowdrey* | c Borde b Surendranath | 6 |
| M.J.K. Smith | b Desai | 98 |
| K.F. Barrington | c sub (M.L. Jaisimha) b Gupte | 8 |
| E.R. Dexter | c Tamhane b Surendranath | 0 |
| R. Illingworth | c Gaekwad b Nadkarni | 50 |
| R. Swetman† | c Baig b Surendranath | 65 |
| F.S. Trueman | st Tamhane b Nadkarni | 1 |
| J.B. Statham | not out | 3 |
| T. Greenhough | c Contractor b Surendranath | 2 |
| Extras | (B 3, LB 8, W 1) | 12 |
| **Total** | | **361** |

| ENGLAND | O | M | R | W | O | M | R | W | FALL OF WICKETS | | | |
|---|---|---|---|---|---|---|---|---|---|---|---|---|
| Trueman | 17 | 6 | 24 | 4 | 14 | 4 | 30 | 3 | | I | E | I |
| Statham | 16·3 | 6 | 24 | 2 | 18 | 4 | 50 | 3 | Wkt | 1st | 1st | 2nd |
| Dexter | 16 | 7 | 24 | 2 | 7 | 1 | 11 | 0 | 1st | 12 | 38 | 5 |
| Greenhough | 29 | 11 | 36 | 2 | 27 | 12 | 47 | 2 | 2nd | 43 | 52 | 17 |
| Illingworth | 1 | 0 | 2 | 0 | 29 | 10 | 43 | 1 | 3rd | 49 | 221 | 44 |
| Barrington | 6 | 0 | 24 | 0 | | | | | 4th | 50 | 232 | 70 |
| INDIA | | | | | | | | | 5th | 67 | 233 | 106 |
| Desai | 33 | 5 | 103 | 2 | | | | | 6th | 72 | 235 | 159 |
| Surendranath | 51·3 | 25 | 75 | 5 | | | | | 7th | 74 | 337 | 163 |
| Gupte | 38 | 9 | 119 | 1 | | | | | 8th | 132 | 347 | 173 |
| Nadkarni | 25 | 11 | 52 | 2 | | | | | 9th | 134 | 358 | 188 |
| | | | | | | | | | 10th | 140 | 361 | 194 |

Umpires: F.S. Lee and E. Davies.

## Chapter 11
# WEST INDIES 1959/60

En route to the West Indies for the 1959/60 series it was decided that Cowdrey should open the innings. Cowdrey's mild comment that he was not very keen was greeted with some scorn by Walter Robins the manager. Robins highlighted that the only other opener in the side was Geoff Pullar who had recently converted from the No 3 position. Cowdrey did not press the point.

May returned to lead a new England party but his wound reopened before the second Test and he flew home after the third Test leaving Cowdrey to captain in the last two. Cowdrey and Dexter were the best batsmen with Cowdrey again undertaking the opening role. Sometimes he batted with grim determination, scoring only when absolutely safe. On other occasions he showed his full range of classical strokes and completely dominated the bowling. In the event he and Pullar were a splendid opening pair.

In the first Test in Bridgetown, Barbados England made 482 in the first innings with Hall and Watson bowling bumpers. Cowdrey brushed a rising ball to second slip to be caught by Sobers for 30. Barrington and Dexter both made centuries but West Indies took the lead with only three wickets down. Sobers 266 and Worrell 197 not out added 399 for the fourth wicket. Worrell's innings lasted eleven hours twenty minutes. England were able to draw.

The second Test at Queen's Park Oval, Port-of-Spain, Trinidad was the decisive match. England made 382 Barrington again making a century; this time M J K Smith also reaching three figures. West Indies when they came to bat were 98 for 8 when bottles began to fly. Roy Swetman brought off a diving catch at the wicket. Conrad Hunte hesitated not thinking he had hit the ball but his hesitation was interpreted, by the record crowd of 30,000, as doubt as to whether the catch had been made. When the umpire rightly gave

*Colin swings a bouncer from Hall to the boundary at Sabina Park in 1960. He made a century and 97.*

Singh run out a sunshade was thrown on to the ground that led to a shower of bottles. Cowdrey was characteristically ambassadorial in the wake of a rioting crowd having stopped a day's play. I wasn't there but having had the pleasure of meeting Conrad Hunte at the Conservative Party Conference some years later, I could not imagine the gentleman I met stirring up a riot. West Indies made only 112 and May declared England's second innings on 230 for 9 setting West Indies 501 runs to win in ten hours. Despite 110 from Kanhai they were dismissed for 244 with 110 minutes to spare.

Cowdrey's batting had made little contribution so far but having opened the batting in the third Test at Sabina Park, Kingston, Jamaica, though hit many times and badly bruised, he stayed throughout the five hours to be undefeated overnight on 75. Next day England came back well with Cowdrey and Trueman adding 45 for the eighth wicket and the last three wickets putting on 107. Cowdrey, ninth out, fought splendidly for six and three quarter hours for 114. Despite 147 from Sobers England restricted the lead to 76. In the second innings Cowdrey and Pullar, having cleared 65 by the close, carried their stand to 177. Cowdrey's 97 after a century in the first innings obviously aroused mixed feelings but he had given one of his finest displays. Cowdrey had cleverly calculated the effect of the length of the bowling. Wearing extra padding he allowed many to strike his person only to dispatch the predictable shorter ball to the long leg boundary. He had driven and hooked with perfect timing. Other batsmen did not fare as well and six fell lbw. However the final wicket survived for 45 minutes on the final morning setting West Indies 230 to square the rubber in 245 minutes. At tea the target had become 115 in 90 minutes with six wickets left. They gave up the chase when Kanhai was sixth out. England failed to take another wicket during the forty five minutes that remained.

Cowdrey took over the captaincy for the fourth Test at Georgetown, British Guiana. Cowdrey and Pullar gave England another useful start to their 295. Slow scoring by the West Indies in making 402 for 8 before declaring allowed England to draw the match. Subba Row and Dexter both scoring centuries. Cowdrey top scored with 65 in the first innings and contributed 27 before being stumped in the second.

The fifth Test, like the second, was played at the Queen's Park Oval, Port-of-Spain, Trinidad. Cowdrey again opened to score 119 in England's first innings total of 393. Sobers was the highest scorer for the West Indies who declared 55 behind. Cowdrey was dismissed in the second innings to his embarrassment. Hall strained his side in running up to bowl the first over and recommenced bowling at half pace. The sudden change of pace induced Cowdrey to turn his third ball into the hands of short leg. A seventh wicket partnership between M J K Smith 96 and wicket keeper Parks undefeated on 101, enabled Cowdrey to declare on 350 for 8 setting the West Indies to make 406 to win at 140 runs an hour. They had reached 209 for 5 when the match ended in a Draw.

|  | Matches | Innings | Not out | Runs | Highest score | Average | 100s | 50s | Caught |
|---|---|---|---|---|---|---|---|---|---|
| This series | 5 | 10 | 1 | 491 | 119 | 54.55 | 2 | 2 | 1 |
| Previous series | 39 | 61 | 3 | 2440 | 160 | 42.07 | 6 | 16 | 48 |
| Cumulative totals | 44 | 71 | 4 | 2931 | 160 | 43.75 | 8 | 18 | 49 |

Test No. 487/36

# WEST INDIES v ENGLAND 1959-60 (1st Test)

Played at Kensington Oval, Bridgetown, Barbados, on 6, 7, 8, 9, 11, 12 January.
Toss: England.  Result: MATCH DRAWN.
Debuts: West Indies – R.G. Scarlett, C.D. Watson; England – D.A. Allen.

Worrell (682 minutes) and Sobers (647 minutes) played the two then longest innings against England and their partnership of 399 in 570 minutes remains the West Indies record for any wicket against England, the West Indies fourth-wicket record in all Tests, and the highest fourth-wicket stand by any country against England. Earlier Alexander had set a West Indies record by holding five catches in an innings and McMorris had been run out off a no-ball.

## ENGLAND

| | | | | |
|---|---|---|---|---|
| G. Pullar | run out | 65 | not out | 46 |
| M.C. Cowdrey | c Sobers b Watson | 30 | not out | 16 |
| K.F. Barrington | c Alexander b Ramadhin | 128 | | |
| P.B.H. May* | c Alexander b Hall | 1 | | |
| M.J.K. Smith | c Alexander b Scarlett | 39 | | |
| E.R. Dexter | not out | 136 | | |
| R. Illingworth | b Ramadhin | 5 | | |
| R. Swetman† | c Alexander b Worrell | 45 | | |
| F.S. Trueman | c Alexander b Ramadhin | 3 | | |
| D.A. Allen | lbw b Watson | 10 | | |
| A.E. Moss | b Watson | 4 | | |
| Extras | (B 4, LB 6, NB 6) | 16 | (B 7, LB 1, W 1) | 9 |
| Total | | 482 | (0 wickets) | 71 |

## WEST INDIES

| | | |
|---|---|---|
| C.C. Hunte | c Swetman b Barrington | 42 |
| E.D.A. St J. McMorris | run out | 0 |
| R.B. Kanhai | b Trueman | 40 |
| G. St A. Sobers | b Trueman | 226 |
| F.M.M. Worrell | not out | 197 |
| B.F. Butcher | c Trueman b Dexter | 13 |
| W.W. Hall | lbw b Trueman | 14 |
| F.C.M. Alexander*† | c Smith b Trueman | 3 |
| R.G. Scarlett | lbw b Dexter | 7 |
| C.D. Watson | did not bat | |
| S. Ramadhin | | |
| Extras | (B 8, LB 7, W 1, NB 5) | 21 |
| Total | (8 wickets declared) | 563 |

| WEST INDIES | O | M | R | W | O | M | R | W | FALL OF WICKETS | | | |
|---|---|---|---|---|---|---|---|---|---|---|---|---|
| Hall | 40 | 9 | 98 | 1 | 6 | 2 | 9 | 0 | | E | WI | E |
| Watson | 32.4 | 6 | 121 | 3 | 8 | 1 | 19 | 0 | Wkt | 1st | 1st | 2nd |
| Worrell | 15 | 2 | 39 | 1 | | | | | 1st | 50 | 6 | – |
| Ramadhin | 54 | 22 | 109 | 3 | 7 | 2 | 11 | 0 | 2nd | 153 | 68 | – |
| Scarlett | 26 | 9 | 46 | 1 | 10 | 4 | 12 | 0 | 3rd | 162 | 102 | – |
| Sobers | 21 | 3 | 53 | 0 | | | | | 4th | 251 | 501 | – |
| Hunte | | | | | 7 | 2 | 9 | 0 | 5th | 291 | 521 | – |
| Kanhai | | | | | 4 | 3 | 2 | 0 | 6th | 303 | 544 | – |
| ENGLAND | | | | | | | | | 7th | 426 | 556 | – |
| Trueman | 47 | 15 | 93 | 4 | | | | | 8th | 439 | 563 | – |
| Moss | 47 | 14 | 116 | 0 | | | | | 9th | 478 | – | – |
| Dexter | 37.4 | 11 | 85 | 2 | | | | | 10th | 482 | – | – |
| Illingworth | 47 | 9 | 106 | 0 | | | | | | | | |
| Allen | 43 | 12 | 82 | 0 | | | | | | | | |
| Barrington | 18 | 3 | 60 | 1 | | | | | | | | |

Umpires: H.B. de C. Jordan and J. Roberts.

Test No. 488/37

# WEST INDIES v ENGLAND 1959–60 (2nd Test)

Played at Queen's Park Oval, Port-of-Spain, Trinidad, on 28, 29, 30 January, 1, 2, 3 February.
Toss: England.   Result: ENGLAND won by 256 runs.
Debuts: West Indies – C.K. Singh.

A dramatic match which was marred when sections of the crowd of 30,000 – a record for any sporting event in the West Indies – threw bottles, rioted, and brought play to a premature close when Singh was run out soon after tea on the third day. Earlier Hall and Watson had been warned by umpires Lloyd and Lee Kow respectively for intimidatory bowling (Law 46). Barrington scored his second hundred in only his second innings against West Indies. England won with 110 minutes to spare after setting West Indies 501 runs to win in ten hours.

### ENGLAND

| | | | | |
|---|---|---|---|---|
| G. Pullar | c Alexander b Watson | 17 | c Worrell b Ramadhin | 28 |
| M.C. Cowdrey | b Hall | 18 | c Alexander b Watson | 5 |
| K.F. Barrington | c Alexander b Hall | 121 | c Alexander b Hall | 49 |
| P.B.H. May* | c Kanhai b Watson | 0 | c and b Singh | 28 |
| E.R. Dexter | c and b Singh | 77 | b Hall | 0 |
| M.J.K. Smith | c Worrell b Ramadhin | 108 | lbw b Watson | 12 |
| R. Illingworth | b Ramadhin | 10 | not out | 41 |
| R. Swetman† | lbw b Watson | 1 | lbw b Singh | 0 |
| F.S. Trueman | lbw b Ramadhin | 7 | c Alexander b Watson | 37 |
| D.A. Allen | not out | 10 | c Alexander b Hall | 16 |
| J.B. Statham | b Worrell | 1 | | |
| Extras | (LB 3, W 1, NB 8) | 12 | (B 6, LB 2. W 4, NB 2) | 14 |
| **Total** | | **382** | (9 wickets declared) | **230** |

### WEST INDIES

| | | | | |
|---|---|---|---|---|
| C.C. Hunte | c Trueman b Statham | 8 | c Swetman b Allen | 47 |
| J.S. Solomon | run out | 23 | c Swetman b Allen | 9 |
| R.B. Kanhai | lbw b Trueman | 5 | c Smith b Dexter | 110 |
| G. St A. Sobers | c Barrington b Trueman | 0 | lbw b Trueman | 31 |
| F.M.M. Worrell | c Swetman b Trueman | 9 | lbw b Statham | 0 |
| B.F. Butcher | lbw b Statham | 9 | lbw b Statham | 9 |
| F.C.M. Alexander *† | lbw b Trueman | 28 | c Trueman b Allen | 7 |
| S. Ramadhin | b Trueman | 23 | lbw b Dexter | 0 |
| C.K. Singh | run out | 0 | c and b Barrington | 11 |
| W.W. Hall | b Statham | 4 | not out | 0 |
| C.D. Watson | not out | 0 | c Allen b Barrington | 0 |
| Extras | (LB 2, W 1) | 3 | (B 11, LB 6, W 2, NB 1) | 20 |
| **Total** | | **112** | | **244** |

| WEST INDIES | O | M | R | W | O | M | R | W |
|---|---|---|---|---|---|---|---|---|
| Hall | 33 | 9 | 92 | 2 | 23.4 | 4 | 50 | 3 |
| Watson | 31 | 5 | 100 | 3 | 19 | 6 | 57 | 3 |
| Worrell | 11.5 | 3 | 2 | 1 | 12 | 5 | 27 | 0 |
| Singh | 23 | 6 | 59 | 1 | 8 | 3 | 28 | 2 |
| Ramadhin | 35 | 12 | 61 | 3 | 28 | 8 | 54 | 1 |
| Sobers | 3 | 0 | 16 | 0 | | | | |
| Solomon | 7 | 0 | 19 | 0 | | | | |
| ENGLAND | | | | | | | | |
| Trueman | 21 | 11 | 35 | 5 | 19 | 9 | 44 | 1 |
| Statham | 19.3 | 8 | 42 | 3 | 25 | 12 | 44 | 2 |
| Allen | 5 | 0 | 9 | 0 | 31 | 13 | 57 | 3 |
| Barrington | 16 | 10 | 15 | 0 | 25.5 | 13 | 34 | 2 |
| Illingworth | 7 | 3 | 8 | 0 | 28 | 14 | 38 | 0 |
| Dexter | | | | | 6 | 3 | 7 | 2 |

| FALL OF WICKETS | | | | |
|---|---|---|---|---|
| | E | WI | E | WI |
| Wkt | 1st | 1st | 2nd | 2nd |
| 1st | 37 | 22 | 18 | 29 |
| 2nd | 42 | 31 | 79 | 107 |
| 3rd | 57 | 31 | 97 | 158 |
| 4th | 199 | 45 | 101 | 159 |
| 5th | 276 | 45 | 122 | 188 |
| 6th | 307 | 73 | 133 | 222 |
| 7th | 308 | 94 | 133 | 222 |
| 8th | 343 | 98 | 201 | 244 |
| 9th | 378 | 108 | 230 | 244 |
| 10th | 382 | 112 | – | 244 |

Umpires: E.N. Lee Kow and E.L. Lloyd.

Test No. 489/38

# WEST INDIES v ENGLAND 1959–60 (3rd Test)

Played at Sabina Park, Kingston, Jamaica, on 17, 18, 19, 20, 22, 23 February.
Toss: England.  Result: MATCH DRAWN.
Debuts: West Indies – S.M. Nurse.

England failed to take a wicket on the third day, McMorris (65*) retiring with a contused lung at 189 for 2 after being hit on the chest by a ball from Statham; he resumed his innings at 329 for 6. After England's last wicket had survived for 45 minutes on the final morning, West Indies required 230 to square the rubber in 245 minutes. At tea their target had become 115 in 90 minutes with six wickets left. They gave up the chase when Kanhai was sixth out and England failed to take the remaining wickets during the subsequent 45 minutes. Six England batsmen were 'lbw' in the second innings, equalling the Test record which they had set in 1955 (*Test No. 411*).

## ENGLAND

| | | | | | |
|---|---|---|---|---|---|
| G. Pullar | c Sobers b Hall | 19 | lbw b Ramadhin | | 66 |
| M.C. Cowdrey | c Scarlett b Ramadhin | 114 | c Alexander b Scarlett | | 97 |
| K.F. Barrington | c Alexander b Watson | 16 | lbw b Solomon | | 4 |
| P.B.H. May* | c Hunte b Hall | 9 | b Hall | | 45 |
| E.R. Dexter | c Alexander b Hall | 25 | b Watson | | 16 |
| M.J.K. Smith | b Hall | 0 | lbw b Watson | | 10 |
| R. Illingworth | c Alexander b Hall | 17 | b Ramadhin | | 6 |
| R. Swetman† | b Hall | 0 | lbw b Watson | | 5 |
| F.S. Trueman | c Solomon b Ramadhin | 17 | lbw b Watson | | 4 |
| D.A. Allen | not out | 30 | not out | | 17 |
| J.B. Statham | b Hall | 13 | lbw b Ramadhin | | 12 |
| Extras | (LB 4, W 10, NB 3) | 17 | (B 8, LB 10, W 3, NB 2) | | 23 |
| **Total** | | **277** | | | **305** |

## WEST INDIES

| | | | | | |
|---|---|---|---|---|---|
| C.C. Hunte | c Illingworth b Statham | 7 | b Trueman | | 40 |
| E.D.A. St J. McMorris | b Barrington | 73 | b Trueman | | 1 |
| R.B. Kanhai | run out | 18 | b Trueman | | 57 |
| G. St A. Sobers | lbw b Trueman | 147 | run out | | 19 |
| S.M. Nurse | c Smith b Illingworth | 70 | b Trueman | | 11 |
| J.S. Solomon | c Swetman b Allen | 8 | (8) not out | | 10 |
| R.G. Scarlett | c Statham b Illingworth | 6 | (6) lbw b Statham | | 12 |
| F.C.M. Alexander*† | b Trueman | 0 | (7) not out | | 7 |
| S. Ramadhin | b Statham | 5 | | | |
| C.D. Watson | b Statham | 3 | | | |
| W.W. Hall | not out | 0 | | | |
| Extras | (B 6, LB 7, W 1, NB 2) | 16 | (B 9, LB 3, W 6) | | 18 |
| **Total** | | **353** | (6 wickets) | | **175** |

| WEST INDIES | O | M | R | W | O | M | R | W | | FALL OF WICKETS | | | |
|---|---|---|---|---|---|---|---|---|---|---|---|---|---|
| | | | | | | | | | | E | WI | E | WI |
| Hall | 31.2 | 8 | 69 | 7 | 26 | 5 | 93 | 1 | Wkt | 1st | 1st | 2nd | 2nd |
| Watson | 29 | 7 | 74 | 1 | 27 | 8 | 62 | 4 | 1st | 28 | 12 | 177 | 11 |
| Ramadhin | 28 | 3 | 78 | 2 | 28.3 | 14 | 38 | 3 | 2nd | 54 | 56 | 177 | 48 |
| Scarlett | 10 | 4 | 13 | 0 | 28 | 12 | 51 | 1 | 3rd | 68 | 299 | 190 | 86 |
| Sobers | 2 | 0 | 14 | 0 | 8 | 2 | 18 | 0 | 4th | 113 | 329 | 211 | 111 |
| Solomon | 4 | 1 | 12 | 0 | 6 | 1 | 20 | 1 | 5th | 113 | 329 | 239 | 140 |
| ENGLAND | | | | | | | | | 6th | 165 | 329 | 258 | 152 |
| Statham | 32.1 | 8 | 76 | 3 | 18 | 6 | 45 | 1 | 7th | 170 | 341 | 269 | – |
| Trueman | 33 | 10 | 82 | 2 | 18 | 4 | 54 | 4 | 8th | 215 | 347 | 269 | – |
| Dexter | 12 | 3 | 38 | 0 | | | | | 9th | 245 | 350 | 280 | – |
| Allen | 28 | 10 | 57 | 1 | 9 | 4 | 19 | 0 | 10th | 277 | 353 | 305 | – |
| Barrington | 21 | 7 | 38 | 1 | 4 | 4 | 0 | 0 | | | | | |
| Illingworth | 30 | 13 | 46 | 2 | 13 | 4 | 35 | 0 | | | | | |
| Cowdrey | | | | | 1 | 0 | 4 | 0 | | | | | |

Umpires: P. Burke and E.N. Lee Kow.

Test No. 490/39

# WEST INDIES v ENGLAND 1959–60 (4th Test)

Played at Bourda, Georgetown, British Guiana, on 9, 10, 11, 12, 14, 15 March.
Toss: England.   Result: MATCH DRAWN.
Debuts: Nil.

Rain delayed the start by 75 minutes. Barrington, struck above the elbow by Hall on the first day, retired at 161 for three after 20 minutes' batting on the second, and resumed at 219 for 7. After Sobers had scored his third hundred of the rubber, West Indies declared with a lead of 107, eight hours of play left, and Watson (torn ankle ligaments) unable to bowl. Subba Row scored his first Test hundred under the handicap of a chipped knuckle.

## ENGLAND

| | | | | |
|---|---|---|---|---|
| G. Pullar | c Alexander b Hall | 33 | lbw b Worrell | 47 |
| M.C. Cowdrey* | c Alexander b Hall | 65 | st Alexander b Singh | 27 |
| R. Subba Row | c Alexander b Sobers | 27 | (4) lbw b Worrell | 100 |
| K.F. Barrington | c Walcott b Sobers | 27 | (7) c Walcott b Worrell | 0 |
| E.R. Dexter | c Hunte b Hall | 39 | (3) c Worrell b Walcott | 110 |
| M.J.K. Smith | b Hall | 0 | (5) c Scarlett b Sobers | 23 |
| R. Illingworth | b Sobers | 4 | (6) c Kanhai b Worrell | 9 |
| R. Swetman† | lbw b Watson | 4 | (9) c Hall b Singh | 3 |
| D.A. Allen | c Alexander b Hall | 55 | (8) not out | 1 |
| F.S. Trueman | b Hall | 6 | | |
| J.B. Statham | not out | 20 | | |
| Extras | (B 5, LB 2, W 2, NB 6) | 15 | (B 6, LB 4, NB 4) | 14 |
| **Total** | | **295** | (8 wickets) | **334** |

## WEST INDIES

| | | |
|---|---|---|
| C.C. Hunte | c Trueman b Allen | 39 |
| E.D.A. St J. McMorris | c Swetman b Statham | 35 |
| R.B. Kanhai | c Dexter b Trueman | 55 |
| G. St A. Sobers | st Swetman b Allen | 145 |
| C.L. Walcott | b Trueman | 9 |
| F.M.M. Worrell | b Allen | 38 |
| F.C.M. Alexander*† | run out | 33 |
| R.G. Scarlett | not out | 29 |
| C.K. Singh | b Trueman | 0 |
| W.W. Hall | not out | 1 |
| C.D. Watson | did not bat | |
| Extras | (B 4, LB 12, NB 2) | 18 |
| **Total** | (8 wickets declared) | **402** |

| WEST INDIES | O | M | R | W | O | M | R | W | | FALL OF WICKETS | | |
|---|---|---|---|---|---|---|---|---|---|---|---|---|
| Hall | 30·2 | 8 | 90 | 6 | 18 | 1 | 79 | 0 | | E | WI | E |
| Watson | 20 | 2 | 56 | 1 | | | | | Wkt | 1st | 1st | 2nd |
| Worrell | 16 | 9 | 22 | 0 | 31 | 12 | 49 | 4 | 1st | 73 | 67 | 40 |
| Scarlett | 22 | 11 | 24 | 0 | 38 | 13 | 63 | 0 | 2nd | 121 | 77 | 110 |
| Singh | 12 | 4 | 29 | 0 | 41·2 | 22 | 50 | 2 | 3rd | 152 | 192 | 258 |
| Sobers | 19 | 1 | 59 | 3 | 12 | 1 | 36 | 1 | 4th | 161 | 212 | 320 |
| Walcott | | | | | 9 | 0 | 43 | 1 | 5th | 169 | 333 | 322 |
| | | | | | | | | | 6th | 175 | 338 | 322 |
| ENGLAND | | | | | | | | | 7th | 219 | 393 | 331 |
| Trueman | 40 | 6 | 116 | 3 | | | | | 8th | 258 | 398 | 334 |
| Statham | 36 | 8 | 79 | 1 | | | | | 9th | 268 | – | – |
| Illingworth | 43 | 11 | 72 | 0 | | | | | 10th | 295 | – | – |
| Barrington | 6 | 2 | 22 | 0 | | | | | | | | |
| Allen | 42 | 11 | 75 | 3 | | | | | | | | |
| Dexter | 5 | 0 | 20 | 0 | | | | | | | | |

Umpires: E.N. Lee Kow and C.P. Kippins.

Test No. 491/40

# WEST INDIES v ENGLAND 1959–60 (5th Test)

Played at Queen's Park Oval, Port-of-Spain, Trinidad, on 25, 26, 28, 29, 30, 31 March.
Toss: England.   Result: MATCH DRAWN.
Debuts: West Indies – C.C. Griffith.

England won their fifth toss of the rubber – the only time that this has been achieved by a side with a change of captain. Barrington (23*) retired hurt at 256 for 3 in the last over of the first day after twice being hit on the knuckles by Hall. Although fit to resume immediately the next morning, he had to wait until the fall of the fourth wicket as the umpires ruled, quite correctly, that a new batsman must go in. Hunte (12*) retired hurt at 24 for 1 when he edged a hook at Trueman into his ear. Smith and Parks (a late addition to the touring party) added 197 to set the present record for England's seventh wicket. West Indies were set 406 to win at 140 runs per hour.

## ENGLAND

| | | | | | |
|---|---|---|---|---|---|
| G. Pullar | c Sobers b Griffith | 10 | c and b Sobers | | 54 |
| M.C. Cowdrey* | c Alexander b Sobers | 119 | c Worrell b Hall | | 0 |
| E.R. Dexter | c and b Sobers | 76 | (4) run out | | 47 |
| R. Subba Row | c Hunte b Hall | 22 | (5) lbw b Ramadhin | | 13 |
| K.F. Barrington | c Alexander b Ramadhin | 69 | (6) c McMorris b Sobers | | 6 |
| M.J.K. Smith | b Ramadhin | 20 | (7) c Alexander b Hunte | | 96 |
| J.M. Parks† | c and b Sobers | 43 | (8) not out | | 101 |
| R. Illingworth | c Sobers b Ramadhin | 0 | | | |
| D.A. Allen | c sub (S.M. Nurse) b Ramadhin | 7 | (3) run out | | 25 |
| F.S. Trueman | not out | 10 | (9) not out | | 2 |
| A.E. Moss | b Watson | 1 | | | |
| Extras | (B 7, NB 9) | 16 | (B 2, LB 3, NB 1) | | 6 |
| Total | | 393 | (7 wickets declared) | | 350 |

## WEST INDIES

| | | | | | |
|---|---|---|---|---|---|
| C.C. Hunte | not out | 72 | st Parks b Illingworth | | 36 |
| E.D.A. St J. McMorris | run out | 13 | lbw b Moss | | 2 |
| F.C.M. Alexander*† | b Allen | 26 | (7) not out | | 4 |
| G. St A. Sobers | b Moss | 92 | (6) not out | | 49 |
| C.L. Walcott | st Parks b Allen | 53 | (4) c Parks b Barrington | | 22 |
| F.M.M. Worrell | b Trueman | 15 | (5) c Trueman b Pullar | | 61 |
| R.B. Kanhai | b Moss | 6 | (3) c Trueman b Illingworth | | 34 |
| S. Ramadhin | c Cowdrey b Dexter | 13 | | | |
| W.W. Hall | b Trueman | 29 | | | |
| C.C. Griffith | not out | 5 | | | |
| C.D. Watson | did not bat | | | | |
| Extras | (B 6, LB 4, NB 4) | 14 | (LB 1) | | 1 |
| Total | (8 wickets declared) | 338 | (5 wickets) | | 209 |

| WEST INDIES | O | M | R | W | O | M | R | W | FALL OF WICKETS | | | | |
|---|---|---|---|---|---|---|---|---|---|---|---|---|---|
| Hall | 24 | 3 | 83 | 1 | 4 | 0 | 16 | 1 | | E | WI | E | WI |
| Griffith | 15 | 2 | 62 | 1 | 9 | 1 | 40 | 0 | Wkt | 1st | 1st | 2nd | 2nd |
| Watson | 18.2 | 3 | 52 | 1 | 14 | 1 | 52 | 0 | 1st | 19 | 26 | 3 | 11 |
| Ramadhin | 34 | 13 | 73 | 4 | 34 | 9 | 67 | 1 | 2nd | 210 | 103 | 69 | 72 |
| Worrell | 8 | 1 | 29 | 0 | 22 | 5 | 44 | 0 | 3rd | 215 | 190 | 102 | 75 |
| Sobers | 20 | 1 | 75 | 3 | 29 | 6 | 84 | 2 | 4th | 268 | 216 | 136 | 107 |
| Walcott | 4 | 2 | 3 | 0 | 7 | 2 | 24 | 0 | 5th | 317 | 227 | 145 | 194 |
| Hunte | | | | | 5 | 1 | 17 | 1 | 6th | 350 | 230 | 148 | – |
| | | | | | | | | | 7th | 350 | 263 | 345 | – |
| ENGLAND | | | | | | | | | 8th | 374 | 328 | – | – |
| Trueman | 37.3 | 6 | 103 | 2 | 5 | 1 | 22 | 0 | 9th | 388 | – | – | – |
| Moss | 34 | 3 | 94 | 2 | 4 | 0 | 16 | 1 | 10th | 393 | – | – | – |
| Allen | 24 | 1 | 61 | 2 | 15 | 2 | 57 | 0 | | | | | |
| Illingworth | 12 | 4 | 25 | 0 | 16 | 3 | 53 | 2 | | | | | |
| Dexter | 4 | 1 | 20 | 1 | | | | | | | | | |
| Barrington | 8 | 0 | 21 | 0 | 8 | 2 | 27 | 1 | | | | | |
| Subba Row | | | | | 1 | 0 | 2 | 0 | | | | | |
| Smith | | | | | 1 | 0 | 15 | 0 | | | | | |
| Pullar | | | | | 1 | 0 | 1 | 1 | | | | | |
| Cowdrey | | | | | 1 | 0 | 15 | 0 | | | | | |

Umpires: H.B. de C. Jordan and C.P. Kippins.

## Chapter 12
# SOUTH AFRICA 1960

The first Test against South Africa in 1960 was at Edgbaston. Cowdrey failed twice on both occasions falling to Adcock but led England to victory by 100 runs with four hours to spare.

In the second Test at Lord's the same mixed fortunes occurred when Cowdrey was out for 4 but England won by an innings and 73 runs. Griffin was the bowler. Later in the innings he became the first bowler to take a hat trick for South Africa. It was also the first hat trick in a Test at Lord's. Less praiseworthy Griffin was called eleven times for throwing during England's innings. It was the first instance in a Test in England and only the third in all tests. Cowdrey did take two great catches at second slip in South Africa's first innings.

The third was at Trent Bridge. Before the series began Cowdrey had been appointed Captain for the first two tests. When it was established that May would not play that season, he was appointed for the rest. At last he regained his form with the bat scoring 67 and 27 in another victory, this time by eight wickets. Following on South Africa lost Skipper McGlew run out for 45 after they had scored 91 in 2 hours. O'Linn played a ball from Moss to extra cover and went for a quick single. Moss dashed across the pitch to chase the ball and McGlew ran into his back. He stumbled and darted for the crease but Statham had picked up and with unerring aim hit the stumps. Cowdrey and other England players near the broken wicket promptly appealed and Elliott, the square leg umpire, signalled out. Elliott's decision was correct because Moss had not deliberately baulked McGlew. Three times Cowdrey called to McGlew to come back and when he did the England captain asked the umpires if it was possible to change the verdict but they were adamant. O'Linn continued until, looking for the shot that would have given him a well-deserved hundred, he was splendidly caught high with the right hand by Cowdrey at second slip off Moss. Cowdrey also caught Carlstein. England only wanted 49 to win and Cowdrey and Subba Row made 25 in the last half hour on Saturday. The weather permitted no play until 3 p.m. on the Monday and when the scores were level both Cowdrey and Dexter fell.

The fourth Test was at Old Trafford. There was no play on the first two days and the match was drawn. Cowdrey made 20 briskly in the first innings and going in first in the second batted quietly until two balls after hitting Adcock for a great six off his toes over mid wicket, he was out for 25.

Cowdrey had not produced many runs so far in the series and opening again in the final Test at the Oval he was out for 11 as England were dismissed for 155. The visitors then made 419. Trevor Goddard, who had opened the batting with skipper McGlew, was dismissed for 99 when Cowdrey dived to his left to pick up the ball. Goddard did not walk and the umpires consulted before giving it out. In a letter dated 5th October 1975 from Dulwich J P Fellows-Smith, who had come in at No 3 and been out for 35, wrote:

> Trevor L Goddard who was my Vice-Captain on the 1960 South African Tour of England is and was the mildest mannered cricketer with whom I had the pleasure of playing for Oxford, Northants, Transvaal and South Africa. Invariably the mildest, perhaps I should say.
>
> When he was 'out' (caught Cowdrey, bowled Statham) for 99 in the 5th Test at the Oval, Goddard threw his bat across the dressing room on his return from the crease. The ball had shortly before been held aloft by the slightly rotund gully fieldsman had, to his mind, undoubtedly hit the turf before being scooped up! Being a Christian and a gentleman, and now an evangelist, Trevor Goddard did not of course accompany his wild gesture with the words some other cricketers might have used. Rather bad luck at the time, for T.L.G. had yet to score his maiden Test century!
>
> Please see the 1961 *Wisden* report on McGlew's run out in the 3rd Test at Trent Bridge. All this and the Griffin throwing episode marred what might otherwise have been a happier tour.
>
> Yours sincerely
>
> Jon Fellows-Smith

Casual readers might be surprised that someone could feel so strongly about an incident in which he was not personally involved fifteen years after the event. Cricketers will not be. Arguably the most famous or infamous, depending on one's point of view, incident of the kind took place way back in 1946 and yet is still a bone of contention among those who are still alive. The match was in the first post second world war Test match between Australia and England at Brisbane. Bradman's own account of the event is still of interest in his autobiography first published in May 1950. "The Don" wrote:

> Then came perhaps the most debated incident of the series. Voce bowled me a ball which was near enough to a yorker. I attempted to chop down on top of it in order to guide the ball wide of the slip fieldsmen. Instead it flew to Ikin at second slip.
>
> In my opinion, the ball touched the bottom of my bat just before hitting the ground and therefore it was not a catch. Accordingly I stood my ground waiting for the game to proceed.
>
> Somewhat belatedly there was an appeal. Without the slightest hesitation umpire Borwick at the bowler's end said, "Not out." He was not even sufficiently doubtful to consult his colleague at square leg. Had he done so the result would have been the same, for Scott wrote an article after the tour in which he said, "It was a bump ball. It hit the ground, a few inches from Bradman's bat."
>
> I am well aware that some of the English players thought it was a catch, and they explained the "belated" appeal by claiming that they did not think an appeal was necessary.
>
> The broadcasters were quite unanimous in their view that it was not a catch. The newspaper writers were divided.
>
> The truth is that nobody outside the fence could possibly give an authoritative opinion.
>
> The incident assumed major importance simply because I went on to score 187, and thus on paper it was claimed that England had been largely penalized.
>
> I want to make it clear that the sole point at issue was whether the ball had finished its downward course before making contact with the bat. The question of whether Ikin caught it did not arise.
>
> This type of decision is never easy for an umpire. I can still recall Frank Chester

giving Hammond not-out at Lord's when I thought he had been clearly caught and bowled by Grimmett.

The women who attend Test matches, and squeal every time a bump ball is held, would give them all out.

I think it is important to record that at the end of the match, Hammond agreed to the reappointment of the two same umpires, and completely clarified his position by saying, "I thought it was a catch, but the umpire may have been right and I may have been wrong."[1]

Such incidents are still a feature of Test match cricket today. Ironically the additional aides, which have been introduced to help the umpire, sometimes add to the controversy. In the summer of 2003 after a catch had been claimed at cover by Zimbabwe, the batsman stood his ground, the "third umpire" signalled "Not Out" only to correct that on his link with the Umpire on the field. Apart from adding chaos to the confusion, it also demonstrated that the commentator's desire for the batsman just to accept the fielder's claim stands no more chance of being universally accepted than it did in 1946 or 1960.

Reverting to Goddard's reaction in the dressing room to Cowdrey's catch, it is important to stress that the incident did not occur *on* the field of play. Goddard had been dropped off consecutive balls from Statham by Cowdrey and Parks and had taken seventy five minutes to add the 18 runs which took him to 99. It was then that Cowdrey diving to his left rolled over as he accepted a difficult slip catch.

In England's second innings Cowdrey was lbw for 155 having put on 290 with Pullar. Although the match ended in a Draw, Cowdrey must be given credit for taking the initiative. He led the way before lunch when in 41 overs his share of a total of 145 was 88 to Pullar's 53. He was only 8 and the total 14 when he offered an easy chance off Pothecary to McLean at second slip. Having survived that he never looked back. He reached what was his first test hundred at the Oval out of 175 and included 22 fours.

---

1. Don Bradman, *Farewell to Cricket*, Hodder & Stoughton, 1950 pp. 128–9.

|  | Matches | Innings | Not out | Runs | Highest score | Average | 100s | 50s | Caught |
|---|---|---|---|---|---|---|---|---|---|
| This series | 5 | 9 | 0 | 312 | 155 | 34.66 | 1 | 1 | 7 |
| Previous series | 44 | 71 | 4 | 2931 | 160 | 43.75 | 8 | 18 | 49 |
| Cumulative totals | 49 | 80 | 4 | 3243 | 160 | 42.67 | 9 | 19 | 56 |

*3000 Runs and 50 catches in Test Cricket*

Test No. 492/90

# ENGLAND v SOUTH AFRICA 1960 (1st Test)

Played at Edgbaston, Birmingham, on 9, 10, 11, 13, 14 June.
Toss: England. Result: ENGLAND won by 100 runs.
Debuts: England – R.W. Barber, P.M. Walker; South Africa – J.P. Fellows-Smith, G.M. Griffin, S.O'Linn.

England included five county captains in Cowdrey, Dexter, Subba Row, Smith and Barber, but no Surrey player for the first time in a home Test since 1949 (*Test No. 316*). Pullar cracked a bone in his left wrist when he fended off an Adcock bouncer in the first innings. He came in last and played one ball single-handed in the second innings. England won with four hours to spare.

## ENGLAND

| | | | | |
|---|---|---|---|---|
| G. Pullar | c McLean b Goddard | 37 | (11) not out | 1 |
| M.C. Cowdrey* | c Waite b Adcock | 3 | (1) b Adcock | 0 |
| E.R. Dexter | b Tayfield | 52 | b Adcock | 26 |
| R. Subba Row | c Waite b Griffin | 56 | (2) c Waite b Tayfield | 32 |
| M.J.K. Smith | c Waite b Adcock | 54 | (4) c O'Linn b Tayfield | 28 |
| J.M. Parks† | c Waite b Adcock | 35 | (5) b Griffin | 4 |
| R. Illingworth | b Tayfield | 1 | (6) c Waite b Adcock | 16 |
| R.W. Barber | lbw b Adcock | 5 | (7) c McLean b Tayfield | 4 |
| P.M. Walker | c Goddard b Adcock | 9 | (8) c Goddard b Griffin | 37 |
| F.S. Trueman | b Tayfield | 11 | (9) b Tayfield | 25 |
| J.B. Statham | not out | 14 | (10) c McLean b Griffin | 22 |
| Extras | (B 4, LB 9, NB 2) | 15 | (B 2, LB 4, NB 2) | 8 |
| **Total** | | **292** | | **203** |

## SOUTH AFRICA

| | | | | |
|---|---|---|---|---|
| D.J. McGlew* | c Parks b Trueman | 11 | c Parks b Statham | 5 |
| T.L. Goddard | c Smith b Statham | 10 | c Walker b Statham | 0 |
| A.J. Pithey | lbw b Statham | 6 | b Illingworth | 17 |
| R.A. McLean | c Statham b Trueman | 21 | lbw b Trueman | 68 |
| J.H.B. Waite† | b Illingworth | 58 | not out | 56 |
| P.R. Carstein | lbw b Trueman | 4 | b Trueman | 10 |
| S. O'Linn | c Cowdrey b Illingworth | 42 | lbw b Barber | 12 |
| J.P. Fellows-Smith | lbw b Illingworth | 18 | lbw b Illingworth | 5 |
| G.M. Griffin | b Trueman | 6 | (10) c Walker b Trueman | 14 |
| H.J. Tayfield | run out | 6 | (9) b Illingworth | 3 |
| N.A.T. Adcock | not out | 1 | b Statham | 7 |
| Extras | (B 2, NB 1) | 3 | (B 7, LB 5) | 12 |
| **Total** | | **186** | | **209** |

| SOUTH AFRICA | O | M | R | W | O | M | R | W |
|---|---|---|---|---|---|---|---|---|
| Adcock | 41.5 | 14 | 62 | 5 | 28 | 8 | 57 | 3 |
| Griffin | 21 | 3 | 61 | 1 | 21 | 4 | 44 | 3 |
| Goddard | 33 | 17 | 47 | 1 | 10 | 5 | 32 | 0 |
| Tayfield | 50 | 19 | 93 | 3 | 27 | 12 | 62 | 4 |
| Fellows-Smith | 5 | 1 | 14 | 0 | | | | |
| ENGLAND | | | | | | | | |
| Statham | 28 | 8 | 67 | 2 | 18 | 5 | 41 | 3 |
| Trueman | 24.5 | 4 | 58 | 4 | 22 | 4 | 58 | 3 |
| Dexter | 1 | 0 | 4 | 0 | 6 | 4 | 4 | 0 |
| Barber | 6 | 0 | 26 | 0 | 10 | 2 | 29 | 1 |
| Illingworth | 17 | 11 | 15 | 3 | 24 | 6 | 57 | 3 |
| Walker | 6 | 1 | 13 | 0 | 4 | 2 | 8 | 0 |

FALL OF WICKETS

| | E | SA | E | SA |
|---|---|---|---|---|
| Wkt | 1st | 1st | 2nd | 2nd |
| 1st | 19 | 11 | 0 | 4 |
| 2nd | 80 | 21 | 42 | 5 |
| 3rd | 100 | 40 | 69 | 58 |
| 4th | 196 | 52 | 74 | 120 |
| 5th | 225 | 61 | 112 | 132 |
| 6th | 2 | 146 | 112 | 156 |
| 7th | 255 | 168 | 118 | 161 |
| 8th | 262 | 179 | 163 | 167 |
| 9th | 275 | 179 | 202 | 200 |
| 10th | 292 | 186 | 203 | 209 |

Umpires: J.G. Langridge and W.E. Phillipson.

Test No. 493/91

# ENGLAND v SOUTH AFRICA 1960 (2nd Test)

Played at Lord's, London, on 23, 24, 25, 27 June.
Toss: England.   Result: ENGLAND won by an innings and 73 runs.
Debuts: South Africa – C. Wesley.

Griffin became the first bowler to take a hat-trick for South Africa when he dismissed Smith with the last ball of one over and Walker and Trueman with the first two balls of his next. It was also the first hat-trick in a Test at Lord's. Griffin was called eleven times by umpire Lee for throwing during England's innings; it was the first instance in a Test in England and only the third in all Tests.

## ENGLAND

| | | |
|---|---|---|
| M.C. Cowdrey* | c McLean b Griffin | 4 |
| R. Subba Row | lbw b Adcock | 90 |
| E.R. Dexter | c McLean b Adcock | 56 |
| K.F. Barrington | lbw b Goddard | 24 |
| M.J.K. Smith | c Waite b Griffin | 99 |
| J.M. Parks† | c Fellows-Smith b Adcock | 3 |
| P.M. Walker | b Griffin | 52 |
| R. Illingworth | not out | 0 |
| F.S. Trueman | b Griffin | 0 |
| J.B. Statham | not out | 2 |
| A.E. Moss | did not bat | |
| Extras | (B 6, LB 14, W 1, NB 11) | 32 |
| Total | (8 wickets declared) | 362 |

## SOUTH AFRICA

| | | | | |
|---|---|---|---|---|
| D.J. McGlew* | lbw b Statham | 15 | b Statham | 17 |
| T.L. Goddard | b Statham | 19 | c Parks b Statham | 24 |
| S. O'Linn | c Walker b Moss | 18 | lbw b Trueman | 8 |
| R.A. McLean | c Cowdrey b Statham | 15 | c Parks b Trueman | 13 |
| J.H.B. Waite† | c Parks b Statham | 3 | lbw b Statham | 0 |
| P.R. Carlstein | c Cowdrey b Moss | 12 | c Parks b Moss | 6 |
| C. Wesley | c Parks b Statham | 11 | b Dexter | 35 |
| J.P. Fellows-Smith | c Parks b Moss | 29 | not out | 27 |
| H.J. Tayfield | c Smith b Moss | 12 | b Dexter | 4 |
| G.M. Griffin | b Statham | 5 | b Statham | 0 |
| N.A.T. Adcock | not out | 8 | b Statham | 2 |
| Extras | (LB 4, NB 1) | 5 | (NB 1) | 1 |
| Total | | 152 | | 137 |

| SOUTH AFRICA | O | M | R | W | O | M | R | W |
|---|---|---|---|---|---|---|---|---|
| Adcock | 36 | 11 | 70 | 3 | | | | |
| Griffin | 30 | 7 | 87 | 4 | | | | |
| Goddard | 31 | 6 | 96 | 1 | | | | |
| Tayfield | 27 | 9 | 64 | 0 | | | | |
| Fellows-Smith | 5 | 0 | 13 | 0 | | | | |
| ENGLAND | | | | | | | | |
| Statham | 20 | 5 | 63 | 6 | 21 | 6 | 34 | 5 |
| Trueman | 13 | 2 | 49 | 0 | 17 | 5 | 44 | 2 |
| Moss | 10.3 | 0 | 35 | 4 | 14 | 1 | 41 | 1 |
| Illingworth | | | | | 1 | 1 | 0 | 0 |
| Dexter | | | | | 4 | 0 | 17 | 2 |

FALL OF WICKETS

| | E | SA | SA |
|---|---|---|---|
| Wkt | 1st | 1st | 2nd |
| 1st | 7 | 33 | 26 |
| 2nd | 103 | 48 | 49 |
| 3rd | 165 | 56 | 49 |
| 4th | 220 | 69 | 50 |
| 5th | 227 | 78 | 63 |
| 6th | 347 | 88 | 72 |
| 7th | 360 | 112 | 126 |
| 8th | 360 | 132 | 132 |
| 9th | – | 138 | 133 |
| 10th | – | 152 | 137 |

Umpires: J.S. Buller and F.S. Lee.

Test No. 494/92

# ENGLAND v SOUTH AFRICA 1960 (3rd Test)

Played at Trent Bridge, Nottingham, on 7, 8, 9, 11 July.
Toss: England.   Result: ENGLAND won by eight wickets.
Debuts: South Africa – J.E. Pothecary.

Waite dislocated his left-hand little finger during England's first innings and O'Linn took over as wicket-keeper, in which position he caught Barrington and Walker. South Africa's total of 88 remains the lowest in any Test at Trent Bridge. McGlew, run out after colliding with the bowler (Moss), was recalled by Cowdrey but umpire Elliott refused to change his decision. Wesley was dismissed first ball in both innings.

## ENGLAND

| | | |
|---|---|---|
| R. Subba Row | b Tayfield | 30 |
| M.C. Cowdrey* | c Fellows-Smith b Goddard | 67 |
| E.R. Dexter | b Adcock | 3 |
| K.F. Barrington | c O'Linn b Goddard | 80 |
| M.J.K. Smith | lbw b Goddard | 0 |
| J.M. Parks† | run out | 16 |
| R. Illingworth | c and b Tayfield | 37 |
| P.M. Walker | c O'Linn b Tayfield | 30 |
| F.S. Trueman | b Goddard | 15 |
| J.B. Statham | b Goddard | 2 |
| A.E. Moss | not out | 3 |
| Extras | (B 2, LB 2) | 4 |
| **Total** | | **287** |

| | | |
|---|---|---|
| | not out | 16 |
| | lbw b Goddard | 27 |
| | c Adcock b Goddard | 0 |
| | not out | 1 |
| | | |
| | | |
| | | |
| | | |
| | | |
| | | |
| | | |
| | (B 4, LB 1) | 5 |
| | (2 wickets) | **49** |

## SOUTH AFRICA

| | | |
|---|---|---|
| D.J. McGlew* | c Parks b Trueman | 0 |
| T.L. Goddard | run out | 16 |
| S. O'Linn | c Walker b Trueman | 1 |
| R.A. McLean | b Statham | 11 |
| P.R. Carlstein | c Walker b Statham | 2 |
| C. Wesley | c Subba Row b Statham | 0 |
| J.P. Fellows-Smith | not out | 31 |
| J.H.B. Waite† | c Trueman b Moss | 1 |
| H.J. Tayfield | b Trueman | 11 |
| J.E. Pothecary | b Trueman | 7 |
| N.A.T. Adcock | b Trueman | 0 |
| Extras | (B 4, LB 4) | 8 |
| **Total** | | **88** |

| | | |
|---|---|---|
| | run out | 45 |
| | b Trueman | 0 |
| | (5) c Cowdrey b Moss | 98 |
| | c Parks b Trueman | 0 |
| | (6) c Cowdrey b Statham | 19 |
| | (7) c Parks b Statham | 0 |
| | (3) c Illingworth b Trueman | 15 |
| | lbw b Moss | 60 |
| | c Parks b Moss | 6 |
| | c Parks b Trueman | 3 |
| | not out | 1 |
| | | |
| | | **247** |

| SOUTH AFRICA | O | M | R | W | O | M | R | W | FALL OF WICKETS | | | | |
|---|---|---|---|---|---|---|---|---|---|---|---|---|---|
| Adcock | 30 | 2 | 86 | 1 | 7.4 | 2 | 16 | 0 | | E | SA | SA | E |
| Pothecary | 20 | 5 | 42 | 0 | 2 | 0 | 15 | 0 | Wkt | 1st | 1st | 2nd | 2nd |
| Fellows-Smith | 5 | 0 | 17 | 0 | | | | | 1st | 57 | 0 | 1 | 48 |
| Goddard | 42 | 17 | 80 | 5 | 5 | 1 | 13 | 2 | 2nd | 82 | 12 | 23 | 48 |
| Tayfield | 28.3 | 11 | 58 | 3 | | | | | 3rd | 129 | 31 | 23 | – |
| ENGLAND | | | | | | | | | 4th | 129 | 33 | 91 | – |
| Trueman | 14.3 | 6 | 27 | 5 | 22 | 3 | 77 | 4 | 5th | 154 | 33 | 122 | – |
| Statham | 14 | 5 | 27 | 3 | 26 | 3 | 71 | 2 | 6th | 229 | 44 | 122 | – |
| Moss | 10 | 3 | 26 | 1 | 15.4 | 3 | 36 | 3 | 7th | 241 | 49 | 231 | – |
| Illingworth | | | | | 19 | 9 | 33 | 0 | 8th | 261 | 68 | 242 | – |
| Barrington | | | | | 3 | 1 | 5 | 0 | 9th | 267 | 82 | 245 | – |
| Dexter | | | | | 6 | 2 | 12 | 0 | 10th | 287 | 88 | 247 | – |
| Walker | | | | | 3 | 0 | 13 | 0 | | | | | |

Umpires: C.S. Elliott and F.S. Lee.

Test No. 495/93

# ENGLAND v SOUTH AFRICA 1960 (4th Test)

Played at Old Trafford, Manchester, on 21 (*no play*), 22 (*no play*), 23, 25, 26 July.
Toss: England.   Result: MATCH DRAWN.
Debuts: England – D.E.V. Padgett.

Manchester's total of blank days of Test cricket was brought to 23 (out of 48 lost on all English grounds) when rain prevented a start until the third day. Goddard ended England's first innings with a spell of 3 for 0 in 56 balls. On the final afternoon England fielded substitutes for Subba Row (fractured thumb), Barrington (pulled thigh muscle) and Statham (tonsillitis). This was England's 16th consecutive Test without a defeat – then their longest unbeaten run.

## ENGLAND

| | | | | |
|---|---|---|---|---|
| G. Pullar | b Pothecary | 12 | c and b Pothecary | 9 |
| R. Subba Row | lbw b Adcock | 27 | | |
| E.R. Dexter | b Pothecary | 38 | c McLean b Pothecary | 22 |
| M.C. Cowdrey* | c Waite b Adcock | 20 | (2) b Adcock | 25 |
| K.F. Barrington | b Goddard | 76 | (7) c Waite b Goddard | 35 |
| D.E.V. Padgett | c Wesley b Pothecary | 5 | (5) c Waite b Adcock | 2 |
| J.M. Parks† | lbw b Goddard | 36 | (6) c and b Goddard | 20 |
| R. Illingworth | not out | 22 | (4) c McLean b Adcock | 5 |
| D.A. Allen | lbw b Goddard | 0 | (8) not out | 14 |
| F.S. Trueman | c Tayfield b Adcock | 10 | (9) not out | 14 |
| J.B. Statham | b Adcock | 0 | | |
| Extras | (B 8, LB 6) | 14 | (B 1, LB 5, NB 1) | 7 |
| **Total** | | **260** | (7 wickets declared) | **153** |

## SOUTH AFRICA

| | | | | |
|---|---|---|---|---|
| D.J. McGlew* | c Subba Row b Trueman | 32 | not out | 26 |
| T.L. Goddard | c Parks b Statham | 8 | not out | 16 |
| A.J. Pithey | c Parks b Statham | 7 | | |
| P.R. Carlstein | b Trueman | 11 | | |
| R.A. McLean | b Allen | 109 | | |
| J.H.B. Waite† | b Statham | 11 | | |
| S. O'Linn | c sub (M.J. Hilton) b Allen | 27 | | |
| C. Wesley | c Trueman b Allen | 3 | | |
| H.J. Tayfield | c Trueman b Allen | 4 | | |
| J.E. Pothecary | b Trueman | 12 | | |
| N.A.T. Adcock | not out | 0 | | |
| Extras | (B 1, LB 4) | 5 | (B 3, NB 1) | 4 |
| **Total** | | **229** | (0 wickets) | **46** |

| SOUTH AFRICA | O | M | R | W | O | M | R | W | FALL OF WICKETS | | | |
|---|---|---|---|---|---|---|---|---|---|---|---|---|
| Adcock | 23 | 5 | 66 | 4 | 27 | 9 | 59 | 3 | | E | SA | E | SA |
| Pothecary | 28 | 3 | 85 | 3 | 32 | 10 | 61 | 2 | Wkt | 1st | 1st | 2nd | 2nd |
| Goddard | 24 | 16 | 26 | 3 | 16 | 5 | 26 | 2 | 1st | 27 | 25 | 23 | – |
| Tayfield | 18 | 3 | 69 | 0 | | | | | 2nd | 85 | 33 | 41 | – |
| ENGLAND | | | | | | | | | 3rd | 108 | 57 | 63 | – |
| Statham | 22 | 11 | 32 | 3 | 4 | 2 | 3 | 0 | 4th | 113 | 62 | 65 | – |
| Trueman | 20 | 2 | 58 | 3 | 6 | 1 | 10 | 0 | 5th | 134 | 92 | 71 | – |
| Dexter | 17 | 5 | 41 | 0 | | | | | 6th | 197 | 194 | 101 | – |
| Allen | 19.5 | 6 | 58 | 4 | 7 | 4 | 5 | 0 | 7th | 239 | 198 | 134 | – |
| Illingworth | 11 | 2 | 35 | 0 | 5 | 3 | 6 | 0 | 8th | 239 | 202 | – | – |
| Pullar | | | | | 1 | 0 | 6 | 0 | 9th | 260 | 225 | – | – |
| Padgett | | | | | 2 | 0 | 8 | 0 | 10th | 260 | 229 | – | – |
| Cowdrey | | | | | 1 | 0 | 4 | 0 | | | | | |

Umpires: J.G. Langridge and N. Oldfield.

Test No. 496/94

# ENGLAND v SOUTH AFRICA 1960 (5th Test)

Played at Kennington Oval, London, on 18, 19, 20, 22, 23 August.
Toss: England.   Result: MATCH DRAWN.
Debuts: South Africa – A.H. McKinnon.

For the second consecutive rubber England won all five tosses – a unique run. When he stumped Pullar, Waite became the first South African to complete the wicket-keeper's double of 1,000 runs and 100 dismissals in Test cricket; W.A.S. Oldfield (Australia) and T.G. Evans (England) were then the only others to achieve this double. The opening partnership of 290 between Pullar and Cowdrey was England's third-highest in all Tests and the fourth-highest by all countries.

### ENGLAND

| | | | | | |
|---|---|---|---|---|---|
| G. Pullar | c Goddard b Pothecary | 59 | st Waite b McKinnon | | 175 |
| M.C. Cowdrey* | b Adcock | 11 | lbw b Goddard | | 155 |
| E.R. Dexter | b Adcock | 28 | b Tayfield | | 16 |
| K.F. Barrington | lbw b Pothecary | 1 | c Carlstein b McKinnon | | 10 |
| M.J.K. Smith | b Adcock | 0 | (6) c Goddard b Tayfield | | 11 |
| D.E.V. Padgett | c Waite b Pothecary | 13 | (7) run out | | 31 |
| J.M. Parks† | c Waite b Pothecary | 23 | (5) c Waite b Adcock | | 17 |
| D.A. Allen | lbw b Adcock | 0 | not out | | 12 |
| F.S. Trueman | lbw b Adcock | 0 | b Goddard | | 24 |
| J.B. Statham | not out | 13 | c Pothecary b Goddard | | 4 |
| T. Greenough | b Adcock | 2 | | | |
| Extras | (B 3, LB 2) | 5 | (B 14, LB 9, W 1) | | 24 |
| **Total** | | **155** | (9 wickets declared) | | **479** |

### SOUTH AFRICA

| | | | | | |
|---|---|---|---|---|---|
| D.J. McGlew* | c Smith b Greenhough | 22 | c Allen b Statham | | 16 |
| T.L. Goddard | c Cowdrey b Statham | 99 | c Cowdrey b Statham | | 28 |
| J.P. Fellows-Smith | c Smith b Dexter | 35 | c Parks b Trueman | | 6 |
| R.A. McLean | lbw b Dexter | 0 | (5) not out | | 32 |
| J.H.B. Waite† | c Trueman b Dexter | 87 | (6) not out | | 1 |
| S. O'Linn | b Trueman | 55 | | | |
| P.R. Carlstein | b Greenhough | 42 | (4) lbw b Trueman | | 13 |
| J.E. Pothecary | run out | 4 | | | |
| H.J. Tayfield | not out | 46 | | | |
| A.H. McKinnon | run out | 22 | | | |
| N.A.T. Adcock | b Trueman | 1 | | | |
| Extras | (B 6, LB 7, NB 3) | 16 | (W 1) | | 1 |
| **Total** | | **419** | (4 wickets) | | **97** |

| SOUTH AFRICA | O | M | R | W | O | M | R | W | | FALL OF WICKETS | | | |
|---|---|---|---|---|---|---|---|---|---|---|---|---|---|
| Adcock | 31·3 | 10 | 65 | 6 | 38 | 8 | 106 | 1 | | E | SA | E | SA |
| Pothecary | 29 | 9 | 58 | 4 | 27 | 5 | 93 | 0 | Wkt | 1st | 1st | 2nd | 2nd |
| Goddard | 14 | 6 | 25 | 0 | 27 | 6 | 69 | 3 | 1st | 27 | 44 | 290 | 21 |
| McKinnon | 2 | 1 | 2 | 0 | 24 | 7 | 62 | 2 | 2nd | 89 | 107 | 339 | 30 |
| Tayfield | | | | | 37 | 14 | 108 | 2 | 3rd | 90 | 107 | 362 | 52 |
| Fellows-Smith | | | | | 4 | 0 | 17 | 0 | 4th | 95 | 222 | 373 | 89 |
| ENGLAND | | | | | | | | | 5th | 107 | 252 | 387 | – |
| Trueman | 31·1 | 4 | 93 | 2 | 10 | 0 | 34 | 2 | 6th | 125 | 326 | 412 | – |
| Statham | 38 | 8 | 96 | 1 | 12 | 1 | 57 | 2 | 7th | 130 | 330 | 447 | – |
| Dexter | 30 | 5 | 79 | 3 | 0·2 | 0 | 0 | 0 | 8th | 130 | 374 | 475 | – |
| Greenhough | 44 | 17 | 99 | 2 | 5 | 2 | 3 | 0 | 9th | 142 | 412 | 479 | – |
| Allen | 28 | 15 | 36 | 0 | 2 | 1 | 2 | 0 | 10th | 155 | 419 | – | – |

Umpires: C.S. Elliott and W.E. Phillipson.

Chapter 13

# AUSTRALIA 1961

Cowdrey expected May to return to captain England against Australia and was surprised to find that he had been appointed captain for the first Test in 1961. May had decided he was not fully fit. The first test at Edgbaston began in inclement weather and England were dismissed cheaply. Australia in better weather did better. In their second innings England were still 200 behind with Pullar out. Then Dexter made a magnificent 180. Subba Row also made a century, in his first Test against Australia. Cowdrey scored only 13 and 14 and curiously played on twice in the match.

Cowdrey came into the second Test at Lord's in great spirits. The previous week-end he had led Kent to within seven runs of victory over the touring side. In a match of three declarations Cowdrey had scored a century on successive days – 149 and 121. I was present on all three days and took my mother to see the second of the two centuries. I had also been present at Lord's earlier in the season for the MCC match against the tourists. Cowdrey came in at No 3 and made 115 magnificent runs. I could well understand why he was happy in his mind. May was back but it was felt that Cowdrey should continue to let May come back to the captaincy gradually after one match in peace. Winning the toss and batting England were all out for 206 on the first day. Cowdrey was out when he tried to avoid a ball from McKenzie which followed him and flicked his gloves. When Australia batted they made 340. A dour Lawry made 130 and Mackay 54. England went for the runs in their second innings but only set Australia 69 to win. In England's second innings Cowdrey presented an easy catch to Mackay in the covers off Misson and was out for 7.

May returned as Captain in the third Test at Headingley. Australia won the toss and did well to reach 187 for 2. Freddie Trueman with the new ball

*Driving Mackay during the MCC v Australia match at Lord's in 1961.*

reduced them to 237 all out. Cowdrey helped get him off to a good start as he caught O'Neill splendidly low down in the gully from the Yorkshireman's first ball. Cowdrey made 93 before walking having been caught on the leg side. Many commented how wonderful it was to walk when seven short of one's century. I remember a club cricketer John Humphreys observing that it was much harder to do so before having scored. England led by 62. Trueman with his "cutters" reduced Australia to 120 all out. Again he was helped by Cowdrey. This time with his sixth wicket by diving to his left and holding Davidson at second slip – another brilliant catch. England made the 59 to win the same evening.

Cowdrey was ill with pleurisy before the next Test and Close replaced him at Old Trafford in a match which Australia won. Cowdrey's absence saves me the mortification of describing in detail how England contrived to lose first by allowing Australia to put on 98 for the last wicket and then succumbing to Benaud, who took 5 for 12 in 25 balls after a magnificent innings from Dexter of 76 had put them apparently back in the driving seat.

Cowdrey returned for the final Test but it was a mistake to do so. After being dismissed caught at the wicket for a duck before lunch he went home in mid-afternoon and spent Friday and Saturday watching the match on television. He returned on Monday to bat quite well in all the circumstances before being out for 3 and then retired to bed again. The match was drawn. It was the end of the series but also, for Cowdrey, the season.

|  | Matches | Innings | Not out | Runs | Highest score | Average | 100s | 50s | Caught |
|---|---|---|---|---|---|---|---|---|---|
| This series | 4 | 8 | 0 | 168 | 93 | 21.00 | 0 | 1 | 4 |
| Previous series | 49 | 80 | 4 | 3243 | 160 | 42.67 | 9 | 19 | 56 |
| Cumulative totals | 53 | 88 | 4 | 3411 | 160 | 40.61 | 9 | 20 | 60 |

Test No. 507/179

# ENGLAND v AUSTRALIA 1961 (1st Test)

Played at Edgbaston, Birmingham, on 8, 9, 10, 12, 13 June.
Toss: England.   Result: MATCH DRAWN.
Debuts: England – J.T. Murray; Australia – W.M. Lawry.

Harvey's 20th hundred in Test matches was Australia's first at Birmingham, their only previous Tests there being in 1902 and 1909. Earlier Mackay had taken the wickets of Barrington, Smith and Subba Row in four balls. On the final day Subba Row became the twelfth England player to score a hundred in his first Test against Australia. Curiously this list includes the first four batsmen of Indian descent to play for England.

### ENGLAND

| | | | | | |
|---|---|---|---|---|---|
| G. Pullar | b Davidson | 17 | c Grout b Misson | | 28 |
| R. Subba Row | c Simpson b Mackay | 59 | b Misson | | 112 |
| E.R. Dexter | c Davidson b Mackay | 10 | st Grout b Simpson | | 180 |
| M.C. Cowdrey* | b Misson | 13 | b Mackay | | 14 |
| K.F. Barrington | c Misson b Mackay | 21 | not out | | 48 |
| M.J.K. Smith | c Lawry b Mackay | 0 | not out | | 1 |
| R. Illingworth | c Grout b Benaud | 15 | | | |
| J.T. Murray† | c Davidson b Benaud | 16 | | | |
| D.A. Allen | run out | 11 | | | |
| F.S. Trueman | c Burge b Benaud | 20 | | | |
| J.B. Statham | not out | 7 | | | |
| Extras | (B 3, LB 3) | 6 | (LB 18) | | 18 |
| **Total** | | **195** | (4 wickets) | | **401** |

### AUSTRALIA

| | | |
|---|---|---|
| W.M. Lawry | c Murray b Illingworth | 57 |
| C.C. McDonald | c Illingworth b Statham | 22 |
| R.N. Harvey | lbw b Allen | 114 |
| N.C. O'Neill | b Statham | 82 |
| P.J.P. Burge | lbw b Allen | 25 |
| R.B. Simpson | c and b Trueman | 76 |
| A.K. Davidson | c and b Illingworth | 22 |
| K.D. Mackay | c Barrington b Statham | 64 |
| R. Benaud* | not out | 36 |
| A.T.W. Grout† | c Dexter b Trueman | 5 |
| F.M. Misson | did not bat | |
| Extras | (B 8, LB 4, NB 1) | 13 |
| **Total** | (9 wickets declared) | **516** |

| AUSTRALIA | O | M | R | W | O | M | R | W | | FALL OF WICKETS | | |
|---|---|---|---|---|---|---|---|---|---|---|---|---|
| Davidson | 26 | 6 | 70 | 1 | 31 | 10 | 60 | 0 | | E | A | E |
| Misson | 15 | 6 | 47 | 1 | 28 | 6 | 82 | 2 | Wkt | 1st | 1st | 2nd |
| Mackay | 29 | 10 | 57 | 4 | 41 | 13 | 87 | 1 | 1st | 36 | 47 | 93 |
| Benaud | 14.3 | 8 | 15 | 3 | 20 | 4 | 67 | 0 | 2nd | 53 | 106 | 202 |
| Simpson | | | | | 34 | 12 | 87 | 1 | 3rd | 88 | 252 | 239 |
| ENGLAND | | | | | | | | | 4th | 121 | 299 | 400 |
| Trueman | 36.5 | 1 | 136 | 2 | | | | | 5th | 121 | 322 | – |
| Statham | 43 | 6 | 147 | 3 | | | | | 6th | 122 | 381 | – |
| Illingworth | 44 | 12 | 110 | 2 | | | | | 7th | 153 | 469 | – |
| Allen | 24 | 4 | 88 | 2 | | | | | 8th | 156 | 501 | – |
| Dexter | 5 | 1 | 22 | 0 | | | | | 9th | 181 | 516 | – |
| | | | | | | | | | 10th | 195 | – | – |

Umpires: J.S. Buller and F.S. Lee.

Test No. 508/180

# ENGLAND v AUSTRALIA 1961 (2nd Test)

Played at Lord's, London, on 22, 23, 24, 26 June.
Toss: England.   Result: AUSTRALIA won by five wickets.
Debuts: Australia – G.D. McKenzie.

England won their twelfth consecutive toss, Cowdrey setting a Test record by winning nine in succession. Statham took his 200th wicket for England when he bowled McDonald. Grout made his hundredth dismissal when he caught Murray. Australia's win, completed at 2.50 p.m. on the fourth day, ended England's then longest unbeaten run of 18 matches starting with the Christchurch Test of 1958-59 (*No. 472*). It was England's first defeat at home since the corresponding fixture in 1956 (*Test No. 426*).

## ENGLAND

| | | | | |
|---|---|---|---|---|
| G. Pullar | b Davidson | 11 | c Grout b Misson | 42 |
| R. Subba Row | lbw b Mackay | 48 | c Grout b Davidson | 8 |
| E.R. Dexter | c McKenzie b Misson | 27 | b McKenzie | 17 |
| M.C. Cowdrey* | c Grout b McKenzie | 16 | c Mackay b Misson | 7 |
| P.B.H. May | c Grout b Davidson | 17 | c Grout b McKenzie | 22 |
| K.F. Barrington | c Mackay b Davidson | 4 | lbw b Davidson | 66 |
| R. Illingworth | b Misson | 13 | c Harvey b Simpson | 0 |
| J.T. Murray† | lbw b Mackay | 18 | c Grout b McKenzie | 25 |
| G.A.R. Lock | c Grout b Davidson | 5 | b McKenzie | 1 |
| F.S. Trueman | b Davidson | 25 | c Grout b McKenzie | 0 |
| J.B. Statham | not out | 11 | not out | 2 |
| Extras | (LB 9, W 2) | 11 | (B 1, LB 10, W 1) | 12 |
| Total | | 206 | | 202 |

## AUSTRALIA

| | | | | |
|---|---|---|---|---|
| W.M. Lawry | c Murray b Dexter | 130 | c Murray b Statham | 1 |
| C.C. McDonald | b Statham | 4 | c Illingworth b Trueman | 14 |
| R.B. Simpson | c Illingworth b Trueman | 0 | (6) c Illingworth b Statham | 15 |
| R.N. Harvey* | c Barrington b Trueman | 27 | (3) c Murray b Trueman | 4 |
| N.C. O'Neill | b Dexter | 1 | (4) b Statham | 0 |
| P.J.P. Burge | c Murray b Statham | 46 | (5) not out | 37 |
| A.K. Davidson | lbw b Trueman | 6 | not out | 0 |
| K.D. Mackay | c Barrington b Illingworth | 54 | | |
| A.T.W. Grout† | lbw b Dexter | 0 | | |
| G.D. McKenzie | b Trueman | 34 | | |
| F.M. Misson | not out | 25 | | |
| Extras | (B 1, LB 12) | 13 | | |
| Total | | 340 | (5 wickets) | 71 |

| AUSTRALIA | O | M | R | W | O | M | R | W | FALL OF WICKETS |
|---|---|---|---|---|---|---|---|---|---|
| Davidson | 24.3 | 6 | 42 | 5 | 24 | 8 | 50 | 2 | |
| McKenzie | 26 | 7 | 81 | 1 | 29 | 13 | 37 | 5 | |
| Misson | 16 | 4 | 48 | 2 | 17 | 2 | 66 | 2 | |
| Mackay | 12 | 3 | 24 | 2 | 8 | 6 | 5 | 0 | |
| Simpson | | | | | 19 | 10 | 32 | 1 | |
| ENGLAND | | | | | | | | | |
| Statham | 44 | 10 | 89 | 2 | 10.5 | 3 | 31 | 3 | |
| Trueman | 34 | 3 | 118 | 4 | 10 | 0 | 40 | 2 | |
| Dexter | 24 | 7 | 56 | 3 | | | | | |
| Lock | 26 | 13 | 48 | 0 | | | | | |
| Illingworth | 11.3 | 5 | 16 | 1 | | | | | |

| Wkt | E 1st | A 1st | E 2nd | A 2nd |
|---|---|---|---|---|
| 1st | 26 | 5 | 33 | 15 |
| 2nd | 87 | 6 | 63 | 15 |
| 3rd | 87 | 81 | 67 | 19 |
| 4th | 111 | 88 | 80 | 19 |
| 5th | 115 | 127 | 127 | 58 |
| 6th | 127 | 194 | 144 | – |
| 7th | 156 | 238 | 191 | – |
| 8th | 164 | 238 | 199 | – |
| 9th | 167 | 291 | 199 | – |
| 10th | 206 | 340 | 202 | – |

Umpires: C.S. Elliott and W.E. Philipson.

Test No. 509/181

# ENGLAND v AUSTRALIA 1961 (3rd Test)

Played at Headingley, Leeds, on 6, 7, 8, July.
Toss: Australia.   Result: ENGLAND won by eight wickets.
Debuts: Nil.

England recalled Jackson for his first Test for twelve years and lost the toss for the first time in 13 matches. Australia bowled 70 balls while England's total stayed at 239, before Lock scored 30 off 20 balls with seven fours in 19 minutes. Trueman had a spell of 5 for 0 in 24 balls in the second innings.

## AUSTRALIA

| | | | | |
|---|---|---|---|---|
| C.C. McDonald | st Murray b Lock | 54 | b Jackson | 1 |
| W.M. Lawry | lbw b Lock | 28 | c Murray b Allen | 28 |
| R.N. Harvey | c Lock b Trueman | 73 | c Dexter b Trueman | 53 |
| N.C. O'Neill | c Cowdrey b Trueman | 27 | c Cowdrey b Trueman | 19 |
| P.J.P. Burge | c Cowdrey b Jackson | 5 | lbw b Allen | 0 |
| K.D. Mackay | lbw b Jackson | 6 | (9) c Murray b Trueman | 0 |
| R.B. Simpson | lbw b Trueman | 2 | (6) b Trueman | 3 |
| A.K. Davidson | not out | 22 | (7) c Cowdrey b Trueman | 7 |
| R. Benaud* | b Trueman | 0 | (8) b Trueman | 0 |
| A.T.W. Grout† | c Murray b Trueman | 3 | c and b Jackson | 7 |
| G.D. McKenzie | b Allen | 8 | not out | 0 |
| Extras | (B 7, LB 2) | 9 | (LB 2) | 2 |
| **Total** | | **237** | | **120** |

## ENGLAND

| | | | | |
|---|---|---|---|---|
| G. Pullar | b Benaud | 53 | not out | 26 |
| R. Subba Row | lbw b Davidson | 35 | b Davidson | 6 |
| M.C. Cowdrey | c Grout b McKenzie | 93 | c Grout b Benaud | 22 |
| P.B.H. May* | c and b Davidson | 26 | not out | 8 |
| E.R. Dexter | b Davidson | 28 | | |
| K.F. Barrington | c Simpson b Davidson | 6 | | |
| J.T. Murray† | b McKenzie | 6 | | |
| F.S. Trueman | c Burge b Davidson | 4 | | |
| G.A.R. Lock | lbw b McKenzie | 30 | | |
| D.A. Allen | not out | 5 | | |
| H.L. Jackson | run out | 8 | | |
| Extras | (LB 5) | 5 | | |
| **Total** | | **299** | (2 wickets) | **62** |

| ENGLAND | O | M | R | W | O | M | R | W | FALL OF WICKETS |
|---|---|---|---|---|---|---|---|---|---|
| Trueman | 22 | 5 | 58 | 5 | 15.5 | 5 | 30 | 6 | | A | E | A | E |
| Jackson | 31 | 11 | 57 | 2 | 13 | 5 | 26 | 2 | Wkt | 1st | 1st | 2nd | 2nd |
| Allen | 28 | 12 | 45 | 1 | 14 | 6 | 30 | 2 | 1st | 65 | 59 | 4 | 14 |
| Lock | 29 | 5 | 68 | 2 | 10 | 1 | 32 | 0 | 2nd | 113 | 145 | 49 | 45 |
| | | | | | | | | | 3rd | 187 | 190 | 99 | – |
| AUSTRALIA | | | | | | | | | 4th | 192 | 223 | 102 | – |
| Davidson | 47 | 23 | 63 | 5 | 11 | 6 | 17 | 1 | 5th | 196 | 239 | 102 | – |
| McKenzie | 27 | 4 | 64 | 3 | 5 | 0 | 15 | 0 | 6th | 203 | 248 | 105 | – |
| Mackay | 22 | 4 | 34 | 0 | 1 | 0 | 8 | 0 | 7th | 203 | 252 | 109 | – |
| Benaud | 39 | 15 | 86 | 1 | 6 | 1 | 22 | 1 | 8th | 204 | 286 | 109 | – |
| Simpson | 14 | 5 | 47 | 0 | | | | | 9th | 208 | 291 | 120 | – |
| | | | | | | | | | 10th | 237 | 299 | 120 | – |

Umpires: J.S. Buller and J.G. Langridge.

Test No. 510/182

# ENGLAND v AUSTRALIA 1961 (4th Test)

Played at Old Trafford, Manchester, on 27, 28, 29, 31 July, 1 August.
Toss: Australia.  Result: AUSTRALIA won by 54 runs.
Debuts: England – J.A. Flavell; Australia - B.C. Booth.

Rain delayed the start until 2.40 p.m. on the first day and brought the total of time lost in post-war Tests at Manchester to 103 hours. Simpson ended England's first innings with a spell of 4 for 2 in 26 balls. Davidson scored 20 runs (604046) off one over from Allen and shared in a last-wicket partnership of 98 with McKenzie. Murray took seven catches to equal T.G. Evans' England record against Australia set in 1956 at Lord's. Benaud bowled his side to victory on the last afternoon with a spell of 5 for 12 in 25 balls.

### AUSTRALIA

| | | | | |
|---|---|---|---|---|
| W.M. Lawry | lbw b Statham | 74 | c Trueman b Allen | 102 |
| R.B. Simpson | c Murray b Statham | 4 | c Murray b Flavell | 51 |
| R.N. Harvey | c Subba Row b Statham | 19 | c Murray b Dexter | 35 |
| N.C. O'Neill | hit wkt b Trueman | 11 | c Murray b Statham | 67 |
| P.J.P. Burge | b Flavell | 15 | c Murray b Dexter | 23 |
| B.C. Booth | c Close b Statham | 46 | lbw b Dexter | 9 |
| K.D. Mackay | c Murray b Statham | 11 | c Close b Allen | 18 |
| A.K. Davidson | c Barrington b Dexter | 0 | not out | 77 |
| R. Benaud* | b Dexter | 2 | lbw b Allen | 1 |
| A.T.W. Grout† | c Murray b Dexter | 2 | c Statham b Allen | 0 |
| G.D. McKenzie | not out | 1 | b Flavell | 32 |
| Extras | (B 4, LB 1) | 5 | (B 6, LB 9, W 2) | 17 |
| **Total** | | **190** | | **432** |

### ENGLAND

| | | | | |
|---|---|---|---|---|
| G. Pullar | b Davidson | 63 | c O'Neill b Davidson | 26 |
| R. Subba Row | c Simpson b Davidson | 2 | b Benaud | 49 |
| E.R. Dexter | c Davidson b McKenzie | 16 | c Grout b Benaud | 76 |
| P.B.H. May* | c Simpson b Davidson | 95 | b Benaud | 0 |
| D.B. Close | lbw b McKenzie | 33 | c O'Neill b Benaud | 8 |
| K.F. Barrington | c O'Neill b Simpson | 78 | lbw b Mackay | 5 |
| J.T. Murray† | c Grout b Mackay | 24 | c Simpson b Benaud | 4 |
| D.A. Allen | c Booth b Simpson | 42 | c Simpson b Benaud | 10 |
| F.S. Trueman | c Harvey b Simpson | 3 | c Benaud b Simpson | 8 |
| J.B. Statham | c Mackay b Simpson | 4 | b Davidson | 8 |
| J.A. Flavell | not out | 0 | not out | 0 |
| Extras | (B 2, LB 4, W 1) | 7 | (B 5. W 2) | 7 |
| **Total** | | **367** | | **201** |

| ENGLAND | O | M | R | W | O | M | R | W | | FALL OF WICKETS | | | |
|---|---|---|---|---|---|---|---|---|---|---|---|---|---|
| Trueman | 14 | 1 | 55 | 1 | 32 | 6 | 92 | 0 | | A | E | A | E |
| Statham | 21 | 3 | 53 | 5 | 44 | 9 | 106 | 1 | Wkt | 1st | 1st | 2nd | 2nd |
| Flavell | 22 | 8 | 61 | 1 | 29·4 | 4 | 65 | 2 | 1st | 8 | 3 | 113 | 40 |
| Dexter | 6·4 | 2 | 16 | 3 | 20 | 4 | 61 | 3 | 2nd | 51 | 43 | 175 | 150 |
| Allen | | | | | 38 | 25 | 58 | 4 | 3rd | 89 | 154 | 210 | 150 |
| Close | | | | | 8 | 1 | 33 | 0 | 4th | 106 | 212 | 274 | 158 |
| | | | | | | | | | 5th | 150 | 212 | 290 | 163 |
| AUSTRALIA | | | | | | | | | 6th | 174 | 272 | 296 | 171 |
| Davidson | 39 | 11 | 70 | 3 | 14·4 | 1 | 50 | 2 | 7th | 185 | 358 | 332 | 171 |
| McKenzie | 38 | 11 | 106 | 2 | 4 | 1 | 20 | 0 | 8th | 185 | 362 | 334 | 189 |
| Mackay | 40 | 9 | 81 | 1 | 13 | 7 | 33 | 1 | 9th | 189 | 367 | 334 | 193 |
| Benaud | 35 | 15 | 80 | 0 | 32 | 11 | 70 | 6 | 10th | 190 | 367 | 432 | 201 |
| Simpson | 11·4 | 4 | 23 | 4 | 8 | 4 | 21 | 1 | | | | | |

Umpires: J.G. Langridge and W.E. Phillipson.

Test No. 511/183

# ENGLAND v AUSTRALIA 1961 (5th Test)

Played at Kennington Oval, London, on 17, 18, 19, 21, 22 August.
Toss: England.   Result: MATCH DRAWN.
Debuts: Nil.

Rain interrupted play on the third and fourth days. Subba Row scored a hundred in his last Test against Australia, having also scored one in his first (*Test No. 507*). Murray's total of 18 dismissals was a new England record for a home rubber and Grout's 21 dismissals set a new record for a rubber in this series.

## ENGLAND

| | | | | | |
|---|---|---|---|---|---|
| G. Pullar | b Davidson | 8 | c Grout b Mackay | | 13 |
| R. Subba Row | lbw b Gaunt | 12 | c and b Benaud | | 137 |
| M.C. Cowdrey | c Grout b Davidson | 0 | (5) c Benaud b Mackay | | 3 |
| P.B.H. May* | c Lawry b Benaud | 71 | c O'Neill b Mackay | | 33 |
| E.R. Dexter | c Grout b Gaunt | 24 | (3) c Gaunt b Mackay | | 0 |
| K.F. Barrington | c Grout b Gaunt | 53 | c O'Neill b Benaud | | 83 |
| J.T. Murray† | c O'Neill b Mackay | 27 | c Grout b Benaud | | 40 |
| G.A.R. Lock | c Grout b Mackay | 3 | c Benaud b Mackay | | 0 |
| D.A. Allen | not out | 22 | not out | | 42 |
| J.B. Statham | b Davidson | 18 | not out | | 9 |
| J.A. Flavell | c Simpson b Davidson | 14 | | | |
| Extras | (B 1, LB 2, W 1) | 4 | (B 6, LB 3, W 1) | | 10 |
| **Total** | | **256** | (8 wickets) | | **370** |

## AUSTRALIA

| | | |
|---|---|---|
| W.M. Lawry | c Murray b Statham | 0 |
| R.B. Simpson | b Allen | 40 |
| R.N. Harvey | lbw b Flavell | 13 |
| N.C. O'Neill | c sub (M.J. Stewart) b Allen | 117 |
| P.J.P. Burge | b Allen | 181 |
| B.C. Booth | c Subba Row b Lock | 71 |
| K.D. Mackay | c Murray b Flavell | 5 |
| A.K. Davidson | lbw b Statham | 17 |
| R. Benaud* | b Allen | 6 |
| A.T.W. Grout† | not out | 30 |
| R.A. Gaunt | b Statham | 3 |
| Extras | (B 10, LB 1) | 11 |
| **Total** | | **494** |

| AUSTRALIA | O | M | R | W | O | M | R | W | | FALL OF WICKETS | | |
|---|---|---|---|---|---|---|---|---|---|---|---|---|
| | | | | | | | | | | E | A | E |
| Davidson | 34.1 | 8 | 83 | 4 | 29 | 7 | 67 | 0 | Wkt | 1st | 1st | 2nd |
| Gaunt | 24 | 3 | 53 | 3 | 22 | 7 | 33 | 0 | 1st | 18 | 0 | 33 |
| Benaud | 17 | 4 | 35 | 1 | 51 | 18 | 113 | 3 | 2nd | 20 | 15 | 33 |
| Mackay | 39 | 14 | 75 | 2 | 68 | 21 | 121 | 5 | 3rd | 20 | 88 | 83 |
| Simpson | 4 | 2 | 6 | 0 | 2 | 0 | 13 | 0 | 4th | 67 | 211 | 90 |
| O'Neill | | | | | 4 | 1 | 13 | 0 | 5th | 147 | 396 | 262 |
| Harvey | | | | | 1 | 1 | 0 | 0 | 6th | 193 | 401 | 283 |
| ENGLAND | | | | | | | | | 7th | 199 | 441 | 283 |
| Statham | 38.5 | 10 | 75 | 3 | | | | | 8th | 202 | 455 | 355 |
| Flavell | 31 | 5 | 105 | 2 | | | | | 9th | 238 | 472 | – |
| Dexter | 24 | 2 | 68 | 0 | | | | | 10th | 256 | 494 | – |
| Allen | 30 | 6 | 133 | 4 | | | | | | | | |
| Lock | 42 | 14 | 102 | 1 | | | | | | | | |

Umpires: C.S. Elliott and F.S. Lee.

## Chapter 14
# PAKISTAN 1962

Cowdrey did not go on the tour of India and Pakistan in 1961/62 and so his next appearance in Test cricket was in the English summer of 1962. Opening again with Pullar he scored 159 in England's only innings in the first Test against Pakistan, at Edgbaston. He was at the wicket for 4 hours and 23 minutes and hit 21 fours taking part with stands with Dexter of 166 in two and a quarter hours and Graveney with whom he added 107 in 87 minutes. Cowdrey had given no indication of a long stay during the first hour when his share of 46 runs was only 12 and even then he offered a chance off D'Souza to first slip where Mushtaq dived unsuccessfully to his right. Thereupon Cowdrey found his best form and hit freely in all directions. England amassed 544 for 5 and won by an innings and 24 runs.

In the second Test at Lord's he made 41 and 20 in a nine wicket victory. He also held three good catches at slip.

Dexter had been Captain in the first two Tests but Cowdrey was at the helm in the third at Headingley, Leeds. He only contributed 7 to a total of 428 which was enough to take England to another win by an innings.

Cowdrey was not playing in the fourth Test at Trent Bridge which was drawn. Dexter was captain.

Dexter continued as captain in the fifth at the Oval although with Cowdrey back. He opened with the Reverend David Sheppard and scored 182.[1] Once again a sedate beginning paid dividends. Having made only 76 in 2 hours before lunch England made 406 for the loss of only two wickets on the first day. Cowdrey and Sheppard gave England a sound start by putting on 117 for the first wicket. Then Cowdrey and Dexter took complete charge,

---

1. This was to be the highest of Cowdrey's 22 test centuries.

adding 248 in two and three quarter hours. Cowdrey was the second to depart at 365 but with one 6 and 23 fours in his 182. Not till he reached 141 did he offer a chance and that was a sharp low one off Fazal to Wallis at slip. Cowdrey himself made a splendid low catch at slip giving Larter the satisfaction of taking his first Test wicket with the fifth ball of his second over. In Pakistan's second innings Imtiaz seemed set for his first century against England when, attempting a drive to take him into three figures, he provided a sharp catch for Cowdrey at slip.

|  | Matches | Innings | Not out | Runs | Highest score | Average | 100s | 50s | Caught |
|---|---|---|---|---|---|---|---|---|---|
| This series | 4 | 5 | 0 | 409 | 182 | 81.80 | 2 | 0 | 9 |
| Previous series | 53 | 88 | 4 | 3411 | 160 | 40.61 | 9 | 20 | 60 |
| Cumulative totals | 57 | 93 | 4 | 3820 | 182 | 42.92 | 11 | 20 | 69 |

Test No. 530/8

# ENGLAND v PAKISTAN 1962 (1st Test)

Played at Edgbaston, Birmingham, on 31 May, 1, 2, 4 June.
Toss: England. Result: ENGLAND won by an innings and 24 runs.
Debuts: Nil.

England won with over a day and half to spare after scoring their highest total for five years. The unbroken partnership of 153 between Parfitt and Allen remains England's highest for the sixth wicket against Pakistan.

## ENGLAND

| | | |
|---|---|---|
| G. Pullar | b D'Souza | 22 |
| M.C. Cowdrey | c Imtiaz b Intikhab | 159 |
| E.R. Dexter* | c Burki b Intikhab | 72 |
| T.W. Graveney | c Ijaz Butt b Mahmood | 97 |
| K.F. Barrington | lbw b Mahmood | 9 |
| P.H. Parfitt | not out | 101 |
| D.A. Allen | not out | 79 |
| G. Millman† | ) | |
| G.A.R. Lock | ) did not bat | |
| F.S. Trueman | ) | |
| J.B. Statham | ) | |
| Extras | (LB 5) | 5 |
| **Total** | (5 wickets declared) | **544** |

## PAKISTAN

| | | | | |
|---|---|---|---|---|
| Hanif Mohammad | c Millman b Allen | 47 | c Cowdrey b Allen | 31 |
| Ijaz Butt | c Lock b Statham | 10 | c Trueman b Allen | 33 |
| Saeed Ahmed | c Graveney b Trueman | 5 | (5) c Parfitt b Lock | 65 |
| Mushtaq Mohammad | c Cowdrey b Lock | 63 | c Millman b Allen | 8 |
| Javed Burki* | c Barrington b Allen | 13 | (6) b Statham | 19 |
| Imtiaz Ahmed† | b Trueman | 39 | (3) c Graveney b Lock | 46 |
| W. Mathias | b Statham | 21 | b Statham | 4 |
| Nasim-ul-Ghani | b Statham | 0 | c Parfitt b Trueman | 35 |
| Intikhab Alam | b Lock | 16 | c Cowdrey b Lock | 0 |
| Mahmood Hussain | b Statham | 0 | c Graveney b Trueman | 22 |
| A. D'Souza | not out | 23 | not out | 9 |
| Extras | (B 8, LB 1) | 9 | (B 1, LB 1) | 2 |
| **Total** | | **246** | | **274** |

| PAKISTAN | O | M | R | W | O | M | R | W |
|---|---|---|---|---|---|---|---|---|
| Mahmood Hussain | 43 | 14 | 130 | 2 | | | | |
| D'Souza | 46 | 9 | 161 | 1 | | | | |
| Intikhab | 25 | 2 | 117 | 2 | | | | |
| Nasim | 30 | 7 | 109 | 0 | | | | |
| Saeed | 2 | 0 | 22 | 0 | | | | |
| ENGLAND | | | | | | | | |
| Statham | 21 | 9 | 54 | 4 | 19 | 6 | 32 | 2 |
| Trueman | 13 | 3 | 59 | 2 | 24 | 5 | 70 | 2 |
| Dexter | 12 | 6 | 23 | 0 | 7 | 2 | 16 | 0 |
| Allen | 32 | 16 | 62 | 2 | 36 | 16 | 73 | 3 |
| Lock | 19 | 8 | 37 | 2 | 36 | 14 | 80 | 3 |
| Parfitt | 2 | 1 | 2 | 0 | | | | |
| Barrington | 2 | 2 | 0 | 0 | | | | |
| Cowdrey | | | | | 1 | 0 | 1 | 0 |

### FALL OF WICKETS

| Wkt | E 1st | P 1st | P 2nd |
|---|---|---|---|
| 1st | 31 | 11 | 60 |
| 2nd | 197 | 30 | 77 |
| 3rd | 304 | 108 | 119 |
| 4th | 330 | 144 | 127 |
| 5th | 391 | 146 | 187 |
| 6th | – | 202 | 199 |
| 7th | – | 206 | 207 |
| 8th | – | 206 | 207 |
| 9th | – | 206 | 257 |
| 10th | – | 246 | 274 |

Umpires: J.S. Buller and C.S. Elliott.

Test No. 531/9

# ENGLAND v PAKISTAN 1962 (2nd Test)

Played at Lord's, London, on 21, 22, 23 June.
Toss: Pakistan. Result: ENGLAND won by nine wickets.
Debuts: England – L.J. Coldwell, M.J. Stewart.

Trueman took his 200th wicket in 47 Test matches when he dismissed Javed Burki and later shared with Graveney in a record ninth-wicket partnership against Pakistan which added 76 runs. Nasim became the first Pakistan batsman to score a Test hundred in England. His fifth-wicket partnership of 197 with Javed Burki was then Pakistan's record for that wicket in all Tests and remains so against England. Nasim was promoted two places as 'night-watchman' and scored his maiden hundred in first-class cricket.

## PAKISTAN

| | | | | |
|---|---|---|---|---|
| Hanif Mohammad | c Cowdrey b Trueman | 13 | lbw b Coldwell | 24 |
| Imtiaz Ahmed† | b Coldwell | 1 | (7) c Trueman b Coldwell | 33 |
| Saeed Ahmed | b Dexter | 10 | b Coldwell | 20 |
| Javed Burki* | c Dexter b Trueman | 5 | (5) lbw b Coldwell | 101 |
| Mustaq Mohammad | c Cowdrey b Trueman | 7 | (4) c Millman b Trueman | 18 |
| Alimuddin | b Coldwell | 9 | (2) c Graveney b Allen | 10 |
| W. Mathias | b Trueman | 15 | (8) c Graveney b Trueman | 1 |
| Nasim-ul-Ghani | c Millman b Trueman | 17 | (6) c Graveney b Coldwell | 101 |
| Mahmood Hussain | c Cowdrey b Coldwell | 1 | b Coldwell | 20 |
| A. D'Souza | not out | 6 | not out | 12 |
| Mohammad Farooq | c Stewart b Trueman | 13 | b Trueman | 1 |
| Extras | (B 1, LB 2) | 3 | (B 6, LB 4, W 4) | 14 |
| **Total** | | **100** | | **355** |

## ENGLAND

| | | | | |
|---|---|---|---|---|
| M.J. Stewart | c Imtiaz b D'Souza | 39 | not out | 34 |
| M.C. Cowdrey | c D'Souza b Farooq | 41 | c Imtiaz b D'Souza | 20 |
| E.R. Dexter* | c Imtiaz b Farooq | 65 | not out | 32 |
| T.W. Graveney | b D'Souza | 153 | | |
| K.F. Barrington | c Imtiaz b Farooq | 0 | | |
| D.A. Allen | lbw b Farooq | 2 | | |
| P.H. Parfitt | b Mahmood | 16 | | |
| G. Millman† | c Hanif b Mahmood | 7 | | |
| G.A.R. Lock | c Mathias b Saeed | 7 | | |
| F.S. Trueman | lbw b Saeed | 29 | | |
| L.J. Coldwell | not out | 0 | | |
| Extras | (B 1, LB 5, NB 5) | 11 | | |
| **Total** | | **370** | (1 wicket) | **86** |

| ENGLAND | O | M | R | W | O | M | R | W | | FALL OF WICKETS | | | |
|---|---|---|---|---|---|---|---|---|---|---|---|---|---|
| Trueman | 17.4 | 6 | 31 | 6 | 33.3 | 6 | 85 | 3 | | P | E | P | E |
| Coldwell | 14 | 2 | 25 | 3 | 41 | 13 | 85 | 6 | Wkt | 1st | 1st | 2nd | 2nd |
| Dexter | 12 | 3 | 41 | 1 | 15 | 4 | 44 | 0 | 1st | 2 | 59 | 36 | 36 |
| Allen | | | | | 15 | 6 | 41 | 1 | 2nd | 23 | 137 | 36 | – |
| Lock | | | | | 14 | 1 | 78 | 0 | 3rd | 25 | 168 | 57 | – |
| Barrington | | | | | 1 | 0 | 8 | 0 | 4th | 31 | 168 | 77 | – |
| | | | | | | | | | 5th | 36 | 184 | 274 | – |
| PAKISTAN | | | | | | | | | 6th | 51 | 221 | 299 | – |
| Mahmood Hussain | 40 | 9 | 106 | 2 | | | | | 7th | 77 | 247 | 300 | – |
| Farooq | 19 | 4 | 70 | 4 | 7 | 1 | 37 | 0 | 8th | 78 | 290 | 333 | – |
| D'Souza | 35.4 | 3 | 147 | 2 | 7 | 0 | 29 | 1 | 9th | 78 | 366 | 354 | – |
| Nasim | 2 | 0 | 15 | 0 | | | | | 10th | 100 | 370 | 355 | – |
| Saeed | 5 | 1 | 21 | 2 | 2 | 0 | 12 | 0 | | | | | |
| Mushtaq | | | | | 1 | 0 | 8 | 0 | | | | | |

Umpires: J.S. Buller and N. Oldfield.

Test No. 532/10

# ENGLAND v PAKISTAN 1962 (3rd Test)

Played at Headingley, Leeds, on 5, 6, 7 July.
Toss: Pakistan.   Result: ENGLAND won by an innings and 117 runs.
Debuts: Pakistan – Javed Akhtar (*his first match in England*).

Cowdrey ended his run of nine consecutive successes with the toss in Test matches. Parfitt and Allen shared what is still England's highest eighth-wicket partnership against Pakistan (99). For the fifth successive Test at Leeds, the match ended within three days' actual play. Pakistan were without Imtiaz Ahmed for the first time in 40 matches since their elevation to full Test status in 1952.

### ENGLAND

| | | |
|---|---|---|
| M.J. Stewart | lbw b Munir | 86 |
| M.C. Cowdrey* | c Saeed b Mahmood | 7 |
| E.R. Dexter | b Mahmood | 20 |
| T.W. Graveney | c Ijaz Butt b Munir | 37 |
| K.F. Barrington | c Mushtaq b Farooq | 1 |
| P.H. Parfitt | c and b Nasim | 119 |
| F.J. Titmus | c and b Munir | 2 |
| J.T. Murray† | c and b Nasim | 29 |
| D.A. Allen | c Ijaz Butt b Munir | 62 |
| F.S. Trueman | lbw b Munir | 20 |
| J.B. Statham | not out | 26 |
| Extras | (B 6, LB 9, W 1, NB 3) | 19 |
| **Total** | | **428** |

### PAKISTAN

| | | | | | |
|---|---|---|---|---|---|
| Alimuddin | c Barrington b Titmus | 50 | c Titmus b Allen | | 60 |
| Ijaz Butt† | b Trueman | 1 | b Trueman | | 6 |
| Saeed Ahmed | c Trueman b Statham | 16 | (5) c Cowdrey b Statham | | 54 |
| Mushtaq Mohammad | c Murray b Dexter | 27 | c Trueman b Allen | | 8 |
| Hanif Mohammad | b Statham | 9 | (6) c Barrington b Allen | | 4 |
| Javed Burki* | b Trueman | 1 | (7) c Murray b Statham | | 21 |
| Nasim-ul-Ghani | c Graveney b Titmus | 5 | (3) lbw b Statham | | 19 |
| Mahmood Hussain | not out | 0 | c and b Dexter | | 0 |
| Munir Malik | b Dexter | 3 | b Statham | | 4 |
| Javed Akhtar | b Dexter | 2 | not out | | 2 |
| Mohammad Farooq | c Statham b Dexter | 8 | c Statham b Trueman | | 0 |
| Extras | (B 8, NB 1) | 9 | (LB 2) | | 2 |
| **Total** | | **131** | | | **180** |

| PAKISTAN | O | M | R | W | O | M | R | W |
|---|---|---|---|---|---|---|---|---|
| Farooq | 28 | 8 | 74 | 1 | | | | |
| Mahmood Hussain | 25 | 5 | 87 | 2 | | | | |
| Munir | 49 | 11 | 128 | 5 | | | | |
| Javed Akhtar | 16 | 5 | 52 | 0 | | | | |
| Nasim | 14 | 2 | 68 | 2 | | | | |
| ENGLAND | | | | | | | | |
| Trueman | 23 | 6 | 55 | 2 | 10.4 | 3 | 33 | 2 |
| Statham | 20 | 9 | 40 | 2 | 20 | 3 | 50 | 4 |
| Dexter | 9.1 | 3 | 10 | 4 | 8 | 1 | 24 | 1 |
| Allen | 9 | 6 | 14 | 0 | 24 | 11 | 47 | 3 |
| Titmus | 4 | 1 | 3 | 2 | 11 | 2 | 20 | 0 |
| Barrington | | | | | 1 | 0 | 4 | 0 |

### FALL OF WICKETS

| | E | P | P |
|---|---|---|---|
| Wkt | 1st | 1st | 2nd |
| 1st | 7 | 13 | 10 |
| 2nd | 43 | 51 | 40 |
| 3rd | 108 | 72 | 57 |
| 4th | 117 | 88 | 130 |
| 5th | 177 | 118 | 136 |
| 6th | 180 | 118 | 163 |
| 7th | 247 | 118 | 178 |
| 8th | 346 | 121 | 179 |
| 9th | 377 | 123 | 179 |
| 10th | 428 | 131 | 180 |

Umpires: J.G. Langridge and W.E. Phillipson.

Test No. 533/11

# ENGLAND v PAKISTAN 1962 (4th Test)

Played at Trent Bridge, Nottingham, on 26 (*no play*), 27, 28, 30, 31 July.
Toss: Pakistan.   Result: MATCH DRAWN.
Debuts: Pakistan – Shahid Mahmood.

After a blank first day, rain reduced play to 195 minutes on the fourth day. Parfitt's hundred was his sixth in seven successive first-class innings against Pakistani bowling and his third in three innings against the tourists within a week. Statham exceeded R.R. Lindwall's record aggregate of Test wickets by a fast bowler (228) when he dismissed Imtiaz.

## ENGLAND

| | | |
|---|---|---:|
| G. Pullar | lbw b Munir | 5 |
| Rev. D.S. Sheppard | c Imtiaz b Intikhab | 83 |
| E.R. Dexter* | c Burki b Fazal | 85 |
| T.W. Graveney | c Intikhab b Fazal | 114 |
| P.H. Parfitt | not out | 101 |
| B.R. Knight | c Saeed b Fazal | 14 |
| F.J. Titmus | not out | 11 |
| J.T. Murray† | ) | |
| F.S. Trueman | ) did not bat | |
| G.A.R. Lock | ) | |
| J.B. Statham | ) | |
| Extras | (LB 13, NB 2) | 15 |
| **Total** | **(5 wickets declared)** | **428** |

## PAKISTAN

| | | | | | |
|---|---|---:|---|---|---:|
| Hanif Mohammad | c Titmus b Trueman | 0 | | c and b Trueman | 3 |
| Shahid Mahmood | c Graveney b Trueman | 16 | (7) | c Statham b Dexter | 9 |
| Mushtaq Mohammad | c Lock b Knight | 55 | | not out | 100 |
| Javed Burki* | c Murray b Knight | 19 | | c sub (C.J. Poole) b Titmus | 28 |
| Saeed Ahmed | c Murray b Statham | 43 | | c Trueman b Lock | 64 |
| Imtiaz Ahmed† | lbw b Trueman | 15 | | lbw b Statham | 1 |
| Alimuddin | b Trueman | 0 | (2) | c Murray b Statham | 11 |
| Nasim-ul-Ghani | c Murray b Knight | 41 | | not out | 0 |
| Intikhab Alam | c Murray b Statham | 14 | | | |
| Fazal Mahmood | lbw b Knight | 2 | | | |
| Munir Malik | not out | 0 | | | |
| Extras | (B 2, LB 10, NB 2) | 14 | | | |
| **Total** | | **219** | | **(6 wickets)** | **216** |

| PAKISTAN | O | M | R | W | O | M | R | W | | FALL OF WICKETS | | |
|---|---:|---:|---:|---:|---:|---:|---:|---:|---|---|---|---|
| Fazal | 60 | 15 | 130 | 3 | | | | | | E | P | P |
| Munir | 34 | 4 | 130 | 1 | | | | | Wkt | 1st | 1st | 2nd |
| Nasim | 20·2 | 1 | 76 | 0 | | | | | 1st | 11 | 0 | 4 |
| Intikhab | 14 | 3 | 49 | 1 | | | | | 2nd | 172 | 39 | 22 |
| Shahid | 6 | 1 | 23 | 0 | | | | | 3rd | 185 | 95 | 78 |
| Saeed | 2 | 0 | 5 | 0 | | | | | 4th | 369 | 98 | 185 |
| ENGLAND | | | | | | | | | 5th | 388 | 120 | 187 |
| Trueman | 24 | 3 | 71 | 4 | 19 | 5 | 35 | 1 | 6th | – | 120 | 216 |
| Statham | 18·1 | 5 | 55 | 2 | 22 | 8 | 47 | 2 | 7th | – | 171 | – |
| Knight | 17 | 1 | 38 | 4 | 21 | 6 | 48 | 0 | 8th | – | 213 | – |
| Lock | 14 | 5 | 19 | 0 | 15 | 4 | 27 | 1 | 9th | – | 217 | – |
| Titmus | 13 | 2 | 22 | 0 | 16 | 7 | 29 | 1 | 10th | – | 219 | – |
| Dexter | | | | | 7 | 0 | 25 | 1 | | | | |
| Parfitt | | | | | 1 | 0 | 5 | 0 | | | | |

Umpires: F.S. Lee and W.E. Phillipson.

Test No. 534/12

# ENGLAND v PAKISTAN 1962 (5th Test)

Played at Kennington Oval, London, on 16, 17, 18, 20 August.
Toss: England. Result: ENGLAND won by ten wickets.
Debuts: England – J.D.F. Larter.

Cowdrey, who scored the highest of his 22 Test hundreds, and Dexter shared what is still England's highest second-wicket partnership against Pakistan (248). Imtiaz became the second batsman after Hanif Mohammad to score 2,000 runs for Pakistan. Larter (6ft 7½in tall) took nine wickets in his first Test match.

## ENGLAND

| | | | | |
|---|---|---|---|---|
| Rev. D.S. Sheppard | c Fazal b Nasim | 57 | not out | 9 |
| M.C. Cowdrey | c Hanif b Fazal | 182 | | |
| E.R. Dexter* | b Fazal | 172 | | |
| K.F. Barrington | not out | 50 | | |
| P.H. Parfitt | c Imtiaz b D'Souza | 3 | | |
| B.R. Knight | b D'Souza | 3 | | |
| R. Illingworth | not out | 2 | | |
| J.T. Murray† | ) | | (2) not out | 14 |
| D.A. Allen | ) did not bat | | | |
| L.J. Coldwell | ) | | | |
| J.D.F. Larter | ) | | | |
| Extras | (B 4, LB 5, NB 2) | 11 | (B 4) | 4 |
| **Total** | (5 wickets declared) | **480** | (0 wickets) | **27** |

## PAKISTAN

| | | | | |
|---|---|---|---|---|
| Ijaz Butt | c Cowdrey b Larter | 10 | run out | 6 |
| Imtiaz Ahmed† | c Murray b Knight | 49 | c Cowdrey b Larter | 98 |
| Mushtaq Mohammad | lbw b Larter | 43 | b Illingworth | 72 |
| Javed Burki* | b Larter | 3 | (6) c Parfitt b Knight | 42 |
| Saeed Ahmed | c Parfitt b Allen | 21 | c Knight b Allen | 4 |
| Hanif Mohammad | b Larter | 46 | (4) c Dexter b Larter | 0 |
| W. Mathias | c Murray b Larter | 0 | run out | 48 |
| A. D'Souza | c Parfitt b Coldwell | 1 | (10) not out | 2 |
| Nasim-ul-Ghani | c Murray b Coldwell | 5 | (8) b Coldwell | 24 |
| Intikhab Alam | not out | 3 | (9) b Larter | 12 |
| Fazal Mahmood | b Coldwell | 0 | b Larter | 5 |
| Extras | (NB 2) | 2 | (B 4, LB 5, NB 1) | 10 |
| **Total** | | **183** | | **323** |

| PAKISTAN | O | M | R | W | O | M | R | W | FALL OF WICKETS |
|---|---|---|---|---|---|---|---|---|---|
| Fazal | 49 | 9 | 192 | 2 | 4 | 1 | 10 | 0 | |
| D'Souza | 42 | 9 | 116 | 2 | 3 | 1 | 8 | 0 | |

| | E | P | P | E |
|---|---|---|---|---|
| Wkt | 1st | 1st | 2nd | 2nd |
| 1st | 117 | 11 | 34 | – |
| 2nd | 365 | 93 | 171 | – |
| 3rd | 441 | 102 | 171 | – |
| 4th | 444 | 115 | 180 | – |
| 5th | 452 | 165 | 186 | – |
| 6th | – | 168 | 250 | – |
| 7th | – | 175 | 294 | – |
| 8th | – | 179 | 316 | – |
| 9th | – | 183 | 316 | – |
| 10th | – | 183 | 323 | – |

| PAKISTAN | O | M | R | W | O | M | R | W |
|---|---|---|---|---|---|---|---|---|
| Intikhab | 38 | 5 | 109 | 0 | | | | |
| Javed Burki | 1 | 0 | 12 | 0 | 1 | 0 | 2 | 0 |
| Nasim | 9 | 1 | 39 | 1 | | | | |
| Saeed | 1 | 0 | 1 | 0 | | | | |
| Mushtaq | | | | | 0.3 | 0 | 3 | 0 |

| ENGLAND | O | M | R | W | O | M | R | W |
|---|---|---|---|---|---|---|---|---|
| Coldwell | 28 | 11 | 53 | 3 | 23 | 4 | 60 | 1 |
| Larter | 25 | 4 | 57 | 5 | 21.1 | 0 | 88 | 4 |
| Allen | 22 | 9 | 33 | 1 | 27 | 14 | 52 | 1 |
| Knight | 9 | 5 | 11 | 1 | 11 | 3 | 33 | 1 |
| Illingworth | 13 | 5 | 27 | 0 | 21 | 9 | 54 | 1 |
| Dexter | | | | | 6 | 1 | 16 | 0 |
| Barrington | | | | | 2 | 0 | 10 | 0 |

Umpires: F.S. Lee and C.S. Elliott.

## Chapter 15
# AUSTRALIA 1962/63

Australia again for the 1962–63 series; this time Vice Captain under Dexter. At the Woolloongabba, Brisbane in a drawn match of many fifties (Wisden recorded that the fourteen equalled the record for the series set at Leeds in 1948) Cowdrey did not manage one of those, scoring 21 and 9. In this match six playing hours per day were stipulated for the first time in Test matches in Australia. Australia won the toss and batted scoring 404. Booth, with 112 at No 6, made the only century of the match. England replied with 389 Benaud taking 6 for 115. Australia declared their second innings at 362 for 4 setting England to make 378 at 63 per hour. They were given a good start by Pullar and Sheppard who put on 114 for the first wicket and Dexter came in to score 99 before being bowled by McKenzie and England finished disappointingly on 278 for 6.

At Melbourne, this time for the second Test, Cowdrey certainly redeemed himself scoring 113 and 58 not out as England won by seven wickets. England's lead had only been 15 with 331 with Davidson taking 6 for 75 but two marvellous slip catches by Cowdrey, dismissing O'Neill and Benaud, helped Trueman take five wickets in dismissing Australia for 248. This was the first Test England had won in Australia since 1954/55. On the last day they scored 226 for the loss of only two wickets – Sheppard for 113 and Dexter for 52 both run out.

In the third at Sydney Australia won by eight wickets drawing level in the series. England won the toss and batted scoring 279 of which Cowdrey made 85. Simpson took 5 for 57. Australia took the lead with 319 Titmus taking 7 for 79 including four wickets for five runs in 58 balls on the second day. When England batted again they were all out for 104 Cowdrey scoring only 8. Davidson took 5 for 25. Thus Australia won on the fourth day.

Both the fourth and fifth Tests were drawn. That at Adelaide Oval lost three hours to rain on the third day and Cowdrey scored 13 and was run out for 32. Although he caught three he also dropped two catches. Giving Harvey lives paved the way for his 154. O'Neill also made 100. Barrington was undefeated with 132 when stumps were drawn.

It was on this ground during this tour that Cowdrey made his highest score – 307 versus South Australia. The fact that it broke a record held by Kent's Frank Woolley was the basis for his personal joy and pride. His car number plate bore testimony to that soon and for ever after.

The fifth at Sydney found Cowdrey opening again, instead of an injured Pullar, in the first innings but he was out for 2 and dropped down to No 5 for the second innings in which he made 53. England came in for some criticism for not making the running in this final test and that may not have helped his next opportunity to succeed, this time Dexter, whose aggregate of 481 was a record by an England captain in Australia, as England's captain. Barrington and Burge made centuries in the sides' first innings. So, for the first time in a five-match series in Australia the series ended with the sides level.

|  | Matches | Innings | Not out | Runs | Highest score | Average | 100s | 50s | Caught |
|---|---|---|---|---|---|---|---|---|---|
| This series | 5 | 10 | 1 | 394 | 113 | 43.77 | 1 | 3 | 6 |
| Previous series | 57 | 93 | 4 | 3820 | 182 | 42.92 | 11 | 20 | 69 |
| Cumulative totals | 62 | 103 | 5 | 4214 | 182 | 43.00 | 12 | 23 | 75 |

*100 test innings and 4,000 runs*

Test No. 535/184

# AUSTRALIA v ENGLAND 1962-63 (1st Test)

Played at Woolloongabba, Brisbane, on 30 November, 1, 3, 4, 5 December.
Toss: Australia.   Result: MATCH DRAWN.
Debuts: England – A.C. Smith.

Six playing hours per day were scheduled for the first time in Test matches in Australia. England were set 378 runs to win at 63 per hour. Fourteen fifties were scored in the match, equalling the record for this series set at Leeds in 1948 (*Test No. 302*).

## AUSTRALIA

| | | | | |
|---|---|---|---|---|
| W.M. Lawry | c Smith b Trueman | 5 | c Sheppard b Titmus | 98 |
| R.B. Simpson | c Trueman b Dexter | 50 | c Smith b Dexter | 71 |
| N.C. O'Neill | c Statham b Trueman | 19 | lbw b Statham | 56 |
| R.N. Harvey | b Statham | 39 | c Statham b Dexter | 57 |
| P.J.P. Burge | c Dexter b Trueman | 6 | not out | 47 |
| B.C. Booth | c Dexter b Titmus | 112 | not out | 19 |
| A.K. Davidson | c Trueman b Barrington | 23 | | |
| K.D. Mackay | not out | 86 | | |
| R. Benaud* | c Smith b Knight | 51 | | |
| G.D. McKenzie | c and b Knight | 4 | | |
| B.N. Jarman† | c Barrington b Knight | 2 | | |
| Extras | (B 5, LB 1, NB 1) | 7 | (B 4, LB 10) | 14 |
| **Total** | | **404** | (4 wickets declared) | **362** |

## ENGLAND

| | | | | |
|---|---|---|---|---|
| G. Pullar | c and b Benaud | 33 | c and b Davidson | 56 |
| Rev. D.S. Sheppard | c McKenzie b Benaud | 31 | c Benaud b Davidson | 53 |
| E.R. Dexter* | b Benaud | 70 | b McKenzie | 99 |
| M.C. Cowdrey | c Lawry b Simpson | 21 | c and b Benaud | 9 |
| K.F. Barrington | c Burge b Benaud | 78 | c McKenzie b Davidson | 23 |
| A.C. Smith† | c Jarman b McKenzie | 21 | | |
| P.H. Parfitt | c Davidson b Benaud | 80 | (6) c Jarman b McKenzie | 4 |
| F.J. Titmus | c Simpson b Benaud | 21 | (7) not out | 3 |
| B.R. Knight | c Davidson b McKenzie | 0 | (8) not out | 4 |
| F.S. Trueman | c Jarman b McKenzie | 19 | | |
| J.B. Statham | not out | 8 | | |
| Extras | (B 4, LB 2, W 1) | 7 | (B 15, LB 10, NB 2) | 27 |
| **Total** | | **389** | (6 wickets) | **278** |

| ENGLAND | O | M | R | W | O | M | R | W | FALL OF WICKETS |
|---|---|---|---|---|---|---|---|---|---|
| Trueman | 18 | 0 | 76 | 3 | 15 | 0 | 59 | 0 | |
| Statham | 16 | 1 | 75 | 1 | 16 | 1 | 67 | 1 | |
| Knight | 17·5 | 2 | 65 | 3 | 14 | 1 | 63 | 0 | |
| Titmus | 33 | 8 | 91 | 1 | 26 | 3 | 81 | 1 | |
| Dexter | 10 | 0 | 46 | 1 | 16 | 0 | 78 | 2 | |
| Barrington | 12 | 3 | 44 | 1 | | | | | |
| AUSTRALIA | | | | | | | | | |
| Davidson | 21 | 4 | 77 | 0 | 20 | 6 | 43 | 3 | |
| McKenzie | 25·3 | 2 | 78 | 3 | 20 | 4 | 61 | 2 | |
| Mackay | 28 | 7 | 55 | 0 | 7 | 0 | 28 | 0 | |
| Benaud | 42 | 12 | 115 | 6 | 27 | 7 | 71 | 1 | |
| Simpson | 18 | 6 | 52 | 1 | 7 | 0 | 48 | 0 | |
| O'Neill | 1 | 0 | 5 | 0 | 2 | 2 | 0 | 0 | |

| Wkt | A 1st | E 1st | A 2nd | E 2nd |
|---|---|---|---|---|
| 1st | 5 | 62 | 136 | 114 |
| 2nd | 46 | 65 | 216 | 135 |
| 3rd | 92 | 145 | 241 | 191 |
| 4th | 101 | 169 | 325 | 257 |
| 5th | 140 | 220 | – | 257 |
| 6th | 194 | 297 | – | 261 |
| 7th | 297 | 361 | – | – |
| 8th | 388 | 362 | – | – |
| 9th | 392 | 362 | – | – |
| 10th | 404 | 389 | – | – |

Umpires: C.J. Egar and E. Wykes.

Test No. 536/185

# AUSTRALIA v ENGLAND 1962–63 (2nd Test)

Played at Melbourne Cricket Ground on 29, 31 December, 1, 2, 3 January.
Toss: Australia.  Result: ENGLAND won by seven wickets.
Debuts: Nil.

England won their first Test in Australia since 1954-55 and with 75 minutes to spare. On the last day they scored 226 runs for the loss of only two wickets – both being run out.

## AUSTRALIA

| | | | | |
|---|---|---|---|---|
| W.M. Lawry | b Trueman | 52 | b Dexter | 57 |
| R.B. Simpson | c Smith b Coldwell | 38 | b Trueman | 14 |
| N.C. O'Neill | c Graveney b Statham | 19 | c Cowdrey b Trueman | 0 |
| R.N. Harvey | b Coldwell | 0 | run out | 10 |
| P.J.P. Burge | lbw b Titmus | 23 | b Statham | 14 |
| B.C. Booth | c Barrington b Titmus | 27 | c Trueman b Statham | 103 |
| A.K. Davidson | c Smith b Trueman | 40 | c Smith b Titmus | 17 |
| K.D. Mackay | lbw b Titmus | 49 | lbw b Trueman | 9 |
| R. Benaud* | c Barrington b Titmus | 36 | c Cowdrey b Trueman | 4 |
| G.D. McKenzie | b Trueman | 16 | b Trueman | 0 |
| B.N. Jarman† | not out | 10 | not out | 11 |
| Extras | (B 2, LB 4) | 6 | (B 4, LB 5) | 9 |
| **Total** | | **316** | | **248** |

## ENGLAND

| | | | | |
|---|---|---|---|---|
| Rev. D.S. Sheppard | lbw b Davidson | 0 | run out | 113 |
| G. Pullar | b Davidson | 11 | c Jarman b McKenzie | 5 |
| E.R. Dexter* | c Simpson b Benaud | 93 | run out | 52 |
| M.C. Cowdrey | c Burge b McKenzie | 113 | not out | 58 |
| K.F. Barrington | lbw b McKenzie | 35 | not out | 0 |
| T.W. Graveney | run out | 41 | | |
| F.J. Titmus | c Jarman b Davidson | 15 | | |
| A.C. Smith† | not out | 6 | | |
| F.S. Trueman | c O'Neill b Davidson | 6 | | |
| J.B. Statham | b Davidson | 1 | | |
| L.J. Coldwell | c Benaud b Davidson | 1 | | |
| Extras | (B 4, LB 4, NB 1) | 9 | (B 5, LB 3, NB 1) | 9 |
| **Total** | | **331** | (3 wickets) | **237** |

| ENGLAND | O | M | R | W | O | M | R | W | | FALL OF WICKETS | | | |
|---|---|---|---|---|---|---|---|---|---|---|---|---|---|
| Trueman | 23 | 1 | 83 | 3 | 20 | 1 | 62 | 5 | | A | E | A | E |
| Statham | 22 | 2 | 83 | 1 | 23 | 1 | 52 | 2 | Wkt | 1st | 1st | 2nd | 2nd |
| Coldwell | 17 | 2 | 58 | 2 | 25 | 2 | 60 | 0 | 1st | 62 | 0 | 30 | 5 |
| Barrington | 6 | 0 | 23 | 0 | 5 | 0 | 22 | 0 | 2nd | 111 | 19 | 30 | 129 |
| Dexter | 6 | 1 | 10 | 0 | 9 | 2 | 18 | 1 | 3rd | 112 | 194 | 46 | 233 |
| Titmus | 15 | 2 | 43 | 4 | 14 | 4 | 25 | 1 | 4th | 112 | 254 | 69 | – |
| Graveney | 3 | 1 | 10 | 0 | | | | | 5th | 155 | 255 | 161 | – |
| AUSTRALIA | | | | | | | | | 6th | 164 | 292 | 193 | – |
| Davidson | 23.1 | 4 | 75 | 6 | 19 | 2 | 53 | 0 | 7th | 237 | 315 | 212 | – |
| McKenzie | 29 | 3 | 95 | 2 | 20 | 3 | 58 | 1 | 8th | 289 | 324 | 228 | – |
| Mackay | 6 | 2 | 17 | 0 | 9 | 0 | 34 | 0 | 9th | 294 | 327 | 228 | – |
| Benaud | 18 | 3 | 82 | 1 | 14 | 1 | 69 | 0 | 10th | 316 | 331 | 248 | – |
| Simpson | 7 | 1 | 34 | 0 | 2 | 0 | 10 | 0 | | | | | |
| O'Neill | 5 | 1 | 19 | 0 | | | | | | | | | |
| Booth | | | | | 0.2 | 0 | 4 | 0 | | | | | |

Umpires: C.J. Egar and W. Smyth.

Test No. 537/186

# AUSTRALIA v ENGLAND 1962–63 (3rd Test)

Played at Sydney Cricket Ground on 11, 12, 14, 15 January.
Toss: England.   Result: AUSTRALIA won by eight wickets.
Debuts: Australia – C.E.J. Guest, B.K. Shepherd.

Australia squared the rubber at 2.15 p.m. on the fourth day. Parfitt kept wicket after Murray injured his shoulder when he caught Lawry. On the second day Titmus took four wickets for five runs in 58 balls.

## ENGLAND

| | | | | |
|---|---|---|---|---|
| G. Pullar | c Benaud b Simpson | 53 | b Davidson | 0 |
| Rev. D.S. Sheppard | c McKenzie b Davidson | 3 | c Simpson b Davidson | 12 |
| E.R. Dexter* | c Lawry b Benaud | 32 | c Simpson b Davidson | 11 |
| M.C. Cowdrey | c Jarman b Simpson | 85 | c Simpson b Benaud | 8 |
| K.F. Barrington | lbw b Davidson | 35 | b McKenzie | 21 |
| P.H. Parfitt | c Lawry b Simpson | 0 | c O'Neill b McKenzie | 28 |
| F.J. Titmus | b Davidson | 32 | c Booth b O'Neill | 6 |
| J.T. Murray† | lbw b Davidson | 0 | not out | 3 |
| F.S. Trueman | b Simpson | 32 | c Jarman b McKenzie | 9 |
| J.B. Statham | c Benaud b Simpson | 0 | b Davidson | 2 |
| L.J. Coldwell | not out | 2 | c Shepherd b Davidson | 0 |
| Extras | (LB 3, W 2) | 5 | (B 2, LB 2) | 4 |
| **Total** | | **279** | | **104** |

## AUSTRALIA

| | | | | |
|---|---|---|---|---|
| W.M. Lawry | c Murray b Coldwell | 8 | b Trueman | 8 |
| R.B. Simpson | b Titmus | 91 | not out | 34 |
| R.N. Harvey | c Barrington b Titmus | 64 | lbw b Trueman | 15 |
| B.C. Booth | c Trueman b Titmus | 16 | not out | 5 |
| N.C. O'Neill | b Titmus | 3 | | |
| B.K. Shepherd | not out | 71 | | |
| B.N. Jarman† | run out | 0 | | |
| A.K. Davidson | c Trueman b Titmus | 15 | | |
| R. Benaud* | c and b Titmus | 15 | | |
| G.D. McKenzie | lbw b Titmus | 4 | | |
| C.E.J. Guest | b Statham | 11 | | |
| Extras | (B 10, LB 11) | 21 | (B 5) | 5 |
| **Total** | | **319** | (2 wickets) | **67** |

| AUSTRALIA | O | M | R | W | O | M | R | W | FALL OF WICKETS |
|---|---|---|---|---|---|---|---|---|---|
| Davidson | 24.5 | 7 | 54 | 4 | 10.6 | 2 | 25 | 5 | |
| McKenzie | 15 | 3 | 52 | 0 | 14 | 3 | 26 | 3 | |
| Guest | 16 | 0 | 51 | 0 | 2 | 0 | 8 | 0 | |
| Benaud | 16 | 2 | 60 | 1 | 19 | 10 | 29 | 1 | |
| Simpson | 15 | 3 | 57 | 5 | 4 | 2 | 5 | 0 | |
| O'Neill | | | | | 7 | 5 | 7 | 1 | |
| ENGLAND | | | | | | | | | |
| Trueman | 20 | 2 | 68 | 0 | 6 | 1 | 20 | 2 | |
| Statham | 21.2 | 2 | 67 | 1 | 3 | 0 | 15 | 0 | |
| Coldwell | 15 | 1 | 41 | 1 | | | | | |
| Titmus | 37 | 14 | 79 | 7 | | | | | |
| Barrington | 8 | 0 | 43 | 0 | | | | | |
| Dexter | | | | | 3.2 | 0 | 27 | 0 | |

| Wkt | E 1st | A 1st | E 2nd | A 2nd |
|---|---|---|---|---|
| 1st | 4 | 14 | 0 | 28 |
| 2nd | 65 | 174 | 20 | 54 |
| 3rd | 132 | 177 | 25 | – |
| 4th | 201 | 187 | 37 | – |
| 5th | 203 | 212 | 53 | – |
| 6th | 221 | 216 | 71 | – |
| 7th | 221 | 242 | 90 | – |
| 8th | 272 | 274 | 100 | – |
| 9th | 272 | 280 | 104 | – |
| 10th | 279 | 319 | 104 | – |

Umpires: W. Smyth and L.P. Rowan.

Test No. 538/187

# AUSTRALIA v ENGLAND 1962–63 (4th Test)

Played at Adelaide Oval on 25, 26, 28, 29, 30 January.
Toss: Australia.   Result: MATCH DRAWN.
Debuts: Nil.

Rain reduced play by three hours on the third day. Barrington became the second batsman after J. Darling in 1897-98 (*Test No. 55*) to reach a hundred in this series of Tests with a six. Statham overtook A.V. Bedser's world record of 236 Test wickets. Davidson pulled a hamstring and was unable to complete his fourth over.

### AUSTRALIA

| | | | | |
|---|---|---|---|---|
| W.M. Lawry | b Illingworth | 10 | c Graveney b Trueman | 16 |
| R.B. Simpson | c Smith b Statham | 0 | c Smith b Dexter | 71 |
| R.N. Harvey | c Statham b Dexter | 154 | c Barrington b Statham | 6 |
| B.C. Booth | c Cowdrey b Titmus | 34 | c Smith b Dexter | 77 |
| N.C. O'Neill | c Cowdrey b Dexter | 100 | c Cowdrey b Trueman | 23 |
| A.K. Davidson | b Statham | 46 | (10) b Statham | 2 |
| B.K. Shepherd | c Trueman b Statham | 10 | (6) c Titmus b Dexter | 13 |
| K.D. Mackay | c Smith b Trueman | 1 | (7) c Graveney b Trueman | 3 |
| R. Benaud* | b Dexter | 16 | (8) c Barrington b Trueman | 48 |
| G.D. McKenzie | c Sheppard b Titmus | 15 | (9) c Smith b Statham | 13 |
| A.T.W. Grout† | not out | 1 | not out | 16 |
| Extras | (LB 5, W 1) | 6 | (B 1, LB 4) | 5 |
| **Total** | | **393** | | **293** |

### ENGLAND

| | | | | |
|---|---|---|---|---|
| G. Pullar | b McKenzie | 9 | c Simpson b McKenzie | 3 |
| Rev. D.S. Sheppard | st Grout b Benaud | 30 | c Grout b Mackay | 1 |
| K.F. Barrington | b Simpson | 63 | not out | 132 |
| M.C. Cowdrey | c Grout b McKenzie | 13 | run out | 32 |
| E.R. Dexter* | c Grout b McKenzie | 61 | c Simpson b Benaud | 10 |
| T.W. Graveney | c Booth b McKenzie | 22 | not out | 36 |
| F.J. Titmus | not out | 59 | | |
| R. Illingworth | c Grout b McKenzie | 12 | | |
| A.C. Smith† | c Lawry b Mackay | 13 | | |
| F.S. Trueman | c Benaud b Mackay | 38 | | |
| J.B. Statham | b Mackay | 1 | | |
| Extras | (B 5, LB 5) | 10 | (B 4, W 5) | 9 |
| **Total** | | **331** | (4 wickets) | **223** |

| ENGLAND | O | M | R | W | O | M | R | W | | FALL OF WICKETS | | | |
|---|---|---|---|---|---|---|---|---|---|---|---|---|---|
| Trueman | 19 | 1 | 54 | 1 | 23.3 | 3 | 60 | 4 | | A | E | A | E |
| Statham | 21 | 5 | 66 | 3 | 21 | 2 | 71 | 3 | Wkt | 1st | 1st | 2nd | 2nd |
| Illingworth | 20 | 3 | 85 | 1 | 5 | 1 | 23 | 0 | 1st | 2 | 17 | 27 | 2 |
| Dexter | 23 | 1 | 94 | 3 | 17 | 0 | 65 | 3 | 2nd | 16 | 84 | 37 | 4 |
| Titmus | 20.1 | 2 | 88 | 2 | 24 | 5 | 69 | 0 | 3rd | 101 | 117 | 170 | 98 |
| | | | | | | | | | 4th | 295 | 119 | 175 | 122 |
| AUSTRALIA | | | | | | | | | 5th | 302 | 165 | 199 | – |
| Davidson | 3.4 | 0 | 30 | 0 | | | | | 6th | 331 | 226 | 205 | – |
| McKenzie | 33 | 3 | 89 | 5 | 14 | 0 | 64 | 1 | 7th | 336 | 246 | 228 | – |
| Mackay | 27.6 | 8 | 80 | 3 | 8 | 2 | 13 | 1 | 8th | 366 | 275 | 254 | – |
| Benaud | 18 | 3 | 82 | 1 | 15 | 3 | 38 | 1 | 9th | 383 | 327 | 258 | – |
| Simpson | 8 | 1 | 40 | 1 | 10 | 1 | 50 | 0 | 10th | 393 | 331 | 293 | |
| O'Neill | | | | | 8 | 0 | 49 | 0 | | | | | |
| Lawry | | | | | 1 | 1 | 0 | 0 | | | | | |
| Harvey | | | | | 1 | 1 | 0 | 0 | | | | | |

Umpires: C.J. Egar and A. Mackley.

Test No. 539/188

# AUSTRALIA v ENGLAND 1962–63 (5th Test)

Played at Sydney Cricket Ground on 15, 16, 18, 19, 20 February.
Toss: England.   Result: MATCH DRAWN.
Debuts: Australia – N.J.N. Hawke.

For the first time a five-match series in Australia ended with the sides level. Dexter's aggregate of 481 remains the record by an England captain in a rubber in Australia.

## ENGLAND

| | | | | |
|---|---|---|---|---|
| Rev. D.S. Sheppard | c and b Hawke | 19 | c Harvey b Benaud | 68 |
| M.C. Cowdrey | c Harvey b Davidson | 2 | (5) c Benaud b Davidson | 53 |
| K.F. Barrington | c Harvey b Benaud | 101 | c Grout b McKenzie | 94 |
| E.R. Dexter* | c Simpson b O'Neill | 47 | st Grout b Benaud | 6 |
| T.W. Graveney | c Harvey b McKenzie | 14 | (6) c and b Davidson | 3 |
| R. Illingworth | c Grout b Davidson | 27 | (2) c Hawke b Benaud | 18 |
| F.J. Titmus | c Grout b Hawke | 34 | not out | 12 |
| F.S. Trueman | c Harvey b Benaud | 30 | c Harvey b McKenzie | 8 |
| A.C. Smith† | b Simpson | 6 | c Simpson b Davidson | 1 |
| D.A. Allen | c Benaud b Davidson | 14 | | |
| J.B. Statham | not out | 17 | | |
| Extras | (B 4, LB 6) | 10 | (B 1, LB 4) | 5 |
| **Total** | | **321** | (8 wickets declared) | **268** |

## AUSTRALIA

| | | | | |
|---|---|---|---|---|
| W.M. Lawry | c Smith b Trueman | 11 | not out | 45 |
| R.B. Simpson | c Trueman b Titmus | 32 | b Trueman | 0 |
| B.C. Booth | b Titmus | 11 | (5) b Allen | 0 |
| N.C. O'Neill | c Graveney b Allen | 73 | c Smith b Allen | 17 |
| P.J.P. Burge | lbw b Titmus | 103 | (6) not out | 52 |
| R.N. Harvey | c sub (P.H. Parfitt) b Statham | 22 | (3) b Allen | 28 |
| A.K. Davidson | c Allen b Dexter | 15 | | |
| R. Benaud* | c Graveney b Allen | 57 | | |
| G.D. McKenzie | c and b Titmus | 0 | | |
| N.J.N. Hawke | c Graveney b Titmus | 14 | | |
| A.T.W. Grout† | not out | 0 | | |
| Extras | (B 6, LB 5) | 11 | (B 4, LB 6) | 10 |
| **Total** | | **349** | (4 wickets) | **152** |

| AUSTRALIA | O | M | R | W | O | M | R | W | FALL OF WICKETS | | | | |
|---|---|---|---|---|---|---|---|---|---|---|---|---|---|
| | | | | | | | | | | E | A | E | A |
| Davidson | 25.6 | 4 | 43 | 3 | 28 | 1 | 80 | 3 | Wkt | 1st | 1st | 2nd | 2nd |
| McKenzie | 27 | 4 | 57 | 1 | 8 | 0 | 39 | 2 | 1st | 5 | 28 | 40 | 0 |
| Hawke | 20 | 1 | 51 | 2 | 9 | 0 | 38 | 0 | 2nd | 39 | 50 | 137 | 39 |
| Benaud | 34 | 9 | 71 | 2 | 30 | 8 | 71 | 3 | 3rd | 129 | 71 | 145 | 70 |
| Simpson | 18 | 4 | 51 | 1 | 4 | 0 | 22 | 0 | 4th | 177 | 180 | 239 | 70 |
| O'Neill | 10 | 0 | 38 | 1 | | | | | 5th | 189 | 231 | 247 | – |
| Harvey | | | | | 3 | 0 | 13 | 0 | 6th | 224 | 271 | 249 | – |
| ENGLAND | | | | | | | | | 7th | 276 | 299 | 257 | – |
| Trueman | 11 | 0 | 33 | 1 | 3 | 0 | 6 | 1 | 8th | 286 | 303 | 268 | – |
| Statham | 18 | 1 | 76 | 1 | 4 | 1 | 8 | 0 | 9th | 293 | 347 | – | – |
| Dexter | 7 | 1 | 24 | 1 | 4 | 1 | 11 | 0 | 10th | 321 | 349 | – | – |
| Titmus | 47.2 | 9 | 103 | 5 | 20 | 7 | 37 | 0 | | | | | |
| Allen | 43 | 15 | 87 | 2 | 19 | 11 | 26 | 3 | | | | | |
| Illingworth | 5 | 1 | 15 | 0 | 10 | 5 | 8 | 0 | | | | | |
| Barrington | | | | | 8 | 3 | 22 | 0 | | | | | |
| Graveney | | | | | 4 | 0 | 24 | 0 | | | | | |

Umpires: C.J. Egar and L.P. Rowan.

Chapter 16

# IN NEW ZEALAND 1963

Cowdrey had enjoyed his second tour of New Zealand more than his first and now on his third visit he showed something of his true class to the islanders. In the first Test at Eden Park, Auckland he made 86 of a first innings total of 562 which took England to an innings win. Barrington, Parfitt and Knight all scored centuries. New Zealand having been dismissed for 258 were then put out for 89.

In the second Test at Basin Reserve, Wellington he made 128 not out in sharing an unbroken partnership of 163 with wicket keeper Smith.[1] England declared at 428 for eight in reply to New Zealand's 194. Cowdrey had damaged a finger on the first day and came into bat at No 8, but changed his grip with remarkable success. In their second innings the home side managed only 187.

In the third, of three Tests, at Lancaster Park, Christchurch, England won by seven wickets. In their first innings England were thirteen short of New Zealand's 266. Trueman had taken 7 for 75. Although the home team's skipper J R Reid had scored 74, no England player reached 50. Cowdrey, with 43, was one of four who made the forties. In the first innings he was No 5 but in the second innings came in at No 3 and was undefeated with 35 when victory came at 173 for 3.

---

1. That established a world Test record for the ninth wicket. It remained an England record for that wicket and had been bettered only by that of Asif Iqbal and Intikhab Alam for Pakistan v. England at The Oval in 1967.

|  | Matches | Innings | Not out | Runs | Highest score | Average | 100s | 50s | Caught |
|---|---|---|---|---|---|---|---|---|---|
| This series | 3 | 4 | 2 | 292 | 128* | 146.00 | 1 | 1 | 1 |
| Previous series | 62 | 103 | 5 | 4214 | 182 | 43.00 | 12 | 23 | 75 |
| Cumulative totals | 65 | 107 | 7 | 4506 | 182 | 45.06 | 13 | 24 | 76 |

Test No. 540/29

# NEW ZEALAND v ENGLAND 1962–63 (1st Test)

Played at Eden Park, Auckland, on 23, 25, 26, 27 February.
Toss: England.  Result: ENGLAND won by an innings and 215 runs.
Debuts: New Zealand – B.W. Sinclair, B.W. Yuile.

England scored their highest total against New Zealand (subsequently bettered), 240 of the runs coming in a partnership between Parfitt and Knight which is still England's highest for the sixth wicket against all countries. An umpiring error allowed Sparling to bowl eleven balls (excluding no balls and wides) in his sixth over. The match ended after 66 minutes of play on the last day.

### ENGLAND

| | | |
|---|---|---|
| Rev. D.S. Sheppard | c Dick b Cameron | 12 |
| R. Illingworth | c Reid b Cameron | 20 |
| K.F. Barrington | c Playle b Cameron | 126 |
| E.R. Dexter* | c Barton b Yuile | 7 |
| M.C. Cowdrey | c Barton b Cameron | 86 |
| P.H. Parfitt | not out | 131 |
| B.R. Knight | b Alabaster | 125 |
| F.J. Titmus | st Dick b Sparling | 26 |
| J.T. Murray† | not out | 9 |
| J.D.F. Larter | } did not bat | |
| L.J. Coldwell | | |
| Extras | (B 18, LB 1, NB 1) | 20 |
| **Total** | **(7 wickets declared)** | **562** |

### NEW ZEALAND

| | | | | | |
|---|---|---|---|---|---|
| G.T. Dowling | b Coldwell | 3 | b Illingworth | | 14 |
| W.R. Playle | c Dexter b Larter | 0 | c Dexter b Coldwell | | 4 |
| P.T. Barton | c Sheppard b Larter | 3 | lbw b Titmus | | 16 |
| J.R. Reid* | b Titmus | 59 | (6) not out | | 21 |
| B.W. Sinclair | c Coldwell b Titmus | 24 | b Larter | | 2 |
| J.T. Sparling | c Murray b Larter | 3 | (4) c Barrington b Illingworth | | 0 |
| A.E. Dick† | run out | 29 | c Illingworth b Larter | | 0 |
| B.W. Yuile | run out | 64 | lbw b Larter | | 1 |
| R.C. Motz | c Murray b Knight | 60 | c and b Illingworth | | 20 |
| J.C. Alabaster | b Knight | 2 | c Titmus b Illingworth | | 0 |
| F.J. Cameron | not out | 0 | b Larter | | 1 |
| Extras | (B 5, LB 3, W 1, NB 2) | 11 | (B 2, LB 8) | | 10 |
| **Total** | | **258** | | | **89** |

| NEW ZEALAND | O | M | R | W | O | M | R | W | FALL OF WICKETS | | | |
|---|---|---|---|---|---|---|---|---|---|---|---|---|
| Motz | 42 | 12 | 98 | 0 | | | | | | E | NZ | NZ |
| Cameron | 43 | 7 | 118 | 4 | | | | | Wkt | 1st | 1st | 2nd |
| Alabaster | 40 | 6 | 130 | 1 | | | | | 1st | 24 | 0 | 15 |
| Yuile | 21 | 4 | 77 | 1 | | | | | 2nd | 45 | 7 | 42 |
| Reid | 28 | 8 | 67 | 0 | | | | | 3rd | 63 | 7 | 42 |
| Sparling | 12 | 2 | 52 | 1 | | | | | 4th | 229 | 62 | 42 |
| ENGLAND | | | | | | | | | 5th | 258 | 71 | 46 |
| Coldwell | 27 | 9 | 66 | 1 | 5 | 2 | 4 | 1 | 6th | 498 | 109 | 46 |
| Larter | 26 | 12 | 51 | 3 | 14.1 | 3 | 26 | 4 | 7th | 535 | 161 | 56 |
| Knight | 10.4 | 2 | 23 | 2 | 10 | 2 | 13 | 0 | 8th | – | 256 | 83 |
| Titmus | 25 | 9 | 44 | 2 | 6 | 5 | 2 | 1 | 9th | – | 258 | 83 |
| Barrington | 12 | 4 | 38 | 0 | | | | | 10th | – | 258 | 89 |
| Dexter | 9 | 4 | 20 | 0 | | | | | | | | |
| Illingworth | 1 | 0 | 5 | 0 | 18 | 7 | 34 | 4 | | | | |

Umpires: R.W.R. Shortt and J.M. Brown.

Test No. 541/30

# NEW ZEALAND v ENGLAND 1962–63 (2nd Test)

Played at Basin Reserve, Wellington, on 1, 2, 4 March.
Toss: England. Result: ENGLAND won by an innings and 47 runs.
Debuts: New Zealand – B.D. Morrison, M.J.F. Shrimpton.

Cowdrey and Smith shared an unbroken partnership of 163 to set a world Test record for the ninth wicket. It remains the England record for that wicket and has been bettered only by the partnership of 190 between Asif Iqbal and Intikhab Alam for Pakistan v England at The Oval in 1967 (*Test No. 623*).

## NEW ZEALAND

| | | | | |
|---|---|---|---|---|
| G.T. Dowling | c Smith b Trueman | 12 | c Knight b Trueman | 2 |
| W.R. Playle | c Smith b Knight | 23 | c and b Illingworth | 65 |
| P.T. Barton | c Cowdrey b Trueman | 0 | c Barrington b Knight | 3 |
| J.R. Reid* | c Smith b Knight | 0 | c Barrington b Titmus | 9 |
| B.W. Sinclair | b Trueman | 4 | c and b Barrington | 36 |
| M.J.F. Shrimpton | lbw b Knight | 28 | c Parfitt b Barrington | 10 |
| A.E. Dick† | c Sheppard b Trueman | 7 | not out | 8 |
| B.W. Yuile | c Illingworth b Titmus | 13 | b Titmus | 0 |
| R.W. Blair | not out | 64 | c Larter b Titmus | 5 |
| B.D. Morrison | run out | 10 | c Larter b Titmus | 0 |
| F.J. Cameron | lbw b Barrington | 12 | lbw b Barrington | 0 |
| Extras | (B 13, LB 5, NB 3) | 21 | (B 13, LB 4, NB 2) | 19 |
| **Total** | | **194** | | **187** |

## ENGLAND

| | | |
|---|---|---|
| Rev. D.S. Sheppard | b Blair | 0 |
| R. Illingworth | c Morrison b Blair | 46 |
| K.F. Barrington | c Dick b Reid | 76 |
| E.R. Dexter* | b Morrison | 31 |
| P.H. Parfitt | c Dick b Morrison | 0 |
| B.R. Knight | c Dick b Cameron | 31 |
| F.J. Titmus | run out | 33 |
| M.C. Cowdrey | not out | 128 |
| F.S. Trueman | b Cameron | 3 |
| A.C. Smith† | not out | 69 |
| J.D.F. Larter | did not bat | |
| Extras | (B 3, LB 6, NB 2) | 11 |
| **Total** | (8 wickets declared) | **428** |

| ENGLAND | O | M | R | W | O | M | R | W | | FALL OF WICKETS | | |
|---|---|---|---|---|---|---|---|---|---|---|---|---|
| Trueman | 20 | 5 | 46 | 4 | 18 | 7 | 27 | 1 | | NZ | E | NZ |
| Larter | 14 | 2 | 52 | 0 | 7 | 1 | 18 | 0 | Wkt | 1st | 1st | 2nd |
| Knight | 21 | 8 | 32 | 3 | 4 | 1 | 7 | 1 | 1st | 32 | 0 | 15 |
| Titmus | 18 | 3 | 40 | 1 | 3 | 1 | 50 | 4 | 2nd | 32 | 77 | 18 |
| Barrington | 2·3 | 1 | 1 | 1 | 11 | 3 | 32 | 3 | 3rd | 35 | 125 | 41 |
| Dexter | 1 | 0 | 2 | 0 | | | | | 4th | 40 | 125 | 122 |
| Illingworth | | | | | 2 | 1 | 34 | 1 | 5th | 61 | 173 | 126 |
| | | | | | | | | | 6th | 74 | 197 | 158 |
| NEW ZEALAND | | | | | | | | | 7th | 96 | 258 | 159 |
| Blair | 33 | 11 | 81 | 2 | | | | | 8th | 129 | 265 | 171 |
| Morrison | 31 | 5 | 129 | 2 | | | | | 9th | 150 | – | 179 |
| Cameron | 43 | 16 | 98 | 2 | | | | | 10th | 194 | – | 187 |
| Reid | 32 | 8 | 73 | 1 | | | | | | | | |
| Yuile | 10 | 1 | 36 | 0 | | | | | | | | |

Umpires: D.P. Dumbleton and W.T. Martin.

Test No. 542/31

# NEW ZEALAND v ENGLAND 1962–63 (3rd Test)

Played at Lancaster Park, Christchurch, on 15, 16, 18, 19 March.
Toss: New Zealand. Result: ENGLAND won by seven wickets.
Debuts: Nil.

Knight completed England's 3-0 victory in this rubber by hitting 14 runs (6, 4, 4) off successive balls from Alabaster. Trueman overtook J.B. Statham's world record of 242 Test wickets and ended his 56th Test with an aggregate of 250.

### NEW ZEALAND

| | | | | |
|---|---|---|---|---|
| G.T. Dowling | c Dexter b Titmus | 40 | c Smith b Larter | 22 |
| W.R. Playle | c Barrington b Trueman | 0 | c Smith b Trueman | 3 |
| B.W. Sinclair | hit wkt b Trueman | 44 | lbw b Larter | 0 |
| J.R. Reid* | c Parfitt b Knight | 74 | b Titmus | 100 |
| P.T. Barton | c Smith b Knight | 11 | lbw b Knight | 12 |
| M.J.F. Shrimpton | c Knight b Trueman | 31 | b Titmus | 8 |
| A.E. Dick† | b Trueman | 16 | c Parfitt b Titmus | 1 |
| R.C. Motz | c Parfitt b Trueman | 7 | b Larter | 3 |
| R.W. Blair | c Parfitt b Trueman | 0 | b Titmus | 0 |
| J.C. Alabaster | not out | 20 | c Parfitt b Trueman | 1 |
| F.J. Cameron | c Smith b Trueman | 1 | not out | 0 |
| Extras | (B 1, LB 9, W 3, NB 9) | 22 | (LB 7, NB 2) | 9 |
| Total | | 266 | | 159 |

### ENGLAND

| | | | | |
|---|---|---|---|---|
| Rev. D.S. Sheppard | b Cameron | 42 | b Alabaster | 31 |
| R. Illingworth | c Dick b Cameron | 2 | | |
| K.F. Barrington | lbw b Motz | 47 | (2) c Reid b Blair | 45 |
| E.R. Dexter* | b Alabaster | 46 | | |
| M.C. Cowdrey | c Motz b Blair | 43 | (3) not out | 35 |
| P.H. Parfitt | lbw b Reid | 4 | (4) c Shrimpton b Alabaster | 31 |
| B.R. Knight | b Blair | 32 | (5) not out | 20 |
| F.J. Titmus | c Dick b Motz | 4 | | |
| F.S. Trueman | c Reid b Alabaster | 11 | | |
| A.C. Smith† | not out | 2 | | |
| J.D.F. Larter | b Motz | 2 | | |
| Extras | (B 4, LB 6, W 5, NB 3) | 18 | (B 9, NB 2) | 11 |
| Total | | 253 | (3 wickets) | 173 |

| ENGLAND | O | M | R | W | O | M | R | W | FALL OF WICKETS | | | | |
|---|---|---|---|---|---|---|---|---|---|---|---|---|---|
| Trueman | 30·2 | 9 | 75 | 7 | 19·4 | 8 | 16 | 2 | | NZ | E | NZ | E |
| Larter | 21 | 5 | 59 | 0 | 23 | 8 | 32 | 3 | Wkt | 1st | 1st | 2nd | 2nd |
| Knight | 23 | 5 | 39 | 2 | 10 | 3 | 38 | 1 | 1st | 3 | 11 | 16 | 70 |
| Titmus | 30 | 13 | 45 | 1 | 21 | 8 | 46 | 4 | 2nd | 83 | 87 | 17 | 96 |
| Dexter | 9 | 3 | 8 | 0 | 10 | 2 | 18 | 0 | 3rd | 98 | 103 | 66 | 149 |
| Barrington | 5 | 0 | 18 | 0 | | | | | 4th | 128 | 186 | 91 | – |
| | | | | | | | | | 5th | 195 | 188 | 129 | – |
| NEW ZEALAND | | | | | | | | | 6th | 234 | 210 | 133 | – |
| Motz | 19·5 | 3 | 68 | 3 | 20 | 6 | 33 | 0 | 7th | 235 | 225 | 151 | – |
| Cameron | 24 | 6 | 47 | 2 | 12 | 3 | 38 | 0 | 8th | 235 | 244 | 154 | – |
| Blair | 24 | 12 | 42 | 2 | 12 | 3 | 34 | 1 | 9th | 251 | 250 | 159 | – |
| Alabaster | 20 | 6 | 47 | 2 | 15·3 | 5 | 57 | 2 | 10th | 266 | 253 | 159 | – |
| Reid | 8 | 1 | 31 | 1 | | | | | | | | | |

Umpires: L.C. Johnston and W.T. Martin.

Chapter 17

# WEST INDIES 1963

Back in England the visitors made sterner opposition in the form of a West Indies side still led by Worrell, with Sobers in the middle order and an opening attack of Hall and Griffith.

The first Test at Old Trafford was won by the strong visiting side by ten wickets. In their first innings West Indies made 501 for 6 declared. When England batted Cowdrey made little contribution being bowled by Hall for 4 in the first innings and succumbing to Gibbs for only 12 in the second.

He did little better in the second Test at Lord's but was involved in one of the most dramatic matches ever. West Indies made 301 in the first innings, Cowdrey taking three catches. Dexter made a memorable 70 in England's reply which came within four of the visitors' total – Cowdrey's score. In the second innings Cowdrey again took three catches and West Indies owed much to Butcher for a magnificent 133. In the final innings Cowdrey suffered a fractured left arm and had to retire hurt when on 19. Rain delayed play on the last day and Cowdrey returned to partner Allen in the final over. Great play was made of Cowdrey's heroism. That has never been in any doubt, not least against the West Indies over his career but in the event he was not required to face a ball. His intention "to bat left-handed, but using only his right arm" must have been the paradox of all time in *The Wisden Book of Test Cricket* compiled and edited by Bill Frindall. Nothing can gainsay the drama of that last over. If experience of life had not taught me to find nothing incredible, such would have been my reaction to this passage in a book largely about prime ministers since 1945.

> ... there was one moment during the Cold War when, had the Soviet Union failed to be deterred, the British war planners at least would have failed to notice. It was

in June 1963 during, ironically enough, the post-Cuba review of readiness procedures. The Russians' "window of opportunity", as it was described to me by a long-serving civil servant on deterrent matters, had to do with a hot (as opposed to a cold) war. During that last over of the Lord's Test Match against the West Indies, when Colin Cowdrey came in with a broken arm and he and David Allen had to hold out against Wes Hall in full cry if the match was to be saved, every single screen of the Ballistic Missile Early Warning System was displaying the live broadcast on BBC Television.[1]

Professor Hennessy told the author that the source he quoted, "Private information", was a very reliable source. In his "Notes" (sadly they are not footnotes, but relegated to the back of the book – p. 573) he helpfully reminds his readers that the gripping last over can be relived by watching the BBC's *The 60s Video* (BBC V 4407, BBC Enterprises, 1993.)

|  | Matches | Innings | Not out | Runs | Highest score | Average | 100s | 50s | Caught |
|---|---|---|---|---|---|---|---|---|---|
| This series | 2 | 4 | 1 | 39 | 19* | 13.00 | 0 | 0 | 6 |
| Previous series | 65 | 107 | 7 | 4506 | 182 | 45.06 | 13 | 24 | 76 |
| Cumulative totals | 67 | 111 | 8 | 4545 | 182 | 44.13 | 13 | 24 | 82 |

---

1. Peter Hennessy, *The Prime minister – the office and its holders since 1945,* Allen Lane The Penguin Press, 2000, p. 143.

Test No. 543/41

## ENGLAND v WEST INDIES 1963 (1st Test)

Played at Old Trafford, Manchester, on 6, 7, 8, 10 June.
Toss: West Indies. Result: WEST INDIES won by ten wickets.
Debuts: England – J.H. Edrich; West Indies – M.C. Carew, D.L. Murray.

West Indies gained their first victory in a Test at Old Trafford. Following their 5-0 defeat of India in 1961-62, this win gave West Indies six consecutive Test victories for the first time. Hunte's 182 not out was then the highest score against England at Manchester. For the first time in England three players from the same county, Stewart, Edrich and Barrington of Surrey, occupied the first three places in England's batting order.

### WEST INDIES

| | | | | |
|---|---|---|---|---|
| C.C. Hunte | c Titmus b Allen | 182 | not out | 1 |
| M.C. Carew | c Andrew b Trueman | 16 | not out | 0 |
| R.B. Kanhai | run out | 90 | | |
| B.F. Butcher | lbw b Trueman | 22 | | |
| G. St A. Sobers | c Edrich b Allen | 64 | | |
| J.S. Solomon | lbw b Titmus | 35 | | |
| F.M.M. Worrell* | not out | 74 | | |
| D.L. Murray† | not out | 7 | | |
| W.W. Hall | ) | | | |
| C.C. Griffith | ) did not bat | | | |
| L.R. Gibbs | ) | | | |
| Extras | (B 3, LB 7, NB 1) | 11 | | |
| **Total** | (6 wickets declared) | **501** | (0 wickets) | **1** |

### ENGLAND

| | | | | |
|---|---|---|---|---|
| M.J. Stewart | c Murray b Gibbs | 37 | c Murray b Gibbs | 87 |
| J.H. Edrich | c Murray b Hall | 20 | c Hunte b Worrell | 38 |
| K.F. Barrington | c Murray b Hall | 16 | (4) b Gibbs | 8 |
| M.C. Cowdrey | b Hall | 4 | (5) c Hunte b Gibbs | 12 |
| E.R. Dexter* | c Worrell b Sobers | 73 | (6) c Murray b Gibbs | 35 |
| D.B. Close | c Hunte b Gibbs | 30 | (7) c Sobers b Gibbs | 32 |
| F.J. Titmus | c Sobers b Gibbs | 0 | (8) b Sobers | 17 |
| D.A. Allen | c Sobers b Gibbs | 5 | (9) b Gibbs | 1 |
| F.S. Trueman | c Worrell b Sobers | 5 | (10) not out | 29 |
| K.V. Andrew† | not out | 3 | (3) c Murray b Sobers | 15 |
| J.B. Statham | b Gibbs | 0 | b Griffith | 7 |
| Extras | (B 2, LB 7, NB 3) | 12 | (B 10, LB 4, NB 1) | 15 |
| **Total** | | **205** | | **296** |

| ENGLAND | O | M | R | W | O | M | R | W |
|---|---|---|---|---|---|---|---|---|
| Trueman | 40 | 7 | 95 | 2 | | | | |
| Statham | 37 | 6 | 121 | 0 | | | | |
| Titmus | 40 | 13 | 105 | 1 | | | | |
| Close | 10 | 2 | 31 | 0 | | | | |
| Allen | 57 | 22 | 122 | 2 | 0·1 | 0 | 1 | 0 |
| Dexter | 12 | 4 | 16 | 0 | | | | |
| WEST INDIES | | | | | | | | |
| Hall | 17 | 4 | 51 | 3 | 14 | 0 | 39 | 0 |
| Griffith | 21 | 4 | 37 | 0 | 8·5 | 4 | 11 | 1 |
| Gibbs | 29·3 | 9 | 59 | 5 | 46 | 16 | 98 | 6 |
| Sobers | 22 | 11 | 34 | 2 | 37 | 4 | 122 | 2 |
| Worrell | 1 | 0 | 12 | 0 | 4 | 2 | 11 | 1 |

### FALL OF WICKETS

| Wkt | WI 1st | E 1st | E 2nd | WI 2nd |
|---|---|---|---|---|
| 1st | 37 | 34 | 93 | – |
| 2nd | 188 | 61 | 131 | – |
| 3rd | 239 | 67 | 160 | – |
| 4th | 359 | 108 | 165 | – |
| 5th | 398 | 181 | 186 | – |
| 6th | 479 | 190 | 231 | – |
| 7th | – | 192 | 254 | – |
| 8th | – | 202 | 256 | – |
| 9th | – | 202 | 268 | – |
| 10th | – | 205 | 296 | – |

Umpires: C.S. Elliott and J.G. Langridge.

Test No. 544/42

# ENGLAND v WEST INDIES 1963 (2nd Test)

Played at Lord's, London, on 20, 21, 22, 24, 25 June.
Toss: West Indies.   Result: MATCH DRAWN.
Debuts: Nil.

This was one of the most dramatic of cricket matches with any of the four results possible as the last ball was being bowled. England needed six runs to win with their last pair together as Allen played Hall's final ball defensively to draw the match. His partner, Cowdrey, had his fractured left arm in plaster and intended to bat left-handed, but using only his right arm, had he been called upon to face the bowling. Hall bowled throughout the 200 minutes of play possible after rain had delayed the start of the last day. Shackleton ended West Indies' first innings by taking three wickets in four balls.

## WEST INDIES

| | | | | |
|---|---|---|---|---|
| C.C. Hunte | c Close b Trueman | 44 | c Cowdrey b Shackleton | 7 |
| E.D.A. St J. McMorris | lbw b Trueman | 16 | c Cowdrey b Trueman | 8 |
| G. St A. Sobers | c Cowdrey b Allen | 42 | (5) c Parks b Trueman | 8 |
| R.B. Kanhai | c Edrich b Trueman | 73 | (3) c Cowdrey b Shackleton | 21 |
| B.F. Butcher | c Barrington b Trueman | 14 | (4) lbw b Shackleton | 133 |
| J.S. Solomon | lbw b Shackleton | 56 | c Stewart b Allen | 5 |
| F.M.M. Worrell* | b Trueman | 0 | c Stewart b Trueman | 33 |
| D.L. Murray† | c Cowdrey b Trueman | 20 | c Parks b Trueman | 2 |
| W.W. Hall | not out | 25 | c Parks b Trueman | 2 |
| C.C. Griffith | c Cowdrey b Shackleton | 0 | b Shackleton | 1 |
| L.R. Gibbs | c Stewart b Shackleton | 0 | not out | 1 |
| Extras | (B 10, LB 1) | 11 | (B 5, LB 2, NB 1) | 8 |
| **Total** | | **301** | | **229** |

## ENGLAND

| | | | | |
|---|---|---|---|---|
| M.J. Stewart | c Kanhai b Griffith | 2 | c Solomon b Hall | 17 |
| J.H. Edrich | c Murray b Griffith | 0 | c Murray b Hall | 8 |
| E.R. Dexter* | lbw b Sobers | 70 | b Gibbs | 2 |
| K.F. Barrington | c Sobers b Worrell | 80 | c Murray b Griffith | 60 |
| M.C. Cowdrey | b Gibbs | 4 | not out | 19 |
| D.B. Close | c Murray b Griffith | 9 | c Murray b Griffith | 70 |
| J.M. Parks† | b Worrell | 35 | lbw b Griffith | 17 |
| F.J. Titmus | not out | 52 | c McMorris b Hall | 11 |
| F.S. Trueman | b Hall | 10 | c Murray b Hall | 0 |
| D.A. Allen | lbw b Griffith | 2 | not out | 4 |
| D. Shackleton | b Griffith | 8 | run out | 4 |
| Extras | (B 8, LB 8, NB 9) | 25 | (B 5, LB 8, NB 3) | 16 |
| **Total** | | **297** | (9 wickets) | **228** |

| ENGLAND | O | M | R | W | O | M | R | W | | FALL OF WICKETS | | | |
|---|---|---|---|---|---|---|---|---|---|---|---|---|---|
| Trueman | 44 | 16 | 100 | 6 | 26 | 9 | 52 | 5 | | WI | E | WI | E |
| Shackleton | 50.2 | 22 | 93 | 3 | 34 | 14 | 72 | 4 | Wkt | 1st | 1st | 2nd | 2nd |
| Dexter | 20 | 6 | 41 | 0 | | | | | 1st | 51 | 2 | 15 | 15 |
| Close | 9 | 3 | 21 | 0 | | | | | 2nd | 64 | 20 | 15 | 27 |
| Allen | 10 | 3 | 35 | 1 | 21 | 7 | 50 | 1 | 3rd | 127 | 102 | 64 | 31 |
| Titmus | | | | | 17 | 3 | 47 | 0 | 4th | 145 | 115 | 84 | 130 |
| | | | | | | | | | 5th | 219 | 151 | 104 | 158 |
| WEST INDIES | | | | | | | | | 6th | 219 | 206 | 214 | 203 |
| Hall | 18 | 2 | 65 | 1 | 40 | 9 | 93 | 4 | 7th | 263 | 235 | 224 | 203 |
| Griffith | 26 | 6 | 91 | 5 | 30 | 7 | 59 | 3 | 8th | 297 | 271 | 226 | 219 |
| Sobers | 18 | 4 | 45 | 1 | 4 | 1 | 4 | 0 | 9th | 297 | 274 | 228 | 228 |
| Gibbs | 27 | 9 | 59 | 1 | 17 | 7 | 56 | 1 | 10th | 301 | 297 | 229 | – |
| Worrell | 13 | 6 | 12 | 2 | | | | | | | | | |

Umpires: J.S. Buller and W.E. Phillipson.

Test No. 545/43

# ENGLAND v WEST INDIES 1963 (3rd Test)

Played at Edgbaston, Birmingham, on 4, 5, 6, 8, 9 July.
Toss: England.  Result: ENGLAND won by 217 runs.
Debuts: England – P.J. Sharpe.

Rain curtailed play on each of the first three days. England's victory maintained their unbeaten run at Edgbaston. Trueman's match analysis of 12 for 119 remains the best by any bowler in a Birmingham Test. His last six wickets were taken in a 24-ball spell which cost him just one scoring stroke for four runs by Gibbs.

### ENGLAND

| | | | | |
|---|---|---|---|---|
| P.E. Richardson | b Hall | 2 | c Murray b Griffith | 14 |
| M.J. Stewart | lbw b Sobers | 39 | c Murray b Griffith | 27 |
| E.R. Dexter* | b Sobers | 29 | (5) st Murray b Gibbs | 57 |
| K.F. Barrington | b Sobers | 9 | (3) b Sobers | 1 |
| D.B. Close | lbw b Sobers | 55 | (4) c Sobers b Griffith | 13 |
| P.J. Sharpe | c Kanhai b Gibbs | 23 | not out | 85 |
| J.M. Parks† | c Murray b Sobers | 12 | c Sobers b Gibbs | 5 |
| F.J. Titmus | c Griffith b Hall | 27 | b Gibbs | 0 |
| F.S. Trueman | b Griffith | 4 | c Gibbs b Sobers | 1 |
| G.A.R. Lock | b Griffith | 1 | b Gibbs | 56 |
| D. Shackleton | not out | 6 | | |
| Extras | (LB 6, NB 3) | 9 | (B 9, LB 9, NB 1) | 19 |
| **Total** | | **216** | (9 wickets declared) | **278** |

### WEST INDIES

| | | | | |
|---|---|---|---|---|
| C.C. Hunte | b Trueman | 18 | c Barrington b Trueman | 5 |
| M.C. Carew | c and b Trueman | 40 | lbw b Shackleton | 1 |
| R.B. Kanhai | c Lock b Shackleton | 32 | c Lock b Trueman | 38 |
| B.F. Butcher | lbw b Dexter | 15 | b Dexter | 14 |
| J.S. Solomon | lbw b Dexter | 0 | (6) c Parks b Trueman | 14 |
| G. St A. Sobers | b Trueman | 19 | (5) c Sharpe b Shackleton | 9 |
| F.M.M. Worrell* | b Dexter | 1 | c Parks b Trueman | 0 |
| D.L. Murray† | not out | 20 | c Parks b Trueman | 3 |
| W.W. Hall | c Sharpe b Dexter | 28 | b Trueman | 0 |
| C.C. Griffith | lbw b Trueman | 5 | lbw b Trueman | 0 |
| L.R. Gibbs | b Trueman | 0 | not out | 4 |
| Extras | (LB 7, W 1) | 8 | (LB 2, W 1) | 3 |
| **Total** | | **186** | | **91** |

| WEST INDIES | O | M | R | W | O | M | R | W |
|---|---|---|---|---|---|---|---|---|
| Hall | 16.4 | 2 | 56 | 2 | 16 | 1 | 47 | 0 |
| Griffith | 21 | 5 | 48 | 2 | 28 | 7 | 55 | 3 |
| Sobers | 31 | 10 | 60 | 5 | 27 | 4 | 80 | 2 |
| Worrell | 14 | 5 | 15 | 0 | 8 | 3 | 28 | 0 |
| Gibbs | 16 | 7 | 28 | 1 | 26.2 | 4 | 49 | 4 |
| **ENGLAND** | | | | | | | | |
| Trueman | 26 | 5 | 75 | 5 | 14.3 | 2 | 44 | 7 |
| Shackleton | 21 | 9 | 60 | 1 | 17 | 4 | 37 | 2 |
| Lock | 2 | 1 | 5 | 0 | | | | |
| Dexter | 20 | 5 | 38 | 4 | 3 | 1 | 7 | 1 |

### FALL OF WICKETS

| Wkt | E 1st | WI 1st | E 2nd | WI 2nd |
|---|---|---|---|---|
| 1st | 2 | 42 | 30 | 2 |
| 2nd | 50 | 79 | 31 | 10 |
| 3rd | 72 | 108 | 60 | 38 |
| 4th | 89 | 109 | 69 | 64 |
| 5th | 129 | 128 | 170 | 78 |
| 6th | 172 | 130 | 184 | 80 |
| 7th | 187 | 130 | 184 | 86 |
| 8th | 194 | 178 | 189 | 86 |
| 9th | 200 | 186 | 278 | 86 |
| 10th | 216 | 186 | – | 91 |

Umpires: C.S. Elliott and L.H. Gray.

Test No. 546/44

# ENGLAND v WEST INDIES 1963 (4th Test)

Played at Headingley, Leeds, on 25, 26, 27, 29 July.
Toss: West Indies. Result: WEST INDIES won by 221 runs.
Debuts: England – J.B. Bolus.

West Indies gained their first Test victory at Headingley at 2.30 p.m. on the fourth day.

## WEST INDIES

| Batsman | 1st innings | | 2nd innings | |
|---|---|---|---|---|
| C.C. Hunte | c Parks b Trueman | 22 | b Trueman | 4 |
| E.D.A. St J. McMorris | c Barrington b Shackleton | 11 | lbw b Trueman | 1 |
| R.B. Kanhai | b Lock | 92 | lbw b Shackleton | 44 |
| B.F. Butcher | c Parks b Dexter | 23 | c Dexter b Shackleton | 78 |
| G. St A. Sobers | c and b Lock | 102 | c Sharpe b Titmus | 52 |
| J.S. Solomon | c Stewart b Trueman | 62 | c Titmus b Shackleton | 16 |
| D.L. Murray† | lbw b Titmus | 34 | (8) c Lock b Titmus | 2 |
| F.M.M. Worrell* | c Close b Lock | 25 | (7) c Parks b Titmus | 0 |
| W.W. Hall | c Shackleton b Trueman | 15 | c Trueman b Titmus | 7 |
| C.C. Griffith | c Stewart b Trueman | 1 | not out | 12 |
| L.R. Gibbs | not out | 0 | c Sharpe b Lock | 6 |
| Extras | (B 4, LB 5, W 1) | 10 | (LB 7) | 7 |
| **Total** | | **397** | | **229** |

## ENGLAND

| Batsman | 1st innings | | 2nd innings | |
|---|---|---|---|---|
| M.J. Stewart | c Gibbs b Griffith | 2 | b Sobers | 0 |
| J.B. Bolus | c Hunte b Hall | 14 | c Gibbs b Sobers | 43 |
| E.R. Dexter* | b Griffith | 8 | lbw b Griffith | 10 |
| K.F. Barrington | c Worrell b Gibbs | 25 | lbw b Sobers | 32 |
| D.B. Close | b Griffith | 0 | c Solomon b Griffith | 56 |
| P.J. Sharpe | c Kanhai b Griffith | 0 | c Kanhai b Gibbs | 13 |
| J.M. Parks† | c Gibbs b Griffith | 22 | lbw b Gibbs | 57 |
| F.J. Titmus | lbw b Gibbs | 33 | st Murray b Gibbs | 5 |
| F.S. Trueman | c Hall b Gibbs | 4 | c Griffith b Gibbs | 5 |
| G.A.R. Lock | b Griffith | 53 | c Murray b Griffith | 1 |
| D. Shackleton | not out | 1 | not out | 1 |
| Extras | (B 4, LB 6, NB 2) | 12 | (B 3, LB 5) | 8 |
| **Total** | | **174** | | **231** |

| ENGLAND | O | M | R | W | O | M | R | W |
|---|---|---|---|---|---|---|---|---|
| Trueman | 46 | 10 | 117 | 4 | 13 | 1 | 46 | 2 |
| Shackleton | 42 | 10 | 88 | 1 | 26 | 2 | 63 | 3 |
| Dexter | 23 | 4 | 68 | 1 | 2 | 0 | 15 | 0 |
| Titmus | 25 | 5 | 60 | 1 | 19 | 2 | 44 | 4 |
| Lock | 28·4 | 9 | 54 | 3 | 7·1 | 0 | 54 | 1 |
| WEST INDIES | | | | | | | | |
| Hall | 13 | 2 | 61 | 1 | 5 | 1 | 12 | 0 |
| Griffith | 21 | 5 | 36 | 6 | 18 | 5 | 45 | 3 |
| Gibbs | 14 | 2 | 50 | 3 | 37·4 | 12 | 76 | 4 |
| Sobers | 6 | 1 | 15 | 0 | 32 | 5 | 90 | 3 |

### FALL OF WICKETS

| Wkt | WI 1st | E 1st | WI 2nd | E 2nd |
|---|---|---|---|---|
| 1st | 28 | 13 | 1 | 0 |
| 2nd | 42 | 19 | 20 | 23 |
| 3rd | 71 | 32 | 85 | 82 |
| 4th | 214 | 32 | 181 | 95 |
| 5th | 287 | 34 | 186 | 130 |
| 6th | 348 | 69 | 188 | 199 |
| 7th | 355 | 87 | 196 | 221 |
| 8th | 379 | 93 | 206 | 224 |
| 9th | 389 | 172 | 212 | 225 |
| 10th | 397 | 174 | 229 | 231 |

Umpires: W.E. Phillipson and J.G. Langridge.

Test No. 547/45

# ENGLAND v WEST INDIES 1963 (5th Test)

Played at Kennington Oval, London, 22, 23, 24, 26 August.
Toss: England.   Result: WEST INDIES won by eight wickets.
Debuts: Nil.

West Indies won the Wisden Trophy by three Tests to one. Although a bruised ankle bone limited his second-innings spell to one over, Trueman set a new record for this series by taking 34 wickets. Murray made 24 dismissals in his first Test rubber. Close kept wicket on the second morning.

## ENGLAND

| | | | | |
|---|---|---|---|---|
| J.B. Bolus | c Murray b Sobers | 33 | c Gibbs b Sobers | 15 |
| J.H. Edrich | c Murray b Sobers | 25 | c Murray b Griffith | 12 |
| E.R. Dexter* | c and b Griffith | 29 | c Murray b Sobers | 27 |
| K.F. Barrington | c Sobers b Gibbs | 16 | b Griffith | 28 |
| D.B. Close | b Griffith | 46 | lbw b Sobers | 4 |
| P.J. Sharpe | c Murray b Griffith | 63 | c Murray b Hall | 83 |
| J.M. Parks† | c Kanhai b Griffith | 19 | lbw b Griffith | 23 |
| F.S. Trueman | b Griffith | 19 | c Sobers b Hall | 5 |
| G.A.R. Lock | hit wkt b Griffith | 4 | b Hall | 0 |
| J.B. Statham | b Hall | 8 | b Hall | 14 |
| D. Shackleton | not out | 0 | not out | 0 |
| Extras | (B 4, LB 2, NB 7) | 13 | (B 5, LB 3, NB 4) | 12 |
| **Total** | | **275** | | **223** |

## WEST INDIES

| | | | | |
|---|---|---|---|---|
| C.C. Hunte | c Parks b Shackleton | 80 | not out | 108 |
| W.V. Rodriguez | c Lock b Statham | 5 | c Lock b Dexter | 28 |
| R.B. Kanhai | b Lock | 30 | c Bolus b Lock | 77 |
| B.F. Butcher | run out | 53 | not out | 31 |
| G. St A. Sobers | run out | 26 | | |
| J.S. Solomon | c Trueman b Statham | 16 | | |
| F.M.M. Worrell* | b Statham | 9 | | |
| D.L. Murray† | c Lock b Trueman | 5 | | |
| W.W. Hall | b Trueman | 2 | | |
| C.C. Griffith | not out | 13 | | |
| L.R. Gibbs | b Trueman | 4 | | |
| Extras | (LB 3) | 3 | (B 4, LB 7) | 11 |
| **Total** | | **246** | (2 wickets) | **255** |

| WEST INDIES | O | M | R | W | O | M | R | W | | FALL OF WICKETS | | | |
|---|---|---|---|---|---|---|---|---|---|---|---|---|---|
| Hall | 22.2 | 2 | 71 | 1 | 16 | 3 | 39 | 4 | | E | WI | E | WI |
| Griffith | 27 | 4 | 71 | 6 | 23 | 7 | 66 | 3 | Wkt | 1st | 1st | 2nd | 2nd |
| Sobers | 21 | 4 | 44 | 2 | 33 | 6 | 77 | 3 | 1st | 59 | 10 | 29 | 78 |
| Gibbs | 27 | 7 | 50 | 1 | 9 | 1 | 29 | 0 | 2nd | 64 | 72 | 31 | 191 |
| Worrell | 5 | 0 | 26 | 0 | | | | | 3rd | 103 | 152 | 64 | – |
| | | | | | | | | | 4th | 115 | 185 | 69 | – |
| ENGLAND | | | | | | | | | 5th | 216 | 198 | 121 | – |
| Trueman | 26.1 | 2 | 65 | 3 | 1 | 1 | 0 | 0 | 6th | 224 | 214 | 173 | – |
| Statham | 22 | 3 | 68 | 3 | 22 | 2 | 54 | 0 | 7th | 254 | 221 | 196 | – |
| Shackleton | 21 | 5 | 37 | 1 | 32 | 7 | 68 | 0 | 8th | 258 | 225 | 196 | – |
| Lock | 29 | 6 | 65 | 1 | 25 | 8 | 52 | 1 | 9th | 275 | 233 | 218 | – |
| Dexter | 6 | 1 | 8 | 0 | 9 | 1 | 34 | 1 | 10th | 275 | 246 | 223 | – |
| Close | | | | | 6 | 0 | 36 | 0 | | | | | |

Umpires: J.S. Buller and A.E.G. Rhodes.

Chapter 18
# INDIA 1963/64

Cowdrey's injury not only put him out of the rest of the series but he had not recovered enough by October to lead the touring party to India, which he had previously been invited to do. Dexter was unavailable so M J K Smith was invited to lead. The touring side was ravaged by injuries. Barrington broke a finger and returned home. It was in such circumstances that Cowdrey joined the party after the team for the second Test had picked itself. He had not held a bat for seven months but after two long nets he returned to the fray for the third test.

The third at Eden Gardens, Calcutta was drawn. India batted first and scored 241 and it was Cowdrey with 107 who secured a modest first innings lead of 26. He was undefeated with 13 in the second innings with England 145 for 2 when time ran out.

The fourth at Feroz Shah Kotla, Delhi was drawn. India batted first and Hanumant Singh scored 105 out of 344 in his first Test innings. Again Cowdrey dominated England's reply with 151 out of 451. In India's second innings, which was still unfinished on 463 for 4 when the match ended, the Indian captain, Nawab of Pataudi Jnr, was undefeated with 203.

The fifth test at Green Park, Kanpur was, like all the others in the series, drawn. Pataudi had won the toss each time. This time Knight and Parfitt scored centuries in England's 559 for 8 declared Cowdrey contributing 38. The match was devoid of interest in its closing stages marked by the fact that wicket keeper Parks and Cowdrey were the ninth and tenth bowlers used by Smith the England captain. This rare combination allowed Durani, who had batted number eight in India's first innings of 266, to score his first fifty in 29 minutes – only one minute slower than the fastest. Nadkarni, who had been undefeated with 52 at number nine in the first innings, came in at number three and was undefeated with 122 when the match ended. For the record Parks took 1 for 43 in his six overs; Cowdrey was wicketless and conceded 34 runs in his five overs. India were 347 for 3 when the match and series ended.

|  | Matches | Innings | Not out | Runs | Highest score | Average | 100s | 50s | Caught |
|---|---|---|---|---|---|---|---|---|---|
| This series | 3 | 4 | 1 | 309 | 151 | 103.00 | 2 | 0 | 4 |
| Previous series | 67 | 111 | 8 | 4545 | 182 | 44.13 | 13 | 24 | 82 |
| Cumulative totals | 70 | 115 | 9 | 4854 | 182 | 45.79 | 15 | 24 | 86 |

Test No. 553/30

# INDIA v ENGLAND 1963–64 (1st Test)

Played at Corporation Stadium, Madras, on 10, 11, 12, 14, 15 January.
Toss: India.   Result: MATCH DRAWN.
Debuts: England – D. Wilson.

England, set to score 29 runs in 265 minutes on a dusting pitch and with several players suffering from stomach indispositions, did well to finish 52 runs short of victory and with five wickets intact. Kunderan scored 170 not out off 91 overs in 330 minutes on the first day and went on to record India's highest score against England (subsequently beaten in this rubber). Nadkarni bowled 21 consecutive maiden overs to establish the record for all first-class cricket. His spell of 131 balls without conceding a run has been beaten only by H.J. Tayfield (137 balls, 16 eight-ball maidens) in Test No. 436.

### INDIA

| | | | | |
|---|---|---|---|---|
| V.L. Mehra | c Parks b Titmus | 17 | run out | 26 |
| B.K. Kunderan† | b Titmus | 192 | lbw b Titmus | 38 |
| D.N. Sardesai | b Titmus | 65 | (4) st Parks b Mortimore | 2 |
| V.L. Manjrekar | c Smith b Knight | 108 | (7) run out | 0 |
| Nawab of Pataudi, jr* | lbw b Titmus | 0 | (6) c Bolus b Titmus | 18 |
| S.A. Durani | lbw b Titmus | 8 | (5) c Parks b Mortimore | 3 |
| M.L. Jaisimha | lbw b Wilson | 51 | (3) b Titmus | 35 |
| A.G. Kripal Singh | not out | 2 | b Wilson | 10 |
| C.G. Borde | not out | 8 | not out | 11 |
| R.G. Nadkarni | ) did not bat | | c Parks b Titmus | 7 |
| V.B. Ranjane | ) | | | |
| Extras | (B 1, LB 5) | 6 | (LB 2) | 2 |
| Total | (7 wickets declared) | 457 | (9 wickets declared) | 152 |

### ENGLAND

| | | | | |
|---|---|---|---|---|
| J.B. Bolus | lbw b Durani | 88 | st Kunderan b Borde | 22 |
| M.J.K. Smith* | c Kunderan b Ranjane | 3 | c Kunderan b Nadkarni | 57 |
| P.J. Sharpe | lbw b Borde | 27 | (7) not out | 31 |
| D. Wilson | c Manjrekar b Durani | 42 | | |
| K.F. Barrington | c and b Borde | 80 | | |
| B.R. Knight | b Durani | 6 | (4) c Kunderan b Kripal Singh | 7 |
| J.M. Parks† | b Borde | 27 | (3) c Kunderan b Nadkarni | 30 |
| F.J. Titmus | c Pataudi b Kripal Singh | 14 | (6) b Kripal Singh | 10 |
| J.B. Mortimore | c and b Borde | 0 | (5) not out | 73 |
| M.J. Stewart | st Kunderan b Borde | 15 | | |
| J.D.F. Larter | not out | 2 | | |
| Extras | (B 6, LB 5, NB 2) | 13 | (B 6, LB 2, NB 3) | 11 |
| Total | | 317 | (5 wickets) | 241 |

| ENGLAND | O | M | R | W | O | M | R | W | FALL OF WICKETS | | | | |
|---|---|---|---|---|---|---|---|---|---|---|---|---|---|
| Larter | 19 | 2 | 62 | 0 | 11 | 3 | 33 | 0 | | I | E | I | E |
| Knight | 27 | 7 | 73 | 1 | 7 | 1 | 22 | 0 | Wkt | 1st | 1st | 2nd | 2nd |
| Wilson | 24 | 6 | 67 | 1 | 4 | 2 | 2 | 1 | 1st | 85 | 12 | 59 | 67 |
| Titmus | 50 | 14 | 116 | 5 | 19·5 | 4 | 46 | 4 | 2nd | 228 | 49 | 77 | 105 |
| Mortimore | 38 | 7 | 110 | 0 | 15 | 3 | 41 | 2 | 3rd | 323 | 116 | 82 | 120 |
| Barrington | 4 | 0 | 23 | 0 | 2 | 0 | 6 | 0 | 4th | 323 | 235 | 100 | 123 |
| INDIA | | | | | | | | | 5th | 343 | 251 | 104 | 155 |
| | | | | | | | | | 6th | 431 | 263 | 106 | – |
| Ranjane | 16 | 2 | 46 | 1 | 2 | 0 | 14 | 0 | 7th | 447 | 287 | 125 | – |
| Jaisimha | 7 | 3 | 16 | 0 | 4 | 2 | 8 | 0 | 8th | – | 287 | 135 | – |
| Borde | 67·4 | 30 | 88 | 5 | 22 | 7 | 44 | 1 | 9th | – | 314 | 152 | – |
| Durani | 43 | 13 | 97 | 3 | 21 | 8 | 64 | 0 | 10th | – | 317 | – | – |
| Nadkarni | 32 | 27 | 5 | 0 | 6 | 4 | 6 | 2 | | | | | |
| Kripal Singh | 25 | 10 | 52 | 1 | 26 | 7 | 66 | 2 | | | | | |
| Manjrekar | | | | | 3 | 0 | 3 | 0 | | | | | |
| Mehra | | | | | 1 | 0 | 2 | 0 | | | | | |
| Sardesai | | | | | 1 | 0 | 14 | 0 | | | | | |
| Pataudi | | | | | 1 | 0 | 9 | 0 | | | | | |

Umpires: I. Gopalakrishnan and S.K. Banerjee.

Test No. 554/31

# INDIA v ENGLAND 1963–64 (2nd Test)

Played at Brabourne Stadium, Bombay, on 21, 22, 23, 25, 26 January.
Toss: India.   Result: MATCH DRAWN.
Debuts: India – B.S. Chandrasekhar, Rajinder Pal; England – J.G. Binks, I.J. Jones, J.S.E. Price.

A superb performance by England earned the touring team a draw after they had been deprived of the services of Barrington (fractured finger), Edrich, Sharpe and Mortimore (stomach disorders). Barrington and Stewart (who retired from the match with dysentery at tea on the first day) took no further part in the tour. England's ten-man team comprised two specialist batsmen, two wicket-keepers, four fast-medium bowlers and two spinners. The partnership of 153 by Borde and Durani remains the highest for the seventh wicket by either side in this series.

### INDIA

| | | | | |
|---|---|---|---|---|
| V.L. Mehra | lbw b Knight | 9 | lbw b Titmus | 35 |
| B.K. Kunderan† | c Wilson b Price | 29 | c Titmus b Price | 16 |
| D.N. Sardesai | b Price | 12 | run out | 66 |
| V.L. Manjrekar | c Binks b Titmus | 0 | (8) not out | 43 |
| Nawab of Pataudi, jr* | c Titmus b Knight | 10 | (4) b Price | 0 |
| M.L. Jaisimha | c Price b Titmus | 23 | (5) c Larter b Knight | 66 |
| C.G. Borde | c Binks b Wilson | 84 | c Smith b Titmus | 7 |
| S.A. Durani | c Binks b Price | 90 | (6) c Knight b Titmus | 3 |
| R.G. Nadkarni | not out | 26 | lbw b Knight | 0 |
| Rajinder Pal | lbw b Larter | 3 | not out | 3 |
| B.S. Chandrasekhar | b Larter | 0 | | |
| Extras | (B 2, LB 9, NB 3) | 14 | (LB 4, W 1, NB 5) | 10 |
| Total | | 300 | (8 wickets declared) | 249 |

### ENGLAND

| | | | | |
|---|---|---|---|---|
| J.B. Bolus | c Chandrasekhar b Durani | 25 | c Pataudi b Durani | 57 |
| M.J.K. Smith* | c Borde b Chandrasekhar | 46 | (4) not out | 31 |
| J.M. Parks | run out | 1 | (5) not out | 40 |
| B.R. Knight | b Chandrasekhar | 12 | | |
| F.J. Titmus | not out | 84 | | |
| D. Wilson | c and b Durani | 1 | (3) c Pataudi b Chandrasekhar | 2 |
| J.G. Binks† | b Chandrasekhar | 10 | (2) c Borde b Jaisimha | 55 |
| J.S.E. Price | b Chandrasekhar | 32 | | |
| J.D.F. Larter | c Borde b Durani | 0 | | |
| I.J. Jones | run out | 5 | | |
| M.J. Stewart | absent ill | – | | |
| Extras | (B 4, LB 7, NB 6) | 17 | (B 12, LB 7, W 1, NB 1) | 21 |
| Total | | 233 | (3 wickets) | 206 |

| ENGLAND | O | M | R | W | O | M | R | W | | FALL OF WICKETS | | | |
|---|---|---|---|---|---|---|---|---|---|---|---|---|---|
| Knight | 20 | 3 | 53 | 2 | 13 | 2 | 28 | 2 | | I | E | I | E |
| Larter | 10·3 | 2 | 35 | 2 | 5 | 0 | 13 | 0 | Wkt | 1st | 1st | 2nd | 2nd |
| Jones | 13 | 0 | 48 | 0 | 11 | 1 | 31 | 0 | 1st | 20 | 42 | 23 | 125 |
| Price | 19 | 2 | 66 | 3 | 17 | 1 | 47 | 2 | 2nd | 55 | 48 | 104 | 127 |
| Titmus | 36 | 17 | 56 | 2 | 46 | 18 | 79 | 3 | 3rd | 56 | 82 | 107 | 134 |
| Wilson | 15 | 5 | 28 | 1 | 23 | 10 | 41 | 0 | 4th | 58 | 91 | 140 | – |
| | | | | | | | | | 5th | 75 | 98 | 152 | – |
| INDIA | | | | | | | | | 6th | 99 | 116 | 180 | – |
| Rajinder Pal | 11 | 4 | 19 | 0 | 2 | 0 | 3 | 0 | 7th | 252 | 184 | 231 | – |
| Jaisimha | 3 | 1 | 9 | 0 | 22 | 9 | 36 | 1 | 8th | 284 | 185 | 231 | – |
| Durani | 38 | 15 | 59 | 3 | 29 | 12 | 35 | 1 | 9th | 300 | 233 | – | – |
| Borde | 34 | 12 | 54 | 0 | 37 | 12 | 38 | 0 | 10th | 300 | – | – | – |
| Chandrasekhar | 40 | 16 | 67 | 4 | 22 | 5 | 40 | 1 | | | | | |
| Nadkarni | 4 | 2 | 8 | 0 | 14 | 11 | 3 | 0 | | | | | |
| Sardesai | | | | | 3 | 2 | 6 | 0 | | | | | |
| Mehra | | | | | 2 | 1 | 1 | 0 | | | | | |
| Pataudi | | | | | 3 | 0 | 23 | 0 | | | | | |

Umpires: H.E. Choudhury and A.M. Mamsa.

Test No. 555/32

# INDIA v ENGLAND 1963–64 (3rd Test)

Played at Eden Gardens, Calcutta, on 29, 30 January, 1, 2, 3 February.
Toss: India. Result: MATCH DRAWN.
Debuts: Nil.

Reinforced by the arrival of Cowdrey and Parfitt, England achieved a first-innings lead of 26. India did not begin their second innings until the fourth day and the match never promised a definite result. 150 minutes of play was lost on the third day when the umpires decided that a shower of rain had rendered the ground unfit.

## INDIA

| | | | | |
|---|---|---|---|---|
| M.L. Jaisimha | c Binks b Price | 33 | c Larter b Titmus | 129 |
| B.K. Kunderan† | c Binks b Price | 23 | lbw b Wilson | 27 |
| D.N. Sardesai | c Binks b Larter | 54 | c and b Parfitt | 36 |
| V.L. Manjrekar | c and b Price | 25 | b Parfitt | 16 |
| R.F. Surti | b Price | 0 | | |
| C.G. Borde | c Cowdrey b Wilson | 21 | c Parks b Titmus | 8 |
| Nawab of Pataudi, jr* | c Binks b Wilson | 2 | (5) c Smith b Larter | 31 |
| S.A. Durani | c Binks b Price | 8 | (7) c Cowdrey b Larter | 25 |
| R.G. Nadkarni | not out | 43 | (8) not out | 10 |
| R.B. Desai | lbw b Titmus | 11 | (9) not out | 2 |
| B.S. Chandrasekhar | c Cowdrey b Knight | 16 | | |
| Extras | (LB 1, NB 4) | 5 | (B 7, LB 5, NB 4) | 16 |
| **Total** | | **241** | (7 wickets declared) | **300** |

## ENGLAND

| | | | | |
|---|---|---|---|---|
| J.B. Bolus | c and b Durani | 39 | c Jaisimha b Borde | 35 |
| J.G. Binks† | c Desai b Durani | 13 | b Durani | 13 |
| M.J.K. Smith* | c Jaisimha b Borde | 19 | not out | 75 |
| M.C. Cowdrey | c Pataudi b Desai | 107 | not out | 13 |
| J.M. Parks | lbw b Nadkarni | 30 | | |
| P.H. Parfitt | c and b Desai | 4 | | |
| D. Wilson | st Kunderan b Chandrasekhar | 1 | | |
| B.R. Knight | c Manjrekar b Nadkarni | 13 | | |
| F.J. Titmus | b Desai | 26 | | |
| J.S.E. Price | not out | 1 | | |
| J.D.F. Larter | c Manjrekar b Desai | 0 | | |
| Extras | (B 6, LB 5, NB 3) | 14 | (B 9) | 9 |
| **Total** | | **267** | (2 wickets) | **145** |

| ENGLAND | O | M | R | W | O | M | R | W |
|---|---|---|---|---|---|---|---|---|
| Knight | 13·2 | 5 | 39 | 1 | 4 | 0 | 33 | 0 |
| Price | 23 | 4 | 73 | 5 | 7 | 0 | 31 | 0 |
| Larter | 18 | 4 | 61 | 1 | 8 | 0 | 27 | 2 |
| Titmus | 15 | 4 | 46 | 1 | 46 | 23 | 67 | 2 |
| Wilson | 16 | 10 | 17 | 2 | 21 | 7 | 55 | 1 |
| Parfitt | | | | | 34 | 16 | 71 | 2 |
| INDIA | | | | | | | | |
| Desai | 22·5 | 3 | 62 | 4 | 5 | 0 | 12 | 0 |
| Surti | 6 | 2 | 8 | 0 | | | | |
| Jaisimha | 4 | 1 | 10 | 0 | 13 | 5 | 32 | 0 |
| Durani | 22 | 7 | 59 | 2 | 8 | 3 | 15 | 1 |
| Borde | 31 | 14 | 40 | 1 | 15 | 5 | 39 | 1 |
| Chandrasekhar | 21 | 5 | 36 | 1 | 8 | 2 | 20 | 0 |
| Nadkarni | 42 | 24 | 38 | 2 | | | | |
| Pataudi | | | | | 3 | 1 | 8 | 0 |
| Sardesai | | | | | 3 | 0 | 10 | 0 |

FALL OF WICKETS

| Wkt | I 1st | E 1st | I 2nd | E 2nd |
|---|---|---|---|---|
| 1st | 47 | 40 | 80 | 30 |
| 2nd | 61 | 74 | 161 | 87 |
| 3rd | 103 | 77 | 217 | – |
| 4th | 103 | 158 | 218 | – |
| 5th | 150 | 175 | 237 | – |
| 6th | 158 | 193 | 272 | – |
| 7th | 169 | 214 | 289 | – |
| 8th | 169 | 258 | – | – |
| 9th | 190 | 267 | – | – |
| 10th | 241 | 267 | – | – |

Umpires: S. Roy and M.V. Nagendra.

Test No. 556/33

# INDIA v ENGLAND 1963–64 (4th Test)

Played at Feroz Shah Kotla, Delhi, on 8, 9, 11, 12, 13 February.
Toss: India.   Result: MATCH DRAWN.
Debuts: India – Hanumant Singh.

Hanumant Singh became the third Indian after L. Amarnath and A.A. Baig to score a hundred against England in his first Test match; he remains the only one to do so in his first innings. Pataudi scored India's only double-century against England; his unbroken partnership of 190 with Borde remains India's highest for the fifth wicket against England and against all countries in India.

### INDIA

| | | | | |
|---|---|---|---|---|
| M.L. Jaisimha | b Titmus | 47 | st Parks b Parfitt | 50 |
| B.K. Kunderan† | b Titmus | 40 | lbw b Price | 100 |
| D.N. Sardesai | c Parks b Mortimore | 44 | b Wilson | 4 |
| Nawab of Pataudi, jr* | b Titmus | 13 | not out | 203 |
| Hanumant Singh | c and b Mortimore | 105 | c Mortimore b Wilson | 23 |
| C.G. Borde | b Price | 26 | not out | 67 |
| S.A. Durani | c Smith b Wilson | 16 | | |
| A.G. Kripal Singh | b Mortimore | 0 | | |
| R.G. Nadkarni | run out | 34 | | |
| R.B. Desai | not out | 14 | | |
| B.S. Chandrasekhar | run out | 0 | | |
| Extras | (LB 3, NB 2) | 5 | (B 5, LB 9, NB 2) | 16 |
| **Total** | | **344** | (4 wickets) | **463** |

### ENGLAND

| | | |
|---|---|---|
| J.B. Bolus | lbw b Kripal Singh | 58 |
| J.H. Edrich | c and b Kripal Singh | 41 |
| M.J.K. Smith* | c Pataudi b Kripal Singh | 37 |
| D. Wilson | c Pataudi b Chandrasekhar | 6 |
| P.H. Parfitt | c Kunderan b Durani | 67 |
| M.C. Cowdrey | lbw b Nadkarni | 151 |
| J.M. Parks† | c sub (P.C. Poddar) b Chandrasekhar | 32 |
| B.R. Knight | c Desai b Nadkarni | 21 |
| J.B. Mortimore | c Hanumant b Nadkarni | 21 |
| F.J. Titmus | not out | 4 |
| J.S.E. Price | b Chandrasekhar | 0 |
| Extras | (B 8, LB 3, NB 2) | 13 |
| **Total** | | **451** |

| ENGLAND | O | M | R | W | O | M | R | W |
|---|---|---|---|---|---|---|---|---|
| Price | 23 | 3 | 71 | 1 | 9 | 1 | 36 | 1 |
| Knight | 11 | 0 | 46 | 0 | 8 | 1 | 47 | 0 |
| Wilson | 22 | 9 | 41 | 1 | 41 | 17 | 74 | 2 |
| Titmus | 49 | 15 | 100 | 3 | 43 | 12 | 105 | 0 |
| Mortimore | 38 | 13 | 74 | 3 | 32 | 11 | 52 | 0 |
| Parfitt | 5 | 2 | 7 | 0 | 19 | 3 | 81 | 1 |
| Smith | | | | | 13 | 0 | 52 | 0 |

| INDIA | O | M | R | W |
|---|---|---|---|---|
| Desai | 9 | 2 | 23 | 0 |
| Jaisimha | 4 | 0 | 14 | 0 |
| Kripal Singh | 36 | 13 | 90 | 3 |
| Chandrasekhar | 34·3 | 11 | 79 | 3 |
| Borde | 12 | 2 | 42 | 0 |
| Durani | 33 | 5 | 93 | 1 |
| Nadkarni | 57 | 30 | 97 | 3 |

### FALL OF WICKETS

| | I | E | I |
|---|---|---|---|
| Wkt | 1st | 1st | 2nd |
| 1st | 81 | 101 | 74 |
| 2nd | 90 | 114 | 101 |
| 3rd | 116 | 134 | 226 |
| 4th | 201 | 153 | 273 |
| 5th | 267 | 268 | – |
| 6th | 283 | 354 | – |
| 7th | 283 | 397 | – |
| 8th | 307 | 438 | – |
| 9th | 344 | 451 | – |
| 10th | 344 | 451 | – |

Umpires: S. Pan and B. Satyaji Rao.

Test No. 557/34

# INDIA v ENGLAND 1963–64 (5th Test)

Played at Green Park, Kanpur, on 15, 16, 18, 19, 20 February.
Toss: India.   Result: MATCH DRAWN.
Debuts: Nil.

Pataudi won the toss for the fifth time in the rubber. England's total remains their highest in India. With the match devoid of interest, Durani reached his first fifty in 29 minutes against the bowling of Cowdrey and Parks. It was one minute slower than the fastest Test fifty which J.T. Brown scored for England against Australia in 1894-95 (*Test No. 46*). Kunderan (525) became the first wicket-keeper to score 500 runs in a Test rubber.

## ENGLAND

| | | |
|---|---|---|
| J.B. Bolus | c Hanumant b Nadkarni | 67 |
| J.H. Edrich | c Pataudi b Borde | 35 |
| M.J.K. Smith* | c Borde b Gupte | 38 |
| B.R. Knight | c Manjrekar b Jaisimha | 127 |
| P.H. Parfitt | lbw b Jaisimha | 121 |
| M.C. Cowdrey | lbw b Pataudi | 38 |
| J.M. Parks† | not out | 51 |
| J.B. Mortimore | b Chandrasekhar | 19 |
| F.J. Titmus | c and b Nadkarni | 5 |
| D. Wilson | not out | 18 |
| J.S.E. Price | did not bat | |
| Extras | (B 29, LB 9, NB 2) | 40 |
| **Total** | (8 wickets declared) | **559** |

## INDIA

| | | | | |
|---|---|---|---|---|
| M.L. Jaisimha | c Parks b Titmus | 5 | c Cowdrey b Titmus | 5 |
| B.K. Kunderan | b Price | 5 | lbw b Parfitt | 55 |
| V.L. Manjrekar | c and b Titmus | 33 | | |
| D.N. Sardesai | c Mortimore b Parfitt | 79 | c Edrich b Parks | 87 |
| Hanumant Singh | c Parks b Titmus | 24 | | |
| Nawab of Pataudi, jr* | b Titmus | 31 | | |
| C.G. Borde | b Titmus | 0 | | |
| S.A. Durani | b Mortimore | 16 | (5) not out | 61 |
| R.G. Nadkarni | not out | 52 | (3) not out | 122 |
| B.P. Gupte | c and b Titmus | 8 | | |
| B.S. Chandrasekhar | b Price | 3 | | |
| Extras | (B 5, LB 1, NB 4) | 10 | (B 5, LB 11, NB 1) | 17 |
| **Total** | | **266** | (3 wickets) | **347** |

| INDIA | O | M | R | W | O | M | R | W | | FALL OF WICKETS | | |
|---|---|---|---|---|---|---|---|---|---|---|---|---|
| Jaisimha | 19 | 4 | 54 | 2 | | | | | | E | I | I |
| Durani | 25 | 8 | 49 | 0 | | | | | Wkt | 1st | 1st | 2nd |
| Chandrasekhar | 36 | 7 | 97 | 1 | | | | | 1st | 63 | 9 | 17 |
| Gupte | 40 | 9 | 115 | 1 | | | | | 2nd | 134 | 17 | 126 |
| Borde | 23 | 4 | 73 | 1 | | | | | 3rd | 174 | 96 | 270 |
| Nadkarni | 57 | 22 | 121 | 2 | | | | | 4th | 365 | 135 | – |
| Pataudi | 3 | 1 | 10 | 1 | | | | | 5th | 458 | 182 | – |
| | | | | | | | | | 6th | 474 | 182 | – |
| ENGLAND | | | | | | | | | 7th | 520 | 188 | – |
| Price | 16·1 | 5 | 32 | 2 | 10 | 2 | 27 | 0 | 8th | 531 | 229 | – |
| Knight | 1 | 0 | 4 | 0 | 2 | 0 | 12 | 0 | 9th | – | 245 | – |
| Titmus | 60 | 37 | 73 | 6 | 34 | 12 | 59 | 1 | 10th | – | 266 | – |
| Mortimore | 48 | 31 | 39 | 1 | 23 | 14 | 28 | 0 | | | | |
| Wilson | 27 | 9 | 47 | 0 | 19 | 10 | 26 | 0 | | | | |
| Parfitt | 30 | 12 | 61 | 1 | 27 | 7 | 68 | 1 | | | | |
| Edrich | | | | | 4 | 1 | 17 | 0 | | | | |
| Bolus | | | | | 3 | 0 | 16 | 0 | | | | |
| Parks | | | | | 6 | 0 | 43 | 1 | | | | |
| Cowdrey | | | | | 5 | 0 | 34 | 0 | | | | |

Umpires: S. Bhattacharya and S.K. Raghunatha Rao.

Chapter 19

# AUSTRALIA 1964

Back home in England for the 1964 season the Australians were the test opponents.

Missing from the touring party were Benaud and Harvey. Benaud was to concentrate on his media activities and was in the commentary box. Harvey's maiden test century at Headingley in the remarkable match in 1948 was the first of many memories for England supporters. Before the first Test a good deal was made of the fact that if Cowdrey was doubtful as a slip fielder, Sharpe's inclusion was essential. No provision seemed to have been made if his injured finger should not mend. Four days before the test I talked to Cowdrey at Gravesend. He still seemed unhappy about the injury but to his mind, should he not be able play in the Test, all would be well, as Sharpe could take his place. A notable feature of the first test was when Titmus, opening the batting in the late withdrawal of Edrich, collided with the bowler when responding to a call for a quick single from Boycott in his first test. Grout, the Australian wicket-keeper, declined to break the wicket and so the improvised opening partnership continued. Benaud, in the commentary box, wholly approved of Grout's decision.

In the first two Tests Cowdrey only managed a top score of 33. In the second Edrich returned fit to score 120.

In the second Test the important thing seemed to me, as we waited for play to start on the fourth day, was Cowdrey's mood. If it were of grandeur England should be able to crack along in style towards a winning total. If, on the other hand, he was in one of his moods of docile humility and self-doubting, England's task would be very much harder. At Trent Bridge we had seen one mood in England's first innings and been given a sickeningly explicit demonstration of the other in the second. My father always said he could soon tell which mood Cowdrey would be in. Today there was to be no time to judge, for Cowdrey, having batted through a good maiden over from McKenzie at the pavilion end and modestly taken a single of Hawke, played a shot to the off that went sour on him, in Hawke's second over, and was caught with professional polish by Burge in the gully.

A back injury kept Cowdrey out of the third Test at Headingley which England lost by seven wickets.

Cowdrey was omitted from the side for the fourth Test at Old Trafford, as was Trueman. It was the first time since his Test career began that Cowdrey had been dropped. In this test Simpson, the Australian captain, continued batting on the third morning to score 311.

Back for the final Test at the Oval Cowdrey came in on a dark August morning and Dexter appealed against the light but even as the umpires conferred the murkiness seemed to brighten a little and the appeal was not allowed. Cowdrey, warmly welcomed on his quick return from exile, looked a disturbingly different batsman from the one who, since the fourth test, had scored so well for Kent and began what one writer said looked more like a struggle with his conscience than an innings. In the event Dexter began to assert himself driving both Corling and McKenzie for fours then hooking the latter to the boundary. Cowdrey could afford to take his time to settle down. He did make one aggressive stroke hitting Hawke straight at Vievers at forward short leg who, at the insistence of his captain, left the field to have the damage done to his right had examined. At luncheon England were 81 for two and Cowdrey in 40 minutes had but three singles to his name. The quick dismissal of Dexter after lunch seemed to take the weight off Cowdrey's mind. With Barrington now as his partner he seemed to have overcome whatever it was that had held him back before the interval and began to play his strokes. He sumptuously off drove McKenzie for four and then took another off his legs to mid wicket raising the hundred after 153 minutes in the 40th over. 19 runs had come in four overs when Cowdrey followed a short delivery from McKenzie round on the leg side. The too fine a touch gave Grout an easy catch. Cowdrey was thus out for only 20 in the first innings. England folded to be all out for 182.

On the second morning Trueman took the ball. In his second over, the last before lunch, he bowled Redpath and had McKenzie caught by Cowdrey at

*Catching Fred Trueman's 300th Test victim, Neil Hawke of Australia, at the Oval in 1964.*

slip next ball – the last before lunch and his 299th test wicket. At that time no-one had taken 300 so there was dual interest in Trueman's first ball after lunch. Neil Hawke survived the hat-trick ball. However, a few overs later he edged Trueman to first slip where Cowdrey again took the catch. My wife remonstrated with me for my reaction frightening our son Michael, born the previous August, who was sitting on my lap watching the cricket. Trueman fell into Cowdrey's arms. England were 197 behind on the first innings and Boycott made his maiden test century in the second. Cowdrey had made 93 not out with England 184 ahead on the penultimate day. Sadly rain prevented play on the final day and the match ended in a draw. During Cowdrey's unbeaten innings he became the seventh to complete 5000 runs in test cricket. It was when a four took his score to 50 after 143 minutes. He joined an elite company – Hammond, Bradman, Hutton, Hobbs, Harvey,

Compton. Thus it was a match for records but with it the series was lost. Cowdrey had had a second successive below par home series against the old enemy. Ironically, as in 1961, his personal contribution for his County against the tourists was notable.

|  | Matches | Innings | Not out | Runs | Highest score | Average | 100s | 50s | Caught |
|---|---|---|---|---|---|---|---|---|---|
| This series | 3 | 5 | 1 | 188 | 93* | 47.00 | 0 | 1 | 2 |
| Previous series | 70 | 115 | 9 | 4854 | 182 | 45.79 | 15 | 24 | 86 |
| Cumulative totals | 73 | 120 | 10 | 5042 | 182 | 45.87 | 15 | 25 | 88 |

*5000 runs*

Cowdrey at first decided that he would not be available for the 1964/65 tour of South Africa and when he eventually decided to make himself available the selectors had already chosen Mike Brearley as an opening batsman. Cowdrey's known reluctance to open made the late change more difficult and Cowdrey did not go. England won under M J K Smith.

Test No. 561/189

# ENGLAND v AUSTRALIA 1964 (1st Test)

Played at Trent Bridge, Nottingham, on 4, 5, 6 *(no play)*, 8, 9 June.
Toss: England.  Result: MATCH DRAWN.
Debuts: England – G. Boycott; Australia – G.E. Corling.

Rain interrupted every day except the fourth, a total of 14¾ hours being lost. Titmus, who improvised as an opening batsman after Edrich had reported unfit shortly before the start, escaped being run out when Grout declined to break the wicket after the batsman had collided with the bowler in responding to a call for a quick single. Boycott fractured a finger when fielding and was unable to bat in the second innings. Australia were set to score 242 runs in 195 minutes but rain ended the match after 45 minutes.

### ENGLAND

| | | | | |
|---|---|---|---|---|
| G. Boycott | c Simpson b Corling | 48 | | |
| F.J. Titmus | c Redpath b Hawke | 16 | lbw b McKenzie | 17 |
| E.R. Dexter* | c Grout b Hawke | 9 | (1) c O'Neill b McKenzie | 68 |
| M.C. Cowdrey | b Hawke | 32 | (3) b McKenzie | 33 |
| K.F. Barrington | c Lawry b Veivers | 22 | (4) lbw b Corling | 33 |
| P.J. Sharpe | not out | 35 | c and b Veivers | 1 |
| J.M. Parks† | c Booth b Veivers | 15 | (5) c Hawke b Veivers | 19 |
| F.S. Trueman | c Simpson b Veivers | 0 | (7) c Grout b McKenzie | 4 |
| D.A. Allen | c Grout b McKenzie | 21 | (8) lbw b McKenzie | 3 |
| L.J. Coldwell | not out | 0 | not out | 0 |
| J.A. Flavell | did not bat | | (9) c Booth b Corling | 7 |
| Extras | (B 5, LB 11, NB 2) | 18 | (B 2, LB 2, W 1, NB 3) | 8 |
| **Total** | **(8 wickets declared)** | **216** | **(9 wickets declared)** | **193** |

### AUSTRALIA

| | | | | |
|---|---|---|---|---|
| W.M. Lawry | c Barrington b Coldwell | 11 | run out | 3 |
| I.R. Redpath | b Trueman | 6 | c Parks b Flavell | 2 |
| N.C. O'Neill | b Allen | 26 | retired hurt | 24 |
| P.J.P. Burge | lbw b Trueman | 31 | not out | 4 |
| B.C. Booth | run out | 0 | not out | 6 |
| R.B. Simpson* | c Barrington b Titmus | 50 | | |
| T.R. Veivers | c Trueman b Flavell | 8 | | |
| G.D. McKenzie | c Parks b Coldwell | 4 | | |
| N.J.N. Hawke | not out | 10 | | |
| A.T.W. Grout† | c Parks b Coldwell | 13 | | |
| G.E. Corling | b Trueman | 3 | | |
| Extras | (LB 1, NB 5) | 6 | (NB 1) | 1 |
| **Total** | | **168** | **(2 wickets)** | **40** |

| AUSTRALIA | O | M | R | W | O | M | R | W | FALL OF WICKETS | | | |
|---|---|---|---|---|---|---|---|---|---|---|---|---|
| McKenzie | 28 | 7 | 53 | 1 | 24 | 5 | 53 | 5 | | E | A | E | A |
| Corling | 23 | 7 | 38 | 1 | 15.5 | 4 | 54 | 2 | Wkt | 1st | 1st | 2nd | 2nd |
| Hawke | 35 | 15 | 68 | 3 | 19 | 5 | 53 | 0 | 1st | 38 | 8 | 90 | 3 |
| Veivers | 16 | 2 | 39 | 3 | 8 | 0 | 25 | 2 | 2nd | 70 | 37 | 95 | 25 |
| | | | | | | | | | 3rd | 90 | 57 | 147 | – |
| **ENGLAND** | | | | | | | | | 4th | 135 | 61 | 174 | – |
| Trueman | 20.3 | 3 | 58 | 3 | 5 | 0 | 28 | 0 | 5th | 141 | 91 | 179 | – |
| Coldwell | 22 | 3 | 48 | 3 | | | | | 6th | 164 | 118 | 180 | – |
| Allen | 16 | 8 | 22 | 1 | | | | | 7th | 165 | 137 | 186 | – |
| Flavell | 16 | 3 | 28 | 1 | 4.2 | 0 | 11 | 1 | 8th | 212 | 141 | 187 | – |
| Titmus | 4 | 1 | 6 | 1 | | | | | 9th | – | 165 | 193 | – |
| | | | | | | | | | 10th | – | 168 | – | – |

Umpires: J.S. Buller and C.S. Elliott.

Test No. 562/190

# ENGLAND v AUSTRALIA 1964 (2nd Test)

Played at Lord's, London, on 18 *(no play)*, 19 *(no play)*, 20, 22, 23 June.
Toss: England.   Result: MATCH DRAWN.
Debuts: England – N. Gifford.

Over half the possible playing time was lost to rain which prevented a start until the third day and ended the match just before 2.30 on the fifth afternoon.

## AUSTRALIA

| | | | | |
|---|---|---|---|---|
| W.M. Lawry | b Trueman | 4 | c Dexter b Gifford | 20 |
| I.R. Redpath | c Parfitt b Coldwell | 30 | lbw b Titmus | 36 |
| N.C. O'Neill | c Titmus b Dexter | 26 | c Parfitt b Trueman | 22 |
| P.J.P. Burge | lbw b Dexter | 1 | c Parfitt b Titmus | 59 |
| B.C. Booth | lbw b Trueman | 14 | not out | 2 |
| R.B. Simpson* | c Parfitt b Trueman | 0 | not out | 15 |
| T.R. Veivers | b Gifford | 54 | | |
| G.D. McKenzie | b Trueman | 10 | | |
| A.T.W. Grout† | c Dexter b Gifford | 14 | | |
| N.J.N. Hawke | not out | 5 | | |
| G.E. Corling | b Trueman | 0 | | |
| Extras | (B 8, LB 5, NB 5) | 18 | (B 8, LB 4, NB 2) | 14 |
| **Total** | | **176** | (4 wickets) | **168** |

## ENGLAND

| | | |
|---|---|---|
| E.R. Dexter* | b McKenzie | 2 |
| J.H. Edrich | c Redpath b McKenzie | 120 |
| M.C. Cowdrey | c Burge b Hawke | 10 |
| K.F. Barrington | lbw b McKenzie | 5 |
| P.H. Parfitt | lbw b Corling | 20 |
| P.J. Sharpe | lbw b Hawke | 35 |
| J.M. Parks† | c Simpson b Hawke | 12 |
| F.J. Titmus | b Corling | 15 |
| F.S. Trueman | b Corling | 8 |
| N. Gifford | c Hawke b Corling | 5 |
| L.J. Coldwell | not out | 6 |
| Extras | (LB 7, NB 1) | 8 |
| **Total** | | **246** |

| ENGLAND | O | M | R | W | O | M | R | W |
|---|---|---|---|---|---|---|---|---|
| Trueman | 25 | 8 | 48 | 5 | 18 | 6 | 52 | 1 |
| Coldwell | 23 | 7 | 51 | 1 | 19 | 4 | 59 | 0 |
| Gifford | 12 | 6 | 14 | 2 | 17 | 9 | 17 | 1 |
| Dexter | 7 | 1 | 16 | 2 | 3 | 0 | 5 | 0 |
| Titmus | 17 | 6 | 29 | 0 | 17 | 7 | 21 | 2 |
| AUSTRALIA | | | | | | | | |
| McKenzie | 26 | 8 | 69 | 3 | | | | |
| Corling | 27.3 | 9 | 60 | 4 | | | | |
| Hawke | 16 | 4 | 41 | 3 | | | | |
| Veivers | 9 | 4 | 17 | 0 | | | | |
| Simpson | 21 | 8 | 51 | 0 | | | | |

### FALL OF WICKETS

| | A | E | A |
|---|---|---|---|
| Wkt | 1st | 1st | 2nd |
| 1st | 8 | 2 | 35 |
| 2nd | 46 | 33 | 76 |
| 3rd | 58 | 42 | 143 |
| 4th | 84 | 83 | 148 |
| 5th | 84 | 138 | – |
| 6th | 88 | 170 | – |
| 7th | 132 | 227 | – |
| 8th | 163 | 229 | – |
| 9th | 167 | 235 | – |
| 10th | 176 | 246 | – |

Umpires: J.F. Crapp and J.S. Buller.

Test No. 563/191

# ENGLAND v AUSTRALIA 1964 (3rd Test)

Played at Headingley, Leeds, on 2, 3, 4, 6 July.
Toss: England.   Result: AUSTRALIA won by seven wickets.
Debuts: Australia – R.M. Cowper.

Australia achieved the only victory of the rubber and so retained the Ashes. Dexter took the second new ball when Australia's first innings total was 187 for 7, and, after struggling against the off-spin of Titmus, Burge (then 38 not out) took his score to 160 and added a further 202 runs. The first seven overs of the new ball conceded 42 runs. In the second innings Titmus, who took the new ball in the absence of the injured Flavell, conceded only 12 runs in his first 24 overs.

### ENGLAND

| | | | | |
|---|---|---|---|---|
| G. Boycott | c Simpson b Corling | 38 | c Simpson b Corling | 4 |
| J.H. Edrich | c Veivers b McKenzie | 3 | c Grout b McKenzie | 32 |
| E.R. Dexter* | c Grout b McKenzie | 66 | (5) c Redpath b Veivers | 17 |
| K.F. Barrington | b McKenzie | 29 | lbw b Veivers | 85 |
| P.H. Parfitt | b Hawke | 32 | (3) c Redpath b Hawke | 6 |
| K. Taylor | c Grout b Hawke | 9 | (8) b Veivers | 15 |
| J.M. Parks† | c Redpath b Hawke | 68 | (6) c Booth b McKenzie | 23 |
| F.J. Titmus | c Burge b McKenzie | 3 | (9) c Cowper b Corling | 14 |
| F.S. Trueman | c Cowper b Hawke | 4 | (10) not out | 12 |
| N. Gifford | not out | 1 | (7) b McKenzie | 1 |
| J.A. Flavell | c Redpath b Hawke | 5 | c Simpson b Corling | 5 |
| Extras | (LB 9, NB 1) | 10 | (B 6, LB 6, W 1, NB 2) | 15 |
| **Total** | | **268** | | **229** |

### AUSTRALIA

| | | | | |
|---|---|---|---|---|
| W.M. Lawry | run out | 78 | c Gifford b Trueman | 1 |
| R.B. Simpson* | b Gifford | 24 | c Barrington b Titmus | 30 |
| I.R. Redpath | b Gifford | 20 | not out | 58 |
| P.J.P. Burge | c sub (A. Rees) b Trueman | 160 | b Titmus | 8 |
| B.C. Booth | st Parks b Titmus | 4 | not out | 12 |
| R.M. Cowper | b Trueman | 2 | | |
| T.R. Veivers | c Parks b Titmus | 8 | | |
| G.D. McKenzie | b Titmus | 0 | | |
| N.J.N. Hawke | c Parfitt b Trueman | 37 | | |
| A.T.W. Grout† | lbw b Titmus | 37 | | |
| G.E. Corling | not out | 2 | | |
| Extras | (B 1, LB 8, W 2, NB 6) | 17 | (B 1, LB 1) | 2 |
| **Total** | | **389** | (3 wickets) | **111** |

| AUSTRALIA | O | M | R | W | O | M | R | W | FALL OF WICKETS | | | |
|---|---|---|---|---|---|---|---|---|---|---|---|---|
| McKenzie | 26 | 7 | 74 | 4 | 28 | 8 | 53 | 3 | | E | A | E | A |
| Hawke | 31.3 | 11 | 75 | 5 | 13 | 1 | 28 | 1 | Wkt | 1st | 1st | 2nd | 2nd |
| Corling | 24 | 7 | 50 | 1 | 17.5 | 6 | 52 | 3 | 1st | 17 | 50 | 13 | 3 |
| Veivers | 17 | 3 | 35 | 0 | 30 | 12 | 70 | 3 | 2nd | 74 | 124 | 88 | 45 |
| Simpson | 5 | 0 | 24 | 0 | 1 | 0 | 11 | 0 | 3rd | 129 | 129 | 145 | 64 |
| | | | | | | | | | 4th | 138 | 154 | 156 | – |
| ENGLAND | | | | | | | | | 5th | 163 | 157 | 169 | – |
| Trueman | 24.3 | 2 | 98 | 3 | 7 | 0 | 28 | 1 | 6th | 215 | 178 | 184 | – |
| Flavell | 29 | 5 | 97 | 0 | | | | | 7th | 232 | 178 | 192 | – |
| Gifford | 34 | 15 | 62 | 2 | 20 | 5 | 47 | 0 | 8th | 260 | 283 | 199 | – |
| Dexter | 19 | 5 | 40 | 0 | 3 | 0 | 9 | 0 | 9th | 263 | 372 | 212 | – |
| Titmus | 50 | 24 | 69 | 4 | 27 | 19 | 25 | 2 | 10th | 268 | 389 | 229 | – |
| Taylor | 2 | 0 | 6 | 0 | | | | | | | | | |

Umpires: W.F.F. Price and C.S. Elliott.

Test No. 564/192

## ENGLAND v AUSTRALIA 1964 (4th Test)

Played at Old Trafford, Manchester, on 23, 24, 25, 27, 28 July.
Toss: Australia.   Result: MATCH DRAWN.
Debuts: England – T.W. Cartwright, F.E. Rumsey.

Australia's total of 656 for 8 declared remains the highest in any Manchester Test. Simpson scored his maiden Test hundred in his 52nd innings; his 311 is still the highest score in an Old Trafford Test and the highest by an Australian captain. Only Bradman (334 in *Test No. 196*) has made a higher score for Australia. His innings lasted 762 minutes and remains the longest against England and the third-longest in all first-class cricket. His partnership of 201 with Lawry set a new Australian first-wicket record against England. Barrington's tenth Test hundred was his first in England and his score of 256 remains England's highest at Manchester. Veivers established a record for this series by bowling 571 balls in an innings, including a spell of 51 overs unchanged. Only S. Ramadhin (588 balls in *Test No. 439*) has bowled more overs in a first-class innings.

### AUSTRALIA

| | | | | |
|---|---|---|---|---|
| W.M. Lawry | run out | 106 | not out | 0 |
| R.B. Simpson* | c Parks b Price | 311 | not out | 4 |
| I.R. Redpath | lbw b Cartwright | 19 | | |
| N.C. O'Neill | b Price | 47 | | |
| P.J.P. Burge | c Price b Cartwright | 34 | | |
| B.C. Booth | c and b Price | 98 | | |
| T.R. Veivers | c Edrich b Rumsey | 22 | | |
| A.T.W. Grout† | c Dexter b Rumsey | 0 | | |
| G.D. McKenzie | not out | 0 | | |
| N.J.N. Hawke | ) did not bat | | | |
| G.E. Corling | ) | | | |
| Extras | (B 1, LB 9, NB 9) | 19 | | |
| Total | (8 wickets declared) | 656 | (0 wickets) | 4 |

### ENGLAND

| | | |
|---|---|---|
| G. Boycott | b McKenzie | 58 |
| J.H. Edrich | c Redpath b McKenzie | 6 |
| E.R. Dexter* | b Veivers | 174 |
| K.F. Barrington | lbw b McKenzie | 256 |
| P.H. Parfitt | c Grout b McKenzie | 12 |
| J.M. Parks† | c Hawke b Veivers | 60 |
| F.J. Titmus | c Simpson b McKenzie | 9 |
| J.B. Mortimore | c Burge b McKenzie | 12 |
| T.W. Cartwright | b McKenzie | 4 |
| J.S.E. Price | b Veivers | 1 |
| F.E. Rumsey | not out | 3 |
| Extras | (B 5, LB 11) | 16 |
| Total | | 611 |

| ENGLAND | O | M | R | W | O | M | R | W |
|---|---|---|---|---|---|---|---|---|
| Rumsey | 35.5 | 4 | 99 | 2 | | | | |
| Price | 45 | 4 | 183 | 3 | | | | |
| Cartwright | 77 | 32 | 118 | 2 | | | | |
| Titmus | 44 | 14 | 100 | 0 | 1 | 1 | 0 | 0 |
| Dexter | 4 | 0 | 12 | 0 | | | | |
| Mortimore | 49 | 13 | 122 | 0 | | | | |
| Boycott | 1 | 0 | 3 | 0 | | | | |
| Barrington | | | | | 1 | 0 | 4 | 0 |
| AUSTRALIA | | | | | | | | |
| McKenzie | 60 | 15 | 153 | 7 | | | | |
| Corling | 46 | 11 | 96 | 0 | | | | |
| Hawke | 63 | 28 | 95 | 0 | | | | |
| Simpson | 19 | 4 | 59 | 0 | | | | |
| Veivers | 95.1 | 36 | 155 | 3 | | | | |
| O'Neill | 10 | 0 | 37 | 0 | | | | |

### FALL OF WICKETS

| Wkt | A 1st | E 1st | A 2nd |
|---|---|---|---|
| 1st | 201 | 15 | – |
| 2nd | 233 | 126 | – |
| 3rd | 318 | 372 | – |
| 4th | 382 | 417 | – |
| 5th | 601 | 560 | – |
| 6th | 646 | 589 | – |
| 7th | 652 | 594 | – |
| 8th | 656 | 602 | – |
| 9th | – | 607 | – |
| 10th | – | 611 | – |

Umpires: J.S. Buller and W.F.F. Price.

Test No. 565/193

# ENGLAND v AUSTRALIA 1964 (5th Test)

Played at Kennington Oval, London, on 13, 14, 15, 17, 18 (*no play*) August.
Toss: England.   Result: MATCH DRAWN.
Debuts: Nil.

Trueman became the first bowler to take 300 wickets in Test matches when he had Hawke caught by Cowdrey at first slip on the third afternoon. Barrington scored his 4,000th run in Test cricket during the first innings and Cowdrey his 5,000th during the second.

### ENGLAND

| | | | | |
|---|---|---|---|---|
| G. Boycott | b Hawke | 30 | c Redpath b Simpson | 113 |
| R.W. Barber | b Hawke | 24 | lbw b McKenzie | 29 |
| E.R. Dexter* | c Booth b Hawke | 23 | c Simpson b McKenzie | 25 |
| M.C. Cowdrey | c Grout b McKenzie | 20 | (5) not out | 93 |
| K.F. Barrington | c Simpson b Hawke | 47 | (6) not out | 54 |
| P.H. Parfitt | b McKenzie | 3 | | |
| J.M. Parks† | c Simpson b Corling | 10 | | |
| F.J. Titmus | c Grout b Hawke | 8 | (4) b McKenzie | 56 |
| F.S. Trueman | c Redpath b Hawke | 14 | | |
| T.W. Cartwright | c Grout b McKenzie | 0 | | |
| J.S.E. Price | not out | 0 | | |
| Extras | (LB 3) | 3 | (B 6, LB 4, NB 1) | 11 |
| **Total** | | **182** | (4 wickets) | **381** |

### AUSTRALIA

| | | |
|---|---|---|
| R.B. Simpson* | c Dexter b Cartwright | 24 |
| W.M. Lawry | c Trueman b Dexter | 94 |
| N.C. O'Neill | c Parfitt b Cartwright | 11 |
| P.J.P. Burge | lbw b Titmus | 25 |
| B.C. Booth | c Trueman b Price | 74 |
| I.R. Redpath | b Trueman | 45 |
| A.T.W. Grout† | b Cartwright | 20 |
| T.R. Veivers | not out | 67 |
| G.D. McKenzie | c Cowdrey b Trueman | 0 |
| N.J.N. Hawke | c Cowdrey b Trueman | 14 |
| G.E. Corling | c Parfitt b Trueman | 0 |
| Extras | (B 4, LB 1) | 5 |
| **Total** | | **379** |

| AUSTRALIA | O | M | R | W | O | M | R | W |
|---|---|---|---|---|---|---|---|---|
| McKenzie | 26 | 6 | 87 | 3 | 38 | 5 | 112 | 3 |
| Corling | 14 | 2 | 32 | 1 | 25 | 4 | 65 | 0 |
| Hawke | 25.4 | 8 | 47 | 6 | 39 | 8 | 89 | 0 |
| Veivers | 6 | 1 | 13 | 0 | 47 | 15 | 90 | 0 |
| Simpson | | | | | 14 | 7 | 14 | 1 |
| ENGLAND | | | | | | | | |
| Trueman | 33.3 | 6 | 87 | 4 | | | | |
| Price | 21 | 2 | 67 | 1 | | | | |
| Cartwright | 62 | 23 | 110 | 3 | | | | |
| Titmus | 42 | 20 | 51 | 1 | | | | |
| Barber | 6 | 1 | 23 | 0 | | | | |
| Dexter | 13 | 1 | 36 | 1 | | | | |

### FALL OF WICKETS

| | E | A | E |
|---|---|---|---|
| Wkt | 1st | 1st | 2nd |
| 1st | 44 | 45 | 80 |
| 2nd | 61 | 57 | 120 |
| 3rd | 82 | 96 | 200 |
| 4th | 111 | 202 | 255 |
| 5th | 117 | 245 | – |
| 6th | 141 | 279 | – |
| 7th | 160 | 343 | – |
| 8th | 173 | 343 | – |
| 9th | 174 | 367 | – |
| 10th | 182 | 379 | – |

Umpires: C.S. Elliott and J.F. Crapp.

Chapter 20

# NEW ZEALAND 1965

In 1965 England played host to two touring sides.

The first was New Zealand under John Reid.

In the first Test at Edgbaston Cowdrey's 85 was in contrast to Barrington's 137 in over seven hours for which he was dropped despite England's victory by nine wickets. The match was played in miserably cold weather and twice

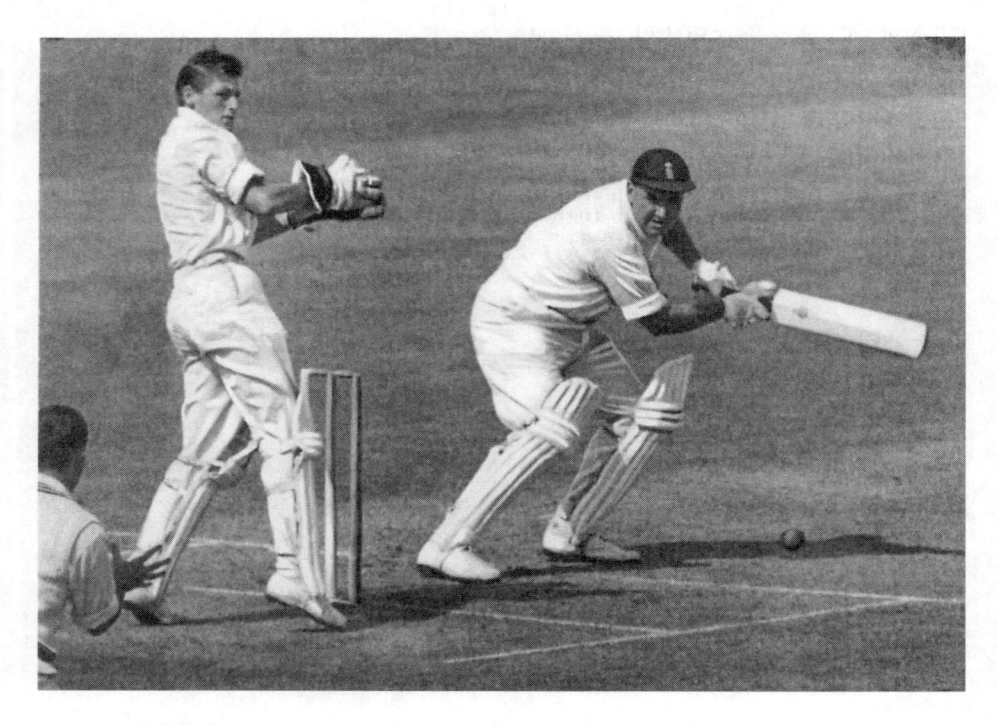

*Colin's late cut executed against the 1965 New Zealanders at Lord's.*

on the second day hot drinks were brought on to the field. Motz took 5 for 108 in England's first innings of 435. New Zealand managed only 116 in their first innings but following on made 413.

At Lord's Cowdrey's 119 clinched a second victory, by seven wickets, despite back trouble. This match was notable as the last Test match in which Fred Trueman played and in which he took his total of wickets to the then record of 307. England won by seven wickets.

In the third Test at Headingley John Edrich accumulated 310 and Barrington, back in favour, made 163. Cowdrey only contributed 13 to England's 546 for 4 declared. England won by an innings and 187 runs taking the series three nil. New Zealand made 193 and 166. In their second innings Titmus took 5 for 19 including four wickets in an over for no run.

|  | Matches | Innings | Not out | Runs | Highest score | Average | 100s | 50s | Caught |
|---|---|---|---|---|---|---|---|---|---|
| This series | 3 | 4 | 1 | 221 | 119 | 73.66 | 1 | 1 | 2 |
| Previous series | 73 | 120 | 10 | 5042 | 182 | 45.87 | 15 | 25 | 88 |
| Cumulative totals | 76 | 124 | 11 | 5263 | 182 | 46.58 | 16 | 26 | 90 |

**Test No. 591/32**

# ENGLAND v NEW ZEALAND 1965 (1st Test)

Played at Edgbaston, Birmingham, on 27, 28, 29, 31 May, 1 June.
Toss: England.   Result: ENGLAND won by nine wickets.
Debuts: Nil.

England maintained their unbeaten record at Birmingham, this being their seventh win in eleven Tests. Barrington's innings occupied 437 minutes and resulted in his omission from the next Test; his score remained at 85 for 62 minutes while 20 overs were bowled. Sutcliffe retired hurt after being hit on the right ear by a Trueman bouncer, came back for the last two minutes before lunch but was unfit to continue afterwards. Congdon retired in the second innings after edging a sweep against Barber into his face but he resumed at 105 for 2. The partnership of 104 between Sutcliffe and Pollard remains New Zealand's highest for the seventh wicket against England. This match was played in miserably cold weather; twice on the second day hot drinks were brought on to the field.

## ENGLAND

| | | | | | |
|---|---|---|---|---|---|
| G. Boycott | c Dick b Motz | 23 | not out | | 44 |
| R.W. Barber | b Motz | 31 | c sub (G.E. Vivian) b Morgan | | 51 |
| E.R. Dexter | c Dick b Motz | 57 | not out | | 0 |
| K.F. Barrington | c Dick b Collinge | 137 | | | |
| M.C. Cowdrey | b Collinge | 85 | | | |
| M.J.K. Smith* | lbw b Collinge | 0 | | | |
| J.M. Parks† | c Cameron b Reid | 34 | | | |
| F.J. Titmus | c Congdon b Motz | 13 | | | |
| T.W. Cartwright | b Motz | 4 | | | |
| F.S. Trueman | c Pollard b Cameron | 3 | | | |
| F.E. Rumsey | not out | 21 | | | |
| Extras | (B 10, LB 6, NB 11) | 27 | (NB 1) | | 1 |
| **Total** | | **435** | (1 wicket) | | **96** |

## NEW ZEALAND

| | | | | | |
|---|---|---|---|---|---|
| G.T. Dowling | b Titmus | 32 | b Barber | | 41 |
| B.F. Congdon | c Smith b Titmus | 24 | b Titmus | | 47 |
| B.W. Sinclair | b Titmus | 14 | st Parks b Barber | | 2 |
| J.R. Reid* | b Trueman | 2 | c Barrington b Titmus | | 44 |
| B. Sutcliffe | retired hurt | 4 | (7) c Titmus b Dexter | | 53 |
| R.W. Morgan | c Parks b Barber | 22 | (5) lbw b Trueman | | 43 |
| A.E. Dick† | c Titmus b Cartwright | 0 | (6) b Barber | | 42 |
| V. Pollard | lbw b Titmus | 4 | not out | | 81 |
| R.C. Motz | c Trueman b Cartwright | 0 | c and b Barber | | 21 |
| R.O. Collinge | c Dexter b Barber | 4 | c Parks b Trueman | | 9 |
| F.J. Cameron | not out | 4 | b Trueman | | 0 |
| Extras | (B 1, LB 1, NB 4) | 6 | (B 17, LB 11, NB 2) | | 30 |
| **Total** | | **116** | | | **413** |

| NEW ZEALAND | O | M | R | W | O | M | R | W |
|---|---|---|---|---|---|---|---|---|
| Collinge | 29.4 | 8 | 63 | 3 | 5 | 1 | 14 | 0 |
| Cameron | 43 | 10 | 117 | 1 | 3 | 0 | 11 | 0 |
| Motz | 43 | 14 | 108 | 5 | 13 | 3 | 34 | 0 |
| Pollard | 18 | 4 | 60 | 0 | 1 | 0 | 5 | 0 |
| Congdon | 7 | 2 | 17 | 0 | 2 | 1 | 6 | 0 |
| Reid | 16 | 5 | 43 | 1 | 5 | 2 | 7 | 0 |
| Morgan | | | | | 1.5 | 0 | 18 | 1 |
| **ENGLAND** | | | | | | | | |
| Rumsey | 9 | 2 | 22 | 0 | 17 | 5 | 32 | 0 |
| Trueman | 18 | 3 | 49 | 1 | 32.4 | 8 | 79 | 3 |
| Titmus | 26 | 17 | 18 | 4 | 59 | 30 | 85 | 2 |
| Cartwright | 7 | 3 | 14 | 2 | 12 | 6 | 12 | 0 |
| Barber | 3 | 2 | 7 | 2 | 45 | 15 | 132 | 4 |
| Barrington | | | | | 5 | 0 | 25 | 0 |
| Dexter | | | | | 5 | 1 | 18 | 1 |

## FALL OF WICKETS

| | E | NZ | NZ | E |
|---|---|---|---|---|
| Wkt | 1st | 1st | 2nd | 2nd |
| 1st | 54 | 54 | 72 | 92 |
| 2nd | 76 | 63 | 105 | – |
| 3rd | 164 | 67 | 131 | – |
| 4th | 300 | 86 | 145 | – |
| 5th | 300 | 97 | 220 | – |
| 6th | 335 | 104 | 249 | – |
| 7th | 368 | 105 | 353 | – |
| 8th | 391 | 108 | 386 | – |
| 9th | 394 | 115 | 413 | – |
| 10th | 435 | – | 413 | – |

Umpires: C.S. Elliott and W.F.F. Price.

**Test No. 592/33**

# ENGLAND v NEW ZEALAND 1965 (2nd Test)

Played at Lord's, London, on 17, 18, 19, 21, 22 June.
Toss: New Zealand. Result: ENGLAND won by seven wickets.
Debuts: England – J.A. Snow.

England won with just 15 minutes to spare after rain had claimed over five hours of play during the last two days. In his 67th and final Test match Frederick Sewards Trueman took his total of Test wickets to 307 – an aggregate which remained unbeaten until 31st January, 1976, when L.R. Gibbs overtook it in his 79th match (*Test No. 769*).

## NEW ZEALAND

| | | | | |
|---|---|---|---|---|
| B.E. Congdon | lbw b Rumsey | 0 | lbw b Titmus | 26 |
| G.T. Dowling | lbw b Rumsey | 12 | b Parfitt | 66 |
| B.W. Sinclair | b Rumsey | 1 | c Parks b Barber | 72 |
| J.R. Reid* | c Parks b Snow | 21 | b Titmus | 22 |
| R.W. Morgan | c Parfitt b Rumsey | 0 | lbw b Rumsey | 35 |
| V. Pollard | c and b Titmus | 55 | run out | 55 |
| A.E. Dick† | b Snow | 7 | c Parks b Snow | 3 |
| B.R. Taylor | b Trueman | 51 | c Smith b Snow | 0 |
| R.C. Motz | c Parks b Titmus | 11 | (10) c Snow b Barber | 8 |
| R.O. Collinge | b Trueman | 7 | (9) c Parks b Barber | 21 |
| F.J. Cameron | not out | 3 | not out | 9 |
| Extras | (B 3, LB 2, NB 2) | 7 | (B 8, LB 12, NB 10) | 30 |
| **Total** | | **175** | | **347** |

## ENGLAND

| | | | | |
|---|---|---|---|---|
| G. Boycott | c Dick b Motz | 14 | lbw b Motz | 76 |
| P.W. Barber | c Dick b Motz | 13 | b Motz | 34 |
| E.R. Dexter | c Dick b Taylor | 62 | (4) not out | 80 |
| M.C. Cowdrey | c sub (T.W. Jarvis) b Collinge | 119 | (5) not out | 4 |
| P.H. Parfitt | c Dick b Cameron | 11 | | |
| M.J.K. Smith* | c sub (T.W. Jarvis) b Taylor | 44 | | |
| J.M. Parks† | b Collinge | 2 | | |
| F.J. Titmus | run out | 13 | (3) c Dick b Motz | 1 |
| F.S. Trueman | b Collinge | 3 | | |
| F.F. Rumsey | b Collinge | 3 | | |
| J.A. Snow | not out | 2 | | |
| Extras | (B 1, LB 7, W 1, NB 12) | 21 | (B 9, LB 5, NB 9) | 23 |
| **Total** | | **307** | (3 wickets) | **218** |

| ENGLAND | O | M | R | W | O | M | R | W | | FALL OF WICKETS | | | |
|---|---|---|---|---|---|---|---|---|---|---|---|---|---|
| | | | | | | | | | | NZ | E | NZ | E |
| Rumsey | 13 | 4 | 25 | 4 | 26 | 10 | 42 | 1 | Wkt | 1st | 1st | 2nd | 2nd |
| Trueman | 19.5 | 8 | 40 | 2 | 26 | 4 | 69 | 0 | 1st | 0 | 18 | 59 | 64 |
| Dexter | 8 | 2 | 27 | 0 | | | | | 2nd | 4 | 38 | 149 | 70 |
| Snow | 11 | 2 | 27 | 2 | 24 | 4 | 53 | 2 | 3rd | 24 | 131 | 196 | 196 |
| Titmus | 15 | 7 | 25 | 2 | 39 | 12 | 71 | 2 | 4th | 28 | 166 | 206 | – |
| Barber | 8 | 2 | 24 | 0 | 28 | 10 | 57 | 3 | 5th | 49 | 271 | 253 | – |
| Parfitt | | | | | 5 | 2 | 25 | 1 | 6th | 62 | 285 | 258 | – |
| | | | | | | | | | 7th | 154 | 292 | 259 | – |
| NEW ZEALAND | | | | | | | | | 8th | 160 | 300 | 293 | – |
| Collinge | 28.2 | 4 | 85 | 4 | 15 | 1 | 43 | 0 | 9th | 171 | 302 | 303 | – |
| Motz | 20 | 1 | 62 | 2 | 19 | 5 | 45 | 3 | 10th | 175 | 307 | 347 | – |
| Taylor | 25 | 4 | 66 | 2 | 10 | 0 | 53 | 0 | | | | | |
| Cameron | 19 | 6 | 40 | 1 | 13 | 0 | 39 | 0 | | | | | |
| Morgan | 8 | 1 | 33 | 0 | 3 | 0 | 11 | 0 | | | | | |
| Reid | | | | | 0 | 0.5 | 0 | 4 | | | | | |

Umpires: J.S. Buller and W.E. Phillipson.

Test No. 593/34

# ENGLAND v NEW ZEALAND 1965 (3rd Test)

Played at Headingley, Leeds, on 8, 9, 10, 12, 13 July.
Toss: England.   Result: ENGLAND won by an innings and 187 runs.
Debuts: Nil.

Edrich scored England's only triple century since 1938, his 310 not out being the highest score by an Englishman in first-class cricket at Leeds. He batted for 532 minutes and hit five sixes and 52 fours – the highest number of boundaries in any Test innings. He was on the field throughout the match. His partnership of 369 in 339 minutes with Barrington remains the highest for any wicket by either country in this series. Titmus took the wickets of Yuile, Taylor, Motz and Collinge for no runs in his 21st over (WOWWOW). England completed their third victory of the rubber after 16 minutes on the fifth morning – just before rain waterlogged the ground.

### ENGLAND

| | | |
|---|---|---|
| R.W. Barber | c Ward b Taylor | 13 |
| J.H. Edrich | not out | 310 |
| K.F. Barrington | c Ward b Motz | 163 |
| M.C. Cowdrey | b Taylor | 13 |
| P.H. Parfitt | b Collinge | 32 |
| M.J.K. Smith* | not out | 2 |
| J.M. Parks† | ) | |
| R. Illingworth | ) | |
| F.J. Titmus | ) did not bat | |
| F.E. Rumsey | ) | |
| J.D.F. Larter | ) | |
| Extras | (B 4, LB 8, NB 1) | 13 |
| **Total** | (4 wickets declared) | **546** |

### NEW ZEALAND

| | | | | |
|---|---|---|---|---|
| G.T. Dowling | c Parks b Larter | 5 | b Rumsey | 41 |
| B.E. Congdon | c Parks b Rumsey | 13 | b Rumsey | 1 |
| B.W. Sinclair | c Smith b Larter | 13 | lbw b Larter | 29 |
| J.R. Reid* | lbw b Illingworth | 54 | c Barrington b Rumsey | 5 |
| R.W. Morgan | b Illingworth | 1 | (6) b Titmus | 21 |
| V. Pollard | run out | 33 | (5) c Cowdrey b Larter | 53 |
| B.W. Yuile | b Larter | 46 | c Cowdrey b Titmus | 12 |
| B.R. Taylor | c Parks b Illingworth | 9 | c and b Titmus | 0 |
| R.C. Motz | c Barber b Illingworth | 3 | c Barrington b Titmus | 0 |
| J.T. Ward† | not out | 0 | (11) not out | 2 |
| R.O. Collinge | b Larter | 8 | (10) b Titmus | 0 |
| Extras | (B 5, LB 2, W 2) | 8 | (NB 2) | 2 |
| **Total** | | **193** | | **166** |

| NEW ZEALAND | O | M | R | W | O | M | R | W | FALL OF WICKETS | | | |
|---|---|---|---|---|---|---|---|---|---|---|---|---|
| Motz | 41 | 8 | 140 | 1 | | | | | | E | NZ | NZ |
| Taylor | 40 | 8 | 140 | 2 | | | | | Wkt | 1st | 1st | 2nd |
| Collinge | 32 | 7 | 87 | 1 | | | | | 1st | 13 | 15 | 4 |
| Yuile | 17 | 5 | 80 | 0 | | | | | 2nd | 382 | 19 | 67 |
| Morgan | 6 | 0 | 28 | 0 | | | | | 3rd | 407 | 53 | 75 |
| Pollard | 11 | 2 | 46 | 0 | | | | | 4th | 516 | 61 | 86 |
| Congdon | 4 | 0 | 12 | 0 | | | | | 5th | – | 100 | 111 |
| ENGLAND | | | | | | | | | 6th | – | 153 | 158 |
| Rumsey | 24 | 6 | 59 | 1 | 15 | 5 | 49 | 3 | 7th | – | 165 | 158 |
| Larter | 28·1 | 6 | 66 | 4 | 22 | 10 | 54 | 2 | 8th | – | 173 | 158 |
| Illingworth | 28 | 14 | 42 | 4 | 7 | 0 | 28 | 0 | 9th | – | 181 | 158 |
| Titmus | 6 | 2 | 16 | 0 | 26 | 17 | 19 | 5 | 10th | – | 193 | 166 |
| Barber | 2 | 0 | 2 | 0 | 14 | 7 | 14 | 0 | | | | |

Umpires: C.S. Elliott and J.F. Crapp.

## Chapter 21
# SOUTH AFRICA 1965

South Africa, the second opponents in 1965, were made of sterner stuff.
Peter van der Merwe led a formidable side.
The first Test at Lord's was drawn. Cowdrey made a modest 29 and 37 but the latter was England's highest score in the second innings of 145 for seven wickets. Colin Bland ran out Barrington and Parks with direct hits on the stumps. These two incidents were worth the admission money.
In the second Test at Trent Bridge South Africa made 269 with a classic 125 in 145 balls from Graeme Pollock. Five for 53 from his elder brother Peter who took another five in the second innings, made it very much the Pollocks match. Cowdrey dominated England's first innings of 240 scoring 105 but was stumped in England's second innings for 20 and at 41 for 5 the end was but doomed resistance and South Africa won by 94 runs.
For the final Test at the Oval South Africa were dismissed for 208. Cowdrey made 58 of England's reply which fell six short and his contribution, which was the top score, took four hours. A Colin Bland century meant that England were set 399 for victory. A fourth wicket partnership between Cowdrey and Barrington put them on track. A Surrey member as well as being a member of Kent CCC I was in a position to wish them well as they went out to resume their partnership after tea needing 109 in 85 minutes. It was not to be as rain soon fell in such proportions as to make any more play impossible. I told my mother that there would be no more play and left to visit my mother-in-law on the Isle of Wight by an earlier train than I had hoped. I was appalled when, at the fall of Barrington's wicket, some sections of the crowd, including members in front of the Pavilion, booed M J K Smith, the England captain, making his way to the crease. Clearly they would have preferred Parks, who had made a speedy 42 in the first innings,

to join Cowdrey in the run chase. What is needed in such circumstances is enthusiastic support not abuse.

And so it was that South Africa won the series.

|  | Matches | Innings | Not out | Runs | Highest score | Average | 100s | 50s | Caught |
|---|---|---|---|---|---|---|---|---|---|
| This series | 3 | 6 | 1 | 327 | 105 | 65.40 | 1 | 2 | 5 |
| Previous series | 76 | 124 | 11 | 5263 | 182 | 46.58 | 16 | 26 | 90 |
| Cumulative totals | 79 | 130 | 12 | 5590 | 182 | 47.37 | 17 | 28 | 95 |

Test No. 594/100

# ENGLAND v SOUTH AFRICA 1965 (1st Test)

Played at Lord's, London on 22, 23, 24, 26, 27 July.
Toss: South Africa. Result: MATCH DRAWN.
Debuts: England – D.J. Brown; South Africa – A. Bacher, J.T. Botten, R. Dumbrill.

Needing 191 runs to win in 235 minutes, England were never on terms with the required scoring rate. With seven wickets down and Edrich unable to resume his innings after being hit on the side of the head by a ball from P.M. Pollock, England did well to draw this 100th match between the two countries. Bland ran out Barrington and Parks with two outstanding pieces of fielding which culminated in direct hits on the stumps.

## SOUTH AFRICA

| | | | | | |
|---|---|---|---|---|---|
| E.J. Barlow | c Barber b Rumsey | 1 | c Parks b Brown | | 52 |
| H.R. Lance | c and b Brown | 28 | c Titmus b Brown | | 9 |
| D.T. Lindsay† | c Titmus b Rumsey | 40 | c Parks b Larter | | 22 |
| R.G. Pollock | c Barrington b Titmus | 56 | b Brown | | 5 |
| K.C. Bland | b Brown | 39 | c Edrich b Barber | | 70 |
| A. Bacher | lbw b Titmus | 4 | b Titmus | | 37 |
| P.L. van der Merwe* | c Barrington b Rumsey | 17 | c Barrington b Rumsey | | 31 |
| R. Dumbrill | b Barber | 3 | c Cowdrey b Rumsey | | 2 |
| J.T. Botten | b Brown | 33 | b Rumsey | | 0 |
| P.M. Pollock | st Parks b Barber | 34 | not out | | 14 |
| H.D. Bromfield | not out | 9 | run out | | 0 |
| Extras | (LB 14, NB 2) | 16 | (B 4, LB 2) | | 6 |
| **Total** | | **280** | | | **248** |

## ENGLAND

| | | | | | |
|---|---|---|---|---|---|
| G. Boycott | c Barlow b Botten | 31 | c and b Dumbrill | | 28 |
| R.W. Barber | b Bromfield | 56 | c Lindsay b P.M. Pollock | | 12 |
| J.H. Edrich | lbw b P.M. Pollock | 0 | retired hurt | | 7 |
| K.F. Barrington | run out | 91 | lbw b Dumbrill | | 18 |
| M.C. Cowdrey | b Dumbrill | 29 | lbw b P.M. Pollock | | 37 |
| M.J.K. Smith* | c Lindsay b Botten | 26 | c Lindsay b Dumbrill | | 13 |
| J.M. Parks† | run out | 32 | c Van der Merwe b Dumbrill | | 7 |
| F.J. Titmus | c P.M. Pollock b Bromfield | 59 | not out | | 9 |
| D.J. Brown | c Bromfield b Dumbrill | 1 | c Barlow b R.G. Pollock | | 5 |
| F.E. Rumsey | b Dumbrill | 3 | not out | | 0 |
| J.D.F. Larter | not out | 0 | | | |
| Extras | (B 1, LB 4, W 1, NB 4) | 10 | (LB 7, W 1, NB 1) | | 9 |
| **Total** | | **338** | (7 wickets) | | **145** |

| ENGLAND | O | M | R | W | O | M | R | W | | FALL OF WICKETS | | | |
|---|---|---|---|---|---|---|---|---|---|---|---|---|---|
| Larter | 26 | 10 | 47 | 0 | 17 | 2 | 67 | 1 | | SA | E | SA | E |
| Rumsey | 30 | 9 | 84 | 3 | 21 | 8 | 49 | 3 | Wkt | 1st | 1st | 2nd | 2nd |
| Brown | 24 | 9 | 44 | 3 | 21 | 11 | 30 | 3 | 1st | 1 | 82 | 55 | 23 |
| Titmus | 29 | 10 | 59 | 2 | 26 | 13 | 36 | 1 | 2nd | 60 | 88 | 62 | 70 |
| Barber | 10·3 | 3 | 30 | 2 | 25 | 5 | 60 | 1 | 3rd | 75 | 88 | 68 | 79 |
| | | | | | | | | | 4th | 155 | 144 | 120 | 113 |
| SOUTH AFRICA | | | | | | | | | 5th | 170 | 240 | 170 | 121 |
| P.M. Pollock | 39 | 12 | 91 | 1 | 20 | 6 | 52 | 2 | 6th | 170 | 240 | 216 | 135 |
| Botten | 33 | 11 | 65 | 2 | 12 | 6 | 25 | 0 | 7th | 178 | 294 | 230 | 140 |
| Barlow | 19 | 6 | 31 | 0 | 9 | 1 | 25 | 0 | 8th | 212 | 314 | 230 | – |
| Bromfield | 25·2 | 5 | 71 | 2 | 5 | 4 | 4 | 0 | 9th | 241 | 338 | 247 | – |
| Dumbrill | 24 | 11 | 31 | 3 | 18 | 8 | 30 | 4 | 10th | 280 | 338 | 248 | – |
| Lance | 5 | 0 | 18 | 0 | | | | | | | | | |
| R.G. Pollock | 5 | 1 | 21 | 0 | 4 | 4 | 0 | 1 | | | | | |

Umpires: J.S. Buller and A.E.G. Rhodes.

Test No. 595/101

# ENGLAND v SOUTH AFRICA 1965 (2nd Test)

Played at Trent Bridge, Nottingham, on 5, 6, 7, 9 August.
Toss: South Africa. Result: SOUTH AFRICA won by 94 runs.
Debuts: Nil.

This was England's first defeat in 15 matches under Smith's captaincy. It was brought about mainly by the performances of the Pollock brothers, Graeme scoring 184 runs and Peter taking 10 for 87 in 48 overs. The former received 145 balls in the first innings, scoring 125 out of 160 with 21 boundaries; the last 91 of his runs were made off 90 balls in 70 minutes while his partner, Van der Merwe, scored 10. Cartwright (fractured thumb) was unable to bowl in the second innings.

### SOUTH AFRICA

| | | | | |
|---|---|---|---|---|
| E.J. Barlow | c Cowdrey b Cartwright | 19 | (4) b Titmus | 76 |
| H.R. Lance | lbw b Cartwright | 7 | c Barber b Snow | 0 |
| D.T. Lindsay† | c Parks b Cartwright | 0 | (1) c Cowdrey b Larter | 9 |
| R.G. Pollock | c Cowdrey b Cartwright | 125 | (5) c Titmus b Larter | 59 |
| K.C. Bland | st Parks b Titmus | 1 | (6) b Snow | 10 |
| A. Bacher | b Snow | 12 | (3) lbw b Larter | 67 |
| P.L. van der Merwe* | run out | 38 | c Parfitt b Larter | 4 |
| R. Dumbrill | c Parfitt b Cartwright | 30 | b Snow | 13 |
| J.T. Botten | c Parks b Larter | 10 | b Larter | 18 |
| P.M. Pollock | c Larter b Cartweight | 15 | not out | 12 |
| A.H. McKinnon | not out | 8 | b Titmus | 9 |
| Extras | (LB 4) | 4 | (B 4, LB 5, NB 3) | 12 |
| **Total** | | **269** | | **289** |

### ENGLAND

| | | | | |
|---|---|---|---|---|
| G. Boycott | c Lance b P.M. Pollock | 0 | b McKinnon | 16 |
| R.W. Barber | c Bacher b Dumbrill | 41 | c Lindsay b P.M. Pollock | 1 |
| K.F. Barrington | b P.M. Pollock | 1 | (5) c Lindsay b P.M. Pollock | 1 |
| F.J. Titmus | c R.G. Pollock b McKinnon | 20 | (3) c Lindsay b McKinnon | 4 |
| M.C. Cowdrey | c Lindsay b Botten | 105 | (6) st Lindsay b McKinnon | 20 |
| P.H. Parfitt | c Dumbrill b P.M. Pollock | 18 | (7) b P.M. Pollock | 86 |
| M.J.K. Smith* | b P.M. Pollock | 32 | (8) lbw b R.G. Pollock | 24 |
| J.M. Parks† | c and b Botten | 6 | (9) not out | 44 |
| J.A. Snow | run out | 3 | (4) b Botten | 0 |
| J.D.F. Larter | b P.M. Pollock | 2 | (11) c Van der Merwe b P.M. Pollock | 10 |
| T.W. Cartwright | not out | 1 | (10) lbw b P.M. Pollock | 0 |
| Extras | (B 1, LB 3. W 1, NB 6) | 11 | (LB 5, W 2, NB 11) | 18 |
| **Total** | | **240** | | **224** |

| ENGLAND | O | M | R | W | O | M | R | W | FALL OF WICKETS | | | |
|---|---|---|---|---|---|---|---|---|---|---|---|---|
| Larter | 17 | 6 | 25 | 1 | 29 | 7 | 68 | 5 | | SA | E | SA | E |
| Snow | 22 | 6 | 63 | 1 | 33 | 6 | 83 | 3 | Wkt | 1st | 1st | 2nd | 2nd |
| Cartwright | 31.3 | 9 | 94 | 6 | | | | | 1st | 16 | 0 | 2 | 1 |
| Titmus | 22 | 8 | 44 | 1 | 19.4 | 5 | 46 | 2 | 2nd | 16 | 8 | 35 | 10 |
| Barber | 9 | 3 | 39 | 0 | 3 | 0 | 20 | 0 | 3rd | 42 | 63 | 134 | 10 |
| Boycott | | | | | 26 | 10 | 60 | 0 | 4th | 43 | 67 | 193 | 13 |
| | | | | | | | | | 5th | 80 | 133 | 228 | 41 |
| SOUTH AFRICA | | | | | | | | | 6th | 178 | 225 | 232 | 59 |
| P.M. Pollock | 23.5 | 8 | 53 | 5 | 24 | 15 | 34 | 5 | 7th | 221 | 229 | 243 | 114 |
| Botten | 23 | 5 | 60 | 2 | 19 | 5 | 58 | 1 | 8th | 242 | 236 | 265 | 207 |
| McKinnon | 28 | 11 | 54 | 1 | 27 | 12 | 50 | 3 | 9th | 252 | 238 | 269 | 207 |
| Dumbrill | 18 | 3 | 60 | 1 | 16 | 4 | 40 | 0 | 10th | 269 | 240 | 289 | 224 |
| R.G. Pollock | 1 | 0 | 2 | 0 | 5 | 2 | 4 | 1 | | | | | |
| Barlow | | | | | 7 | 1 | 20 | 0 | | | | | |

Umpires: C.S. Elliott and J.F. Crapp.

Test No. 596/102

# ENGLAND v SOUTH AFRICA 1965 (3rd Test)

Played at Kennington Oval, London, on 26, 27, 28, 30, 31 August.
Toss: England. Result: MATCH DRAWN.
Debuts: England – K. Higgs.

England needed 91 runs to win with 70 minutes left when heavy rain ensured that South Africa won their second rubber in England, the first being in 1935. Higgs took the wicket of Lindsay with his 16th ball in Test cricket. Recalled after an interval of two years and 20 Tests, Statham took seven wickets in his final match to bring his tally to 252 wickets in 70 Tests – an aggregate at the time exceeded only by F.S. Trueman (307).

## SOUTH AFRICA

| | | | | |
|---|---|---|---|---|
| E.J. Barlow | lbw b Statham | 18 | b Statham | 18 |
| D.T. Lindsay† | lbw b Higgs | 4 | b Brown | 17 |
| A. Bacher | lbw b Higgs | 28 | c Smith b Statham | 70 |
| R.G. Pollock | b Titmus | 12 | run out | 34 |
| K.C. Bland | lbw b Statham | 39 | c Titmus b Higgs | 127 |
| H.R. Lance | lbw b Statham | 69 | b Higgs | 53 |
| P.L. van der Merwe* | c Barrington b Higgs | 20 | b Higgs | 0 |
| R. Dumbrill | c Smith b Higgs | 14 | c Barrington b Brown | 36 |
| J.T. Botten | c Cowdrey b Statham | 0 | b Titmus | 4 |
| P.M. Pollock | b Statham | 3 | not out | 9 |
| A.H. McKinnon | not out | 0 | b Higgs | 14 |
| Extras | (NB 1) | 1 | (B 1, LB 7, NB 2) | 10 |
| **Total** | | **208** | | **392** |

## ENGLAND

| | | | | |
|---|---|---|---|---|
| R.W. Barber | st Lindsay b McKinnon | 40 | c and b P.M. Pollock | 22 |
| W.E. Russell | lbw b P.M. Pollock | 0 | c Bacher b McKinnon | 70 |
| K.F. Barrington | b Botten | 18 | (4) lbw b P.M. Pollock | 73 |
| M.C. Cowdrey | c Barlow b P.M. Pollock | 58 | (5) not out | 78 |
| P.H. Parfitt | c and b McKinnon | 24 | (3) lbw b Botten | 46 |
| M.J.K. Smith* | lbw b P.M. Pollock | 7 | not out | 10 |
| D.J. Brown | c Dumbrill b McKinnon | 0 | | |
| J.M. Parks† | c Bland b Botten | 42 | | |
| F.J. Titmus | not out | 2 | | |
| K. Higgs | b P.M. Pollock | 2 | | |
| J.B. Statham | b P.M. Pollock | 0 | | |
| Extras | (LB 6, W 3) | 9 | (LB 6, NB 3) | 9 |
| **Total** | | **202** | (4 wickets) | **308** |

| ENGLAND | O | M | R | W | O | M | R | W | FALL OF WICKETS | | | | |
|---|---|---|---|---|---|---|---|---|---|---|---|---|---|
| Statham | 24.2 | 11 | 40 | 5 | 29 | 1 | 105 | 2 | | SA | E | SA | E |
| Brown | 22 | 4 | 63 | 0 | 23 | 3 | 63 | 2 | Wkt | 1st | 1st | 2nd | 2nd |
| Higgs | 24 | 4 | 47 | 4 | 41.1 | 10 | 96 | 4 | 1st | 21 | 1 | 28 | 39 |
| Titmus | 26 | 12 | 57 | 1 | 27 | 3 | 74 | 1 | 2nd | 23 | 42 | 61 | 138 |
| Barber | | | | | 13 | 1 | 44 | 0 | 3rd | 60 | 76 | 123 | 144 |
| | | | | | | | | | 4th | 86 | 125 | 164 | 279 |
| SOUTH AFRICA | | | | | | | | | 5th | 109 | 141 | 260 | – |
| P.M. Pollock | 25.1 | 7 | 43 | 5 | 32.2 | 7 | 93 | 2 | 6th | 156 | 142 | 260 | – |
| Botten | 27 | 6 | 56 | 2 | 24 | 4 | 73 | 1 | 7th | 196 | 198 | 343 | – |
| Barlow | 11 | 1 | 27 | 0 | 6 | 1 | 22 | 0 | 8th | 197 | 198 | 367 | – |
| Dumbrill | 6 | 2 | 11 | 0 | 9 | 1 | 30 | 0 | 9th | 207 | 200 | 371 | – |
| McKinnon | 27 | 11 | 50 | 3 | 31 | 7 | 70 | 1 | 10th | 208 | 202 | 392 | – |
| Lance | 2 | 0 | 6 | 0 | 2 | 0 | 11 | 0 | | | | | |

Umpires: J.S. Buller and W.F.F. Price.

Chapter 22
# AUSTRALIA 1965/66

Next was the 1965/66 tour of Australia. It was Cowdrey's fourth tour and his third as Vice Captain, as M J K Smith retained the captaincy.

Sadly Cowdrey missed the first Test with what had come to be described as a "viral infection". At all events he was unfit to play and his replacement Eric Russell was unable to bat because of a hand injury and England following-on were thankful to bad weather in holding on for a draw.

Cowdrey was back for the Melbourne Test, a venue of happy memories, and he made a classic 104. Bobby Simpson and E W Swanton were two admirers from different camps. It was his fourth against Australia and his third at Melbourne. However, despite England making 558 Australia ensured that this second Test was also drawn.

At Sydney soon after England won by an innings and 93. In their first innings Bob Barber made a riveting 185. Cowdrey made a duck but he took two catches in both innings.

At Adelaide Australia fought back and Cowdrey and Barrington found themselves together again at 33 for three. Tragically Cowdrey misheard wicket-keeper Grout's call of "Watch the one" as Barrington saying "Come on", was sent back and run out for 38. England's 241 was soon put in the shade by an opening partnership of 244 from Lawry and Simpson. In England's second innings much again depended on Cowdrey and Barrington but Cowdrey was caught at the wicket for 35. Although Barrington in his final appearance at Adelaide Oval made 102, in the process scoring his tenth consecutive fifty on the ground, England lost.

There was still the final Test at Melbourne. In the first innings Cowdrey made 79 and Barrington made another century. England's 485 for nine declared paled in the face of Bob Cowper's 307. The match was drawn.

*Cover driving Chappell at Adelaide, February 1966.*

|  | Matches | Innings | Not out | Runs | Highest score | Average | 100s | 50s | Caught |
|---|---|---|---|---|---|---|---|---|---|
| This series | 4 | 6 | 1 | 267 | 104 | 53.40 | 1 | 1 | 5 |
| Previous series | 79 | 130 | 12 | 5590 | 182 | 47.37 | 17 | 28 | 95 |
| Cumulative totals | 83 | 136 | 13 | 5857 | 182 | 47.62 | 18 | 29 | 100 |

## *100 Catches*

Test No. 597/194

# AUSTRALIA v ENGLAND 1965-66 (1st Test)

Played at Woolloongabba, Brisbane, on 10, 11 (*no play*), 13, 14, 15 December.
Toss: Australia.  Result: MATCH DRAWN.
Debuts: Australia – P.J. Allan, K.D. Walters.

Rain restricted play on the first day to 111 minutes and washed out the second completely. Lawry, having survived a confident appeal for a catch at the wicket off Brown's seventh ball of the innings, batted 419 minutes and hit 23 fours. Walters was the fifth Australian to score a hundred in the first innings of his first Test; all five instances have been against England. At 19 years 357 days, Walters was the third-youngest Australian after R.N. Harvey and A. Jackson to score a Test hundred. Russell, who began the match with a fractured thumb, split the webbing of his right hand when fielding.

## AUSTRALIA

| | | |
|---|---|---:|
| W.M. Lawry | c Parks b Higgs | 166 |
| I.R. Redpath | b Brown | 17 |
| R.M. Cowper | c Barrington b Brown | 22 |
| P.J.P. Burge | b Brown | 0 |
| B.C. Booth* | c and b Titmus | 16 |
| K.D. Walters | c Parks b Higgs | 155 |
| T.R. Veivers | not out | 56 |
| N.J.N. Hawke | not out | 6 |
| P.I. Philpott | ) | |
| A.T.W. Grout† | ) did not bat | |
| P.J. Allan | ) | |
| Extras | (LB 2, NB 3) | 5 |
| **Total** | (6 wickets declared) | **443** |

## ENGLAND

| | | | | |
|---|---|---:|---|---:|
| R.W. Barber | c Walters b Hawke | 5 | c Veivers b Walters | 34 |
| G. Boycott | b Philpott | 45 | not out | 63 |
| J.H. Edrich | c Lawry b Philpott | 32 | c Veivers b Philpott | 37 |
| K.F. Barrington | b Hawke | 53 | c Booth b Cowper | 38 |
| M.J.K. Smith* | b Allan | 16 | not out | 10 |
| J.M. Parks† | c Redpath b Philpott | 52 | | |
| F.J. Titmus | st Grout b Philpott | 60 | | |
| D.A. Allen | c Cowper b Walters | 3 | | |
| D.J. Brown | b Philpott | 3 | | |
| K. Higgs | lbw b Allan | 4 | | |
| W.E. Russell | not out | 0 | | |
| Extras | (B 4, NB 3) | 7 | (B 2, LB 2) | 4 |
| **Total** | | **280** | (3 wickets) | **186** |

| ENGLAND | O | M | R | W | O | M | R | W |
|---|---|---|---|---|---|---|---|---|
| Brown | 21 | 4 | 71 | 3 | | | | |
| Higgs | 30 | 6 | 102 | 2 | | | | |
| Titmus | 38 | 9 | 99 | 1 | | | | |
| Allen | 39 | 12 | 108 | 0 | | | | |
| Barber | 5 | 0 | 42 | 0 | | | | |
| Boycott | 4 | 0 | 16 | 0 | | | | |
| AUSTRALIA | | | | | | | | |
| Allan | 21 | 6 | 58 | 2 | 3 | 0 | 25 | 0 |
| Hawke | 16 | 7 | 44 | 2 | 10 | 2 | 16 | 0 |
| Walters | 10 | 1 | 25 | 1 | 5 | 1 | 22 | 1 |
| Philpott | 28.1 | 3 | 90 | 5 | 14 | 1 | 62 | 1 |
| Cowper | 7 | 4 | 7 | 0 | 6 | 0 | 20 | 1 |
| Veivers | 11 | 1 | 49 | 0 | 12 | 0 | 37 | 0 |

## FALL OF WICKETS

| | A | E | E |
|---|---|---|---|
| Wkt | 1st | 1st | 2nd |
| 1st | 51 | 5 | 46 |
| 2nd | 90 | 75 | 114 |
| 3rd | 90 | 86 | 168 |
| 4th | 125 | 115 | – |
| 5th | 312 | 191 | – |
| 6th | 431 | 221 | – |
| 7th | – | 232 | – |
| 8th | – | 253 | – |
| 9th | – | 272 | – |
| 10th | – | 280 | – |

Umpires: C.J. Egar and L.P. Rowan.

Test No. 598/195

# AUSTRALIA v ENGLAND 1965–66 (2nd Test)

Played at Melbourne Cricket Ground on 30, 31 December, 1, 3, 4 January.
Toss: Australia.   Result: MATCH DRAWN.
Debuts: Nil.

Simpson, Australia's appointed captain, had recovered from the fractured wrist which prevented him from playing in the 1st Test. For a variety of reasons both sides had a complete change of opening bowlers for this match. Boycott and Barber scored 98 in 77 minutes for England's first wicket. Cowdrey's hundred was his fourth against Australia and his third at Melbourne. McKenzie bowled 35·5 overs but earlier in the innings retired after bowling five balls of an over. On the fourth day Barrington deputised for Parks (stomach upset) from the start of the innings until tea and caught Simpson. Parks returned after the interval but rain ended play after nine minutes. Parks missed a vital stumping chance off Barber when Burge was 34 and Australia 204 for 4 in the second innings.

## AUSTRALIA

| | | | | | |
|---|---|---|---|---|---|
| R.B. Simpson* | c Edrich b Allen | 59 | c Barrington b Knight | | 67 |
| W.M. Lawry | c Cowdrey b Allen | 88 | c Smith b Barber | | 78 |
| P.J.P. Burge | b Jones | 5 | (4) c Edrich b Boycott | | 120 |
| R.M. Cowper | c Titmus b Jones | 99 | (3) lbw b Jones | | 5 |
| B.C. Booth | lbw b Jones | 23 | b Allen | | 10 |
| K.D. Walters | c Parks b Knight | 22 | c and b Barrington | | 115 |
| T.R. Veivers | run out | 19 | st Parks b Boycott | | 3 |
| P.I. Philpott | b Knight | 10 | b Knight | | 2 |
| A.T.W. Grout† | c Barber b Knight | 11 | c Allen b Barrington | | 16 |
| G.D. McKenzie | not out | 12 | run out | | 2 |
| A.N. Connolly | c Parks b Knight | 0 | not out | | 0 |
| Extras | (B 2, LB 7, NB 1) | 10 | (B 1, LB 3, W 1 NB 3) | | 8 |
| **Total** | | **358** | | | **426** |

## ENGLAND

| | | |
|---|---|---|
| G. Boycott | c McKenzie b Walters | 51 | not out | 5 |
| R.W. Barber | c Grout b McKenzie | 48 | not out | 0 |
| J.H. Edrich | c and b Veivers | 109 | | |
| K.F. Barrington | c Burge b Veivers | 63 | | |
| M.C. Cowdrey | c Connolly b Cowper | 104 | | |
| M.J.K. Smith* | c Grout b McKenzie | 41 | | |
| J.M. Parks† | c Cowper b McKenzie | 71 | | |
| B.R. Knight | c Simpson b McKenzie | 1 | | |
| F.J. Titmus | not out | 56 | | |
| D.A. Allen | c Grout b Connolly | 2 | | |
| I.J. Jones | b McKenzie | 1 | | |
| Extras | (B 4, LB 5, W 2) | 11 | | |
| **Total** | | **558** | (0 wickets) | 5 |

| ENGLAND | O | M | R | W | O | M | R | W | FALL OF WICKETS | | | |
|---|---|---|---|---|---|---|---|---|---|---|---|---|
| Jones | 24 | 4 | 92 | 3 | 20 | 1 | 92 | 1 | | A | E | A | E |
| Knight | 26·5 | 2 | 84 | 4 | 21 | 4 | 61 | 2 | Wkt | 1st | 1st | 2nd | 2nd |
| Titmus | 31 | 7 | 93 | 0 | 22 | 6 | 43 | 0 | 1st | 93 | 98 | 120 | – |
| Allen | 20 | 4 | 55 | 2 | 18 | 3 | 48 | 1 | 2nd | 109 | 110 | 141 | – |
| Barber | 6 | 1 | 24 | 0 | 17 | 0 | 87 | 1 | 3rd | 203 | 228 | 163 | – |
| Barrington | | | | | 7·4 | 0 | 47 | 2 | 4th | 262 | 333 | 176 | – |
| Boycott | | | | | 9 | 0 | 32 | 2 | 5th | 297 | 409 | 374 | – |
| Smith | | | | | 2 | 0 | 8 | 0 | 6th | 318 | 443 | 382 | – |
| | | | | | | | | | 7th | 330 | 447 | 385 | – |
| AUSTRALIA | | | | | | | | | 8th | 342 | 540 | 417 | – |
| McKenzie | 35·2 | 3 | 134 | 5 | 1 | 0 | 2 | 0 | 9th | 352 | 551 | 426 | – |
| Connolly | 37 | 5 | 125 | 1 | 1 | 0 | 3 | 0 | 10th | 358 | 558 | 426 | – |
| Philpott | 30 | 2 | 133 | 0 | | | | | | | | | |
| Walters | 10 | 2 | 32 | 1 | | | | | | | | | |
| Simpson | 16 | 4 | 61 | 0 | | | | | | | | | |
| Veivers | 12 | 3 | 46 | 2 | | | | | | | | | |
| Cowper | 3 | 0 | 16 | 1 | | | | | | | | | |

Umpires: C.J. Egar and W. Smyth.

Test No. 599/196

## AUSTRALIA v ENGLAND 1965–66 (3rd Test)

Played at Sydney Cricket Ground on 7, 8, 10, 11 January.
Toss: England. Result: ENGLAND won by an innings and 93 runs.
Debuts: Nil.

England beat Australia for the first time in eleven matches since the 2nd Test at Melbourne in 1962-63. The opening partnership of 234 in 240 minutes between Boycott and Barber was England's third-highest against Australia. Barber reached his only Test hundred in 200 minutes. He batted 291 minutes, faced 272 balls and hit 19 fours in making his highest score in first-class cricket; it remains the highest score by an England batsman on the first day of a Test against Australia. Edrich completed his second successive Test hundred with a six. Titmus scored his 1,000th run and completed the 'double' in his 40th Test. Brown took the wickets of Sincock, Hawke and Grout with the second, seventh, and eighth balls of his first over with the second new ball.

### ENGLAND

| | | |
|---|---|---|
| G. Boycott | c and b Philpott | 84 |
| R.W. Barber | b Hawke | 185 |
| J.H. Edrich | c and b Philpott | 103 |
| K.F. Barrington | c McKenzie b Hawke | 1 |
| M.C. Cowdrey | c Grout b Hawke | 0 |
| M.J.K. Smith* | c Grout b Hawke | 6 |
| D.J. Brown | c Grout b Hawke | 1 |
| J.M. Parks† | c Grout b Hawke | 13 |
| F.J. Titmus | c Grout b Walters | 14 |
| D.A. Allen | not out | 50 |
| I.J. Jones | b Hawke | 16 |
| Extras | (B 3, LB 8, W 2, NB 2) | 15 |
| **Total** | | **488** |

### AUSTRALIA

| | | | | |
|---|---|---|---|---|
| W.M. Lawry | c Parks b Jones | 0 | c Cowdrey b Brown | 33 |
| G. Thomas | c Titmus b Brown | 51 | c Cowdrey b Titmus | 25 |
| R.M. Cowper | st Parks b Allen | 60 | c Boycott b Titmus | 0 |
| P.J.P. Burge | c Parks b Brown | 6 | run out | 1 |
| B.C. Booth* | c Cowdrey b Jones | 8 | b Allen | 27 |
| D.J. Sincock | c Parks b Brown | 29 | (7) c Smith b Allen | 27 |
| K.D. Walters | st Parks b Allen | 23 | (6) not out | 35 |
| N.J.N. Hawke | c Barber b Brown | 0 | (9) c Smith b Titmus | 2 |
| A.T.W. Grout† | b Brown | 0 | (10) c Smith b Allen | 3 |
| G.D. McKenzie | c Cowdrey b Barber | 24 | (11) c Barber b Titmus | 12 |
| P.I. Philpott | not out | 5 | (8) lbw b Allen | 5 |
| Extras | (B 7, LB 8) | 15 | (B 3, LB 1) | 4 |
| **Total** | | **221** | | **174** |

| AUSTRALIA | O | M | R | W | O | M | R | W | | FALL OF WICKETS | | |
|---|---|---|---|---|---|---|---|---|---|---|---|---|
| McKenzie | 25 | 2 | 113 | 0 | | | | | | E | A | A |
| Hawke | 33·7 | 6 | 105 | 7 | | | | | Wkt | 1st | 1st | 2nd |
| Walters | 10 | 1 | 38 | 1 | | | | | 1st | 234 | 0 | 46 |
| Philpott | 28 | 3 | 86 | 2 | | | | | 2nd | 303 | 81 | 50 |
| Sincock | 20 | 1 | 98 | 0 | | | | | 3rd | 309 | 91 | 51 |
| Cowper | 6 | 1 | 33 | 0 | | | | | 4th | 309 | 105 | 86 |
| | | | | | | | | | 5th | 317 | 155 | 86 |
| ENGLAND | | | | | | | | | 6th | 328 | 174 | 119 |
| Jones | 20 | 6 | 51 | 2 | 7 | 0 | 35 | 0 | 7th | 358 | 174 | 131 |
| Brown | 17 | 1 | 63 | 5 | 11 | 2 | 32 | 1 | 8th | 395 | 174 | 135 |
| Boycott | 3 | 1 | 8 | 0 | | | | | 9th | 433 | 203 | 140 |
| Titmus | 23 | 8 | 40 | 0 | 17·3 | 4 | 40 | 4 | 10th | 488 | 221 | 174 |
| Barber | 2·1 | 1 | 2 | 1 | 5 | 0 | 16 | 0 | | | | |
| Allen | 19 | 5 | 42 | 2 | 20 | 8 | 47 | 4 | | | | |

Umpires: C.J. Egar and L.P. Rowan.

Test No. 600/197

# AUSTRALIA v ENGLAND 1965–66 (4th Test)

Played at Adelaide Oval on 28, 29, 31 January, 1 February.
Toss: England.   Result: AUSTRALIA won by an innings and 9 runs.
Debuts: Australia – K.R. Stackpole.

Australia's opening partnership of 244 in 260 minutes between Simpson and Lawry remains their highest for the first wicket against England and against all opponents in Australia. Simpson batted for 547 minutes and hit a six and 18 fours. Barrington, in his final Test appearance at Adelaide, extended his unique run of success by scoring his tenth consecutive fifty in first-class matches on that ground: 104, 52, 52*, 63, 132* (in 1962-63); 69, 51, 63, 60, 102 (in 1965-66).

## ENGLAND

| | | | | |
|---|---|---|---|---|
| G. Boycott | c Chappell b Hawke | 22 | lbw b McKenzie | 12 |
| R.W. Barber | b McKenzie | 0 | c Grout b Hawke | 19 |
| J.H. Edrich | c Simpson b McKenzie | 5 | c Simpson b Hawke | 1 |
| K.F. Barrington | lbw b Walters | 60 | c Chappell b Hawke | 102 |
| M.C. Cowdrey | run out | 38 | c Grout b Stackpole | 35 |
| M.J.K. Smith* | b Veivers | 29 | c McKenzie b Stackpole | 5 |
| J.M. Parks† | c Stackpole b McKenzie | 49 | run out | 16 |
| F.J. Titmus | lbw b McKenzie | 33 | c Grout b Hawke | 53 |
| D.A. Allen | c Simpson b McKenzie | 2 | not out | 5 |
| D.J. Brown | c Thomas b McKenzie | 1 | c and b Hawke | 0 |
| I.J. Jones | not out | 0 | c Lawry b Veivers | 8 |
| Extras | (LB 2) | 2 | (LB 2, NB 8) | 10 |
| **Total** | | **241** | | **266** |

## AUSTRALIA

| | | |
|---|---|---|
| R.B. Simpson* | c Titmus b Jones | 225 |
| W.M. Lawry | b Titmus | 119 |
| G. Thomas | b Jones | 52 |
| T.R. Veivers | c Parks b Jones | 1 |
| P.J.P. Burge | c Parks b Jones | 27 |
| K.D. Walters | c Parks b Brown | 0 |
| I.M. Chappell | c Edrich b Jones | 17 |
| K.R. Stackpole | c Parks b Jones | 43 |
| N.J.N. Hawke | not out | 20 |
| A.T.W. Grout† | b Titmus | 4 |
| G.D. McKenzie | lbw b Titmus | 1 |
| Extras | (B 4, LB 3) | 7 |
| **Total** | | **516** |

| AUSTRALIA | O | M | R | W | O | M | R | W |
|---|---|---|---|---|---|---|---|---|
| McKenzie | 21.7 | 4 | 48 | 6 | 18 | 4 | 53 | 1 |
| Hawke | 23 | 2 | 69 | 1 | 21 | 6 | 54 | 5 |
| Walters | 14 | 0 | 50 | 1 | 9 | 0 | 47 | 0 |
| Stackpole | 5 | 0 | 30 | 0 | 14 | 3 | 33 | 2 |
| Chappell | 4 | 1 | 18 | 0 | 22 | 4 | 53 | 0 |
| Veivers | 13 | 3 | 24 | 1 | 3.7 | 0 | 16 | 1 |
| ENGLAND | | | | | | | | |
| Jones | 29 | 3 | 118 | 6 | | | | |
| Brown | 28 | 4 | 109 | 1 | | | | |
| Boycott | 7 | 3 | 33 | 0 | | | | |
| Titmus | 37 | 6 | 116 | 3 | | | | |
| Allen | 21 | 1 | 103 | 0 | | | | |
| Barber | 4 | 0 | 30 | 0 | | | | |

FALL OF WICKETS

| | E | A | E |
|---|---|---|---|
| Wkt | 1st | 1st | 2nd |
| 1st | 7 | 244 | 23 |
| 2nd | 25 | 331 | 31 |
| 3rd | 33 | 333 | 32 |
| 4th | 105 | 379 | 114 |
| 5th | 150 | 383 | 123 |
| 6th | 178 | 425 | 163 |
| 7th | 210 | 480 | 244 |
| 8th | 212 | 501 | 253 |
| 9th | 222 | 506 | 257 |
| 10th | 241 | 516 | 266 |

Umpires: C.J. Egar and L.P. Rowan.

Test No. 601/198

# AUSTRALIA v ENGLAND 1965–66 (5th Test)

Played at Melbourne Cricket Ground on 11, 12, 14, 15 (*no play*), 16 February.
Toss: England.   Result: MATCH DRAWN.
Debuts: Nil.

Cowper scored Australia's only triple hundred in a home Test. He hit 20 fours and batted for 727 minutes to record the longest first-class innings in Australia, the longest innings against England overseas, and the fourth-longest innings in all first-class cricket. Barrington hit his 122nd ball for six to complete his second consecutive Test hundred in 148 minutes. He was the first to reach a hundred with a six twice in Tests between England and Australia (also *Test No. 538*).

### ENGLAND

| | | | | |
|---|---|---|---|---|
| G. Boycott | c Stackpole b McKenzie | 17 | lbw b McKenzie | 1 |
| R.W. Barber | run out | 17 | b McKenzie | 20 |
| J.H. Edrich | c McKenzie b Walters | 85 | b McKenzie | 3 |
| K.F. Barrington | c Grout b Walters | 115 | not out | 32 |
| M.C. Cowdrey | c Grout b Walters | 79 | not out | 11 |
| M.J.K. Smith* | c Grout b Walters | 0 | | |
| J.M. Parks† | run out | 89 | | |
| F.J. Titmus | not out | 42 | | |
| B.R. Knight | c Grout b Hawke | 13 | | |
| D.J. Brown | c and b Chappell | 12 | | |
| I.J. Jones | not out | 4 | | |
| Extras | (B 9, LB 2, NB 1) | 12 | (LB 2) | 2 |
| Total | (9 wickets declared) | **485** | (3 wickets) | **69** |

### AUSTRALIA

| | | |
|---|---|---|
| W.M. Lawry | c Edrich b Jones | 108 |
| R.B. Simpson* | b Brown | 4 |
| G. Thomas | c Titmus b Jones | 19 |
| R.M. Cowper | b Knight | 307 |
| K.D. Walters | c and b Barber | 60 |
| I.M. Chappell | c Parks b Jones | 19 |
| K.R. Stackpole | b Knight | 9 |
| T.R. Veivers | b Titmus | 4 |
| N.J.N. Hawke | not out | 0 |
| A.T.W. Grout† | ⎱ did not bat | |
| G.D. McKenzie | ⎰ | |
| Extras | (B 6, LB 5, NB 2) | 13 |
| Total | (8 wickets declared) | **543** |

| AUSTRALIA | O | M | R | W | O | M | R | W |
|---|---|---|---|---|---|---|---|---|
| McKenzie | 26 | 5 | 100 | 1 | 6 | 2 | 17 | 3 |
| Hawke | 35 | 5 | 109 | 1 | 4 | 1 | 22 | 0 |
| Walters | 19 | 3 | 53 | 4 | 2 | 0 | 16 | 0 |
| Simpson | 5 | 1 | 20 | 0 | | | | |
| Stackpole | 10 | 2 | 43 | 0 | 3 | 0 | 10 | 0 |
| Veivers | 15 | 3 | 78 | 0 | | | | |
| Chappell | 17 | 4 | 70 | 1 | 2 | 0 | 20 | 0 |
| ENGLAND | | | | | | | | |
| Brown | 31 | 3 | 134 | 1 | | | | |
| Jones | 29 | 1 | 145 | 3 | | | | |
| Knight | 36·2 | 4 | 105 | 2 | | | | |
| Titmus | 42 | 12 | 86 | 1 | | | | |
| Barber | 16 | 0 | 60 | 1 | | | | |

### FALL OF WICKETS

| Wkt | E 1st | A 1st | E 2nd |
|---|---|---|---|
| 1st | 36 | 15 | 6 |
| 2nd | 41 | 36 | 21 |
| 3rd | 219 | 248 | 34 |
| 4th | 254 | 420 | – |
| 5th | 254 | 481 | – |
| 6th | 392 | 532 | – |
| 7th | 419 | 543 | – |
| 8th | 449 | 543 | – |
| 9th | 474 | – | – |
| 10th | – | – | – |

Umpires: C.J. Egar and L.P. Rowan.

## Chapter 23
# IN NEW ZEALAND 1966

The following tour of New Zealand in 1966 involved three four-day drawn Tests.

In the first at Christchurch Cowdrey was out for a duck but when New Zealand batted he caught skipper Chapple at second slip to become the second non-wicket keeper after W R Hammond to hold 100 catches in Test cricket – on almost the same spot where Hammond had taken his hundredth catch. It was a remarkable record given his opening fears in that regard.

In the second at Carisbrook, Dunedin Cowdrey made 89 not out in England's only innings.

In the third at Eden Park Auckland Cowdrey made 59 and 27.

|  | Matches | Innings | Not out | Runs | Highest score | Average | 100s | 50s | Caught |
|---|---|---|---|---|---|---|---|---|---|
| This series | 3 | 5 | 1 | 196 | 89* | 49.00 | 0 | 2 | 2 |
| Previous series | 83 | 136 | 13 | 5857 | 182 | 47.62 | 18 | 29 | 100 |
| Cumulative totals | 86 | 141 | 14 | 6053 | 182 | 47.66 | 18 | 31 | 102 |

*6,000 runs*

Test No. 602/35

# NEW ZEALAND v ENGLAND 1965–66 (1st Test)

Played at Lancaster Park, Christchurch on 25, 26, 28 February, 1 March.
Toss: England.   Result: MATCH DRAWN.
Debuts: New Zealand – G.P. Bilby, N. Puna.

Cowdrey became the second non-wicket-keeper after W.R. Hammond to hold 100 catches in Test cricket when he caught Chapple at second slip.

## ENGLAND

| | | | | |
|---|---|---|---|---|
| G. Boycott | c Petrie b Motz | 4 | run out | 4 |
| W.E. Russell | b Motz | 30 | b Bartlett | 25 |
| J.H. Edrich | c Bartlett b Motz | 2 | lbw b Cunis | 2 |
| M.C. Cowdrey | c Bilby b Cunis | 0 | c Pollard b Motz | 21 |
| M.J.K. Smith* | c Puna b Pollard | 54 | c Bilby b Puna | 87 |
| P.H. Parfitt | c Congdon b Bartlett | 54 | not out | 46 |
| J.M. Parks† | c Petrie b Chapple | 30 | not out | 4 |
| D.A. Allen | c Chapple b Bartlett | 88 | | |
| D.J. Brown | b Cunis | 44 | | |
| K. Higgs | not out | 8 | | |
| I.J. Jones | b Bartlett | 0 | | |
| Extras | (B 6, LB 6, NB 16) | 28 | (B 4, LB 1, NB 7) | 12 |
| **Total** | | **342** | (5 wickets declared) | **201** |

## NEW ZEALAND

| | | | | |
|---|---|---|---|---|
| G.P. Bilby | c Parks b Higgs | 28 | c Parks b Brown | 3 |
| M.J.F. Shrimpton | c Parks b Brown | 11 | c Smith b Allen | 13 |
| B.E. Congdon | c Smith b Jones | 104 | c Cowdrey b Higgs | 4 |
| B.W. Sinclair | c and b Higgs | 23 | c Parks b Higgs | 0 |
| V. Pollard | lbw b Higgs | 23 | not out | 6 |
| M.E. Chapple* | c Cowdrey b Jones | 15 | (7) c Parks b Higgs | 0 |
| G.A. Bartlett | c Parks b Brown | 0 | (8) c Brown b Parfitt | 0 |
| E.C. Petrie† | c Parks b Brown | 55 | (6) lbw b Higgs | 1 |
| R.C. Motz | c Parks b Jones | 58 | c Russell b Parfitt | 2 |
| R.S. Cunis | not out | 8 | not out | 16 |
| N. Puna | c Smith b Jones | 1 | | |
| Extras | (B 7, LB 13, NB 1) | 21 | (B 2, LB 1) | 3 |
| **Total** | | **347** | (8 wickets) | **48** |

| NEW ZEALAND | O | M | R | W | O | M | R | W |
|---|---|---|---|---|---|---|---|---|
| Motz | 31 | 9 | 83 | 3 | 20 | 6 | 38 | 1 |
| Bartlett | 33.2 | 6 | 63 | 3 | 14 | 2 | 44 | 1 |
| Cunis | 31 | 9 | 63 | 2 | 19 | 3 | 58 | 1 |
| Puna | 18 | 6 | 54 | 0 | 14 | 6 | 49 | 1 |
| Chapple | 9 | 3 | 24 | 1 | | | | |
| Pollard | 5 | 1 | 27 | 1 | | | | |
| ENGLAND | | | | | | | | |
| Brown | 30 | 3 | 80 | 3 | 4 | 2 | 6 | 1 |
| Jones | 28.4 | 9 | 71 | 4 | 7 | 3 | 13 | 0 |
| Higgs | 30 | 6 | 51 | 3 | 9 | 7 | 5 | 4 |
| Allen | 40 | 14 | 80 | 0 | 19 | 15 | 8 | 1 |
| Boycott | 12 | 6 | 30 | 0 | | | | |
| Parfitt | 3 | 0 | 14 | 0 | 6 | 3 | 5 | 2 |
| Parks | | | | | 3 | 1 | 8 | 0 |

### FALL OF WICKETS

| Wkt | E 1st | NZ 1st | E 2nd | NZ 2nd |
|---|---|---|---|---|
| 1st | 19 | 39 | 18 | 5 |
| 2nd | 28 | 41 | 32 | 19 |
| 3rd | 47 | 112 | 48 | 21 |
| 4th | 47 | 181 | 68 | 21 |
| 5th | 160 | 202 | 193 | 22 |
| 6th | 160 | 203 | – | 22 |
| 7th | 209 | 237 | – | 22 |
| 8th | 316 | 326 | – | 32 |
| 9th | 342 | 344 | – | – |
| 10th | 342 | 347 | – | – |

Umpires: W.T. Martin and F.R. Goodall.

Test No. 603/36

# NEW ZEALAND v ENGLAND 1965–66 (2nd Test)

Played at Carisbrook, Dunedin, on 4, 5, 7, 8 March.
Toss: New Zealand.   Result: MATCH DRAWN.
Debuts: Nil.

Motz hit 22 runs (064066) off Allen's 26th over to establish the record for the most runs by one batsman off a six-ball over in Test matches. Rain restricted play to 3¼ hours on the first day and to just over two hours on the third.

## NEW ZEALAND

| | | | | |
|---|---|---|---|---|
| G.P. Bilby | c Murray b Jones | 3 | c Parfitt b Higgs | 21 |
| M.J.F. Shrimpton | c Boycott b Higgs | 38 | (6) b Allen | 0 |
| B.E. Congdon | c Murray b Jones | 0 | b Parfitt | 19 |
| B.W. Sinclair* | b Knight | 33 | c Knight b Jones | 39 |
| V. Pollard | c Murray b Higgs | 8 | (2) b Higgs | 2 |
| R.W. Morgan | c Murray b Higgs | 0 | (5) c Smith b Allen | 3 |
| G.A. Bartlett | c Parfitt b Allen | 6 | c Knight b Allen | 4 |
| E.C. Petrie† | c Smith b Jones | 28 | not out | 13 |
| R.C. Motz | c Higgs b Knight | 57 | b Jones | 1 |
| R.S. Cunis | c Boycott b Allen | 8 | lbw b Allen | 9 |
| N. Puna | not out | 3 | not out | 18 |
| Extras | (B 4, LB 4) | 8 | (B 10, LB 6, NB 2) | 18 |
| **Total** | | **192** | (9 wickets) | **147** |

## ENGLAND

| | | |
|---|---|---|
| G. Boycott | b Bartlett | 5 |
| W.E. Russell | b Motz | 11 |
| J.H. Edrich | c Bilby b Cunis | 36 |
| M.C. Cowdrey | not out | 89 |
| M.J.K. Smith* | c Pollard b Bartlett | 20 |
| P.H. Parfitt | c Pollard b Puna | 4 |
| J.T. Murray† | c Sinclair b Puna | 50 |
| B.R. Knight | c Bartlett b Motz | 12 |
| D.A. Allen | b Cunis | 9 |
| K. Higgs | not out | 0 |
| I.J. Jones | did not bat | |
| Extras | (B 4, LB 6, NB 8) | 18 |
| **Total** | (8 wickets declared) | **254** |

| ENGLAND | O | M | R | W | O | M | R | W | FALL OF WICKETS | | | |
|---|---|---|---|---|---|---|---|---|---|---|---|---|
| Jones | 26 | 11 | 46 | 3 | 15 | 4 | 32 | 2 | | NZ | E | NZ |
| Higgs | 20 | 6 | 29 | 3 | 13 | 7 | 12 | 2 | Wkt | 1st | 1st | 2nd |
| Knight | 32 | 14 | 41 | 2 | 3 | 1 | 3 | 0 | 1st | 4 | 9 | 8 |
| Allen | 27·4 | 9 | 68 | 2 | 33 | 17 | 46 | 4 | 2nd | 6 | 32 | 27 |
| Parfitt | | | | | 17 | 6 | 30 | 1 | 3rd | 66 | 72 | 66 |
| Edrich | | | | | 1 | 0 | 6 | 0 | 4th | 83 | 103 | 75 |
| | | | | | | | | | 5th | 83 | 119 | 75 |
| NEW ZEALAND | | | | | | | | | 6th | 92 | 200 | 79 |
| Motz | 32 | 7 | 76 | 2 | | | | | 7th | 100 | 213 | 100 |
| Bartlett | 29 | 4 | 70 | 2 | | | | | 8th | 170 | 241 | 102 |
| Cunis | 28 | 7 | 49 | 2 | | | | | 9th | 181 | – | 112 |
| Puna | 14 | 2 | 40 | 2 | | | | | 10th | 192 | – | – |
| Pollard | 1 | 0 | 1 | 0 | | | | | | | | |

Umpires: W.T. Martin and W.J.C. Gwynne.

Test No. 604/37

# NEW ZEALAND v ENGLAND 1965–66 (3rd Test)

Played at Eden Park, Auckland, on 11, 12, 14, 15 March.
Toss: New Zealand. Result: MATCH DRAWN.
Debuts: Nil.

England needed 204 runs to win in 4½ hours. Edrich was taken ill with appendicitis after the first day and operated upon before the start of the second. Brown severely strained his back and was unable to complete his ninth over.

### NEW ZEALAND

| | | | | | |
|---|---|---|---|---|---|
| T.W. Jarvis | c Parks b Jones | 39 | c Parks b Jones | | 0 |
| M.J.F. Shrimpton | b Brown | 6 | lbw b Brown | | 0 |
| B.E. Congdon | lbw b Higgs | 64 | run out | | 23 |
| B.W. Sinclair* | c Russell b Jones | 114 | b Higgs | | 9 |
| R.W. Morgan | c Smith b Allen | 5 | lbw b Knight | | 25 |
| V. Pollard | c Knight b Allen | 2 | c Parks b Jones | | 25 |
| E.C. Petrie† | c Smith b Higgs | 12 | (8) b Higgs | | 6 |
| R.C. Motz | c Jones b Allen | 16 | (7) c Smith b Jones | | 14 |
| B.R. Taylor | b Allen | 18 | b Higgs | | 6 |
| R.S. Cunis | not out | 6 | c sub (J.T. Murray) b Allen | | 8 |
| N. Puna | c Russell b Allen | 7 | not out | | 2 |
| Extras | (B 1, LB 4, NB 2) | 7 | (B 2, LB 7, NB 2) | | 11 |
| **Total** | | **296** | | | **129** |

### ENGLAND

| | | | | | |
|---|---|---|---|---|---|
| P.H. Parfitt | b Taylor | 3 | b Taylor | | 30 |
| W.E. Russell | lbw b Motz | 56 | c Petrie b Taylor | | 1 |
| M.C. Cowdrey | run out | 59 | lbw b Puna | | 27 |
| M.J.K. Smith* | b Taylor | 18 | lbw b Cunis | | 30 |
| J.M. Parks† | lbw b Taylor | 38 | not out | | 45 |
| B.R. Knight | c Taylor b Pollard | 25 | not out | | 13 |
| D.A. Allen | not out | 7 | | | |
| D.J. Brown | b Pollard | 0 | | | |
| K. Higgs | c Petrie b Pollard | 0 | | | |
| I.J. Jones | b Cunis | 0 | | | |
| J.H. Edrich | absent ill | – | | | |
| Extras | (B 11, LB 3, NB 2) | 16 | (B 4, LB 4, NB 5) | | 13 |
| **Total** | | **222** | (4 wickets) | | **159** |

| ENGLAND | O | M | R | W | O | M | R | W |
|---|---|---|---|---|---|---|---|---|
| Brown | 18 | 6 | 32 | 1 | 8.1 | 3 | 8 | 1 |
| Jones | 21 | 4 | 52 | 2 | 25 | 9 | 28 | 3 |
| Higgs | 28 | 13 | 33 | 2 | 28 | 11 | 27 | 3 |
| Allen | 47.5 | 12 | 123 | 5 | 23.3 | 7 | 34 | 1 |
| Knight | 16 | 7 | 40 | 0 | 18 | 9 | 21 | 1 |
| Parfitt | 2 | 0 | 9 | 0 | | | | |
| NEW ZEALAND | | | | | | | | |
| Motz | 15 | 4 | 42 | 1 | 16 | 1 | 32 | 0 |
| Taylor | 21 | 6 | 46 | 3 | 12 | 4 | 20 | 2 |
| Cunis | 25.5 | 8 | 45 | 1 | 18 | 5 | 33 | 1 |
| Puna | 22 | 2 | 70 | 0 | 12 | 4 | 27 | 1 |
| Pollard | 5 | 2 | 3 | 3 | 14 | 3 | 30 | 0 |
| Shrimpton | | | | | 2 | 1 | 1 | 0 |
| Jarvis | | | | | 1 | 0 | 3 | 0 |

### FALL OF WICKETS

| | NZ | E | NZ | E |
|---|---|---|---|---|
| Wkt | 1st | 1st | 2nd | 2nd |
| 1st | 22 | 3 | 0 | 2 |
| 2nd | 99 | 121 | 0 | 50 |
| 3rd | 142 | 128 | 20 | 79 |
| 4th | 153 | 175 | 48 | 112 |
| 5th | 189 | 195 | 68 | – |
| 6th | 237 | 215 | 88 | – |
| 7th | 262 | 215 | 109 | – |
| 8th | 264 | 219 | 118 | – |
| 9th | 288 | 222 | 121 | – |
| 10th | 296 | – | 129 | – |

Umpires: W.T. Martin and R.W.R. Shortt.

Chapter 24

# WEST INDIES 1966

1966 in England was a historic sporting year. I was fortunate to be present at every one of England's matches in the soccer World Cup. It was a memorable year for Cowdrey too but not for reasons of unalloyed joy.

The West Indies were the visitors. They were a formidable side led by Garry Sobers, the greatest all rounder to grace the game.

In the first Test at Old Trafford West Indies made their mark with 484, Hunte and Sobers scoring centuries, and by bowling out England twice, largely by Lance Gibbs, they won by an innings. Colin Milburn's meaty 94 on his debut was a bright spot. Cowdrey's 69 in the second innings offered the only real resistance. England had lost in three days.

M J K Smith was axed as Captain. Popular with the players and a prolific scorer in County cricket, his own contribution with the bat in the highest company was found wanting. He was never to Captain England again. Generally England have appointed the Captain before the team. Australia notably select their team and then the Captain. England's contrary procedure dates back to the appointment of an amateur, fortunately often gifted and inspirational, who then had a say in the choice of the team. The distinction is that every member of an Australian team was worth his place *as a player*. The different procedure was to be perpetuated later by J M Brearley being chosen largely as a Captain, but when opening the batting with Boycott his staying quality was like chalk compared with cheese.

At all events it was Cowdrey at the helm again for the second Test at Lord's. Graveney was also recalled. He made 96 in England's first innings after West Indies had been dismissed for 269. In their second innings they were only nine ahead with five wickets down. Cowdrey came in for criticism for not putting Sobers under any pressure, relying on his bowlers to dismiss the No 7, Sobers's cousin, David Holford. In the event both Sobers and Holford made centuries. England were set to make 264 in four hours but Cowdrey failed for the second time in the match and it was a typical Milburn undefeated century that saved the day. It was a great Test match but a disappointing result for England.

England began the third Test at Trent Bridge in fine fettle. West Indies were all out for 235. However having lost three for 13 on the first evening Cowdrey joined Graveney in a fight-back that was to continue the following morning. Graveney made 109 and Cowdrey 96. The lead of 90 was effectively dismissed and West Indies were able to declare at 482 for five. England were beaten by 139. So England, under Cowdrey's renewed leadership, were two down with two to play.

The fourth Test at Headingley was no less disastrous. With Barber back in the side but not used as a bowler until West Indies were over 300 and Sobers well set, Cowdrey was widely criticised. West Indies amassed 500 for nine. England could not cope with Hall and Griffith. They followed on 260 behind but were all out for 205. The match was over before tea on the fourth day. Cowdrey had made 17 and 12.

Cowdrey was replaced as Captain by Brian Close for the fifth Test and was dropped from the side. I attended that match which England won. I remember particularly Amiss coming in where Cowdrey should have been. It was a delight to see Murray's wicket-keeping and one can pay his batting no greater compliment than to say it was hard to distinguish him from Graveney when in partnership they both made centuries. So much for the ploy of playing a wicket-keeper on the strength of his greater ability as a batsman. Higgs made a notable tail-ender. A particular irony that struck me was the tremendous coverage and acclaim that was given to Close's catching of Sobers in the West Indies second innings. Typically he had stood unmoved at short square leg as Sobers swung at a ball on the leg side. The ball intended for the boundary popped up and Close took a dolly catch. He was, of course, only able to do so having stood his ground rather than ducking for cover as most first class cricketers do in such circumstances. The irony? It was precisely the circumstances in which Cowdrey had taken the first of his 122 catches in Test cricket.

There was no winter tour in 1966/67 and Cowdrey was able to rest and reflect while he waited for the 1967 series.

## WEST INDIES 1966

|  | Matches | Innings | Not out | Runs | Highest score | Average | 100s | 50s | Caught |
|---|---|---|---|---|---|---|---|---|---|
| This series | 4 | 8 | 0 | 252 | 96 | 31.50 | 0 | 2 | 3 |
| Previous series | 86 | 141 | 14 | 6053 | 182 | 47.66 | 18 | 31 | 102 |
| Cumulative totals | 90 | 149 | 14 | 6305 | 182 | 46.70 | 18 | 33 | 105 |

Test No. 605/46

# ENGLAND v WEST INDIES 1966 (1st Test)

Played at Old Trafford, Manchester, on 2, 3, 4 June.
Toss: West Indies.  Result: WEST INDIES won by an innings and 40 runs.
Debuts: England – C. Milburn; West Indies – D.A.J. Holford.

Hunte square cut the first ball of the rubber for four runs. England were beaten in three days for the first time since 1938 (*Test No. 265*) and it was their first such defeat in a five-day Test. The weather was hot throughout.

### WEST INDIES

| | | |
|---|---|---|
| C.C. Hunte | c Smith b Higgs | 135 |
| E.D.A. St J. McMorris | c Russell b Higgs | 11 |
| R.B. Kanhai | b Higgs | 0 |
| B.F. Butcher | c Parks b Titmus | 44 |
| S.M. Nurse | b Titmus | 49 |
| G. St A. Sobers* | c Cowdrey b Titmus | 161 |
| D.A.J. Holford | c Smith b Allen | 32 |
| D.W. Allan† | lbw b Titmus | 1 |
| C.C. Griffith | lbw b Titmus | 30 |
| W.W. Hall | b Allen | 1 |
| L.R. Gibbs | not out | 1 |
| Extras | (B 8, LB 10, NB 1) | 19 |
| **Total** | | **484** |

### ENGLAND

| | | | | |
|---|---|---|---|---|
| C. Milburn | run out | 0 | b Gibbs | 94 |
| W.E. Russell | c Sobers b Gibbs | 26 | b Griffith | 20 |
| K.F. Barrington | c and b Griffith | 5 | c Nurse b Holford | 30 |
| M.C. Cowdrey | c and b Gibbs | 12 | c Butcher b Sobers | 69 |
| M.J.K. Smith* | c Butcher b Gibbs | 5 | b Gibbs | 6 |
| J.M. Parks† | c Nurse b Holford | 43 | c and b Sobers | 11 |
| F.J. Titmus | b Holford | 15 | c Butcher b Sobers | 12 |
| D.A. Allen | c Sobers b Gibbs | 37 | c Allan b Gibbs | 1 |
| D.J. Brown | b Gibbs | 14 | c Sobers b Gibbs | 10 |
| K. Higgs | c Sobers b Holford | 1 | st Allan b Gibbs | 5 |
| I.J. Jones | not out | 0 | not out | 0 |
| Extras | (B 1, LB 4, NB 4) | 9 | (B 11, LB 1, NB 7) | 19 |
| **Total** | | **167** | | **277** |

| ENGLAND | O | M | R | W | O | M | R | W |
|---|---|---|---|---|---|---|---|---|
| Jones | 28 | 6 | 100 | 0 | | | | |
| Brown | 28 | 4 | 84 | 0 | | | | |
| Higgs | 31 | 5 | 94 | 3 | | | | |
| Allen | 31·1 | 8 | 104 | 2 | | | | |
| Titmus | 35 | 10 | 83 | 5 | | | | |
| WEST INDIES | | | | | | | | |
| Hall | 14 | 6 | 43 | 0 | 5 | 0 | 28 | 0 |
| Griffith | 10 | 3 | 28 | 1 | 6 | 1 | 25 | 1 |
| Sobers | 7 | 1 | 16 | 0 | 42 | 11 | 87 | 3 |
| Gibbs | 28·1 | 13 | 37 | 5 | 41 | 16 | 69 | 5 |
| Holford | 15 | 4 | 34 | 3 | 14 | 2 | 49 | 1 |

### FALL OF WICKETS

| Wkt | WI 1st | E 1st | E 2nd |
|---|---|---|---|
| 1st | 38 | 11 | 53 |
| 2nd | 42 | 24 | 142 |
| 3rd | 116 | 42 | 166 |
| 4th | 215 | 48 | 184 |
| 5th | 283 | 65 | 203 |
| 6th | 410 | 85 | 217 |
| 7th | 411 | 143 | 218 |
| 8th | 471 | 153 | 268 |
| 9th | 482 | 163 | 276 |
| 10th | 484 | 167 | 277 |

Umpires: J.S. Buller and C.S. Elliott.

Test No. 606/47

# ENGLAND v WEST INDIES 1966 (2nd Test)

Played at Lord's, London, on 16, 17, 18, 20, 21 June.
Toss: West Indies. Result: MATCH DRAWN.
Debuts: England – B.L. D'Oliveira.

England needed to score 284 runs in 240 minutes. The unbroken partnership of 274 between Sobers and his cousin, Holford, remains the highest for West Indies' sixth wicket in all Tests. Milburn and Graveney recorded England's highest fifth-wicket partnership against West Indies (130 unbroken). Both Holford and Milburn scored hundreds in their second Test match. Parks made his 100th dismissal as a wicket-keeper and completed the double of 1,000 runs and 100 dismissals when he caught Kanhai.

### WEST INDIES

| | | | | | |
|---|---|---|---|---|---|
| C.C. Hunte | c Parks b Higgs | 18 | c Milburn b Knight | | 13 |
| M.C. Carew | c Parks b Higgs | 2 | c Knight b Higgs | | 0 |
| R.B. Kanhai | c Titmus b Higgs | 25 | c Parks b Knight | | 40 |
| B.F. Butcher | c Milburn b Knight | 49 | lbw b Higgs | | 3 |
| S.M. Nurse | b D'Oliveira | 64 | c Parks b D'Oliveira | | 35 |
| G. St A. Sobers* | lbw b Knight | 46 | not out | | 163 |
| D.A.J. Holford | b Jones | 26 | not out | | 105 |
| D.W. Allan† | c Titmus b Higgs | 13 | | | |
| C.C. Griffith | lbw b Higgs | 5 | | | |
| W.W. Hall | not out | 8 | | | |
| L.R. Gibbs | c Parks b Higgs | 4 | | | |
| Extras | (B 2, LB 7) | 9 | (LB 8, NB 2) | | 10 |
| **Total** | | **269** | (5 wickets declared) | | **369** |

### ENGLAND

| | | | | | |
|---|---|---|---|---|---|
| G. Boycott | c Griffith b Gibbs | 60 | c Allan b Griffith | | 25 |
| C. Milburn | lbw b Hall | 6 | not out | | 126 |
| T.W. Graveney | c Allan b Hall | 96 | (6) not out | | 30 |
| K.F. Barrington | b Sobers | 19 | (3) b Griffith | | 5 |
| M.C. Cowdrey* | c Gibbs b Hall | 9 | (4) c Allan b Hall | | 5 |
| J.M. Parks† | lbw b Carew | 91 | (5) b Hall | | 0 |
| B.L. D'Oliveira | run out | 27 | | | |
| B.R. Knight | b Griffith | 6 | | | |
| F.J. Titmus | c Allan b Hall | 6 | | | |
| K. Higgs | c Holford b Gibbs | 13 | | | |
| I.J. Jones | not out | 0 | | | |
| Extras | (B 7, LB 10, NB 5) | 22 | (B 4, LB 2) | | 6 |
| **Totals** | | **355** | (4 wickets) | | **197** |

| ENGLAND | O | M | R | W | O | M | R | W |
|---|---|---|---|---|---|---|---|---|
| Jones | 21 | 3 | 64 | 1 | 25 | 2 | 95 | 0 |
| Higgs | 33 | 9 | 91 | 6 | 34 | 5 | 82 | 2 |
| Knight | 21 | 0 | 63 | 2 | 30 | 3 | 106 | 2 |
| Titmus | 5 | 0 | 18 | 0 | 19 | 3 | 30 | 0 |
| D'Oliveira | 14 | 5 | 24 | 1 | 25 | 7 | 46 | 1 |
| WEST INDIES | | | | | | | | |
| Sobers | 39 | 12 | 89 | 1 | 8 | 4 | 8 | 0 |
| Hall | 36 | 2 | 106 | 4 | 14 | 1 | 65 | 2 |
| Griffith | 28 | 4 | 79 | 1 | 11 | 2 | 43 | 2 |
| Gibbs | 37·3 | 18 | 48 | 2 | 13 | 4 | 40 | 0 |
| Carew | 3 | 0 | 11 | 1 | | | | |
| Holford | | | | | 9 | 1 | 35 | 0 |

### FALL OF WICKETS

| | WI | E | WI | E |
|---|---|---|---|---|
| Wkt | 1st | 1st | 2nd | 2nd |
| 1st | 8 | 8 | 2 | 37 |
| 2nd | 42 | 123 | 22 | 43 |
| 3rd | 53 | 164 | 25 | 67 |
| 4th | 119 | 198 | 91 | 67 |
| 5th | 205 | 203 | 95 | – |
| 6th | 213 | 251 | – | – |
| 7th | 252 | 266 | – | – |
| 8th | 252 | 296 | – | – |
| 9th | 261 | 355 | – | – |
| 10th | 269 | 355 | – | – |

Umpires: J.S. Buller and W.F.F. Price.

Test No. 607/48

# ENGLAND v WEST INDIES 1966 (3rd Test)

Played at Trent Bridge, Nottingham, on 30 June, 1, 2, 4, 5 July.
Toss: West Indies. Result: WEST INDIES won by 139 runs.
Debuts: England – D.L. Underwood.

England, needing to score 393 runs in 389 minutes, were all out at 4.14 p.m. Graveney scored his third hundred in consecutive Test appearances at Nottingham. Butcher, who batted for 461 minutes and hit 22 fours, shared in century partnerships for three successive wickets.

### WEST INDIES

| | | | | |
|---|---|---|---|---|
| C.C. Hunte | lbw b Higgs | 9 | c Graveney b D'Oliveira | 12 |
| P.D. Lashley | c Parks b Snow | 49 | lbw b D'Oliveira | 23 |
| R.B. Kanhai | c Underwood b Higgs | 32 | c Cowdrey b Higgs | 63 |
| B.F. Butcher | b Snow | 5 | not out | 209 |
| S.M. Nurse | c Illingworth b Snow | 93 | lbw b Higgs | 53 |
| G. St A. Sobers* | c Parks b Snow | 3 | c Underwood b Higgs | 94 |
| D.A.J. Holford | lbw b D'Oliveira | 11 | not out | 17 |
| J.L. Hendriks† | b D'Oliveira | 2 | | |
| C.C. Griffith | c Cowdrey b Higgs | 14 | | |
| W.W. Hall | b Higgs | 12 | | |
| L.R. Gibbs | not out | 0 | | |
| Extras | (B 3, LB 2) | 5 | (LB 6, W 5) | 11 |
| **Total** | | **235** | (5 wickets declared) | **482** |

### ENGLAND

| | | | | |
|---|---|---|---|---|
| G. Boycott | lbw b Sobers | 0 | c Sobers b Griffith | 71 |
| C. Milburn | c Sobers b Hall | 7 | c Griffith b Hall | 12 |
| W.E. Russell | b Hall | 4 | c Sobers b Gibbs | 11 |
| T.W. Graveney | c Holford b Sobers | 109 | c Hendriks b Griffith | 32 |
| M.C. Cowdrey* | c Hendriks b Griffith | 96 | c Sobers b Gibbs | 32 |
| J.M. Parks† | c Butcher b Sobers | 11 | c Lashley b Hall | 7 |
| B.L. D'Oliveira | b Hall | 76 | lbw b Griffith | 54 |
| R. Illingworth | c Lashley b Griffith | 0 | c Lashley b Sobers | 4 |
| K. Higgs | c Lashley b Sobers | 5 | c Sobers b Gibbs | 4 |
| J.A. Snow | b Hall | 0 | b Griffith | 3 |
| D.L. Underwood | not out | 12 | not out | 10 |
| Extras | (LB 2, NB 3) | 5 | (B 8, LB 2, NB 3) | 13 |
| **Total** | | **325** | | **253** |

| ENGLAND | O | M | R | W | O | M | R | W |
|---|---|---|---|---|---|---|---|---|
| Snow | 25 | 7 | 82 | 4 | 38 | 10 | 117 | 0 |
| Higgs | 25·4 | 3 | 71 | 4 | 38 | 6 | 109 | 3 |
| D'Oliveira | 30 | 14 | 51 | 2 | 34 | 8 | 77 | 2 |
| Underwood | 2 | 1 | 5 | 0 | 43 | 15 | 86 | 0 |
| Illingworth | 8 | 1 | 21 | 0 | 25 | 7 | 82 | 0 |
| WEST INDIES | | | | | | | | |
| Sobers | 49 | 12 | 90 | 4 | 31 | 6 | 71 | 1 |
| Hall | 34·3 | 8 | 105 | 4 | 16 | 3 | 52 | 2 |
| Griffith | 20 | 5 | 62 | 2 | 13·3 | 3 | 34 | 4 |
| Gibbs | 23 | 9 | 40 | 0 | 48 | 16 | 83 | 3 |
| Holford | 8 | 2 | 23 | 0 | | | | |

### FALL OF WICKETS

| Wkt | WI 1st | E 1st | WI 2nd | E 2nd |
|---|---|---|---|---|
| 1st | 19 | 0 | 29 | 32 |
| 2nd | 68 | 10 | 65 | 71 |
| 3rd | 80 | 13 | 175 | 125 |
| 4th | 140 | 182 | 282 | 132 |
| 5th | 144 | 221 | 455 | 142 |
| 6th | 180 | 238 | – | 176 |
| 7th | 190 | 247 | – | 181 |
| 8th | 215 | 255 | – | 222 |
| 9th | 228 | 260 | – | 240 |
| 10th | 235 | 325 | – | 253 |

Umpires: C.S. Elliott and A. Jepson.

Test No. 608/49

## ENGLAND v WEST INDIES 1966 (4th Test)

Played at Headingley, Leeds, on 4, 5, 6, 8 August.
Toss: West Indies. Result: WEST INDIES won by an innings and 55 runs.
Debuts: Nil.

West Indies retained the Wisden Trophy, completing their third victory of the rubber at 3.07 p.m. on the fourth day. Sobers scored his third hundred of the rubber and hit 103 runs between lunch and tea on the second day. His highest Test innings in England took 240 minutes, included 24 fours and took him past 5,000 runs in Tests, 2,000 runs against England, 500 runs in the rubber and 1,000 runs for the tour. His partnership of 265 in 240 minutes with Nurse remains the West Indies fifth-wicket record in all Tests.

### WEST INDIES

| | | |
|---|---|---|
| C.C. Hunte | lbw b Snow | 48 |
| P.D. Lashley | b Higgs | 9 |
| R.B. Kanhai | c Graveney b Underwood | 45 |
| B.F. Butcher | c Parks b Higgs | 38 |
| S.M. Nurse | c Titmus b Snow | 137 |
| G. St A. Sobers* | b Barber | 174 |
| D.A.J. Holford | b Higgs | 24 |
| C.C. Griffith | b Higgs | 0 |
| J.L. Hendriks† | not out | 9 |
| W.W. Hall | b Snow | 1 |
| L.R. Gibbs | not out | 2 |
| Extras | (B 1, LB 12) | 13 |
| **Total** | (9 wickets declared) | **500** |

### ENGLAND

| | | | | | |
|---|---|---|---|---|---|
| G. Boycott | c Holford b Hall | 12 | c Hendriks b Lashley | | 14 |
| R.W. Barber | c Hendriks b Griffith | 6 | b Sobers | | 55 |
| C. Milburn | not out | 29 | (7) b Gibbs | | 42 |
| T.W. Graveney | b Hall | 8 | b Gibbs | | 19 |
| M.C. Cowdrey* | b Hall | 17 | lbw b Gibbs | | 12 |
| B.L. D'Oliveira | c Hall b Griffith | 88 | (3) c Butcher b Sobers | | 7 |
| J.M. Parks† | lbw b Sobers | 2 | (6) c Nurse b Gibbs | | 16 |
| F.J. Titmus | c Hendriks b Sobers | 6 | b Gibbs | | 22 |
| K. Higgs | c Nurse b Sobers | 49 | c Hunte b Sobers | | 7 |
| D.L. Underwood | c Gibbs b Sobers | 0 | c Kanhai b Gibbs | | 0 |
| J.A. Snow | c Holford b Sobers | 0 | not out | | 0 |
| Extras | (B 12, LB 11) | 23 | (B 8, LB 1, NB 2) | | 11 |
| **Total** | | **240** | | | **205** |

| ENGLAND | O | M | R | W | O | M | R | W | | FALL OF WICKETS | | |
|---|---|---|---|---|---|---|---|---|---|---|---|---|
| | | | | | | | | | | WI | E | E |
| Snow | 42 | 6 | 146 | 3 | | | | | Wkt | 1st | 1st | 2nd |
| Higgs | 43 | 11 | 94 | 4 | | | | | 1st | 37 | 10 | 28 |
| D'Oliveira | 19 | 3 | 52 | 0 | | | | | 2nd | 102 | 18 | 70 |
| Titmus | 22 | 7 | 59 | 0 | | | | | 3rd | 122 | 42 | 84 |
| Underwood | 24 | 9 | 81 | 1 | | | | | 4th | 154 | 49 | 109 |
| Barber | 14 | 2 | 55 | 1 | | | | | 5th | 419 | 63 | 129 |
| WEST INDIES | | | | | | | | | 6th | 467 | 83 | 133 |
| Hall | 17 | 5 | 47 | 3 | 8 | 2 | 24 | 0 | 7th | 467 | 179 | 184 |
| Griffith | 12 | 2 | 37 | 2 | 12 | 0 | 52 | 0 | 8th | 489 | 238 | 205 |
| Sobers | 19.3 | 4 | 41 | 5 | 20.1 | 5 | 39 | 3 | 9th | 491 | 240 | 205 |
| Gibbs | 20 | 5 | 49 | 0 | 19 | 6 | 39 | 6 | 10th | – | 240 | 205 |
| Holford | 10 | 3 | 43 | 0 | 9 | 0 | 39 | 0 | | | | |
| Lashley | | | | | 3 | 2 | 1 | 1 | | | | |

Umpires: J.S. Buller and C.S. Elliott.

Test No. 609/50

# ENGLAND v WEST INDIES 1966 (5th Test)

Played at Kennington Oval, London, on 18, 19, 20, 22 August.
Toss: West Indies. Result: ENGLAND won by an innings and 34 runs.
Debuts: England – D.L. Amiss.

Sobers won the toss for the fifth time in the rubber. England's last three wickets added a record 361 runs and for the first time in Test cricket the last three batsmen scored one hundred and two fifties. The partnership of 217 in 235 minutes between Graveney and Murray remains England's highest for the eighth wicket against West Indies and second-highest in all Tests. Higgs and Snow each scored their maiden fifties in first-class cricket and their partnership of 128 in 140 minutes was only two runs short of the England tenth-wicket record by R.E. Foster and W. Rhodes against Australia in 1903–04 (*Test No. 78*).

### WEST INDIES

| | | | | |
|---|---|---:|---|---:|
| C.C. Hunte | b Higgs | 1 | c Murray b Snow | 7 |
| E.D.A. St J. McMorris | b Snow | 14 | c Murray b Snow | 1 |
| R.B. Kanhai | c Graveney b Illingworth | 104 | b D'Oliveira | 15 |
| B.F. Butcher | c Illingworth b Close | 12 | c Barber b Illingworth | 60 |
| S.M. Nurse | c Graveney b D'Oliveira | 0 | c Edrich b Barber | 70 |
| G. St A. Sobers* | c Graveney b Barber | 81 | (7) c Close b Snow | 0 |
| D.A.J. Holford | c D'Oliveira b Illingworth | 5 | (6) run out | 7 |
| J.L. Hendriks† | b Barber | 0 | b Higgs | 0 |
| C.C. Griffith | c Higgs b Barber | 4 | not out | 29 |
| W.W. Hall | not out | 30 | c D'Oliveira b Illingworth | 17 |
| L.R. Gibbs | c Murray b Snow | 12 | c and b Barber | 3 |
| Extras | (B 1, LB 3, NB 1) | 5 | (B 1, LB 14, NB 1) | 16 |
| **Total** | | **268** | | **225** |

### ENGLAND

| | | |
|---|---|---:|
| G. Boycott | b Hall | 4 |
| R.W. Barber | c Nurse b Sobers | 36 |
| J.H. Edrich | c Hendriks b Sobers | 35 |
| T.W. Graveney | run out | 165 |
| D.L. Amiss | lbw b Hall | 17 |
| B.L. D'Oliveira | b Hall | 4 |
| D.B. Close* | run out | 4 |
| R. Illingworth | c Hendriks b Griffith | 3 |
| J.T. Murray† | lbw b Sobers | 112 |
| K. Higgs | c and b Holford | 63 |
| J.A. Snow | not out | 59 |
| Extras | (B 8, LB 14, NB 3) | 25 |
| **Total** | | **527** |

| ENGLAND | O | M | R | W | O | M | R | W | FALL OF WICKETS |
|---|---:|---:|---:|---:|---:|---:|---:|---:|---|
| Snow | 20.5 | 1 | 66 | 2 | 13 | 5 | 40 | 3 | |
| Higgs | 17 | 4 | 52 | 1 | 15 | 6 | 18 | 1 | |
| D'Oliveira | 21 | 7 | 35 | 1 | 17 | 4 | 44 | 1 | |
| Close | 9 | 2 | 21 | 1 | 3 | 1 | 7 | 0 | |
| Barber | 15 | 3 | 49 | 3 | 22.1 | 2 | 78 | 2 | |
| Illingworth | 15 | 7 | 40 | 2 | 15 | 9 | 22 | 2 | |
| WEST INDIES | | | | | | | | | |
| Hall | 31 | 8 | 85 | 3 | | | | | |
| Griffith | 32 | 7 | 78 | 1 | | | | | |
| Sobers | 54 | 23 | 104 | 3 | | | | | |
| Holford | 25.5 | 1 | 79 | 1 | | | | | |
| Gibbs | 44 | 16 | 115 | 0 | | | | | |
| Hunte | 13 | 2 | 41 | 0 | | | | | |

| Wkt | WI 1st | E 1st | WI 2nd |
|---|---:|---:|---:|
| 1st | 1 | 6 | 5 |
| 2nd | 56 | 72 | 12 |
| 3rd | 73 | 85 | 50 |
| 4th | 74 | 126 | 107 |
| 5th | 196 | 130 | 137 |
| 6th | 218 | 150 | 137 |
| 7th | 218 | 166 | 142 |
| 8th | 223 | 383 | 168 |
| 9th | 223 | 399 | 204 |
| 10th | 268 | 527 | 225 |

Umpires: J.S. Buller and C.S. Elliott.

Chapter 25
# PAKISTAN 1967

Close continued as Captain in 1967 with continued success. England beat India three-nil in the first series of the summer. He followed this by leading the side in the drawn match with Pakistan at Lord's.

There had been a growing demand for Cowdrey's return as a player. He was having a most successful season with the bat in both County and Gillette Cup matches. The disappointing draw in the first Test prompted his recall, as opening batsman, as one of six changes in the team for the second Test at Trent Bridge. Cowdrey's contribution to a ten wicket win was 14 and 2 not out.

Cowdrey's contribution at the Oval was 16 and 9 to an eight wicket win. Close also opened in this match scoring 6 and 8, a chest infection having laid Boycott low on the morning of the match.

Cowdrey's return to Test cricket had hardly been a resounding success. Close's leadership of Yorkshire, in their successful attempt to hold the County championship, was to lead to Cowdrey's reinstatement as Captain for the 1967/68 tour of the West Indies.

On the eve of the final test the Counties' Executive Committee unanimously agreed that Yorkshire had been guilty of unfair play and that Close, as the instigator of those tactics, should be severely censured. The full MCC Committee vetoed his appointment for the forthcoming West Indies tour. It was in such circumstances that Cowdrey began his fourth term as Captain of England.

|  | Matches | Innings | Not out | Runs | Highest score | Average | 100s | 50s | Caught |
|---|---|---|---|---|---|---|---|---|---|
| This series | 2 | 4 | 1 | 41 | 16 | 13.66 | 0 | 0 | 1 |
| Previous series | 90 | 149 | 14 | 6305 | 182 | 46.70 | 18 | 33 | 105 |
| Cumulative totals | 92 | 153 | 15 | 6346 | 182 | 45.99 | 18 | 33 | 106 |

Test No. 621/13

# ENGLAND v PAKISTAN 1967 (1st Test)

Played at Lord's, London, on 27, 28, 29, 31 July, 1 August.
Toss: England.  Result: MATCH DRAWN.
Debuts: Pakistan – Salim Altaf, Wasim Bari.

Five wickets fell for nine runs after Barrington and Graveney had established England's third-wicket record against Pakistan with a partnership of 201 in 223 minutes. Hanif's 187 not out, scored off 556 balls in 542 minutes, included 21 fours, was then Pakistan's highest score against England, and represented 55% of their total. His partnership of 130 in 191 minutes with Asif is still Pakistan's record for the eighth wicket against all countries. Set 257 runs in 210 minutes, Pakistan scored only 88 in 165 minutes off 62 overs, 32 of which were maidens. Rain claimed 3 hours 37 minutes of the match.

### ENGLAND

| | | | | | |
|---|---|---|---|---|---|
| C. Milburn | c Wasim b Asif | 3 | c Asif b Majid | | 32 |
| W.E. Russell | b Intikhab | 43 | b Majid | | 12 |
| K.F. Barrington | c Wasim b Asif | 148 | b Intikhab | | 14 |
| T.W. Graveney | b Salim | 81 | c Ibadulla b Asif | | 30 |
| B.L. D'Oliveira | c Intikhab b Mushtaq | 59 | not out | | 81 |
| D.B. Close* | c sub (Ghulam Abbas) b Salim | 4 | st Wasim b Nasim | | 36 |
| J.T. Murray† | b Salim | 0 | c and b Nasim | | 0 |
| R. Illingworth | b Asif | 4 | c and b Nasim | | 9 |
| K. Higgs | lbw b Mushtaq | 14 | c Hanif b Intikhab | | 1 |
| J.A. Snow | b Mushtaq | 0 | c Hanif b Mushtaq | | 7 |
| R.N.S. Hobbs | not out | 1 | not out | | 1 |
| Extras | (LB 5, NB 7) | 12 | (B 12, LB 5, NB 1) | | 18 |
| Total | | 369 | (9 wickets declared) | | 241 |

### PAKISTAN

| | | | | | |
|---|---|---|---|---|---|
| Khalid Ibadulla | b Higgs | 8 | c Close b Illingworth | | 32 |
| Javed Burki | lbw b Higgs | 31 | c and b Barrington | | 13 |
| Mushtaq Mohammad | c Murray b Higgs | 4 | (4) not out | | 30 |
| Hanif Mohammad* | not out | 187 | | | |
| Majid Khan | c and b Hobbs | 5 | (3) c Close b Barrington | | 5 |
| Nasim-ul-Ghani | c D'Oliveira b Snow | 2 | | | |
| Saeed Ahmed | c Graveney b Snow | 6 | (5) not out | | 6 |
| Intikhab Alam | lbw b Illingworth | 17 | | | |
| Asif Iqbal | c Barrington b Illingworth | 76 | | | |
| Wasim Bari† | c Close b Barrington | 13 | | | |
| Salim Altaf | c Milburn b Snow | 2 | | | |
| Extras | (B 1, LB 2) | 3 | (B 1, LB 1) | | 2 |
| Total | | 354 | (3 wickets) | | 88 |

| PAKISTAN | O | M | R | W | O | M | R | W | FALL OF WICKETS | | | |
|---|---|---|---|---|---|---|---|---|---|---|---|---|
| Salim | 33 | 6 | 74 | 3 | 0.3 | 0 | 4 | 0 | | E | P | E | P |
| Asif | 28 | 10 | 76 | 3 | 21 | 5 | 50 | 1 | Wkt | 1st | 1st | 2nd | 2nd |
| Ibadulla | 3 | 0 | 5 | 0 | | | | | 1st | 5 | 19 | 33 | 27 |
| Majid | 11 | 2 | 28 | 0 | 10 | 1 | 32 | 2 | 2nd | 82 | 25 | 48 | 39 |
| Nasim | 12 | 1 | 36 | 0 | 13 | 3 | 32 | 3 | 3rd | 283 | 67 | 76 | 77 |
| Intikhab | 29 | 3 | 86 | 1 | 30 | 7 | 70 | 2 | 4th | 283 | 76 | 95 | – |
| Mushtaq | 11.3 | 3 | 23 | 3 | 16 | 4 | 35 | 1 | 5th | 287 | 91 | 199 | – |
| Saeed | 11 | 3 | 29 | 0 | | | | | 6th | 287 | 99 | 201 | – |
| ENGLAND | | | | | | | | | 7th | 292 | 139 | 215 | – |
| Snow | 45.1 | 11 | 120 | 3 | 4 | 2 | 6 | 0 | 8th | 352 | 269 | 220 | – |
| Higgs | 39 | 12 | 81 | 3 | 6 | 3 | 6 | 0 | 9th | 354 | 310 | 239 | – |
| D'Oliveira | 15 | 7 | 17 | 0 | | | | | 10th | 369 | 354 | – | – |
| Illingworth | 31 | 14 | 48 | 2 | 15 | 11 | 10 | 1 | | | | | |
| Hobbs | 35 | 16 | 46 | 1 | 16 | 9 | 28 | 0 | | | | | |
| Barrington | 11 | 1 | 29 | 1 | 13 | 2 | 23 | 2 | | | | | |
| Close | 6 | 3 | 10 | 0 | 8 | 5 | 13 | 0 | | | | | |

Umpire: C.S. Elliott and A. Jepson.

Test No. 622/14

# ENGLAND v PAKISTAN 1967 (2nd Test)

Played at Trent Bridge, Nottingham, on 10, 11, 12, 14 (*no play*), 15 August.
Toss: Pakistan.   Result: ENGLAND won by ten wickets.
Debuts: England – G.G. Arnold, A.P.E. Knott; Pakistan – Niaz Ahmed.

Barrington reached his hundred off 344 balls and altogether batted for 409 minutes. The Nottingham Fire Brigade pumped 100,000 gallons of water off the ground after a violent thunderstorm soon after 5 p.m. on the first day had transformed the playing area into a lake. Play was able to restart at 12.45 p.m. on the second day. Alan Bull, a young recruit to the Nottinghamshire playing staff who was not destined to play in a first-class match, fielded substitute for D'Oliveira and caught Asif at long on. This was Hanif's first defeat in ten Tests as captain.

## PAKISTAN

| | | | | | |
|---|---|---|---|---|---|
| Khalid Ibadulla | c Knott b Higgs | 2 | | c Knott b Close | 5 |
| Javed Burki | lbw b Arnold | 1 | | c Knott b Higgs | 3 |
| Saeed Ahmed | c Knott b Arnold | 44 | | c Arnold b Underwood | 68 |
| Mushtaq Mohammad | b Higgs | 29 | (6) | lbw b Underwood | 0 |
| Hanif Mohammad* | c Titmus b Underwood | 16 | | c Knott b Higgs | 4 |
| Majid Khan | lbw b D'Oliveira | 17 | (7) | c Close b Underwood | 5 |
| Asif Iqbal | b Higgs | 18 | (8) | c sub (A. Bull) b Titmus | 1 |
| Nasim-ul-Ghani | run out | 11 | (4) | c Close b Titmus | 6 |
| Intikhab Alam | c Knott b Arnold | 0 | | c Knott b Underwood | 16 |
| Wasim Bari† | b Higgs | 0 | | c Barrington b Underwood | 3 |
| Niaz Ahmed | not out | 0 | | not out | 1 |
| Extras | (LB 1, NB 1) | 2 | | (LB 1, NB 1) | 2 |
| **Total** | | **140** | | | **114** |

## ENGLAND

| | | |
|---|---|---|
| G. Boycott | b Asif | 15 | not out | 1 |
| M.C. Cowdrey | c Majid b Nasim | 14 | not out | 2 |
| K.F. Barrington | not out | 109 | | |
| T.W. Graveney | c Niaz b Ibadulla | 28 | | |
| B.L. D'Oliveira | run out | 7 | | |
| D.B. Close* | c Wasim b Niaz | 41 | | |
| F.J. Titmus | lbw b Asif | 13 | | |
| A.P.E. Knott† | c Hanif b Mushtaq | 0 | | |
| G.G. Arnold | lbw b Niaz | 14 | | |
| K. Higgs | not out | 0 | | |
| D.L. Underwood | did not bat | | | |
| Extras | (B 3, LB 3, W 1, NB 4) | 11 | | |
| **Total** | (8 wickets declared) | **252** | (0 wickets) | **3** |

| ENGLAND | O | M | R | W | O | M | R | W | | FALL OF WICKETS | | | |
|---|---|---|---|---|---|---|---|---|---|---|---|---|---|
| Arnold | 17 | 5 | 35 | 3 | 5 | 3 | 5 | 0 | | P | E | P | E |
| Higgs | 19 | 12 | 35 | 4 | 6 | 1 | 8 | 2 | Wkt | 1st | 1st | 2nd | 2nd |
| D'Oliveira | 18 | 9 | 27 | 1 | | | | | 1st | 3 | 21 | 4 | – |
| Close | 3 | 0 | 12 | 0 | 4 | 1 | 11 | 1 | 2nd | 21 | 31 | 35 | – |
| Titmus | 7 | 3 | 12 | 0 | 23 | 11 | 36 | 2 | 3rd | 65 | 75 | 60 | – |
| Underwood | 5 | 2 | 17 | 1 | 26 | 8 | 52 | 5 | 4th | 82 | 92 | 71 | – |
| | | | | | | | | | 5th | 104 | 187 | 76 | – |
| PAKISTAN | | | | | | | | | 6th | 116 | 213 | 89 | – |
| Asif | 39 | 10 | 72 | 2 | | | | | 7th | 140 | 214 | 93 | – |
| Niaz | 37 | 10 | 72 | 2 | | | | | 8th | 140 | 251 | 99 | – |
| Nasim | 8 | 2 | 20 | 1 | | | | | 9th | 140 | – | 113 | – |
| Saeed | 2 | 2 | 0 | 0 | 1 | 1 | 0 | 0 | 10th | 140 | – | 114 | – |
| Intikhab | 7 | 2 | 19 | 0 | | | | | | | | | |
| Ibadulla | 32 | 13 | 42 | 1 | | | | | | | | | |
| Mushtaq | 9·3 | 3 | 16 | 1 | 1·1 | 0 | 3 | 0 | | | | | |

Umpires: J.S. Buller and W.F.F. Price.

Test No. 623/15

# ENGLAND v PAKISTAN 1967 (3rd Test)

Played at Kennington Oval, London, on 24, 25, 26, 28 August.
Toss: England. Result: ENGLAND won by eight wickets.
Debuts: Pakistan – Ghulam Abbas.

Barrington's 19th Test hundred was his third in successive Tests and his first in a Test on his county ground. He thus became the first to score a Test hundred on each of England's six current Test grounds. It was his 52nd score of 50 or more and equalled L. Hutton's world Test record. Asif's 146 off 244 balls in 200 minutes included two sixes and 21 fours. His partnership of 190 in 170 minutes with Intikhab remains the highest for the ninth wicket in all Test cricket. England won at 5.11 on the fourth evening.

### PAKISTAN

| | | | | |
|---|---|---|---|---|
| Hanif Mohammad* | b Higgs | 3 | (5) c Knott b Higgs | 18 |
| Mohammad Ilyas | b Arnold | 2 | c Cowdrey b Higgs | 1 |
| Saeed Ahmed | b Arnold | 38 | c Knott b Higgs | 0 |
| Majid Khan | c Knott b Arnold | 6 | b Higgs | 0 |
| Mashtaq Mohammad | lbw b Higgs | 66 | (7) c D'Oliveira b Underwood | 17 |
| Javed Burki | c D'Oliveira b Titmus | 27 | (8) b Underwood | 7 |
| Ghulam Abbas | c Underwood b Titmus | 12 | (6) c Knott b Higgs | 0 |
| Asif Iqbal | c Close b Arnold | 26 | (9) st Knott b Close | 146 |
| Intikhab Alam | b Higgs | 20 | (10) b Titmus | 51 |
| Wasim Bari† | c Knott b Arnold | 1 | (1) b Titmus | 12 |
| Salim Altaf | not out | 7 | not out | 0 |
| Extras | (B 5, LB 2, NB 1) | 8 | (B 1, LB 1, NB 1) | 3 |
| **Total** | | **216** | | **255** |

### ENGLAND

| | | | | |
|---|---|---|---|---|
| M.C. Cowdrey | c Mushtaq b Majid | 16 | c Intikhab b Asif | 9 |
| D.B. Close* | c Wasim b Asif | 6 | b Asif | 8 |
| K.F. Barrington | c Wasim b Salim | 142 | not out | 13 |
| T.W. Graveney | c Majid b Intikhab | 77 | | |
| D.L. Amiss | c Saeed b Asif | 26 | (4) not out | 3 |
| B.L. D'Oliveira | c Mushtaq b Asif | 3 | | |
| F.J. Titmus | c sub (Niaz Ahmed) b Mushtaq | 65 | | |
| A.P.E. Knott† | c Ilyas b Mushtaq | 28 | | |
| G.G. Arnold | c Majid b Mushtaq | 59 | | |
| K. Higgs | b Mushtaq | 7 | | |
| D.L. Underwood | not out | 2 | | |
| Extras | (LB 4, NB 5) | 9 | (NB 1) | 1 |
| **Total** | | **440** | (2 wickets) | **34** |

| ENGLAND | O | M | R | W | O | M | R | W | FALL OF WICKETS | | | | |
|---|---|---|---|---|---|---|---|---|---|---|---|---|---|
| Arnold | 29 | 9 | 58 | 5 | 17 | 5 | 49 | 0 | | P | E | P | E |
| Higgs | 29 | 10 | 61 | 3 | 20 | 7 | 58 | 5 | Wkt | 1st | 1st | 2nd | 2nd |
| D'Oliveira | 17 | 6 | 41 | 0 | | | | | 1st | 3 | 16 | 1 | 17 |
| Close | 5 | 1 | 15 | 0 | 1 | 0 | 4 | 1 | 2nd | 5 | 35 | 5 | 20 |
| Titmus | 13 | 6 | 21 | 2 | 29.1 | 8 | 64 | 2 | 3rd | 17 | 176 | 5 | – |
| Underwood | 9 | 5 | 12 | 0 | 26 | 12 | 48 | 2 | 4th | 74 | 270 | 26 | – |
| Barrington | | | | | 8 | 2 | 29 | 0 | 5th | 138 | 276 | 26 | – |
| | | | | | | | | | 6th | 155 | 276 | 41 | – |
| PAKISTAN | | | | | | | | | 7th | 182 | 323 | 53 | – |
| Salim | 40 | 14 | 94 | 1 | 2 | 1 | 8 | 0 | 8th | 188 | 416 | 65 | – |
| Asif | 42 | 19 | 66 | 3 | 4 | 1 | 14 | 2 | 9th | 194 | 437 | 255 | – |
| Majid | 10 | 0 | 29 | 1 | | | | | 10th | 216 | 440 | 255 | – |
| Mushtaq | 26.4 | 7 | 80 | 4 | | | | | | | | | |
| Saeed | 21 | 5 | 69 | 0 | 2 | 0 | 7 | 0 | | | | | |
| Intikhab | 28 | 3 | 93 | 1 | | | | | | | | | |
| Hanif | | | | | 0.2 | 0 | 4 | 0 | | | | | |

Umpires: W.F.F. Price and H. Yarnold.

## Chapter 26
# WEST INDIES 1967/68

Playing the West Indies at home was difficult enough. To do so in their Caribbean islands was an even more difficult proposition. This was the task that faced Cowdrey in 1967/68. He began by having a two-day squad session at Crystal Palace. Common place today that was an innovation in the sixties. On the tour he was considerably helped by having Les Ames as Manager.

In the first Test at Port-of-Spain starting as underdogs they came very close to winning by an innings a drawn match. Cowdrey contributed 72 to their 244 for two on the first day and although he was out first thing on the second, England amassed 568.

England again batted first in the second Test. Cowdrey made 101 of their 376. West Indies replied with 143. Following on they were facing defeat by an innings when at 204 for four Butcher was caught on the leg side by Parks off D'Oliveira. Butcher waited for the decision and walked when given out. Whether the crowd interpreted his hesitation as disputing the confirmation that the catch had carried or not, the outcome was an outbreak of bottle-throwing. When the police used tear gas Cowdrey had to lead his players from the field. A letter from Copse Hill, Wimbledon on 27 October 1975 recalled this Sabina Park Test match. "Although we were surrounded entirely by West Indians, and they are, as you will know, very excitable, we did not hear a single voice in favour of the rioters, who were roundly condemned by all." The resultant chaos meant a delay of seventy-five minutes and a loss of momentum. In the end on 68 for eight, to which Cowdrey contributed 0, they narrowly avoided defeat.

The third Test at Bridgetown ended in a draw. Cowdrey came in at the fall of the first wicket at 172. He was soon out for 1–174 for 2. England were 100 ahead on the first innings but the match was drawn.

In the fourth Test at Port-of-Spain West Indies made 526 for seven but Cowdrey led the fight back scoring 148 his sixth century against the West Indies. In their second innings Sobers astonishingly declared setting England 215 to win in 165 minutes at 78 an hour. During the tea interval there was much discussion about the possibility of victory. In the event Cowdrey made 71 leaving only 38 to win. Boycott timed his contribution to perfection in scoring an undefeated 80.

The fifth Test was played in Georgetown Guyana. West Indies batted and made 414 to which Sobers contributed 152. England made 43 less Cowdrey making 59 and Boycott 116. West Indies second innings was graced by 95 not out from Sobers. England began the sixth and final day needing 330 to win; in the event their fight for survival. At 41 for five Cowdrey was joined by Knott. Cowdrey stayed until after tea scoring 82. Knott was there at the end and the Kentish element in the rearguard action pleased many observers.

The team returned home triumphant. Cowdrey's return had been an undoubted success.

The MCC tour of West Indies under the captaincy of Cowdrey and the management of Ames was undoubtedly one of the high spots of Cowdrey's career. The team was unbeaten and the test series won.

|  | Matches | Innings | Not out | Runs | Highest score | Average | 100s | 50s | Caught |
|---|---|---|---|---|---|---|---|---|---|
| This series | 5 | 8 | 0 | 534 | 148 | 66.75 | 2 | 4 | 3 |
| Previous series | 92 | 153 | 15 | 6346 | 182 | 45.99 | 18 | 33 | 106 |
| Cumulative totals | 97 | 161 | 15 | 6880 | 182 | 47.12 | 20 | 37 | 109 |

Test No. 628/51

# WEST INDIES v ENGLAND 1967–68 (1st Test)

Played at Queen's Park Oval, Port-of-Spain, Trinidad, on 19, 20, 22, 23, 24 January.
Toss: England. Result: MATCH DRAWN.
Debuts: West Indies – G.S. Camacho.

England's total was their second-highest in the West Indies. Barrington reached his hundred with a six; it was his fourth century in consecutive Tests. Lloyd became the fourth West Indies batsman to score a hundred in his first match against England. West Indies followed on for the first time in their 14 matches under the captaincy of Sobers. Brown dismissed Butcher, Murray and Griffith in the last over before tea but Hall partnered Sobers throughout the final session and avoided the possibility of an innings defeat. Their unbroken partnership of 63 remains the West Indies record for the ninth wicket against England.

### ENGLAND

| | | |
|---|---|---|
| G. Boycott | lbw b Holford | 68 |
| J.H. Edrich | c Murray b Gibbs | 25 |
| M.C. Cowdrey* | c Murray b Griffith | 72 |
| K.F. Barrington | c Griffith b Gibbs | 143 |
| T.W. Graveney | b Gibbs | 118 |
| J.M. Parks† | lbw b Sobers | 42 |
| B.L. D'Oliveira | b Griffith | 32 |
| F.J. Titmus | lbw b Griffith | 15 |
| D.J. Brown | not out | 22 |
| R.N.S. Hobbs | c Butcher b Griffith | 2 |
| I.J. Jones | c Murray b Griffith | 2 |
| Extras | (B 8, LB 11, W 1, NB 7) | 27 |
| **Total** | | **568** |

### WEST INDIES

| | | | | |
|---|---|---|---|---|
| S.M. Nurse | c Graveney b Titmus | 41 | b Titmus | 42 |
| G.S. Camacho | c Graveney b Brown | 22 | c Graveney b Barrington | 43 |
| R.B. Kanhai | c Cowdrey b D'Oliveira | 85 | (4) c and b Hobbs | 37 |
| B.F. Butcher | lbw b Brown | 14 | (3) lbw b Brown | 52 |
| C.H. Lloyd | b Jones | 118 | c Titmus b Jones | 2 |
| G. St A. Sobers* | c Graveney b Barrington | 17 | (7) not out | 33 |
| D.A.J. Holford | run out | 4 | (6) b Titmus | 1 |
| D.L. Murray† | c D'Oliveira b Hobbs | 16 | lbw b Brown | 0 |
| C.C. Griffith | c Parks b Jones | 18 | b Brown | 0 |
| W.W. Hall | not out | 10 | not out | 26 |
| L.R. Gibbs | b Jones | 1 | | |
| Extras | (B 4, LB 6, NB 7) | 17 | (LB 5, NB 2) | 7 |
| **Total** | | **363** | (8 wickets) | **243** |

| WEST INDIES | O | M | R | W | O | M | R | W |
|---|---|---|---|---|---|---|---|---|
| Hall | 28 | 5 | 92 | 0 | | | | |
| Sobers | 26 | 5 | 83 | 1 | | | | |
| Griffith | 29.5 | 13 | 69 | 5 | | | | |
| Gibbs | 63 | 15 | 147 | 3 | | | | |
| Holford | 43 | 1 | 121 | 1 | | | | |
| Lloyd | 8 | 3 | 17 | 0 | | | | |
| Camacho | 3 | 1 | 12 | 0 | | | | |
| ENGLAND | | | | | | | | |
| Brown | 22 | 3 | 65 | 2 | 14 | 4 | 27 | 3 |
| Jones | 19 | 5 | 63 | 3 | 15 | 3 | 32 | 1 |
| D'Oliveira | 27 | 13 | 49 | 1 | 5 | 2 | 21 | 0 |
| Titmus | 34 | 9 | 91 | 1 | 27 | 13 | 42 | 2 |
| Hobbs | 15 | 1 | 34 | 1 | 13 | 2 | 44 | 1 |
| Barrington | 18 | 6 | 44 | 1 | 15 | 0 | 69 | 1 |
| Cowdrey | | | | | 1 | 0 | 1 | 0 |

### FALL OF WICKETS

| Wkt | E 1st | WI 1st | WI 2nd |
|---|---|---|---|
| 1st | 80 | 50 | 70 |
| 2nd | 110 | 102 | 100 |
| 3rd | 244 | 124 | 164 |
| 4th | 432 | 240 | 167 |
| 5th | 471 | 290 | 178 |
| 6th | 511 | 294 | 180 |
| 7th | 527 | 329 | 180 |
| 8th | 554 | 352 | 180 |
| 9th | 566 | 357 | – |
| 10th | 568 | 363 | – |

Umpires: H.B. de C. Jordan and R. Gosein.

**Test No. 629/52**

# WEST INDIES v ENGLAND 1967–68 (2nd Test)

Played at Sabina Park, Kingston, Jamaica, on 8, 9, 10, 12, 13, 14 February.
Toss: England.   Result: MATCH DRAWN.
Debuts: Nil.

West Indies followed on for the second Test running after Snow dismissed Sobers first ball for the second time in successive innings in which he had bowled to him. Butcher's second innings dismissal in mid-afternoon on the fourth day sparked off a bottle-throwing riot with West Indies 204 for 5 and needing 29 runs to avoid an innings defeat. Play resumed after tea and it was agreed that the 75 minutes lost would be played on an extra (sixth) day.

## ENGLAND

| | | | | |
|---|---|---|---|---|
| G. Boycott | b Hall | 17 | b Sobers | 0 |
| J.H. Edrich | c Kanhai b Sobers | 96 | b Hall | 6 |
| M.C. Cowdrey* | c Murray b Gibbs | 101 | lbw b Sobers | 0 |
| K.F. Barrington | c and b Holford | 63 | lbw b Griffith | 13 |
| T.W. Graveney | b Hall | 30 | c Griffith b Gibbs | 21 |
| J.M. Parks† | c Sobers b Holford | 3 | lbw b Gibbs | 3 |
| B.L. D'Oliveira | st Murray b Holford | 0 | not out | 13 |
| F.J. Titmus | lbw b Hall | 19 | c Camacho b Gibbs | 4 |
| D.J. Brown | c Murray b Hall | 14 | b Sobers | 0 |
| J.A. Snow | b Griffith | 10 | | |
| I.J. Jones | not out | 0 | | |
| Extras | (B 12, LB 7, NB 4) | 23 | (B 8) | 8 |
| **Total** | | **376** | (8 wickets) | **68** |

## WEST INDIES

| | | | | |
|---|---|---|---|---|
| G.S. Camacho | b Snow | 5 | b D'Oliveira | 25 |
| D.L. Murray† | c D'Oliveira b Brown | 0 | (8) lbw b Brown | 14 |
| R.B. Kanhai | c Graveney b Snow | 26 | c Edrich b Jones | 36 |
| S.M. Nurse | b Jones | 22 | (2) b Snow | 73 |
| C.H. Lloyd | not out | 34 | b Brown | 7 |
| G. St A. Sobers* | lbw b Snow | 0 | not out | 113 |
| B.F. Butcher | c Parks b Snow | 21 | (4) c Parks b D'Oliveira | 25 |
| D.A.J. Holford | c Parks b Snow | 6 | (7) lbw b Titmus | 35 |
| C.C. Griffith | c D'Oliveira b Snow | 8 | lbw b Jones | 14 |
| W.W. Hall | b Snow | 0 | c Parks b Jones | 0 |
| L.R. Gibbs | c Parks b Jones | 0 | not out | 1 |
| Extras | (B 12, LB 5, W 1, NB 3) | 21 | (B 33, LB 10, NB 5) | 48 |
| **Total** | | **143** | (9 wickets declared) | **391** |

| WEST INDIES | O | M | R | W | O | M | R | W | | FALL OF WICKETS | | | |
|---|---|---|---|---|---|---|---|---|---|---|---|---|---|
| Hall | 27 | 5 | 63 | 4 | 3 | 2 | 3 | 1 | | E | WI | WI | E |
| Griffith | 31·2 | 7 | 72 | 1 | 5 | 2 | 13 | 1 | Wkt | 1st | 1st | 2nd | 2nd |
| Sobers | 31 | 11 | 55 | 1 | 16·5 | 7 | 33 | 3 | 1st | 49 | 5 | 102 | 0 |
| Gibbs | 47 | 18 | 91 | 1 | 14 | 11 | 11 | 3 | 2nd | 178 | 5 | 122 | 0 |
| Holford | 33 | 10 | 71 | 3 | | | | | 3rd | 279 | 51 | 164 | 19 |
| | | | | | | | | | 4th | 310 | 80 | 174 | 19 |
| ENGLAND | | | | | | | | | 5th | 318 | 80 | 204 | 38 |
| Brown | 13 | 1 | 34 | 1 | 33 | 9 | 65 | 2 | 6th | 318 | 120 | 314 | 51 |
| Snow | 21 | 7 | 49 | 7 | 27 | 4 | 91 | 1 | 7th | 351 | 126 | 351 | 61 |
| Jones | 14·1 | 4 | 39 | 2 | 30 | 4 | 90 | 3 | 8th | 352 | 143 | 388 | 68 |
| D'Oliveira | | | | | 32 | 12 | 51 | 2 | 9th | 376 | 142 | 388 | — |
| Titmus | | | | | 7 | 2 | 32 | 1 | 10th | 376 | 143 | — | — |
| Barrington | | | | | 6 | 1 | 14 | 0 | | | | | |

Umpires: D. Sang Hue and H.B. de C. Jordan.

Test No. 630/53

# WEST INDIES v ENGLAND 1967–68 (3rd Test)

Played at Kensington Oval, Bridgetown, Barbados, on 29 February, 1, 2, 4, 5 March.
Toss: West Indies. Result: MATCH DRAWN.
Debuts: England – P.I. Pocock.

## WEST INDIES

| | | | | |
|---|---|---|---|---|
| S.M. Nurse | c Cowdrey b Brown | 26 | c Parks b Snow | 19 |
| G.S. Camacho | c Graveney b Barrington | 57 | lbw b Snow | 18 |
| R.B. Kanhai | c Parks b Snow | 12 | lbw b Snow | 12 |
| B.F. Butcher | lbw b Snow | 86 | run out | 60 |
| C.H. Lloyd | c and b Pocock | 20 | not out | 113 |
| G. St A. Sobers* | c Jones b Snow | 68 | b Brown | 19 |
| D.A.J. Holford | c Graveney b Snow | 0 | | |
| D.L. Murray† | c Parks b Brown | 27 | (7) c Snow b Pocock | 18 |
| C.C. Griffith | not out | 16 | (8) not out | 8 |
| W.W. Hall | c Barrington b Snow | 2 | | |
| L.R. Gibbs | b Jones | 14 | | |
| Extras | (B 1, LB 14, NB 6) | 21 | (B 8, LB 3, NB 6) | 17 |
| **Total** | | **349** | (6 wickets) | **284** |

## ENGLAND

| | | |
|---|---|---|
| J.H. Edrich | c Murray b Griffith | 146 |
| G. Boycott | lbw b Sobers | 90 |
| M.C. Cowdrey* | c Sobers b Griffith | 1 |
| K.F. Barrington | c Butcher b Hall | 17 |
| T.W. Graveney | c Sobers b Gibbs | 55 |
| J.M. Parks† | lbw b Gibbs | 0 |
| B.L. D'Oliveira | b Hall | 51 |
| D.J. Brown | b Griffith | 1 |
| J.A. Snow | c Nurse b Gibbs | 37 |
| P.I. Pocock | b Sobers | 6 |
| I.J. Jones | not out | 1 |
| Extras | (B 16, LB 9, NB 19) | 44 |
| **Total** | | **449** |

| ENGLAND | O | M | R | W | O | M | R | W |
|---|---|---|---|---|---|---|---|---|
| Brown | 32 | 10 | 66 | 2 | 11 | 0 | 61 | 1 |
| Snow | 35 | 11 | 86 | 5 | 10 | 2 | 39 | 3 |
| D'Oliveira | 19 | 5 | 36 | 0 | 4 | 0 | 19 | 0 |
| Pocock | 28 | 11 | 55 | 1 | 13 | 0 | 78 | 1 |
| Jones | 21·1 | 3 | 56 | 1 | 11 | 3 | 53 | 0 |
| Barrington | 8 | 1 | 29 | 1 | 4 | 0 | 17 | 0 |

| WEST INDIES | O | M | R | W |
|---|---|---|---|---|
| Sobers | 41 | 10 | 76 | 2 |
| Hall | 32 | 8 | 98 | 2 |
| Griffith | 24 | 6 | 71 | 3 |
| Gibbs | 47·5 | 16 | 98 | 3 |
| Holford | 32 | 9 | 52 | 0 |
| Lloyd | 3 | 0 | 10 | 0 |
| Nurse | 1 | 1 | 0 | 0 |

### FALL OF WICKETS

| Wkt | WI 1st | E 1st | WI 2nd |
|---|---|---|---|
| 1st | 54 | 172 | 38 |
| 2nd | 67 | 174 | 49 |
| 3rd | 163 | 210 | 79 |
| 4th | 198 | 319 | 180 |
| 5th | 252 | 319 | 217 |
| 6th | 252 | 349 | 274 |
| 7th | 315 | 354 | – |
| 8th | 315 | 411 | – |
| 9th | 319 | 439 | – |
| 10th | 349 | 449 | – |

Umpires: H.B. de C. Jordan and D. Sang Hue.

Test No. 631/54

# WEST INDIES v ENGLAND 1967–68 (4th Test)

Played at Queen's Park Oval, Port-of-Spain, Trinidad, on 14, 15, 16, 18, 19 March.
Toss: West Indies.   Result: ENGLAND won by seven wickets.
Debuts: Nil.

Butcher, whose leg-breaks had been allowed only one spell of six overs in his previous 31 Test matches, took five wickets for 15 runs in a spell of ten overs. Carew set a West Indies record by bowling 16 consecutive maidens. England, set to score 215 runs in 165 minutes, won with three minutes to spare.

## WEST INDIES

| | | | | |
|---|---|---|---|---|
| G.S. Camacho | c Knott b Brown | 87 | c Graveney b Snow | 31 |
| M.C. Carew | c Lock b Brown | 36 | not out | 40 |
| S.M. Nurse | c Edrich b Barrington | 136 | run out | 9 |
| R.B. Kanhai | c Barrington b Lock | 153 | not out | 2 |
| C.H. Lloyd | b Jones | 43 | | |
| G. St A. Sobers* | c Jones b Brown | 48 | | |
| B.F. Butcher | not out | 7 | | |
| W.V. Rodriguez | b Jones | 0 | | |
| D.L. Murray† | not out | 5 | | |
| C.C. Griffith | ) did not bat | | | |
| L.R. Gibbs | ) | | | |
| Extras | (LB 6, NB 5) | 11 | (B 1, LB 7, NB 2) | 10 |
| **Total** | (7 wickets declared) | **526** | (2 wickets declared) | **92** |

## ENGLAND

| | | | | |
|---|---|---|---|---|
| J.H. Edrich | c Lloyd b Carew | 32 | b Rodriguez | 29 |
| G. Boycott | c Nurse b Rodriguez | 62 | not out | 80 |
| M.C. Cowdrey* | c Murray b Butcher | 148 | c Sobers b Gibbs | 71 |
| K.F. Barrington | lbw b Gibbs | 48 | | |
| T.W. Graveney | c Murray b Rodriguez | 8 | (4) b Gibbs | 2 |
| B.L. D'Oliveira | b Rodriguez | 0 | (5) not out | 12 |
| A.P.E. Knott† | not out | 69 | | |
| J.A. Snow | b Butcher | 0 | | |
| D.J. Brown | c Murray b Butcher | 0 | | |
| G.A.R. Lock | lbw b Butcher | 3 | | |
| I.J. Jones | b Butcher | 1 | | |
| Extras | (B 13, LB 11, W 2, NB 7) | 33 | (B 11, LB 6, NB 4) | 21 |
| **Total** | | **404** | (3 wickets) | **215** |

| ENGLAND | O | M | R | W | O | M | R | W | | FALL OF WICKETS | | | |
|---|---|---|---|---|---|---|---|---|---|---|---|---|---|
| Brown | 27 | 2 | 107 | 3 | 10 | 2 | 33 | 0 | | WI | E | WI | E |
| Snow | 20 | 3 | 68 | 0 | 9 | 0 | 29 | 1 | Wkt | 1st | 1st | 2nd | 2nd |
| Jones | 29 | 1 | 108 | 2 | 11 | 2 | 20 | 0 | 1st | 119 | 86 | 66 | 55 |
| D'Oliveira | 15 | 2 | 62 | 0 | | | | | 2nd | 142 | 112 | 88 | 173 |
| Lock | 32 | 3 | 129 | 1 | | | | | 3rd | 415 | 245 | – | 182 |
| Barrington | 10 | 2 | 41 | 1 | | | | | 4th | 421 | 260 | – | – |
| WEST INDIES | | | | | | | | | 5th | 506 | 260 | – | – |
| Sobers | 36 | 8 | 87 | 0 | 14 | 0 | 48 | 0 | 6th | 513 | 373 | – | – |
| Griffith | 3 | 1 | 7 | 0 | | | | | 7th | 514 | 377 | – | – |
| Gibbs | 57 | 24 | 68 | 1 | 16·4 | 1 | 76 | 2 | 8th | – | 377 | – | – |
| Rodriguez | 35 | 4 | 145 | 3 | 10 | 1 | 34 | 1 | 9th | – | 381 | – | – |
| Carew | 25 | 18 | 23 | 1 | 7 | 2 | 19 | 0 | 10th | – | 404 | – | – |
| Butcher | 13·4 | 2 | 34 | 5 | 5 | 1 | 17 | 0 | | | | | |
| Lloyd | 4 | 2 | 7 | 0 | | | | | | | | | |
| Nurse | 2 | 2 | 0 | 0 | | | | | | | | | |

Umpires: D. Sang Hue and R. Gosein.

Test No. 632/55

# WEST INDIES v ENGLAND 1967–68 (5th Test)

Played at Bourda, Georgetown, Guyana, on 28, 29, 30 March, 1, 2, 3 April.
Toss: West Indies. Result: MATCH DRAWN.
Debuts: Nil.

Sobers became the first to score 6,000 runs in Tests for West Indies. Pocock batted for 82 minutes before scoring his first run – the second-longest instance in Test cricket. His partnership of 109 with Lock, who made his highest Test score on his final appearance for England, remains the highest for the ninth wicket in this series. Snow took 27 wickets in the rubber (in only four Tests) to beat England's previous best in the West Indies – 21 by F.S. Trueman in 1959–60.

### WEST INDIES

| | | | | |
|---|---|---|---|---|
| S.M. Nurse | c Knott b Snow | 17 | lbw b Snow | 49 |
| G.S. Camacho | c and b Jones | 14 | c Graveney b Snow | 26 |
| R.B. Kanhai | c Edrich b Pocock | 150 | c Edrich b Jones | 22 |
| B.F. Butcher | run out | 18 | (6) c Lock b Pocock | 18 |
| G. St A. Sobers* | c Cowdrey b Barrington | 152 | not out | 95 |
| C.H. Lloyd | b Lock | 31 | (4) c Knott b Snow | 1 |
| D.A.J. Holford | lbw b Snow | 1 | (8) b Lock | 3 |
| D.L. Murray† | c Knott b Lock | 8 | (7) c Boycott b Pocock | 16 |
| L.A. King | b Snow | 8 | b Snow | 20 |
| W.W. Hall | not out | 5 | b Snow | 7 |
| L.R. Gibbs | b Snow | 1 | b Snow | 0 |
| Extras | (LB 3, W 2, NB 4) | 9 | (B 1, LB 2, W 1, NB 3) | 7 |
| **Total** | | **414** | | **264** |

### ENGLAND

| | | | | |
|---|---|---|---|---|
| J.H. Edrich | c Murray b Sobers | 0 | c Gibbs b Sobers | 6 |
| G. Boycott | c Murray b Hall | 116 | b Gibbs | 30 |
| M.C. Cowdrey* | lbw b Sobers | 59 | lbw b Gibbs | 82 |
| T.W. Graveney | c Murray b Hall | 27 | c Murray b Gibbs | 0 |
| K.F. Barrington | c Kanhai b Sobber | 4 | c Lloyd b Gibbs | 0 |
| B.L. D'Oliveira | c Nurse b Holford | 27 | c and b Gibbs | 2 |
| A.P.E. Knott† | lbw b Holford | 7 | not out | 73 |
| J.A. Snow | b Gibbs | 0 | lbw b Sobers | 1 |
| G.A.R. Lock | b King | 89 | c King b Sobers | 2 |
| P.I. Pocock | c and b King | 13 | c Lloyd b Gibbs | 0 |
| I.J. Jones | not out | 0 | not out | 0 |
| Extras | (B 12, LB 14, NB 3) | 29 | (B 9, W 1) | 10 |
| **Total** | | **371** | (9 wickets) | **206** |

| ENGLAND | O | M | R | W | O | M | R | W |
|---|---|---|---|---|---|---|---|---|
| Snow | 27.4 | 2 | 82 | 4 | 15.2 | 0 | 60 | 6 |
| Jones | 31 | 5 | 114 | 1 | 17 | 1 | 81 | 1 |
| D'Oliveira | 8 | 1 | 27 | 0 | 8 | 0 | 28 | 0 |
| Pocock | 38 | 11 | 78 | 1 | 17 | 1 | 66 | 2 |
| Lock | 28 | 7 | 61 | 2 | 9 | 1 | 22 | 1 |
| Barrington | 18 | 4 | 43 | 1 | | | | |
| WEST INDIES | | | | | | | | |
| Sobers | 37 | 15 | 72 | 3 | 31 | 16 | 53 | 3 |
| Hall | 19 | 3 | 71 | 2 | 13 | 6 | 26 | 0 |
| King | 38.2 | 11 | 79 | 2 | 9 | 1 | 11 | 0 |
| Holford | 31 | 10 | 54 | 2 | 17 | 9 | 37 | 0 |
| Gibbs | 33 | 9 | 59 | 1 | 40 | 20 | 60 | 6 |
| Butcher | 5 | 3 | 7 | 0 | 10 | 7 | 9 | 0 |

FALL OF WICKETS

| Wkt | WI 1st | E 1st | WI 2nd | E 2nd |
|---|---|---|---|---|
| 1st | 29 | 13 | 78 | 33 |
| 2nd | 35 | 185 | 84 | 37 |
| 3rd | 72 | 185 | 86 | 37 |
| 4th | 322 | 194 | 133 | 39 |
| 5th | 385 | 240 | 171 | 41 |
| 6th | 387 | 252 | 201 | 168 |
| 7th | 399 | 257 | 216 | 198 |
| 8th | 400 | 259 | 252 | 200 |
| 9th | 412 | 368 | 264 | 206 |
| 10th | 414 | 371 | 264 | – |

Umpires: H.B. de C. Jordan and C.P. Kippins.

Chapter 27

# AUSTRALIA 1968

Cowdrey began the 1968 season as the Captain who had led a successful tour and test series in the West Indies. He was confirmed as Captain for the whole series against Australia under Bill Lawry.

The first Test left England needing 413 for victory and they lost by 159 runs. Cowdrey contributed only 4 and 11.

The second Test at Lord's was the two hundredth between the two teams. Rain marred the opening day but Milburn made a characteristic 83 and Cowdrey a less flamboyant 45. England declared at 351 for seven. Cowdrey took a splendid catch at slip to dismiss Redpath early on. When he took two more to end the innings for only 78, he broke Hammond's test record of 110 catches. Unfortunately more rain stopped England from pressing home their advantage and the match was drawn.

The third Test at Edgbaston was Cowdrey's hundredth Test and he was the first player to hold that record. Once again rain interfered but on the second day ended with Cowdrey on 95 having pulled a hamstring and had Boycott to run for him. The next morning, still clearly handicapped, he took half an hour to get the five singles needed to mark his hundredth test in the most appropriate way. He was out soon after for 104. During his innings Cowdrey became the second batsman after W R Hammond to score 7,000 runs in test cricket. Graveney, who assumed the captaincy when Cowdrey was unable to field, with 96 took England to 409 and Australia again were helped by rain in saving the game.

The hamstring injury caused Cowdrey to miss the fourth Test at Headingley in which Graveney was Captain. England settled for a draw which ensured that Australia kept the Ashes.

Cowdrey was back for the Oval Test and England who made 494. Edrich

*Batting in the fifth Test against Australia at the Oval in 1968.*

made 164 and D'Oliveira 158. Australia began well but were eventually set 352 to win and were 86 for five at lunch on the last day. Then came a thunderstorm which flooded the ground and had apparently saved Australia from defeat once again. Cowdrey went out to the middle to survey the apparently hopeless scene and surmised that if the water could be cleared, they could play again by five o'clock. He instigated an appeal for volunteers and hundreds – including Bob, to whom this book is dedicated – did the trick encouraged by Cowdrey. Play recommenced at a quarter to five and Cowdrey went straight on the offensive with Illingworth and Underwood but neither made any impression on the saturated wicket. With time getting shorter and shorter Cowdrey brought D'Oliveira into the attack and in his third over he dismissed Jarman. Cowdrey immediately restored Underwood to the pavilion end and aided by a drying pitch, he ran through the Australian tail to enable England to have the consolation of squaring the rubber. Cowdrey's contribution with the bat was minimal on this occasion –

16 and 35. In the first innings he was out lbw to Mallett's fifth ball in test cricket and in the second was bowled to give the bowler the fifth of five wickets on his debut.

Cowdrey had little time for celebration as he had to attend a meeting at Lord's the same evening to help pick the team to tour South Africa in 1967/68. Much of the discussion centred on D'Oliveira who had come to English cricket from South Africa. In the event the Selectors left D'Oliveira out. A storm of adverse publicity followed. In September Cartwright, who had been selected, was forced to withdraw because of further back problems. It was in these paradoxical circumstances that D'Olivera was included in the touring party. A pro-apartheid South African government led by prime minister Vorster denounced the MCC and made clear his opposition to a team "being thrust upon us".

|  | Matches | Innings | Not out | Runs | Highest score | Average | 100s | 50s | Caught |
|---|---|---|---|---|---|---|---|---|---|
| This series | 4 | 6 | 0 | 215 | 104 | 35.83 | 1 | 0 | 4 |
| Previous series | 97 | 161 | 15 | 6880 | 182 | 47.12 | 20 | 37 | 109 |
| Cumulative totals | 101 | 167 | 15 | 7095 | 182 | 46.68 | 21 | 37 | 113 |

*7000 runs and 100 in one-hundredth test*

Test No. 637/199

# ENGLAND v AUSTRALIA 1968 (1st Test)

Played at Old Trafford, Manchester, on 6, 7, 8, 10, 11 June.
Toss: Australia. Result: AUSTRALIA won by 159 runs.
Debuts: Nil.

Australia won at 1.02 p.m. on the fifth day.

## AUSTRALIA

| | | | | | |
|---|---|---|---|---|---|
| W.M. Lawry* | c Boycott b Barber | 81 | c Pocock b D'Oliveira | | 16 |
| I.R. Redpath | lbw b Snow | 8 | lbw b Snow | | 8 |
| R.M. Cowper | b Snow | 0 | c and b Pocock | | 37 |
| K.D. Walters | lbw b Barber | 81 | lbw b Pocock | | 86 |
| A.P. Sheahan | c D'Oliveira b Snow | 88 | c Graveney b Pocock | | 8 |
| I.M. Chappell | run out | 73 | c Knott b Pocock | | 9 |
| B.N. Jarman† | c and b Higgs | 12 | b Pocock | | 41 |
| N.J.N. Hawke | c Knott b Snow | 5 | c Edrich b Pocock | | 0 |
| G.D. McKenzie | c Cowdrey b D'Oliveira | 0 | c Snow b Barber | | 0 |
| J.W. Gleeson | c Knott b Higgs | 0 | run out | | 2 |
| A.N. Connolly | not out | 0 | not out | | 2 |
| Extras | (LB 7, NB 2) | 9 | (B 2, LB 9) | | 11 |
| **Total** | | **357** | | | **220** |

## ENGLAND

| | | | | | |
|---|---|---|---|---|---|
| J.H. Edrich | run out | 49 | c Jarman b Cowper | | 38 |
| G. Boycott | c Jarman b Cowper | 35 | c Redpath b McKenzie | | 11 |
| M.C. Cowdrey* | c Lawry b McKenzie | 4 | c Jarman b McKenzie | | 11 |
| T.W. Graveney | c McKenzie b Cowper | 2 | c Jarman b Gleeson | | 33 |
| D.L. Amiss | c Cowper b McKenzie | 0 | b Cowper | | 0 |
| R.W. Barber | c Sheahan b McKenzie | 20 | c Cowper b Hawke | | 46 |
| B.L. D'Oliveira | b Connolly | 9 | not out | | 87 |
| A.P.E. Knott† | c McKenzie b Cowper | 5 | lbw b Connolly | | 4 |
| J.A. Snow | not out | 18 | c Lawry b Connolly | | 2 |
| K. Higgs | lbw b Cowper | 2 | c Jarman b Gleeson | | 0 |
| P.I. Pocock | c Redpath b Gleeson | 6 | lbw b Gleeson | | 10 |
| Extras | (B 9, LB 3, W 3) | 15 | (B 5, LB 6) | | 11 |
| **Total** | | **165** | | | **253** |

| ENGLAND | O | M | R | W | O | M | R | W | FALL OF WICKETS | | | |
|---|---|---|---|---|---|---|---|---|---|---|---|---|
| Snow | 34 | 5 | 97 | 4 | 17 | 2 | 51 | 1 | | A | E | A | E |
| Higgs | 35·3 | 11 | 80 | 2 | 23 | 8 | 41 | 0 | Wkt | 1st | 1st | 2nd | 2nd |
| D'Oliveira | 25 | 11 | 38 | 1 | 5 | 3 | 7 | 1 | 1st | 29 | 86 | 24 | 13 |
| Pocock | 25 | 5 | 77 | 0 | 33 | 10 | 79 | 6 | 2nd | 29 | 87 | 24 | 25 |
| Barber | 11 | 0 | 56 | 2 | 10 | 1 | 31 | 1 | 3rd | 173 | 89 | 106 | 91 |
| | | | | | | | | | 4th | 174 | 90 | 122 | 91 |
| AUSTRALIA | | | | | | | | | 5th | 326 | 97 | 140 | 105 |
| McKenzie | 28 | 11 | 33 | 3 | 18 | 3 | 52 | 2 | 6th | 341 | 120 | 211 | 185 |
| Hawke | 15 | 7 | 18 | 0 | 8 | 4 | 15 | 1 | 7th | 351 | 137 | 211 | 214 |
| Connolly | 28 | 15 | 26 | 1 | 13 | 4 | 35 | 2 | 8th | 353 | 137 | 214 | 218 |
| Gleeson | 6·3 | 2 | 21 | 1 | 30 | 14 | 44 | 3 | 9th | 357 | 144 | 214 | 219 |
| Cowper | 26 | 11 | 48 | 4 | 39 | 12 | 82 | 2 | 10th | 357 | 165 | 220 | 253 |
| Chappell | 1 | 0 | 4 | 0 | 2 | 0 | 14 | 0 | | | | | |

Umpires: J.S. Buller and C.S. Elliott.

Test No. 638/200

# ENGLAND v AUSTRALIA 1968 (2nd Test)

Played at Lord's, London, on 20, 21, 22, 24, 25 June.
Toss: England. Result: MATCH DRAWN.
Debuts: Nil.

After England had won their 103rd toss against Australia, rain reduced the playing time in this 200th match of the original series of Tests by over half, a total of 15 hours 3 minutes being lost, although some play was possible on each of the five days. Barrington (damaged finger) retired hurt at 271 for 5 when 61* and resumed at 330 for 6. Australia's total of 78 was their lowest since South Africa dismissed them for 75 in 1949-50 (*Test No. 320*). Cowdrey overtook W.R. Hammond's world Test record of 110 catches when he caught Gleeson at 1st slip. Knight took his 1,000th first-class wicket when he dismissed Sheahan. Jarman, who had fractured his right index finger when keeping wicket, retired after being hit on the same finger by the first ball he received.

## ENGLAND

| | | |
|---|---|---|
| J.H. Edrich | c Cowper b McKenzie | 7 |
| G. Boycott | c Sheahan b McKenzie | 49 |
| C. Milburn | c Walters b Gleeson | 83 |
| M.C. Cowdrey* | c Cowper b McKenzie | 45 |
| K.F. Barrington | c Jarman b Connolly | 75 |
| T.W. Graveney | c Jarman b Connolly | 14 |
| B.R. Knight | not out | 27 |
| A.P.E. Knott† | run out | 33 |
| J.A. Snow | not out | 0 |
| D.J. Brown | ) did not bat | |
| D.L. Underwood | ) | |
| Extras | (B 7, LB 5, W 1, NB 5) | 18 |
| **Total** | (7 wickets declared) | **351** |

## AUSTRALIA

| | | | | |
|---|---|---|---|---|
| W.M. Lawry* | c Knott b Brown | 0 | c Brown b Snow | 28 |
| I.R. Redpath | c Cowdrey b Brown | 4 | b Underwood | 53 |
| R.M. Cowper | c Graveney b Snow | 8 | c Underwood b Barrington | 32 |
| K.D. Walters | c Knight b Brown | 26 | b Underwood | 0 |
| A.P. Sheahan | c Knott b Knight | 6 | not out | 0 |
| I.M. Chappell | lbw b Knight | 7 | not out | 12 |
| N.J.N. Hawke | c Cowdrey b Knight | 2 | | |
| G.D. McKenzie | b Brown | 5 | | |
| J.W. Gleeson | c Cowdrey b Brown | 14 | | |
| B.N. Jarman† | retired hurt | 0 | | |
| A.N. Connolly | not out | 0 | | |
| Extras | (LB 2, NB 4) | 6 | (NB 2) | 2 |
| **Total** | | **78** | (4 wickets) | **127** |

| AUSTRALIA | O | M | R | W | O | M | R | W | | FALL OF WICKETS | | |
|---|---|---|---|---|---|---|---|---|---|---|---|---|
| McKenzie | 45 | 18 | 111 | 3 | | | | | | E | A | A |
| Hawke | 35 | 7 | 82 | 0 | | | | | Wkt | 1st | 1st | 2nd |
| Connolly | 26·3 | 8 | 55 | 2 | | | | | 1st | 10 | 1 | 66 |
| Walters | 3 | 2 | 2 | 0 | | | | | 2nd | 142 | 12 | 93 |
| Cowper | 8 | 2 | 40 | 0 | | | | | 3rd | 147 | 23 | 97 |
| Gleeson | 27 | 11 | 43 | 1 | | | | | 4th | 244 | 46 | 115 |
| | | | | | | | | | 5th | 271 | 52 | – |
| ENGLAND | | | | | | | | | 6th | 330 | 58 | – |
| Snow | 9 | 5 | 14 | 1 | 12 | 5 | 30 | 1 | 7th | 351 | 63 | – |
| Brown | 14 | 5 | 42 | 5 | 19 | 9 | 40 | 0 | 8th | – | 78 | – |
| Knight | 10·4 | 5 | 16 | 3 | 16 | 9 | 35 | 0 | 9th | – | 78 | – |
| Underwood | | | | | 18 | 15 | 8 | 2 | 10th | – | – | – |
| Barrington | | | | | 2 | 0 | 12 | 1 | | | | |

Umpires: J.S. Buller and A.E. Fagg.

Test No. 639/201

# ENGLAND v AUSTRALIA 1968 (3rd Test)

Played at Edgbaston, Birmingham, on 11 (*no play*), 12, 13, 15, 16 July.
Toss: England.   Result: MATCH DRAWN.
Debuts: Nil.

Cowdrey celebrated his becoming the first to appear in 100 Test matches by scoring his 21st hundred for England. He pulled a muscle in his left leg and used Boycott as his runner when he had scored 58. Two runs later he became the second batsman after W.R. Hammond to score 7,000 runs in Test cricket. Graveney assumed the captaincy when Cowdrey was unable to field. After scoring Australia's first six runs, Lawry retired when his right-hand little finger was fractured by a ball in Snow's opening over. McKenzie deputised as captain when Australia fielded again. Rain ended the match at 12.30 p.m. when Australia needed 262 runs to win in 270 minutes.

## ENGLAND

| | | | | |
|---|---|---|---|---|
| J.H. Edrich | c Taber b Freeman | 88 | c Cowper b Freeman | 64 |
| G. Boycott | lbw b Gleeson | 36 | c Taber b Connolly | 31 |
| M.C. Cowdrey* | b Freeman | 104 | | |
| K.F. Barrington | lbw b Freeman | 0 | | |
| T.W. Graveney | b Connolly | 96 | (3) not out | 39 |
| B.R. Knight | c Chappell b Connolly | 6 | (4) b Connolly | 1 |
| A.P.E. Knott† | b McKenzie | 4 | (5) not out | 4 |
| R. Illingworth | lbw b Gleeson | 27 | | |
| D.J. Brown | b Connolly | 0 | | |
| J.A. Snow | c Connolly b Freeman | 19 | | |
| D.L. Underwood | not out | 14 | | |
| Extras | (B 4, LB 6, W 1, NB 4) | 15 | (LB 2, NB 1) | 3 |
| **Total** | | **409** | (3 wickets declared) | **142** |

## AUSTRALIA

| | | | | |
|---|---|---|---|---|
| W.M. Lawry* | retired hurt | 6 | | |
| I.R. Redpath | b Brown | 0 | lbw b Snow | 22 |
| R.M. Cowper | b Snow | 57 | (1) not out | 25 |
| I.M. Chappell | b Knight | 71 | (3) not out | 18 |
| K.D. Walters | c and b Underwood | 46 | | |
| A.P. Sheahan | b Underwood | 4 | | |
| H.B. Taber† | c Barrington b Illingworth | 16 | | |
| E.W. Freeman | b Illingworth | 6 | | |
| G.D. McKenzie | not out | 0 | | |
| J.W. Gleeson | c Illingworth b Underwood | 3 | | |
| A.N. Connolly | b Illingworth | 0 | | |
| Extras | (B 1, LB 10, NB 2) | 13 | (LB 1, NB 2) | 3 |
| **Total** | | **222** | (1 wicket) | **68** |

| AUSTRALIA | O | M | R | W | O | M | R | W | FALL OF WICKETS | | | | |
|---|---|---|---|---|---|---|---|---|---|---|---|---|---|
| McKenzie | 47 | 14 | 115 | 1 | 18 | 1 | 57 | 0 | | E | A | E | A |
| Freeman | 30·5 | 8 | 78 | 4 | 9 | 2 | 23 | 1 | Wkt | 1st | 1st | 2nd | 2nd |
| Connolly | 35 | 8 | 84 | 3 | 15 | 3 | 59 | 2 | 1st | 80 | 10 | 57 | 44 |
| Gleeson | 46 | 19 | 84 | 2 | | | | | 2nd | 188 | 121 | 131 | – |
| Cowper | 7 | 1 | 25 | 0 | | | | | 3rd | 189 | 165 | 134 | – |
| Walters | 7 | 3 | 8 | 0 | | | | | 4th | 282 | 176 | – | – |
| ENGLAND | | | | | | | | | 5th | 293 | 213 | – | – |
| Snow | 17 | 3 | 46 | 1 | 9 | 1 | 32 | 1 | 6th | 323 | 213 | – | – |
| Brown | 13 | 2 | 44 | 1 | 6 | 1 | 15 | 0 | 7th | 374 | 219 | – | – |
| Knight | 14 | 2 | 34 | 1 | | | | | 8th | 374 | 222 | – | – |
| Underwood | 25 | 9 | 48 | 3 | 8 | 4 | 14 | 0 | 9th | 376 | 222 | – | – |
| Illingworth | 22 | 10 | 37 | 3 | 5·2 | 2 | 4 | 0 | 10th | 409 | – | – | – |

Umpires: C.S. Elliott and H. Yarnold.

Test No. 640/202

## ENGLAND v AUSTRALIA 1968 (4th Test)

Played at Headingley, Leeds, on 25, 26, 27, 29, 30 July.
Toss: Australia.   Result: MATCH DRAWN.
Debuts: England – K.W.R. Fletcher, R.M. Prideaux; Australia – R.J. Inverarity.

With Cowdrey and Lawry both injured, Graveney and Jarman were called upon to make their only appearances as Test captains. Australia retained the Ashes when England failed to score 326 runs in 295 minutes. Underwood's score of 45 not out is the highest by an England No. 11 against Australia.

### AUSTRALIA

| | | | | | |
|---|---|---|---|---|---|
| R.J. Inverarity | b Snow | 8 | lbw b Illingworth | | 34 |
| R.M. Cowper | b Snow | 27 | st Knott b Illingworth | | 5 |
| I.R. Redpath | b Illingworth | 92 | c Edrich b Snow | | 48 |
| K.D. Walters | c Barrington b Underwood | 42 | c Graveney b Snow | | 56 |
| I.M. Chappell | b Brown | 65 | c Barrington b Underwood | | 81 |
| A.P. Sheahan | c Knott b Snow | 38 | st Knott b Illingworth | | 31 |
| B.N. Jarman*† | c Dexter b Brown | 10 | st Knott b Illingworth | | 4 |
| E.W. Freeman | b Underwood | 21 | b Illingworth | | 10 |
| G.D. McKenzie | lbw b Underwood | 5 | c Snow b Illingworth | | 10 |
| J.W. Gleeson | not out | 2 | c Knott b Underwood | | 7 |
| A.N. Connolly | c Graveney b Underwood | 0 | not out | | 0 |
| Extras | (LB 4, NB 1) | 5 | (B 13, LB 8, NB 5) | | 26 |
| **Total** | | **315** | | | **312** |

### ENGLAND

| | | | | | |
|---|---|---|---|---|---|
| J.H. Edrich | c Jarman b McKenzie | 62 | c Jarman b Connolly | | 65 |
| R.M. Prideaux | c Freeman b Gleeson | 64 | b McKenzie | | 2 |
| E.R. Dexter | b McKenzie | 10 | b Connolly | | 38 |
| T.W. Graveney* | c Cowper b Connolly | 37 | c and b Cowper | | 41 |
| K.F. Barrington | b Connolly | 49 | not out | | 46 |
| K.W.R. Fletcher | c Jarman b Connolly | 0 | not out | | 23 |
| A.P.E. Knott† | lbw b Freeman | 4 | | | |
| R. Illingworth | c Gleeson b Connolly | 6 | | | |
| J.A. Snow | b Connolly | 0 | | | |
| D.J. Brown | b Cowper | 14 | | | |
| D.L. Underwood | not out | 45 | | | |
| Extras | (B 1, LB 7, NB 3) | 11 | (LB 7, NB 8) | | 15 |
| **Total** | | **302** | (4 wickets) | | **230** |

| ENGLAND | O | M | R | W | O | M | R | W | | FALL OF WICKETS | | | |
|---|---|---|---|---|---|---|---|---|---|---|---|---|---|
| Snow | 35 | 3 | 98 | 3 | 24 | 3 | 51 | 2 | | A | E | A | E |
| Brown | 35 | 4 | 99 | 2 | 27 | 5 | 79 | 0 | Wkt | 1st | 1st | 2nd | 2nd |
| Illingworth | 29 | 15 | 47 | 1 | 51 | 22 | 87 | 6 | 1st | 10 | 123 | 28 | 4 |
| Underwood | 27·4 | 13 | 41 | 4 | 45·1 | 22 | 52 | 2 | 2nd | 104 | 136 | 81 | 81 |
| Dexter | 7 | 0 | 25 | 0 | 1 | 0 | 3 | 0 | 3rd | 152 | 141 | 119 | 134 |
| Barrington | | | | | 6 | 1 | 14 | 0 | 4th | 188 | 209 | 198 | 168 |
| | | | | | | | | | 5th | 248 | 215 | 273 | – |
| AUSTRALIA | | | | | | | | | 6th | 267 | 235 | 281 | – |
| McKenzie | 39 | 20 | 61 | 2 | 25 | 2 | 65 | 1 | 7th | 307 | 237 | 283 | – |
| Freeman | 22 | 6 | 60 | 1 | 6 | 1 | 25 | 0 | 8th | 309 | 241 | 296 | – |
| Gleeson | 25 | 5 | 68 | 1 | 11 | 4 | 26 | 0 | 9th | 315 | 241 | 311 | – |
| Connolly | 39 | 13 | 72 | 5 | 31 | 10 | 68 | 2 | 10th | 315 | 302 | 312 | – |
| Cowper | 18 | 10 | 24 | 1 | 5 | 0 | 22 | 1 | | | | | |
| Chappell | 4 | 1 | 6 | 0 | 5 | 3 | 6 | 0 | | | | | |
| Inverarity | | | | | 1 | 0 | 3 | 0 | | | | | |

Umpires: J.S. Buller and A.E. Fagg.

Test No. 641/203

# ENGLAND v AUSTRALIA 1968 (5th Test)

Played at Kennington Oval, London, on 22, 23, 24, 26, 27 August.
Toss: England.   Result: ENGLAND won by 226 runs.
Debuts: Australia – A.A. Mallett.

England won with just five minutes to spare when Inverarity padded up to a ball from Underwood after batting throughout Australia's 250-minute innings. Rain brought the players in to lunch a minute early on the final day. During the interval a freak storm completely flooded the playing area but the sun's reappearance, combined with heroic efforts by a groundstaff reinforced with volunteers from the crowd, enabled play to resume at 4.45 p.m. with Australia's score 86 for 5. Until D'Oliveira bowled Jarman at 5.24 p.m. they seemed to have saved the match. Cowdrey brought Underwood back to bowl the next over from the pavilion end and Mallett and McKenzie fell to the first and sixth balls. Gleeson survived until 5.48 p.m. Seven minutes later Inverarity made his fatal lapse and England had taken five wickets and bowled 20·3 overs in the last hour of play. Earlier Mallett had dismissed Cowdrey with his fifth ball in Test cricket.

### ENGLAND

| | | | | | |
|---|---|---|---|---|---|
| J.H. Edrich | b Chappell | 164 | c Lawry b Mallett | | 17 |
| C. Milburn | b Connolly | 8 | c Lawry b Connolly | | 18 |
| E.R. Dexter | b Gleeson | 21 | b Connolly | | 28 |
| M.C. Cowdrey* | lbw b Mattett | 16 | b Mallett | | 35 |
| T.W. Graveney | c Redpath b McKenzie | 63 | run out | | 12 |
| B.L. D'Oliveira | c Inverarity b Mallett | 158 | c Gleeson b Connolly | | 9 |
| A.P.E. Knott† | c Jarman b Mallett | 28 | run out | | 34 |
| R. Illingworth | lbw b Connolly | 8 | b Gleeson | | 10 |
| J.A. Snow | run out | 4 | c Sheahan b Gleeson | | 13 |
| D.L. Underwood | not out | 9 | not out | | 1 |
| D.J. Brown | c Sheahan b Gleeson | 2 | b Connolly | | 1 |
| Extras | (B 1, LB 11, W 1) | 13 | (LB 3) | | 3 |
| **Total** | | **494** | | | **181** |

### AUSTRALIA

| | | | | | |
|---|---|---|---|---|---|
| W.M. Lawry* | c Knott b Snow | 135 | c Milburn b Brown | | 4 |
| R.J. Inverarity | c Milburn b Snow | 1 | lbw b Underwood | | 56 |
| I.R. Redpath | c Cowdrey b Snow | 67 | lbw b Underwood | | 8 |
| I.M. Chappell | c Knott b Brown | 10 | lbw b Underwood | | 2 |
| K.D. Walters | c Knott b Brown | 5 | c Knott b Underwood | | 1 |
| A.P. Sheahan | b Illingworth | 14 | c Snow b Illingworth | | 24 |
| B.N. Jarman† | st Knott b Illingworth | 0 | b D'Oliveira | | 21 |
| G.D. McKenzie | b Brown | 12 | (9) c Brown b Underwood | | 0 |
| A.A. Mallett | not out | 43 | (8) c Brown b Underwood | | 0 |
| J.W. Gleeson | c Dexter b Underwood | 19 | b Underwood | | 5 |
| A.N. Connolly | b Underwood | 3 | not out | | 0 |
| Extras | (B 4, LB 7, NB 4) | 15 | (LB 4) | | 4 |
| **Total** | | **324** | | | **125** |

| AUSTRALIA | O | M | R | W | O | M | R | W | FALL OF WICKETS | | | | |
|---|---|---|---|---|---|---|---|---|---|---|---|---|---|
| McKenzie | 40 | 8 | 87 | 1 | 4 | 0 | 14 | 0 | | E | A | E | A |
| Connolly | 57 | 12 | 127 | 2 | 22·4 | 2 | 65 | 4 | Wkt | 1st | 1st | 2nd | 2nd |
| Walters | 6 | 2 | 17 | 0 | | | | | 1st | 28 | 7 | 23 | 4 |
| Gleeson | 41·2 | 8 | 109 | 2 | 7 | 2 | 22 | 2 | 2nd | 84 | 136 | 53 | 13 |
| Mallett | 36 | 11 | 87 | 3 | 25 | 4 | 77 | 2 | 3rd | 113 | 151 | 67 | 19 |
| Chappell | 21 | 5 | 54 | 1 | | | | | 4th | 238 | 161 | 90 | 29 |
| | | | | | | | | | 5th | 359 | 185 | 114 | 65 |
| ENGLAND | | | | | | | | | 6th | 421 | 188 | 126 | 110 |
| Snow | 35 | 12 | 67 | 3 | 11 | 5 | 22 | 0 | 7th | 458 | 237 | 149 | 110 |
| Brown | 22 | 5 | 63 | 3 | 8 | 3 | 19 | 1 | 8th | 468 | 269 | 179 | 110 |
| Illingworth | 48 | 15 | 87 | 1 | 28 | 18 | 29 | 1 | 9th | 489 | 302 | 179 | 120 |
| Underwood | 54·3 | 21 | 89 | 2 | 31·3 | 19 | 50 | 7 | 10th | 494 | 324 | 181 | 125 |
| D'Oliveira | 4 | 2 | 3 | 0 | 5 | 4 | 1 | 1 | | | | | |

Umpires: C.S. Elliott and A.E. Fagg.

Chapter 28

# PAKISTAN 1968/69

Out of the frying pan of South Africa the England touring party were sent instead to the fire of Pakistan for the winter tour of 1968/69.

The first Test at Lahore was frequently interrupted by the crowd invading the playing area and minor riots and skirmishes. Cowdrey scored his twenty-second test century. The match ended in a draw. Graveney captained England during the final innings while Cowdrey went to hospital to have treatment to a jarred nerve in his right forearm.

I have been grateful for help in writing this book by various newspapers publishing letters of mine asking readers for their recollections of my subject. Some responses were particularly poignant and none more so than the following from Miss Marjory E Fyson the Founder of the Sunrise School for the Blind, Lahore. Writing on 5th October 1975 from Porlock in Somerset, what she said was in pleasing contrast to riots and graphically describes how test cricketers do much more than play cricket on tour:

> I saw your little request in the *Daily Telegraph* about Colin Cowdrey's Test days.
> 
> He came to Lahore and he and Graveney, Edrich, Murray and that nice physiotherapist came to my blind school, Sunrise School for the Blind in Ravi Road, Lahore. Our blind boys play the best blind cricket in the world, a very fast hard game invented by a Manchester VSO we had, Brian Mainwaring. The wickets are empty oil drums, the ball is brass full of bits of metal, and the bats very heavy wood with a 'mowing the dasies' action. The boys ran properly between the wickets, banging on the drum to show they are back in the crease. Fielders hear the ball and the constant banging on the drums by wicket-keeper and bowler, and are able if clever to get batsmen run out. This game can be umpired entirely by the blind themselves.

The England players played with our boys. I have two nice slides of Cowdrey and Graveney playing, but not a sunny day for once. Ghulam Ilahi, a blind boy of ours, bowled out Edrich!

The next day four of the boys came with me to Cowdrey's room at the Intercontinental Hotel, and there was Brian Johnston, Ames and at times Brown and Snow. Cowdrey, dear chap, was so chatty and we made a very good tape recording of him talking to the boys, mostly about Sobers. It was a real thrill for the blind boys, as you can imagine. He has such a good voice, and we all took to him. I have retired now, but whenever I go back to Lahore I always make a point of turning on this little interview again.

The blind boys have a good wireless and listen to all Test matches. They have phenomenal memories of who made how many runs when, and so on. But actually to meet Cowdrey and talk to him was a marvellous treat for them — and me!

At Dacca they had the only riot-free match of the series but the crowd was controlled by student leaders of East Pakistan. Again it was a draw but England finished the stronger of the two teams.

At trouble-torn Karachi for the third and final Test. Pitch invasions continued. The match could not continue on the third day. Beforehand England amassed 502 for 7 with Milburn and Graveney both making centuries. Cowdrey only made 14 but Knott was within four of what would have been his first Test century when play stopped. The team flew home a day later than Cowdrey who had returned because his father-in-law had died. A few weeks later Milburn lost his left eye in a car accident.

1969 was to prove another frustrating year for Colin Cowdrey. On 25 May he was appointed Captain of England for the summer. I watched him on television playing in a Sunday match for Kent against Glamorgan at Mote Park, Maidstone. The wicket was damp and Kent were struggling until Cowdrey arrived. As so often was the case he made batting look easier. He had reached 39 when setting off for a quick single he slipped to the ground and a loud crack was heard. He had snapped an Achilles tendon. Carried off he was sent to St Nicholas's Hospital, Plumstead for an operation the next day. He left three days later in plaster.

Thus Cowdrey played no Test cricket in the summer of 1969.

|  | Matches | Innings | Not out | Runs | Highest score | Average | 100s | 50s | Caught |
|---|---|---|---|---|---|---|---|---|---|
| This series | 3 | 4 | 0 | 133 | 100 | 33.25 | 1 | 0 | 0 |
| Previous series | 101 | 167 | 15 | 7095 | 182 | 46.68 | 21 | 37 | 113 |
| Cumulative totals | 104 | 171 | 15 | 7228 | 182 | 46.33 | 22 | 37 | 113 |

Test No. 647/16

# PAKISTAN v ENGLAND 1968–69 (1st Test)

Played at Lahore Stadium on 21, 22, 23, 24 February.
Toss: England.   Result: MATCH DRAWN.
Debuts: Pakistan – Aftab Gul, Asif Masood; England – R.M.H. Cottam.

Cowdrey's 22nd and last Test hundred equalled the England record held by W.R. Hammond. It was made in a match frequently interrupted by crowd invasions of the playing area and by minor riots and skirmishes. Pakistan were set to score 323 runs in 295 minutes. Graveney captained England throughout the final innings when Cowdrey went to hospital for treatment to a jarred nerve in the right forearm.

### ENGLAND

| | | | | | |
|---|---|---|---|---|---|
| J.H. Edrich | c Asif Masood b Intikhab | 54 | c Majid b Asif Masood | 8 |
| R.M. Prideaux | c Shafqat b Asif Masood | 9 | b Majid | 5 |
| M.C. Cowdrey* | c Wasim b Majid | 100 | c Wasim b Asif Masood | 12 |
| T.W. Graveney | c Asif Iqbal b Intikhab | 13 | run out | 12 |
| K.W.R. Fletcher | c Intikhab b Saeed | 20 | b Majid | 83 |
| B.L. D'Oliveira | c Ilyas b Intikhab | 26 | c Mushtaq b Saeed | 5 |
| A.P.E. Knott† | lbw b Saeed | 52 | b Asif Masood | 30 |
| D.L. Underwood | c Intikhab b Saeed | 0 | c Aftab b Mushtaq | 6 |
| D.J. Brown | b Saeed | 7 | not out | 44 |
| P.I. Pocock | b Intikhab | 12 | b Saeed | 1 |
| R.M.H. Cottam | not out | 4 | | |
| Extras | (B 4, LB 2, NB 3) | 9 | (B 6, LB 9, NB 4) | 19 |
| **Total** | | **306** | (9 wickets declared) | **225** |

### PAKISTAN

| | | | | | |
|---|---|---|---|---|---|
| Mohammad Ilyas | lbw b Brown | 0 | c Fletcher b Brown | 1 |
| Aftab Gul | c D'Oliveira b Brown | 12 | c Pocock b Underwood | 29 |
| Saeed Ahmed* | c Knott b D'Oliveira | 18 | b Cottam | 39 |
| Asif Iqbal | c D'Oliveira b Cottam | 70 | c and b Cottam | 0 |
| Mushtaq Mohammad | c Fletcher b Cottam | 4 | not out | 34 |
| Hanif Mohammad | b Brown | 7 | (7) not out | 23 |
| Majid Khan | c Pocock b Underwood | 18 | (6) c Pocock b Brown | 68 |
| Shafqat Rana | c Knott b Cottam | 30 | | |
| Intikhab Alam | c D'Oliveira b Pocock | 12 | | |
| Wasim Bari† | not out | 14 | | |
| Asif Masood | b Cottam | 11 | | |
| Extras | (B 8, LB 4, NB 1) | 13 | (B 3, LB 5, NB 1) | 9 |
| **Total** | | **209** | (5 wickets) | **203** |

| PAKISTAN | O | M | R | W | O | M | R | W | | FALL OF WICKETS | | | |
|---|---|---|---|---|---|---|---|---|---|---|---|---|---|
| Asif Masood | 21 | 5 | 59 | 1 | 25 | 4 | 68 | 3 | | E | P | E | P |
| Asif Iqbal | 4 | 2 | 11 | 0 | | | | | Wkt | 1st | 1st | 2nd | 2nd |
| Majid | 18 | 8 | 25 | 1 | 20 | 5 | 41 | 2 | 1st | 41 | 0 | 8 | 6 |
| Intikhab | 40·1 | 8 | 117 | 4 | 15 | 5 | 29 | 0 | 2nd | 92 | 32 | 25 | 71 |
| Saeed | 20 | 5 | 64 | 4 | 15·5 | 3 | 44 | 2 | 3rd | 113 | 32 | 41 | 71 |
| Mushtaq | 14 | 6 | 15 | 0 | 9 | 1 | 24 | 1 | 4th | 182 | 52 | 46 | 71 |
| Shafqat | 2 | 0 | 6 | 0 | | | | | 5th | 219 | 72 | 68 | 156 |
| | | | | | | | | | 6th | 246 | 119 | 136 | – |
| ENGLAND | | | | | | | | | 7th | 257 | 145 | 151 | – |
| Brown | 14 | 0 | 43 | 3 | 15 | 4 | 47 | 2 | 8th | 287 | 176 | 201 | – |
| Cottam | 22·2 | 5 | 50 | 4 | 13 | 1 | 35 | 2 | 9th | 294 | 187 | 225 | – |
| D'Oliveira | 8 | 2 | 28 | 1 | | | | | 10th | 306 | 209 | – | – |
| Underwood | 16 | 4 | 36 | 1 | 19 | 8 | 29 | 1 | | | | | |
| Pocock | 10 | 3 | 39 | 1 | 16 | 4 | 41 | 0 | | | | | |
| Fletcher | | | | | 8 | 2 | 31 | 0 | | | | | |
| Graveney | | | | | 6 | 0 | 11 | 0 | | | | | |
| Prideaux | | | | | 2 | 2 | 0 | 0 | | | | | |

Umpires: Shujauddin and Munawar Hussain.

**Test No. 648/17**

# PAKISTAN v ENGLAND 1968–69 (2nd Test)

Played at Dacca Stadium on 28 February, 1, 2, 3, March.
Toss: Pakistan. Result: MATCH DRAWN.
Debuts: Nil.

The only riot-free match of this rubber was played in front of crowds controlled by the student leaders of East Pakistan and without either police or army presence.

### PAKISTAN

| | | | | |
|---|---|---|---|---|
| Mohammad Ilyas | c Knott b Snow | 20 | c Snow b Cottam | 21 |
| Salahuddin | c Brown b Snow | 6 | lbw b Underwood | 5 |
| Saeed Ahmed* | b Brown | 19 | (5) c Knott b Underwood | 33 |
| Asif Iqbal | b Brown | 44 | (3) b Underwood | 16 |
| Mushtaq Mohammad | c Cottam b Snow | 52 | (4) c D'Oliveira b Underwood | 31 |
| Majid Khan | c Knott b Brown | 27 | not out | 49 |
| Hanif Mohammad | lbw b Snow | 8 | lbw b Underwood | 8 |
| Intikhab Alam | lbw b Underwood | 25 | not out | 19 |
| Wasim Bari† | c Knott b Cottam | 14 | | |
| Niaz Ahmed | not out | 16 | | |
| Pervez Sajjad | b Cottam | 2 | | |
| Extras | (B 4, LB 4, NB 5) | 13 | (LB 5, NB 8) | 13 |
| **Total** | | **246** | (6 wickets declared) | **195** |

### ENGLAND

| | | | | |
|---|---|---|---|---|
| J.H. Edrich | c Mushtaq b Intikhab | 24 | not out | 12 |
| R.M. Prideaux | c Hanif b Pervez | 4 | not out | 18 |
| T.W. Graveney | b Pervez | 46 | | |
| K.W.R. Fletcher | c Hanif b Saeed | 16 | | |
| M.C. Cowdrey* | lbw b Pervez | 7 | | |
| B.L. D'Oliveira | not out | 114 | | |
| A.P.E. Knott† | c and b Pervez | 2 | | |
| D.J. Brown | c Hanif b Saeed | 4 | | |
| J.A. Snow | c Majid b Niaz | 9 | | |
| D.L. Underwood | c Ilyas b Mushtaq | 22 | | |
| R.M.H. Cottam | c Hanif b Saeed | 4 | | |
| Extras | (B 14, LB 8) | 22 | (B 2, NB 1) | 3 |
| **Total** | | **274** | (0 wickets) | **33** |

| ENGLAND | O | M | R | W | O | M | R | W |
|---|---|---|---|---|---|---|---|---|
| Snow | 25 | 5 | 70 | 4 | 12 | 7 | 15 | 0 |
| Brown | 23 | 8 | 51 | 3 | 6 | 1 | 18 | 0 |
| Underwood | 27 | 13 | 45 | 1 | 44 | 15 | 94 | 5 |
| Cottam | 27·1 | 6 | 52 | 2 | 30 | 17 | 43 | 1 |
| D'Oliveira | 8 | 1 | 15 | 0 | 9 | 2 | 12 | 0 |
| PAKISTAN | | | | | | | | |
| Niaz | 10 | 4 | 20 | 1 | 2 | 0 | 2 | 0 |
| Majid | 11 | 4 | 15 | 0 | | | | |
| Pervez | 37 | 8 | 75 | 4 | 3 | 2 | 1 | 0 |
| Saeed | 37·4 | 15 | 59 | 3 | 3 | 2 | 4 | 0 |
| Intikhab | 26 | 7 | 65 | 1 | 4 | 0 | 19 | 0 |
| Mushtaq | 11 | 3 | 18 | 1 | | | | |
| Asif | | | | | 4 | 2 | 2 | 0 |
| Hanif | | | | | 3 | 2 | 1 | 0 |
| Ilyas | | | | | 1 | 0 | 1 | 0 |

### FALL OF WICKETS

| Wkt | P 1st | E 1st | P 2nd | E 2nd |
|---|---|---|---|---|
| 1st | 16 | 17 | 8 | – |
| 2nd | 39 | 61 | 48 | – |
| 3rd | 55 | 96 | 50 | – |
| 4th | 123 | 100 | 97 | – |
| 5th | 168 | 113 | 129 | – |
| 6th | 184 | 117 | 147 | – |
| 7th | 186 | 130 | – | – |
| 8th | 211 | 170 | – | – |
| 9th | 237 | 236 | – | – |
| 10th | 246 | 274 | – | – |

Umpires: Shujauddin and Gulzar.

Test No. 649/18

# PAKISTAN v ENGLAND 1968–69 (3rd Test)

Played at National Stadium, Karachi, on 6, 7, 8 March.
Toss: England.   Result: MATCH DRAWN – abandoned because of rioting.
Debuts: Pakistan – Sarfraz Nawaz.

Rioting compelled the abandonment of this match on the penultimate morning. The playing area was invaded when Knott needed four runs for his first hundred in Test cricket. Earlier Milburn, who had joined the M.C.C. team from Western Australia where he had been playing in the Sheffield Shield, reached his hundred off 163 balls. It was his first innings in Pakistan and his last in Test cricket. Within a few weeks he had lost his left eye as a result of a car accident near Northampton.

### ENGLAND
| | | |
|---|---|---|
| C. Milburn | c Wasim b Asif Masood | 139 |
| J.H. Edrich | c Saeed b Intikhab | 32 |
| T.W. Graveney | c Asif Iqbal b Intikhab | 105 |
| M.C. Cowdrey* | c Hanif b Intikhab | 14 |
| K.W.R. Fletcher | b Mushtaq | 38 |
| B.L. D'Oliveira | c Aftab b Mushtaq | 16 |
| A.P.E. Knott† | not out | 96 |
| J.A. Snow | b Asif Masood | 9 |
| D.J. Brown | not out | 25 |
| D.L. Underwood | ) did not bat | |
| R.N.S. Hobbs | ) | |
| Extras | (B 5, LB 12, NB 11) | 28 |
| **Total** | (7 wickets) | **502** |

### PAKISTAN
Aftab Gul
Hanif Mohamad
Mushtaq Mohammad
Asif Iqbal
Saeed Ahmed*
Majid Khan
Shafqat Rana
Intikhab Alam
Wasim Bari†
Asif Masood
Sarfraz Nawaz

| PAKISTAN | O | M | R | W |
|---|---|---|---|---|
| Asif Masood | 28 | 2 | 94 | 2 |
| Majid | 20 | 5 | 51 | 0 |
| Sarfraz | 34 | 6 | 78 | 0 |
| Intikhab | 48 | 4 | 129 | 3 |
| Saeed | 22 | 5 | 53 | 0 |
| Mushtaq | 23·1 | 5 | 69 | 2 |

Umpires: Shujauddin and Daud Khan.

FALL OF WICKETS
| | E |
|---|---|
| Wkt | 1st |
| 1st | 78 |
| 2nd | 234 |
| 3rd | 286 |
| 4th | 309 |
| 5th | 360 |
| 6th | 374 |
| 7th | 427 |
| 8th | – |
| 9th | – |
| 10th | – |

Chapter 29

# AUSTRALIA 1970/71

The 1970 season started badly for Cowdrey but after two centuries in the Tunbridge Wells week he was recalled to the England team for the second match against the Rest of the World which was to compensate for the cancelled South African tour. He made 64 in the second innings at Trent Bridge where England won by eight-wickets.

In the third match at Edgbaston the Captain for the coming Australian tour was announced. Cowdrey had been Captain and successfully so up until the mishap on the Sunday afternoon at Maidstone. Ray Illingworth had been appointed in his absence and had done well against the West Indies and New Zealand. The Selectors decided to ask Illingworth to continue and for the fifth time Cowdrey was offered the position of Vice Captain. Eventually Cowdrey accepted.

There could be no compensation for the loss of a lifetime's ambition but Kent winning the championship at the end of that season must have been the next best thing.

And so Cowdrey set out for his fifth tour of Australia in 1970/71. It was not a harmonious one.

He began the Test series miserably. His 28 which made him at the time the most prolific scorer in test cricket was a poor contribution to England's 464. He was better in the second Test at Perth where he made 40 and 1 in a second drawn match. He was selected for the Melbourne Test which was abandoned. But dropped for the fourth at Sydney.

Fletcher, who replaced Cowdrey, injured his wrist and that enabled Cowdrey to be included for the fifth test at Melbourne. It was something of a disaster. In Australia's first innings he dropped four slip catches. In the second he dropped another.

## AUSTRALIA 1970/71

Cowdrey was not included for the final two Tests.

|  | Matches | Innings | Not out | Runs | Highest score | Average | 100s | 50s | Caught |
|---|---|---|---|---|---|---|---|---|---|
| This series | 3 | 4 | 0 | 82 | 40 | 20.50 | 0 | 0 | 3 |
| Previous series | 104 | 171 | 15 | 7228 | 182 | 46.33 | 22 | 37 | 113 |
| Cumulative totals | 107 | 175 | 15 | 7310 | 182 | 45.69 | 22 | 37 | 116 |

Test No. 674/204

# AUSTRALIA v ENGLAND 1970–71 (1st Test)

Played at Woolloongabba, Brisbane, on 27, 28, 29 November, 1, 2 December.
Toss: Australia.   Result: MATCH DRAWN.
Debuts: Australia – T.J. Jenner, R.W. Marsh, A.L. Thomson; England – B.W. Luckhurst, K. Shuttleworth.

Stackpole, favoured by a run out decision when he had scored 18, became the first to score a double century in an Australia v England Test at Brisbane; only Bradman (twice) has played a higher innings there. Stackpole batted for 440 minutes and hit a six and 25 fours. Australia's last seven first innings wickets fell for 15 runs in 47 minutes – Underwood claiming those of Redpath, Sheahan and Walters in seven balls without conceding a run. Cowdrey passed W.R. Hammond's world Test record aggregate of 7,249 runs when he had scored 22.

## AUSTRALIA

| | | | | |
|---|---|---|---|---|
| W.M. Lawry* | c Knott b Snow | 4 | c Snow b Fletcher | 84 |
| K.R. Stackpole | c Knott b Snow | 207 | c Knott b Shuttleworth | 8 |
| I.M. Chappell | run out | 59 | st Knott b Illingworth | 10 |
| K.D. Walters | b Underwood | 112 | c Luckhurst b Snow | 7 |
| I.R. Redpath | c Illingworth b Underwood | 22 | c and b Underwood | 28 |
| A.P. Sheahan | c Knott b Underwood | 0 | c Shuttleworth b Snow | 36 |
| R.W. Marsh† | b Snow | 9 | b Shuttleworth | 14 |
| T.J. Jenner | c Cowdrey b Snow | 0 | c Boycott b Shuttleworth | 2 |
| G.D. McKenzie | not out | 3 | b Shuttleworth | 1 |
| J.W. Gleeson | c Cowdrey b Snow | 0 | b Shuttleworth | 6 |
| A.L. Thomson | b Snow | 0 | not out | 4 |
| Extras | (B 7, LB 4, NB 6) | 17 | (B 4, LB 3, NB 7) | 14 |
| **Total** | | **433** | | **214** |

## ENGLAND

| | | | | |
|---|---|---|---|---|
| G. Boycott | c Marsh b Gleeson | 37 | c and b Jenner | 16 |
| B.W. Luckhurst | run out | 74 | not out | 20 |
| A.P.E. Knott† | c Lawry b Walters | 73 | | |
| J.H. Edrich | c Chappell b Jenner | 79 | | |
| M.C. Cowdrey | c Chappell b Gleeson | 28 | | |
| K.W.R. Fletcher | c Marsh b McKenzie | 34 | | |
| B.L. D'Oliveira | c Sheahan b McKenzie | 57 | | |
| R. Illingworth* | c Marsh b Thomson | 8 | | |
| J.A. Snow | c Marsh b Walters | 34 | | |
| D.L. Underwood | not out | 2 | | |
| K. Shuttleworth | c Lawry b Walters | 7 | | |
| Extras | (B 2, LB 7, NB 22) | 31 | (LB 3) | 3 |
| **Total** | | **464** | (1 wicket) | **39** |

| ENGLAND | O | M | R | W | O | M | R | W | FALL OF WICKETS |
|---|---|---|---|---|---|---|---|---|---|
| Snow | 32.3 | 6 | 114 | 6 | 20 | 3 | 48 | 2 | | A | E | A | E |
| Shuttleworth | 27 | 6 | 81 | 0 | 17.5 | 2 | 47 | 5 | Wkt | 1st | 1st | 2nd | 2nd |
| D'Oliveira | 16 | 2 | 63 | 0 | 7 | 5 | 7 | 0 | 1st | 12 | 92 | 30 | 39 |
| Illingworth | 11 | 1 | 47 | 0 | 18 | 11 | 19 | 1 | 2nd | 163 | 136 | 47 | – |
| Underwood | 28 | 6 | 101 | 3 | 20 | 10 | 23 | 1 | 3rd | 372 | 245 | 64 | – |
| Cowdrey | 1 | 0 | 10 | 0 | 2 | 0 | 8 | 0 | 4th | 418 | 284 | 137 | – |
| Fletcher | | | | | 9 | 1 | 48 | 1 | 5th | 418 | 336 | 152 | – |
| | | | | | | | | | 6th | 421 | 346 | 193 | – |
| AUSTRALIA | | | | | | | | | 7th | 422 | 371 | 199 | – |
| McKenzie | 28 | 5 | 90 | 2 | 3 | 0 | 6 | 0 | 8th | 433 | 449 | 201 | – |
| Thomson | 43 | 8 | 136 | 1 | 4 | 0 | 20 | 0 | 9th | 433 | 456 | 208 | – |
| Gleeson | 42 | 15 | 97 | 2 | | | | | 10th | 433 | 464 | 214 | – |
| Jenner | 24 | 5 | 86 | 1 | 4.6 | 2 | 9 | 1 | | | | | |
| Stackpole | 4 | 0 | 12 | 0 | 4 | 3 | 1 | 0 | | | | | |
| Walters | 5.5 | 0 | 12 | 3 | | | | | | | | | |

Umpires: L.P. Rowan and T.F. Brooks.

Test No. 675/205

# AUSTRALIA v ENGLAND 1970–71 (2nd Test)

Played at W.A.C.A. Ground, Perth, on 11, 12, 13, 15, 16 December.
Toss: Australia.   Result: MATCH DRAWN.
Debuts: Australia – G.S. Chappell; England – P. Lever.

Perth's first Test match attracted nearly 85,000 spectators and produced receipts approaching £50,000. Luckhurst, his thumb damaged early in his innings, scored a hundred in his second Test. G.S. Chappell became the sixth Australian to score a hundred in his first Test innings. When Australia were asked to score 245 runs in 145 minutes, Lawry managed only six runs in the first 68 minutes; the second of them was his 5,000th in Test cricket and the third was his 2,000th against England.

## ENGLAND

| | | | | |
|---|---|---|---|---|
| G. Boycott | c McKenzie b Gleeson | 70 | st Marsh b Gleeson | 50 |
| B.W. Luckhurst | b McKenzie | 131 | c Stackpole b Walters | 19 |
| J.H. Edrich | run out | 47 | not out | 115 |
| A.P.E. Knott† | c Stackpole b Thomson | 24 | (8) not out | 30 |
| K.W.R. Fletcher | b Walters | 22 | (4) lbw b Gleeson | 0 |
| M.C. Cowdrey | c and b G.S. Chappell | 40 | (5) c Marsh b Thomson | 1 |
| B.L. D'Oliveira | c Stackpole b Thomson | 8 | (6) b Gleeson | 31 |
| R. Illingworth* | b McKenzie | 34 | (7) c Marsh b Stackpole | 29 |
| J.A. Snow | not out | 4 | | |
| K. Shuttleworth | b McKenzie | 2 | | |
| P. Lever | b McKenzie | 2 | | |
| Extras | (LB 8, W 1, NB 4) | 13 | (B 2, LB 3, NB 7) | 12 |
| **Total** | | **397** | (6 wickets declared) | **287** |

## AUSTRALIA

| | | | | |
|---|---|---|---|---|
| W.M. Lawry* | c Illingworth b Snow | 0 | not out | 38 |
| K.R. Stackpole | c Lever b Snow | 5 | c sub (J.H. Hampshire) b Snow | 0 |
| I.M. Chappell | c Knott b Snow | 50 | c sub (J.H. Hampshire) b Snow | 17 |
| K.D. Walters | c Knott b Lever | 7 | b Lever | 8 |
| I.R. Redpath | c and b Illingworth | 171 | not out | 26 |
| A.P. Sheahan | run out | 2 | | |
| G.S. Chappell | c Luckhurst b Shuttleworth | 108 | | |
| R.W. Marsh† | c D'Oliveira b Shuttleworth | 44 | | |
| G.D. McKenzie | c Lever b D'Oliveira | 7 | | |
| J.W. Gleeson | c Knott b Snow | 15 | | |
| A.L. Thomson | not out | 12 | | |
| Extras | (B 5, LB 4, NB 10) | 19 | (B 4, LB 4, NB 3) | 11 |
| **Total** | | **440** | (3 wickets) | **100** |

| AUSTRALIA | O | M | R | W | O | M | R | W | | FALL OF WICKETS | | | |
|---|---|---|---|---|---|---|---|---|---|---|---|---|---|
| McKenzie | 31·4 | 4 | 66 | 4 | 18 | 2 | 50 | 0 | | E | A | E | A |
| Thomson | 24 | 4 | 118 | 2 | 25 | 3 | 71 | 1 | Wkt | 1st | 1st | 2nd | 2nd |
| G.S. Chappell | 24 | 4 | 54 | 1 | 4 | 1 | 17 | 0 | 1st | 171 | 5 | 60 | 0 |
| Gleeson | 32 | 10 | 78 | 1 | 32 | 11 | 68 | 3 | 2nd | 243 | 8 | 98 | 20 |
| Walters | 11 | 1 | 35 | 1 | 7 | 1 | 26 | 1 | 3rd | 281 | 17 | 98 | 40 |
| Stackpole | 11 | 2 | 33 | 0 | 15 | 3 | 43 | 1 | 4th | 291 | 105 | 101 | – |
| | | | | | | | | | 5th | 310 | 107 | 152 | – |
| ENGLAND | | | | | | | | | 6th | 327 | 326 | 209 | – |
| Snow | 33·5 | 3 | 143 | 4 | 9 | 4 | 17 | 2 | 7th | 389 | 393 | – | – |
| Shuttleworth | 28 | 4 | 105 | 2 | 3 | 1 | 9 | 0 | 8th | 389 | 408 | – | – |
| Lever | 21 | 3 | 78 | 1 | 5 | 2 | 10 | 1 | 9th | 393 | 426 | – | – |
| D'Oliveira | 17 | 1 | 41 | 1 | 4 | 2 | 5 | 0 | 10th | 397 | 440 | – | – |
| Illingworth | 13 | 2 | 43 | 1 | 4 | 2 | 12 | 0 | | | | | |
| Boycott | 1 | 0 | 7 | 0 | | | | | | | | | |
| Fletcher | 1 | 0 | 4 | 0 | 4 | 0 | 18 | 0 | | | | | |
| Cowdrey | | | | | 3 | 0 | 18 | 0 | | | | | |

Umpires: L.P. Rowan and T.F. Brooks.

**The 3rd Test at Melbourne Cricket Ground, scheduled for 31 December, 1, 2, 4, 5 January was abandoned on the third day without a ball being bowled**

Test No. 676/206

# AUSTRALIA v ENGLAND 1970–71 (4th Test)

Played at Sydney Cricket Ground on 9, 10, 11, 13, 14 January.
Toss: England.   Result: ENGLAND won by 299 runs.
Debuts: England – R.G.D. Willis.

England achieved their largest victory against Australia by a runs margin since 1936–37 (*Test No. 255*). Lawry carried his bat through a completed Test innings – the first Australian to do so at Sydney and the second after W.M. Woodfull to achieve this feat twice.

## ENGLAND

| | | | | |
|---|---|---|---|---|
| G. Boycott | c Gleeson b Connolly | 77 | not out | 142 |
| B.W. Luckhurst | lbw b Gleeson | 38 | c I.M. Chappell b McKenzie | 5 |
| J.H. Edrich | c Gleeson b G.S. Chappell | 55 | run out | 12 |
| K.W.R. Fletcher | c Walters b Mallett | 23 | c Stackpole b Mallett | 8 |
| B.L. D'Oliveira | c Connolly b Mallett | 0 | c I.M. Chappell b G.S. Chappell | 56 |
| R. Illingworth* | b Gleeson | 25 | st Marsh b Mallett | 53 |
| A.P.E. Knott† | st Marsh b Mallett | 6 | not out | 21 |
| J.A. Snow | c Lawry b Gleeson | 37 | | |
| P. Lever | c Connolly b Mallett | 36 | | |
| D.L. Underwood | c G.S. Chappell b Gleeson | 0 | | |
| R.G.D. Willis | not out | 15 | | |
| Extras | (B 5, LB 2, W 1, NB 12) | 20 | (B 9, LB 4, NB 9) | 22 |
| Total | | 332 | (5 wickets declared) | 319 |

## AUSTRALIA

| | | | | |
|---|---|---|---|---|
| W.M. Lawry* | c Edrich b Lever | 9 | not out | 60 |
| I.M. Chappell | c Underwood b Snow | 12 | c D'Oliveira b Snow | 0 |
| I.R. Redpath | c Fletcher b D'Oliveira | 64 | c Edrich b Snow | 6 |
| K.D. Walters | c Luckhurst b Illingworth | 55 | c Knott b Lever | 3 |
| G.S. Chappell | c and b Underwood | 15 | b Snow | 2 |
| K.R. Stackpole | c Boycott b Underwood | 33 | c Lever b Snow | 30 |
| R.W. Marsh† | c D'Oliveira b Underwood | 8 | c Willis b Snow | 0 |
| A.A. Mallett | b Underwood | 4 | c Knott b Willis | 6 |
| G.D. McKenzie | not out | 11 | retired hurt | 6 |
| J.W. Gleeson | c Fletcher b D'Oliveira | 0 | b Snow | 0 |
| A.N. Connolly | b Lever | 14 | c Knott b Snow | 0 |
| Extras | (NB 11) | 11 | (B 2, NB 1) | 3 |
| Total | | 236 | | 116 |

| AUSTRALIA | O | M | R | W | O | M | R | W | | FALL OF WICKETS | | | |
|---|---|---|---|---|---|---|---|---|---|---|---|---|---|
| | | | | | | | | | | E | A | E | A |
| McKenzie | 15 | 3 | 74 | 0 | 15 | 0 | 65 | 1 | Wkt | 1st | 1st | 2nd | 2nd |
| Connolly | 13 | 2 | 43 | 1 | 14 | 1 | 38 | 0 | 1st | 116 | 14 | 7 | 1 |
| Gleeson | 29 | 7 | 83 | 4 | 23 | 4 | 54 | 0 | 2nd | 130 | 38 | 35 | 11 |
| G.S. Chappell | 11 | 4 | 30 | 1 | 15 | 5 | 24 | 1 | 3rd | 201 | 137 | 48 | 14 |
| Mallett | 16.7 | 5 | 40 | 4 | 19 | 1 | 85 | 2 | 4th | 205 | 160 | 181 | 21 |
| Walters | 3 | 1 | 11 | 0 | 2 | 0 | 14 | 0 | 5th | 208 | 189 | 276 | 66 |
| Stackpole | 7 | 2 | 31 | 0 | 6 | 1 | 17 | 0 | 6th | 219 | 199 | – | 66 |
| ENGLAND | | | | | | | | | 7th | 262 | 208 | – | 86 |
| Snow | 14 | 6 | 23 | 1 | 17.5 | 5 | 40 | 7 | 8th | 291 | 208 | – | 116 |
| Willis | 9 | 2 | 26 | 0 | 3 | 2 | 1 | 1 | 9th | 291 | 219 | – | 116 |
| Lever | 8.6 | 1 | 31 | 2 | 11 | 1 | 24 | 1 | 10th | 332 | 236 | – | – |
| Underwood | 22 | 7 | 66 | 4 | 8 | 2 | 17 | 0 | | | | | |
| Illingworth | 14 | 3 | 59 | 1 | 9 | 5 | 9 | 0 | | | | | |
| D'Oliveira | 9 | 2 | 20 | 2 | 7 | 3 | 16 | 0 | | | | | |
| Fletcher | | | | | 1 | 0 | 6 | 0 | | | | | |

Umpires: L.P. Rowan and T.F. Brooks.

Test No. 677/207

# AUSTRALIA v ENGLAND 1970-71 (5th Test)

Played at Melbourne Cricket Ground on 21, 22, 23, 25, 26 January.
Toss: Australia.   Result: MATCH DRAWN.
Debuts: Australia – J.R.F. Duncan, K.J. O'Keeffe.

This additional Test match was arranged after the 3rd Test had been abandoned without a ball being bowled; it replaced the touring team's four-day return match with Victoria and a one-day game at Euroa. Lawry's declaration temporarily deprived Marsh of the opportunity of becoming the first Australian wicket-keeper to score a Test hundred. Luckhurst scored his second hundred of the rubber despite fracturing his left little finger early in his innings. The third day produced receipts of £25,070 – then a world record.

## AUSTRALIA

| | | | | | |
|---|---|---|---|---|---|
| K.R. Stackpole | c Lever b D'Oliveira | 30 | c Knott b Willis | | 18 |
| W.M. Lawry* | c Snow b Willis | 56 | c sub (K. Shuttleworth) b Snow | | 42 |
| I.M. Chappell | c Luckhurst b Snow | 111 | b Underwood | | 30 |
| I.R. Redpath | b Snow | 72 | c Knott b Snow | | 5 |
| K.D. Walters | b Underwood | 55 | not out | | 39 |
| G.S. Chappell | c Edrich b Willis | 3 | not out | | 20 |
| R.W. Marsh† | not out | 92 | | | |
| K.J. O'Keeffe | c Luckhurst b Illingworth | 27 | | | |
| J.W. Gleeson | c Cowdrey b Willis | 5 | | | |
| J.R.F. Duncan | c Edrich b Illingworth | 3 | | | |
| A.L. Thomson | not out | 0 | | | |
| Extras | (B 10, LB 17, NB 12) | 39 | (B 8, LB 3, NB 4) | | 15 |
| **Total** | (9 wickets declared) | **493** | (4 wickets declared) | | **169** |

## ENGLAND

| | | | | | |
|---|---|---|---|---|---|
| G. Boycott | c Redpath b Thomson | 12 | not out | | 76 |
| B.W. Luckhurst | b Walters | 109 | | | |
| J.H. Edrich | c Marsh b Thomson | 9 | (2) not out | | 74 |
| M.C. Cowdrey | c and b Gleeson | 13 | | | |
| B.L. D'Oliveira | c Marsh b Thomson | 117 | | | |
| R. Illingworth* | c Redpath b Gleeson | 41 | | | |
| A.P.E. Knott† | lbw b Stackpole | 19 | | | |
| J.A. Snow | b I.M. Chappell | 1 | | | |
| P. Lever | run out | 19 | | | |
| D.L. Underwood | c and b Gleeson | 5 | | | |
| R.G.D. Willis | not out | 5 | | | |
| Extras | (B 17, LB 14, NB 11) | 42 | (B 1, LB 8, NB 2) | | 11 |
| **Total** | | **392** | (0 wickets) | | **161** |

| ENGLAND | O | M | R | W | O | M | R | W |
|---|---|---|---|---|---|---|---|---|
| Snow | 29 | 6 | 94 | 2 | 12 | 4 | 21 | 2 |
| Lever | 25 | 6 | 79 | 0 | 12 | 1 | 53 | 0 |
| D'Oliveira | 22 | 6 | 71 | 1 | | | | |
| Willis | 20 | 5 | 73 | 3 | 10 | 1 | 42 | 1 |
| Underwood | 19 | 4 | 78 | 1 | 12 | 0 | 38 | 1 |
| Illingworth | 13 | 0 | 59 | 2 | | | | |
| AUSTRALIA | | | | | | | | |
| Thomson | 34 | 5 | 110 | 3 | 11 | 5 | 26 | 0 |
| Duncan | 14 | 4 | 30 | 0 | | | | |
| G.S. Chappell | 8 | 0 | 21 | 0 | 5 | 0 | 19 | 0 |
| O'Keeffe | 31 | 11 | 71 | 0 | 19 | 3 | 45 | 0 |
| Gleeson | 25 | 7 | 60 | 3 | 3 | 1 | 18 | 0 |
| Stackpole | 17.5 | 4 | 41 | 1 | 13 | 2 | 28 | 0 |
| Walters | 5 | 2 | 7 | 1 | 7 | 1 | 14 | 0 |
| I.M. Chappell | 3 | 0 | 10 | 1 | | | | |

FALL OF WICKETS

| Wkt | A 1st | E 1st | A 2nd | E 2nd |
|---|---|---|---|---|
| 1st | 64 | 40 | 51 | – |
| 2nd | 266 | 64 | 84 | – |
| 3rd | 269 | 88 | 91 | – |
| 4th | 310 | 228 | 132 | – |
| 5th | 314 | 306 | – | – |
| 6th | 374 | 340 | – | – |
| 7th | 471 | 354 | – | – |
| 8th | 477 | 362 | – | – |
| 9th | 480 | 379 | – | – |
| 10th | – | 392 | – | – |

Umpires: L.P. Rowan and M.G. O'Connell.

Test No. 678/208

## AUSTRALIA v ENGLAND 1970–71 (6th Test)

Played at Adelaide Oval on 29, 30 January, 1, 2, 3 February.
Toss: England. Result: MATCH DRAWN.
Debuts: Australia – D.K. Lillee.

After deciding not to enforce the follow-on, England set Australia to score 469 runs in 500 minutes. Boycott and Edrich became the third opening pair to share century partnerships in both innings of a Test against Australia; the others were J.B. Hobbs and H. Sutcliffe, and L. Hutton and C. Washbrook (twice). Lillee took five wickets in his first Test innings.

### ENGLAND

| | | | | |
|---|---|---|---|---|
| G. Boycott | run out | 58 | not out | 119 |
| J.H. Edrich | c Stackpole b Lillee | 130 | b Thomson | 40 |
| K.W.R. Fletcher | b Thomson | 80 | b Gleeson | 5 |
| A.P.E. Knott† | c Redpath b Lillee | 7 | | |
| B.L. D'Oliveira | c Marsh b G.S. Chappell | 47 | (4) c Walters b Thomson | 5 |
| J.H. Hampshire | c Lillee b G.S. Chappell | 55 | (5) lbw b Thomson | 3 |
| R. Illingworth* | b Lillee | 24 | (6) not out | 48 |
| J.A. Snow | b Lillee | 38 | | |
| P. Lever | b Thomson | 5 | | |
| D.L. Underwood | not out | 1 | | |
| R.G.D. Willis | c Walters b Lillee | 4 | | |
| Extras | (B 1, LB 5, W 4, NB 11) | 21 | (LB 4, W 1, NB 8) | 13 |
| Total | | 470 | (4 wickets declared) | 233 |

### AUSTRALIA

| | | | | |
|---|---|---|---|---|
| K.R. Stackpole | b Underwood | 87 | b Snow | 136 |
| W.M. Lawry* | c Knott b Snow | 10 | c Knott b Willis | 21 |
| I.M. Chappell | c Knott b Lever | 28 | c Willis b Underwood | 104 |
| I.R. Redpath | c Lever b Illingworth | 9 | not out | 21 |
| K.D. Walters | c Knott b Lever | 8 | not out | 36 |
| G.S. Chappell | c Edrich b Lever | 0 | | |
| R.W. Marsh† | c Knott b Willis | 28 | | |
| A.A. Mallett | c Illingworth b Snow | 28 | | |
| J.W. Gleeson | c Boycott b Willis | 16 | | |
| D.K. Lillee | c Boycott b Lever | 10 | | |
| A.L. Thomson | not out | 6 | | |
| Extras | (LB 2, NB 3) | 5 | (B 2, LB 3, NB 5) | 10 |
| Total | | 235 | (3 wickets) | 328 |

| AUSTRALIA | O | M | R | W | O | M | R | W | FALL OF WICKETS | | | |
|---|---|---|---|---|---|---|---|---|---|---|---|---|
| | | | | | | | | | | E | A | E | A |
| Thomson | 29.7 | 6 | 94 | 2 | 19 | 2 | 79 | 3 | Wkt | 1st | 1st | 2nd | 2nd |
| Lillee | 28.3 | 0 | 84 | 5 | 7 | 0 | 40 | 0 | 1st | 107 | 61 | 103 | 65 |
| Walters | 9 | 2 | 29 | 0 | 3 | 0 | 5 | 0 | 2nd | 276 | 117 | 128 | 267 |
| G.S. Chappell | 18 | 1 | 54 | 2 | 5 | 0 | 27 | 0 | 3rd | 289 | 131 | 143 | 271 |
| Gleeson | 19 | 1 | 78 | 0 | 16 | 1 | 69 | 1 | 4th | 289 | 141 | 151 | – |
| Mallett | 20 | 1 | 63 | 0 | 1 | 1 | 0 | 0 | 5th | 385 | 145 | – | – |
| Stackpole | 12 | 2 | 47 | 0 | | | | | 6th | 402 | 163 | – | – |
| ENGLAND | | | | | | | | | 7th | 458 | 180 | – | – |
| Snow | 21 | 4 | 73 | 2 | 17 | 3 | 60 | 1 | 8th | 465 | 219 | – | – |
| Lever | 17.1 | 2 | 49 | 4 | 17 | 4 | 49 | 0 | 9th | 465 | 221 | – | – |
| Underwood | 21 | 6 | 45 | 1 | 35 | 7 | 85 | 1 | 10th | 470 | 235 | – | – |
| Willis | 12 | 3 | 49 | 2 | 13 | 1 | 48 | 1 | | | | | |
| Illingworth | 5 | 2 | 14 | 1 | 14 | 7 | 32 | 0 | | | | | |
| D'Oliveira | | | | | 15 | 4 | 28 | 0 | | | | | |
| Fletcher | | | | | 4 | 0 | 16 | 0 | | | | | |

Umpires: T.F. Brooks and M.G. O'Connell.

Test No. 679/209

# AUSTRALIA v ENGLAND 1970–71 (7th Test)

Played at Sydney Cricket Ground on 12, 13, 14, 16, 17 February.
Toss: Australia.   Result: ENGLAND won by 62 runs.
Debuts: Australia – A.R. Dell, K.H. Eastwood.

England regained the Ashes at 12.36 p.m. on the fifth day of this six-day Test after the longest rubber in Test history. Chappell emulated P.S. McDonnell, G. Giffen and R.B. Simpson when he invited the opposition to bat in his first Test as Australia's captain. Crowd disturbances around 5.00 p.m. on the second day, after Snow had hit Jenner on the head with a short-pitched ball, led to Illingworth leading the England team off the field. They returned when the playing area had been cleared of missiles. In the second innings Snow fractured and dislocated his right little finger when he collided with the fencing in trying to catch Stackpole. Knott's total of 24 dismissals remains the England record for any rubber. No 'lbw' appeal was upheld against an Australian batsman in the entire rubber.

### ENGLAND

| | | | | |
|---|---|---|---|---|
| J.H. Edrich | c G.S. Chappell b Dell | 30 | c I.M. Chappell b O'Keeffe | 57 |
| B.W. Luckhurst | c Redpath b Walters | 0 | c Lillee b O'Keeffe | 59 |
| K.W.R. Fletcher | c Stackpole b O'Keeffe | 33 | c Stackpole b Eastwood | 20 |
| J.H. Hampshire | c Marsh b Lillee | 10 | c I.M. Chappell b O'Keeffe | 24 |
| B.L. D'Oliveira | b Dell | 1 | c I.M. Chappell b Lillee | 47 |
| R. Illingworth* | b Jenner | 42 | lbw b Lillee | 29 |
| A.P.E. Knott† | c Stackpole b O'Keeffe | 27 | b Dell | 15 |
| J.A. Snow | b Jenner | 7 | c Stackpole b Dell | 20 |
| P. Lever | c Jenner b O'Keeffe | 4 | c Redpath b Jenner | 17 |
| D.L. Underwood | not out | 8 | c Marsh b Dell | 0 |
| R.G.D. Willis | b Jenner | 11 | not out | 2 |
| Extras | (B 4, LB 4, W 1, NB 2) | 11 | (B 3, LB 3, NB 6) | 12 |
| Total | | 184 | | 302 |

### AUSTRALIA

| | | | | |
|---|---|---|---|---|
| K.H. Eastwood | c Knott b Lever | 5 | b Snow | 0 |
| K.R. Stackpole | b Snow | 6 | b Illingworth | 67 |
| R.W. Marsh† | c Willis b Lever | 4 | (7) b Underwood | 16 |
| I.M. Chappell* | b Willis | 25 | (3) c Knott b Lever | 6 |
| I.R. Redpath | c and b Underwood | 59 | (4) c Hampshire b Illingworth | 14 |
| K.D. Walters | st Knott b Underwood | 42 | (5) c D'Oliveira b Willis | 1 |
| G.S. Chappell | b Willis | 65 | (6) st Knott b Illingworth | 30 |
| K.J. O'Keeffe | c Knott b Illingworth | 3 | c sub (K. Shuttleworth) b D'Oliveira | 12 |
| T.J. Jenner | b Lever | 30 | c Fletcher b Underwood | 4 |
| D.K. Lillee | c Knott b Willis | 6 | c Hampshire b D'Oliveira | 0 |
| A.R. Dell | not out | 3 | not out | 3 |
| Extras | (LB 5, W 1, NB 10) | 16 | (B 2, NB 5) | 7 |
| Total | | 264 | | 160 |

| AUSTRALIA | O | M | R | W | O | M | R | W | FALL OF WICKETS | | | | |
|---|---|---|---|---|---|---|---|---|---|---|---|---|---|
| Lillee | 13 | 5 | 32 | 1 | 14 | 0 | 43 | 2 | | E | A | E | A |
| Dell | 16 | 8 | 32 | 2 | 26·7 | 3 | 65 | 3 | Wkt | 1st | 1st | 2nd | 2nd |
| Walters | 4 | 0 | 10 | 1 | 5 | 0 | 18 | 0 | 1st | 5 | 11 | 94 | 0 |
| G.S. Chappell | 3 | 0 | 9 | 0 | | | | | 2nd | 60 | 13 | 130 | 22 |
| Jenner | 16 | 3 | 42 | 3 | 21 | 5 | 39 | 1 | 3rd | 68 | 32 | 158 | 71 |
| O'Keeffe | 24 | 8 | 48 | 3 | 26 | 8 | 96 | 3 | 4th | 69 | 66 | 165 | 82 |
| Eastwood | | | | | 5 | 0 | 21 | 1 | 5th | 98 | 147 | 234 | 96 |
| Stackpole | | | | | 3 | 1 | 8 | 0 | 6th | 145 | 162 | 251 | 131 |
| | | | | | | | | | 7th | 156 | 178 | 276 | 142 |
| ENGLAND | | | | | | | | | 8th | 165 | 235 | 298 | 154 |
| Snow | 18 | 2 | 68 | 1 | 2 | 1 | 7 | 1 | 9th | 165 | 239 | 299 | 154 |
| Lever | 14·6 | 3 | 43 | 3 | 12 | 2 | 23 | 1 | 10th | 184 | 264 | 302 | 160 |
| D'Oliveira | 12 | 2 | 24 | 0 | 5 | 1 | 15 | 2 | | | | | |
| Willis | 12 | 1 | 58 | 3 | 9 | 1 | 32 | 1 | | | | | |
| Underwood | 16 | 3 | 39 | 2 | 13·6 | 5 | 28 | 2 | | | | | |
| Illingworth | 11 | 3 | 16 | 1 | 20 | 7 | 39 | 3 | | | | | |
| Fletcher | | | | | 1 | 0 | 9 | 0 | | | | | |

Umpires: L.P. Rowan and T.F. Brooks.

Chapter 30

# IN NEW ZEALAND 1971

In New Zealand Cowdrey was restored to the side for the second Test at Eden Park, Auckland where he made 54 in the first innings. Cunis took 6 for 76. In the second innings despite a cold and leg injury his stand with Knott for the fifth wicket reached 76 helping to make the game safe and achieve a one nil victory in the series. It was very much Knott's match as he scored 101 and 96. Burgess made 104 in New Zealand's first innings.

|  | Matches | Innings | Not out | Runs | Highest score | Average | 100s | 50s | Caught |
|---|---|---|---|---|---|---|---|---|---|
| This series | 1 | 2 | 0 | 99 | 54 | 49.50 | 0 | 1 | 0 |
| Previous series | 107 | 175 | 15 | 7310 | 182 | 45.69 | 22 | 37 | 116 |
| Cumulative totals | 108 | 177 | 15 | 7409 | 182 | 45.73 | 22 | 38 | 116 |

Test No. 685/41

# NEW ZEALAND v ENGLAND 1970–71 (1st Test)

Played at Lancaster Park, Christchurch, on 25, 26, 27 February, 1 March.
Toss: New Zealand.   Result: ENGLAND won by eight wickets.
Debuts: England – R.W. Taylor.

New Zealand were dismissed for the lowest total in any Test at Christchurch and their third-lowest against England. Underwood took his 1,000th first-class wicket when he dismissed Shrimpton in the second innings. His match analysis of 12 for 97 is the record for any Test at Christchurch. C.S. Elliott, in New Zealand on a Churchill Fellowship, was invited to umpire by the New Zealand Cricket Council.

### NEW ZEALAND

| | | | | |
|---|---|---|---|---|
| G.T. Dowling* | c Edrich b Underwood | 13 | c Luckhurst b Lever | 1 |
| B.A.G. Murray | c Taylor b Shuttleworth | 1 | b Shuttleworth | 1 |
| B.E. Congdon | c Taylor b Shuttleworth | 1 | b Underwood | 55 |
| R.W. Morgan | c Luckhurst b Shuttleworth | 6 | (5) b Underwood | 0 |
| M.J.F. Shrimpton | c Fletcher b Underwood | 0 | (6) c Illingworth b Underwood | 8 |
| G.M. Turner | b Underwood | 11 | (4) b Underwood | 76 |
| V. Pollard | b Wilson | 18 | lbw b Underwood | 34 |
| K.J. Wadsworth† | c Fletcher b Underwood | 0 | c Fletcher b Wilson | 1 |
| R.S. Cunis | b Underwood | 0 | b Shuttleworth | 35 |
| H.J. Howarth | st Taylor b Underwood | 0 | c Illingworth b Underwood | 25 |
| R.O. Collinge | not out | 3 | not out | 7 |
| Extras | (B 9, LB 1, W 1, NB 1) | 12 | (B 6, LB 3, W 1, NB 1) | 11 |
| **Total** | | **65** | | **254** |

### ENGLAND

| | | | | |
|---|---|---|---|---|
| B.W. Luckhurst | c Wadsworth b Collinge | 10 | not out | 29 |
| J.H. Edrich | lbw b Cunis | 12 | c Wadsworth b Collinge | 2 |
| K.W.R. Fletcher | b Collinge | 4 | c Howarth b Collinge | 2 |
| J.H. Hampshire | c Turner b Howarth | 40 | not out | 51 |
| B.L. D'Oliveira | b Shrimpton | 100 | | |
| R. Illingworth* | b Shrimpton | 36 | | |
| R.W. Taylor† | st Wadsworth b Howarth | 4 | | |
| D. Wilson | c Murray b Howarth | 5 | | |
| P. Lever | b Howarth | 4 | | |
| K. Shuttleworth | b Shrimpton | 5 | | |
| D.L. Underwood | not out | 0 | | |
| Extras | (B 1, LB 9, NB 1) | 11 | (B 1, LB 4) | 5 |
| **Total** | | **231** | (2 wickets) | **89** |

| ENGLAND | O | M | R | W | O | M | R | W |
|---|---|---|---|---|---|---|---|---|
| Lever | 5 | 4 | 1 | 0 | 15 | 3 | 30 | 1 |
| Shuttleworth | 8 | 1 | 14 | 3 | 12 | 1 | 27 | 2 |
| D'Oliveira | 3 | 1 | 2 | 0 | | | | |
| Underwood | 11·6 | 7 | 12 | 6 | 32·3 | 7 | 85 | 6 |
| Illingworth | 6 | 3 | 12 | 0 | 17 | 5 | 45 | 0 |
| Wilson | 4 | 2 | 12 | 1 | 21 | 6 | 56 | 1 |
| NEW ZEALAND | | | | | | | | |
| Collinge | 12 | 2 | 39 | 2 | 7 | 2 | 20 | 2 |
| Cunis | 13 | 2 | 44 | 1 | 8 | 0 | 17 | 0 |
| Howarth | 19 | 7 | 46 | 4 | 4 | 0 | 17 | 0 |
| Pollard | 9 | 3 | 45 | 0 | 3 | 1 | 9 | 0 |
| Shrimpton | 11·5 | 0 | 35 | 3 | 3 | 0 | 21 | 0 |
| Congdon | 3 | 0 | 11 | 0 | | | | |

### FALL OF WICKETS

| Wkt | NZ 1st | E 1st | NZ 2nd | E 2nd |
|---|---|---|---|---|
| 1st | 4 | 20 | 1 | 3 |
| 2nd | 7 | 26 | 6 | 11 |
| 3rd | 19 | 31 | 83 | – |
| 4th | 28 | 95 | 83 | – |
| 5th | 33 | 188 | 99 | – |
| 6th | 54 | 213 | 151 | – |
| 7th | 54 | 220 | 152 | – |
| 8th | 62 | 224 | 209 | – |
| 9th | 62 | 231 | 231 | – |
| 10th | 65 | 231 | 254 | – |

Umpires: C.S. Elliott and W.T. Martin.

Test No. 686/42

# NEW ZEALAND v ENGLAND 1970–71 (2nd Test)

Played at Eden Park, Auckland, on 5, 6, 7, 8 March.
Toss: New Zealand.   Result: MATCH DRAWN.
Debuts: New Zealand – M.G. Webb.

New Zealand were unable to include either B.A.G. Murray or V. Pollard in their team as neither would play on a Sunday. Burgess scored his second hundred in successive Test innings and shared with Shrimpton a New Zealand fifth-wicket record partnership against England of 141. Knott narrowly missed becoming the first wicket-keeper to score a hundred in each innings of a Test. His partnership of 149 with Lever remains the highest for the seventh wicket in this series.

## ENGLAND

| | | | | |
|---|---|---|---|---|
| J.H. Edrich | c Morgan b Webb | 1 | c Burgess b Collinge | 24 |
| B.W. Luckhurst | c Dowling b Cunis | 14 | c Wadsworth b Webb | 15 |
| M.C. Cowdrey | c Congdon b Cunis | 54 | (6) b Collinge | 45 |
| J.H. Hampshire | c Turner b Cunis | 9 | (3) c Wadsworth b Cunis | 0 |
| B.L. D'Oliveira | c Morgan b Congdon | 58 | (9) b Collinge | 5 |
| R. Illingworth* | c Wadsworth b Cunis | 0 | (4) c Turner b Collinge | 22 |
| A.P.E. Knott† | b Collinge | 101 | (5) b Cunis | 96 |
| P. Lever | c Wadsworth b Cunis | 64 | (7) lbw b Howarth | 0 |
| K. Shuttleworth | c Wadsworth b Cunis | 0 | (8) c Wadsworth b Morgan | 11 |
| R.G.D. Willis | c Burgess b Collinge | 7 | lbw b Cunis | 3 |
| D.L. Underwood | not out | 1 | not out | 8 |
| Extras | (B 1, LB 4, NB 7) | 12 | (B 5, LB 3) | 8 |
| **Total** | | **321** | | **237** |

## NEW ZEALAND

| | | | | |
|---|---|---|---|---|
| G.M. Turner | c and b Underwood | 65 | not out | 8 |
| G.T. Dowling* | c and b Underwood | 53 | not out | 31 |
| B.E. Congdon | b Underwood | 0 | | |
| R.W. Morgan | c and b Underwood | 8 | | |
| M.G. Burgess | c Edrich b Willis | 104 | | |
| M.J.F. Shrimpton | lbw b Underwood | 46 | | |
| K.J. Wadsworth† | c Hampshire b Willis | 16 | | |
| R.S. Cunis | not out | 5 | | |
| H.J. Howarth | not out | 2 | | |
| R.O. Collinge | ⎫ did not bat | | | |
| M.G. Webb | ⎭ | | | |
| Extras | (B 7, LB 4, NB 3) | 14 | (LB 1) | 1 |
| **Total** | (7 wickets declared) | **313** | (0 wickets) | **40** |

| NEW ZEALAND | O | M | R | W | O | M | R | W | FALL OF WICKETS | | | | |
|---|---|---|---|---|---|---|---|---|---|---|---|---|---|
| Webb | 18 | 0 | 94 | 1 | 11 | 0 | 50 | 1 | | E | NZ | E | NZ |
| Collinge | 18·6 | 5 | 51 | 2 | 19 | 6 | 41 | 4 | Wkt | 1st | 1st | 2nd | 2nd |
| Cunis | 24 | 4 | 76 | 6 | 21·7 | 5 | 52 | 3 | 1st | 8 | 91 | 26 | – |
| Howarth | 7 | 0 | 41 | 0 | 21 | 8 | 37 | 1 | 2nd | 38 | 91 | 27 | – |
| Congdon | 2 | 0 | 18 | 1 | | | | | 3rd | 59 | 121 | 62 | – |
| Shrimpton | 3 | 0 | 29 | 0 | 6 | 0 | 33 | 0 | 4th | 111 | 142 | 67 | – |
| Morgan | | | | | 6 | 0 | 16 | 1 | 5th | 111 | 283 | 143 | – |
| | | | | | | | | | 6th | 145 | 302 | 152 | – |
| ENGLAND | | | | | | | | | 7th | 294 | 307 | 177 | – |
| Lever | 19 | 3 | 43 | 0 | 2 | 0 | 6 | 0 | 8th | 297 | – | 199 | – |
| Shuttleworth | 17 | 3 | 49 | 0 | 4 | 0 | 12 | 0 | 9th | 317 | – | 218 | – |
| Willis | 14 | 2 | 54 | 2 | 6 | 1 | 15 | 0 | 10th | 321 | – | 237 | – |
| Underwood | 38 | 12 | 108 | 5 | 2 | 2 | 0 | 0 | | | | | |
| Illingworth | 18 | 4 | 45 | 0 | | | | | | | | | |
| Luckhurst | | | | | 2 | 0 | 6 | 0 | | | | | |

Umpires: E.C.A. MacKintosh and R.W.R. Shortt.

Chapter 31

# PAKISTAN 1971

Back home in England for the 1971 season Cowdrey showed such form on the County circuit that he was retained in the Test team for the first match versus Pakistan at Edgbaston. Scoring only 16 and 34 he was discarded and in June pneumonia ended his season.

|  | Matches | Innings | Not out | Runs | Highest score | Average | 100s | 50s | Caught |
|---|---|---|---|---|---|---|---|---|---|
| This series | 1 | 2 | 0 | 50 | 34 | 25.00 | 0 | 0 | 1 |
| Previous series | 108 | 177 | 15 | 7409 | 182 | 45.73 | 22 | 38 | 116 |
| Cumulative totals | 109 | 179 | 15 | 7459 | 182 | 45.48 | 22 | 38 | 117 |

Test No. 687/19

# ENGLAND v PAKISTAN 1971 (1st Test)

Played at Edgbaston, Birmingham on 3, 4, 5, 7, 8 June.
Toss: Pakistan.   Result: MATCH DRAWN.
Debuts: Pakistan – Imran Khan.

Following-on for the first time against Pakistan, England (184 for 3) were still 71 runs behind the highest total ever made in a Test at Edgbaston when rain eventually allowed the fifth day's play to start at 5.06 p.m. Bad light ended the match with 3·1 of a mandatory 18 overs still to be bowled. Zaheer scored Pakistan's first double century against England and his partnership of 291 with Mushtaq is still Pakistan's record for the second wicket in all first-class cricket. His score of 274 remains the highest for Pakistan against England and the highest by any batsman playing his first innings against England. Pakistan's total is the highest by either country in this series, as is the partnership of 159 between Knott and Lever for the seventh wicket. Aftab (0*) retired at 1 for 0 after being struck on the head by Ward's third ball of the innings. He resumed at 469 for 5.

### PAKISTAN

| | | |
|---|---|---|
| Aftab Gul | b D'Oliveira | 28 |
| Sadiq Mohammad | c and b Lever | 17 |
| Zaheer Abbas | c Luckhurst b Illingworth | 274 |
| Mushtaq Mohammad | c Cowdrey b Illingworth | 100 |
| Majid Khan | c Lever b Illingworth | 35 |
| Asif Iqbal | not out | 104 |
| Intikhab Alam* | c Underwood b D'Oliveira | 9 |
| Imran Khan | run out | 5 |
| Wasim Bari † | not out | 4 |
| Asif Masood | ) did not bat | |
| Pervez Sajjad | ) | |
| Extras | (B 6, LB 14, NB 12) | 32 |
| **Total** | (7 wickets declared) | **608** |

### ENGLAND

| | | | | | |
|---|---|---|---|---|---|
| J.H. Edrich | c Zaheer b Asif Masood | 0 | c Wasim b Asif Masood | | 15 |
| B.W. Luckhurst | c Sadiq b Pervez | 35 | not out | | 108 |
| M.C. Cowdrey | b Asif Masood | 16 | b Asif Masood | | 34 |
| D.L. Amiss | b Asif Masood | 4 | c Pervez b Asif Masood | | 22 |
| B.L. D'Oliveira | c Mushtaq b Intikhab | 73 | c Mushtaq b Asif Iqbal | | 22 |
| R. Illingworth* | b Intikhab | 1 | c Wasim b Asif Masood | | 1 |
| A.P.E. Knott† | b Asif Masood | 116 | not out | | 4 |
| P. Lever | c Pervez b Asif Masood | 47 | | | |
| K. Shuttleworth | c Imran b Pervez | 21 | | | |
| D.L. Underwood | not out | 9 | | | |
| A. Ward | c Mushtaq b Pervez | 0 | | | |
| Extras | (B 16, LB 6, W 3, NB 6) | 31 | (B 4, LB 5, W 6, NB 8) | | 23 |
| **Total** | | **353** | (5 wickets) | | **229** |

| ENGLAND | O | M | R | W | O | M | R | W | | FALL OF WICKETS | | |
|---|---|---|---|---|---|---|---|---|---|---|---|---|
| | | | | | | | | | | P | E | E |
| Ward | 29 | 3 | 115 | 0 | | | | | Wkt | 1st | 1st | 2nd |
| Lever | 38 | 7 | 126 | 1 | | | | | 1st | 68 | 0 | 34 |
| Shuttleworth | 23 | 2 | 83 | 0 | | | | | 2nd | 359 | 29 | 114 |
| D'Oliveira | 38 | 17 | 78 | 2 | | | | | 3rd | 441 | 46 | 169 |
| Underwood | 41 | 13 | 102 | 0 | | | | | 4th | 456 | 112 | 218 |
| Illingworth | 26 | 5 | 72 | 3 | | | | | 5th | 469 | 127 | 221 |
| PAKISTAN | | | | | | | | | 6th | 567 | 148 | – |
| Asif Masood | 34 | 6 | 111 | 5 | 23·5 | 7 | 49 | 4 | 7th | 581 | 307 | – |
| Imran | 23 | 9 | 36 | 0 | 5 | 0 | 19 | 0 | 8th | – | 324 | – |
| Majid | 4 | 1 | 8 | 0 | | | | | 9th | – | 351 | – |
| Intikhab | 31 | 13 | 82 | 2 | 20 | 8 | 52 | 0 | 10th | – | 353 | – |
| Pervez | 15·5 | 6 | 46 | 3 | 14 | 4 | 27 | 0 | | | | |
| Mushtaq | 13 | 3 | 39 | 0 | 8 | 2 | 23 | 0 | | | | |
| Asif Iqbal | | | | | 20 | 6 | 36 | 1 | | | | |

Umpires: C.S. Elliott and T.W. Spencer.

Test No. 688/20

# ENGLAND v PAKISTAN 1971 (2nd Test)

Played at Lord's, London, on 17, 18, 19 *(no play)*, 21, 22 June.
Toss: England.   Result: MATCH DRAWN.
Debuts: England – R.A. Hutton.

Rain claimed 17 hours 17 minutes of playing time during the match; play started at 3.30 p.m. on the first day, at 2.30 p.m. on the fourth, not at all on the third, and there was only 23 minutes of cricket on the second. Price dismissed Wasim Bari and Asif Masood with successive balls but was denied the chance of a hat-trick by Pervez's illness. Luckhurst shared in century opening partnerships in both innings.

## ENGLAND

| | | | | |
|---|---|---|---|---|
| G. Boycott | not out | 121 | | |
| B.W. Luckhurst | c Wasim b Salim | 46 | (1) not out | 53 |
| J.H. Edrich | c Asif Masood b Pervez | 37 | | |
| D.L. Amiss | not out | 19 | | |
| R.A. Hutton | ) | | (2) not out | 58 |
| B.L. D'Oliveira | ) | | | |
| R. Illingworth* | ) | | | |
| A.P.E. Knott† | ) did not bat | | | |
| P. Lever | ) | | | |
| N. Gifford | ) | | | |
| J.S.E. Price | ) | | | |
| Extras | (B 6, LB 2, W 5, NB 5) | 18 | (B 1, LB 1, NB 4) | 6 |
| **Total** | (2 wickets declared) | **241** | (0 wickets) | **117** |

## PAKISTAN

| | | |
|---|---|---|
| Aftab Gul | c Knott b Hutton | 33 |
| Sadiq Mohammad | c Knott b D'Oliveira | 28 |
| Zaheer Abbas | c Hutton b Lever | 40 |
| Mushtaq Mohammad | c Amiss b Hutton | 2 |
| Asif Iqbal | c Knott b Gifford | 9 |
| Majid Khan | c Edrich b Price | 9 |
| Intikhab Alam* | c Gifford b Lever | 18 |
| Wasim Bari† | c Knott b Price | 0 |
| Salim Altaf | not out | 0 |
| Asif Masood | b Price | 0 |
| Pervez Sajjad | absent ill | – |
| Extras | (LB 5, W 1, NB 3) | 9 |
| **Total** | | **148** |

| PAKISTAN | O | M | R | W | O | M | R | W |
|---|---|---|---|---|---|---|---|---|
| Asif Masood | 21 | 3 | 60 | 0 | 3 | 1 | 3 | 0 |
| Salim | 19 | 5 | 42 | 1 | 5 | 2 | 11 | 0 |
| Asif Iqbal | 13 | 2 | 24 | 0 | 4 | 1 | 11 | 0 |
| Majid | 4 | 0 | 16 | 0 | 6 | 2 | 7 | 0 |
| Intikhab | 20 | 2 | 64 | 0 | 9 | 1 | 26 | 0 |
| Pervez | 6 | 2 | 17 | 1 | | | | |
| Mushtaq | | | | | 11 | 3 | 31 | 0 |
| Sadiq | | | | | 5 | 1 | 17 | 0 |
| Aftab | | | | | 1 | 0 | 4 | 0 |
| Zaheer | | | | | 1 | 0 | 1 | 0 |
| ENGLAND | | | | | | | | |
| Price | 11·4 | 5 | 29 | 3 | | | | |
| Lever | 16 | 3 | 38 | 2 | | | | |
| Gifford | 12 | 6 | 13 | 1 | | | | |
| Illingworth | 7 | 6 | 1 | 0 | | | | |
| Hutton | 16 | 5 | 36 | 2 | | | | |
| D'Oliveira | 10 | 5 | 22 | 1 | | | | |

FALL OF WICKETS

| Wkt | E 1st | P 1st | E 2nd |
|---|---|---|---|
| 1st | 124 | 57 | – |
| 2nd | 205 | 66 | – |
| 3rd | – | 97 | – |
| 4th | – | 117 | – |
| 5th | – | 119 | – |
| 6th | – | 146 | – |
| 7th | – | 148 | – |
| 8th | – | 148 | – |
| 9th | – | 148 | – |
| 10th | – | – | – |

Umpires: A.E. Fagg and A.E.G. Rhodes.

# ENGLAND v PAKISTAN 1971 (3rd Test)

Played at Headingley, Leeds, on 8, 9, 10, 12, 13 July.
Toss: England.   Result: ENGLAND won by 25 runs.
Debuts: Nil.

England won the rubber at 3.49 on the fifth afternoon when Pakistan narrowly failed to score 231 runs in 385 minutes. Boycott's tenth Test hundred was his third in successive innings. Only 159 runs were scored off 107.4 overs on the third day (Pakistan 142 for 6, England 17 for 1) – the slowest full day of Test cricket in England. Wasim Bari equalled the Test record by holding eight catches in the match, which ended when Lever took three wickets in four balls.

## ENGLAND

| Batsman | Dismissal | Runs | Dismissal | Runs |
|---|---|---|---|---|
| G. Boycott | c Wasim b Intikhab | 112 | c Mushtaq b Asif Masood | 13 |
| B.W. Luckhurst | c Wasim b Salim | 0 | c Wasim b Asif Masood | 0 |
| J.H. Edrich | c Wasim b Asif Masood | 2 | c Mashtaq b Intikhab | 33 |
| D.L. Amiss | c Wasim b Pervez | 23 | c and b Saeed | 56 |
| B.L. D'Oliveira | b Intikhab | 74 | c Wasim b Salim | 72 |
| A.P.E. Knott† | b Asif Masood | 10 | c Zaheer b Intikhab | 7 |
| R. Illingworth* | b Asif Iqbal | 20 | c Wasim b Salim | 45 |
| R.A. Hutton | c Sadiq b Asif Iqbal | 28 | c Zaheer b Intikhab | 4 |
| R.N.S. Hobbs | c Wasim b Asif Iqbal | 6 | b Salim | 0 |
| P. Lever | c Salim b Intikhab | 19 | b Salim | 8 |
| N. Gifford | not out | 3 | not out | 2 |
| Extras | (B 5, LB 5, NB 9) | 19 | (B 6, LB 11, W 2, NB 5) | 24 |
| **Total** | | **316** | | **264** |

## PAKISTAN

| Batsman | Dismissal | Runs | Dismissal | Runs |
|---|---|---|---|---|
| Aftab Gul | b Gifford | 27 | c Hobbs b Illingworth | 18 |
| Sadiq Mohammad | c Knott b Gifford | 28 | c and b D'Oliveira | 91 |
| Zaheer Abbas | c Edrich b Lever | 72 | c Luckhurst b Illingworth | 0 |
| Mushtaq Mohammad | c Knott b Hutton | 57 | c Edrich b Illingworth | 5 |
| Saeed Ahmed | c Knott b D'Oliveira | 22 | c D'Oliveira b Gifford | 5 |
| Asif Iqbal | c Hutton b D'Oliveira | 14 | st Knott b Gifford | 33 |
| Intikhab Alam* | c Hobbs b D'Oliveira | 17 | c Hutton b D'Oliveira | 4 |
| Wasim Bari† | c Edrich b Gifford | 63 | c Knott b Lever | 10 |
| Salim Altaf | c Knott b Hutton | 22 | not out | 8 |
| Asif Masood | c and b Hutton | 0 | c Knott b Lever | 1 |
| Pervez Sajjad | not out | 9 | lbw b Lever | 0 |
| Extras | (B 6, LB 11, W 1, NB 1) | 19 | (B 17, LB 9, W 1, NB 3) | 30 |
| **Total** | | **350** | | **205** |

| PAKISTAN | O | M | R | W | O | M | R | W |
|---|---|---|---|---|---|---|---|---|
| Asif Masood | 18 | 2 | 75 | 2 | 20 | 7 | 46 | 2 |
| Salim | 20.1 | 4 | 46 | 1 | 14.3 | 9 | 11 | 4 |
| Asif Iqbal | 13 | 2 | 37 | 3 | | | | |
| Pervez | 20 | 2 | 65 | 1 | 16 | 3 | 46 | 0 |
| Intikhab | 27.1 | 12 | 51 | 3 | 36 | 10 | 91 | 3 |
| Saeed | 4 | 0 | 13 | 0 | 15 | 4 | 30 | 1 |
| Mushtaq | 3 | 1 | 10 | 0 | 6 | 1 | 16 | 0 |
| **ENGLAND** | | | | | | | | |
| Lever | 31 | 9 | 65 | 1 | 3.3 | 1 | 10 | 3 |
| Hutton | 41 | 8 | 72 | 3 | 6 | 0 | 18 | 0 |
| Gifford | 53.4 | 26 | 69 | 3 | 34 | 14 | 51 | 2 |
| Illingworth | 28 | 14 | 31 | 0 | 26 | 11 | 58 | 3 |
| Hobbs | 20 | 5 | 48 | 0 | 4 | 0 | 22 | 0 |
| D'Oliveira | 36 | 18 | 46 | 3 | 15 | 7 | 16 | 2 |

### FALL OF WICKETS

| Wkt | E 1st | P 1st | E 2nd | P 2nd |
|---|---|---|---|---|
| 1st | 4 | 54 | 0 | 25 |
| 2nd | 10 | 69 | 21 | 25 |
| 3rd | 74 | 198 | 112 | 54 |
| 4th | 209 | 198 | 120 | 65 |
| 5th | 234 | 223 | 142 | 160 |
| 6th | 234 | 249 | 248 | 184 |
| 7th | 283 | 256 | 252 | 187 |
| 8th | 286 | 313 | 252 | 203 |
| 9th | 294 | 313 | 262 | 205 |
| 10th | 316 | 350 | 264 | 205 |

Umpires: A.E. Fagg and D.J. Constant.

## Chapter 32
# AUSTRALIA 1974/75

And that seemed to be that. Cowdrey was not finished but his Test career patently was. 1972 was the season in which he reached his hundred hundreds in successive matches at Maidstone. He finished the season with an average just short of 50. In 1974 he scored five centuries in County cricket and another in the Gillette Cup.

For the 1974/75 tour of Australia Cowdrey was not selected. An irony was that the person chosen to lead the party was Mike Denness his successor as Kent Captain.

Cowdrey was left to watch the series on television. In the first Test Lillee and Thomson not only blasted England aside but had injured Amiss and Edrich to such an extent that was likely to render them both unfit for the second test. Six weeks after their arrival a supplement to the party was thought advisable but budding a newcomer was not. The tour committee unanimously chose Cowdrey – the *players'* choice. Denness telephoned him and he readily agreed to help. He flew out two days later to join his sixth tour of Australia.

He was asked to bat No 3 in the second Test. Cowdrey survived for 125 minutes making 22. England's 208 was no match for Australia's reply of 481. In the second innings Cowdrey opened with Lloyd who had generously agreed to take Thomson. His reward after two hours was to be laid low necessitating an ambulance on the field. Cowdrey was out for 41 soon afterwards. England lost by nine wickets. 22 and 41 were creditable scores in such circumstances.

In the third Test at Melbourne Cowdrey was in partnership with Edrich. Cowdrey's defence won admiration but in nearly four hours at the crease he made only 35. In a closely fought match England made 242 and then dismissed

Australia for 241. England then scored 244 of which Cowdrey contributed only 8. Australia were thus set 246 to win and finished on 238 for eight.

Sydney for the fourth Test was nothing like as close. Denness omitted himself from the side because he had failed so frequently. Edrich was captaining the side. Again Cowdrey batted for over an hour before falling again to Thomson for 22 in England's inadequate reply of 295 to Australia's 405. Then Redpath and Greg Chappell dominated, enabling Australia to declare at 289 for 4. England managed only 228 losing by 171 runs. Cowdrey managed only 1.

At Adelaide, with Denness back, it was the same old story. Cowdrey was in for some time in the first innings for 26 but out quickly in the second for 3. John Woodcock of *The Times* wrote "When he hooked Thomson for four to long leg he was the first England batsman to do so on the tour." This was Cowdrey's 42nd appearance against Australia beating a record previously held jointly by Rhodes and Hobbs. Australia with 304 and 272 for 5 declared were too good for England's 172 and 241 and won by 163 runs. A silver lining was Knott scoring the second hundred by a wicket keeper in this series, Ames having scored the first in 1934. As Knott had become the second wicket-keeper after T G Evans to make 200 dismissals in Test cricket when he caught Ian Chappell in the first innings, everyone in Kent was justifiably proud.

The sixth and final test at Melbourne provided some consolation for England if not for Cowdrey. Australia were dismissed for 152. With Lloyd unfit Cowdrey again opened. He lasted overnight but having reached 7 the following morning was out caught off his gloves at the wicket. England, with Thomson unable to play, amassed 529 and won by an innings and four runs, Australia being all out for 373 in their second innings. Cowdrey caught McCosker at slip taking his total to 120.

And so Cowdrey's one hundred and fourteenth and final match in test cricket ended in victory at Melbourne, which had been the scene of so many fine innings including the first of his twenty two centuries and the one he regarded as "the innings of my life" – the first in 1954.

It was his sixth tour. A letter from E R O'Brien from Wollongong, New South Wales on 12 January 1976, replying to mine in the *Sydney Morning Herald* of 1 March 1975, said that I could be assured that Colin is most popular down-under. He continued: "I was so thrilled 1975; saw him in the limelight with the 151 against the Aussies. [This was a reference to a momentous innings after Colin had announced his retirement. Longing for one more good innings at Canterbury, he came in against Australia apparently coasting to an early victory. In the event Kent scored the required 354 for six wickets with the scoreboard reading Cowdrey 151 not out and Woolmer 71 not out.] I write to him now and again. I see he is on the 'Cricketer' Board of Directors. The contacts of my age group (64 years) all agree: the Colin, not only was a MASTER but such a 'Great' off the field with the youngsters."

The reporter for the *Daily Telegraph* on 14 February 1975 wrote "My last sight of Melbourne Cricket Ground was an impromptu little gathering on the outfield in front of the banner reading 'MCC fans thank Colin – six tours.' The central figure, wearing a large straw sun-hat, was signing endless autographs posing for photographs and exchanging friendly talk with young and old in the way that has made him as popular a cricketer as has ever visited Australia."

|  | Matches | Innings | Not out | Runs | Highest score | Average | 100s | 50s | Caught |
|---|---|---|---|---|---|---|---|---|---|
| This series | 5 | 9 | 0 | 165 | 41 | 18.33 | 0 | 0 | 3 |
| Previous series | 109 | 179 | 15 | 7459 | 182 | 45.48 | 22 | 38 | 117 |
| Cumulative totals | 114 | 188 | 15 | 7624 | 182 | 44.06 | 22 | 38 | 120 |

Test No. 750/215

# AUSTRALIA v ENGLAND 1974–75 (1st Test)

Played at Woolloongabba, Brisbane, on 29, 30 November, 1, 3, 4 December.
Toss: Australia. Result: AUSTRALIA won by 166 runs.
Debuts: Australia – W.J. Edwards.

With 80 minutes of the last day to spare, Australia completed their fifth victory in eight post-war Tests against England at Brisbane. Knott overtook the world Test record of 173 catches by T.G. Evans when he caught R. Edwards in the second innings. Greig's hundred was the first for England at Brisbane since 1936–37.

## AUSTRALIA

| | | | | |
|---|---|---|---|---|
| I.R. Redpath | b Willis | 5 | b Willis | 25 |
| W.J. Edwards | c Amiss b Hendrick | 4 | c Knott b Willis | 5 |
| I.M. Chappell* | c Greig b Willis | 90 | c Fletcher b Underwood | 11 |
| G.S. Chappell | c Fletcher b Underwood | 58 | b Underwood | 71 |
| R. Edwards | c Knott b Underwood | 32 | c Knott b Willis | 53 |
| K.D. Walters | c Lever b Willis | 3 | not out | 62 |
| R.W. Marsh† | c Denness b Hendrick | 14 | not out | 46 |
| T.J. Jenner | c Lever b Willis | 12 | | |
| D.K. Lillee | c Knott b Greig | 15 | | |
| M.H.N. Walker | not out | 41 | | |
| J.R. Thomson | run out | 23 | | |
| Extras | (LB 4, NB 8) | 12 | (B 1, LB 7, W 1, NB 6) | 15 |
| Total | | 309 | (5 wickets declared) | 288 |

## ENGLAND

| | | | | |
|---|---|---|---|---|
| D.L. Amiss | c Jenner b Thomson | 7 | c Walters b Thomson | 25 |
| B.W. Luckhurst | c Marsh b Thomson | 1 | c I.M. Chappell b Lillee | 3 |
| J.H. Edrich | c I.M. Chappell b Thomson | 48 | b Thomson | 6 |
| M.H. Denness* | lbw b Walker | 6 | c Walters b Thomson | 27 |
| K.W.R. Fletcher | b Lillee | 17 | c G.S. Chappell b Jenner | 19 |
| A.W. Greig | c Marsh b Lillee | 110 | b Thomson | 2 |
| A.P.E. Knott† | c Jenner b Walker | 12 | b Thomson | 19 |
| P. Lever | c I.M. Chappell b Walker | 4 | c Redpath b Lillee | 14 |
| D.L. Underwood | c Redpath b Walters | 25 | c Walker b Jenner | 30 |
| R.G.D. Willis | not out | 13 | not out | 3 |
| M. Hendrick | c Redpath b Walker | 4 | b Thomson | 0 |
| Extras | (B 5, LB 2, W 3, NB 8) | 18 | (B 8, LB 3, W 2, NB 5) | 18 |
| Total | | 265 | | 166 |

| ENGLAND | O | M | R | W | O | M | R | W | FALL OF WICKETS | | | | |
|---|---|---|---|---|---|---|---|---|---|---|---|---|---|
| Willis | 21·5 | 3 | 56 | 4 | 15 | 3 | 45 | 3 | | A | E | A | E |
| Lever | 16 | 1 | 53 | 0 | 18 | 4 | 58 | 0 | Wkt | 1st | 1st | 2nd | 2nd |
| Hendrick | 19 | 3 | 64 | 2 | 13 | 2 | 47 | 0 | 1st | 7 | 9 | 15 | 18 |
| Greig | 16 | 2 | 70 | 1 | 13 | 2 | 60 | 0 | 2nd | 10 | 10 | 39 | 40 |
| Underwood | 20 | 6 | 54 | 2 | 26 | 6 | 63 | 2 | 3rd | 110 | 33 | 59 | 44 |
| | | | | | | | | | 4th | 197 | 57 | 173 | 92 |
| AUSTRALIA | | | | | | | | | 5th | 202 | 130 | 190 | 94 |
| Lillee | 23 | 6 | 73 | 2 | 12 | 2 | 25 | 2 | 6th | 205 | 162 | – | 94 |
| Thomson | 21 | 5 | 59 | 3 | 17·5 | 3 | 46 | 6 | 7th | 228 | 168 | – | 115 |
| Walker | 24·5 | 2 | 73 | 4 | 9 | 4 | 32 | 0 | 8th | 229 | 226 | – | 162 |
| Walters | 6 | 1 | 18 | 1 | 2 | 2 | 0 | 0 | 9th | 257 | 248 | – | 163 |
| Jenner | 6 | 1 | 24 | 0 | 16 | 5 | 45 | 2 | 10th | 309 | 265 | – | 166 |

Umpires: T.F. Brooks and R.C. Bailhache.

Test No. 751/216

# AUSTRALIA v ENGLAND 1974–75 (2nd Test)

Played at W.A.C.A. Ground, Perth, on 13, 14, 15, 17 December.
Toss: Australia.   Result: AUSTRALIA won by nine wickets.
Debuts: Nil.

Australia's first win against England in Perth was gained with a day and 50 minutes to spare. Hand fractures sustained by Amiss and Edrich in the first Test resulted in Cowdrey making his first Test appearance since June 1971 just four days after arriving in Australia. This was his sixth tour of that continent, equalling the record of J. Briggs. Walters scored 100 runs between tea and the close of play on the second day; he took his score to 103* with a six off the last ball of the session. G.S. Chappell set the present record (seven) for the most catches by a non-wicket-keeper in a Test match. He was the third after S.J.E. Loxton and R.N. Harvey to hold four in an England innings in this series. Lloyd retired at 52 for 0 in the second innings, after being hit in the stomach by a ball from Thomson, and resumed at 106 for 2.

## ENGLAND

| | | | | |
|---|---|---|---|---|
| D. Lloyd | c G.S. Chappell b Thomson | 49 | c G.S. Chappell b Walker | 35 |
| B.W. Luckhurst | c Mallett b Walker | 27 | (7) c Mallett b Lillee | 23 |
| M.C. Cowdrey | b Thomson | 22 | (2) lbw b Thomson | 41 |
| A.W. Greig | c Mallett b Walker | 23 | c G.S. Chappell b Thomson | 32 |
| K.W.R. Fletcher | c Redpath b Lillee | 4 | c Marsh b Thomson | 0 |
| M.H. Denness* | c G.S. Chappell b Lillee | 2 | (3) c Redpath b Thomson | 20 |
| A.P.E. Knott† | c Redpath b Walters | 51 | (6) c G.S. Chappell b Lillee | 18 |
| F.J. Titmus | c Redpath b Walters | 10 | c G.S. Chappell b Mallett | 61 |
| C.M. Old | c G.S. Chappell b I.M. Chappell | 7 | c Thomson b Mallett | 43 |
| G.G. Arnold | run out | 1 | c Mallett b Thomson | 4 |
| R.G.D. Willis | not out | 4 | not out | 0 |
| Extras | (W 3, NB 5) | 8 | (LB 4, W 1, NB 11) | 16 |
| **Total** | | **208** | | **293** |

## AUSTRALIA

| | | | | |
|---|---|---|---|---|
| I.R. Redpath | st Knott b Titmus | 41 | not out | 12 |
| W.J. Edwards | c Lloyd b Greig | 30 | lbw b Arnold | 0 |
| I.M. Chappell* | c Knott b Arnold | 25 | not out | 11 |
| G.S. Chappell | c Greig b Willis | 62 | | |
| R. Edwards | b Arnold | 115 | | |
| K.D. Walters | c Fletcher b Willis | 103 | | |
| R.W. Marsh† | c Lloyd b Titmus | 41 | | |
| M.H.N. Walker | c Knott b Old | 19 | | |
| D.K. Lillee | b Old | 11 | | |
| A.A. Mallett | c Knott b Old | 0 | | |
| J.R. Thomson | not out | 11 | | |
| Extras | (B 7, LB 14, NB 2) | 23 | | |
| **Total** | | **481** | (1 wicket) | **23** |

| AUSTRALIA | O | M | R | W | O | M | R | W | FALL OF WICKETS | | | | |
|---|---|---|---|---|---|---|---|---|---|---|---|---|---|
| Lillee | 16 | 4 | 48 | 2 | 22 | 5 | 59 | 2 | | E | A | E | A |
| Thomson | 15 | 6 | 45 | 2 | 25 | 4 | 93 | 5 | Wkt | 1st | 1st | 2nd | 2nd |
| Walker | 20 | 5 | 49 | 2 | 24 | 7 | 76 | 1 | 1st | 44 | 64 | 62 | 4 |
| Mallett | 10 | 3 | 35 | 0 | 11·1 | 4 | 32 | 2 | 2nd | 99 | 101 | 106 | – |
| Walters | 2·3 | 0 | 13 | 2 | 9 | 4 | 17 | 0 | 3rd | 119 | 113 | 124 | – |
| I.M. Chappell | 2 | 0 | 10 | 1 | | | | | 4th | 128 | 192 | 124 | – |
| | | | | | | | | | 5th | 132 | 362 | 154 | – |
| ENGLAND | | | | | | | | | 6th | 132 | 416 | 156 | – |
| Willis | 22 | 0 | 91 | 2 | 2 | 0 | 8 | 0 | 7th | 194 | 449 | 219 | – |
| Arnold | 27 | 1 | 129 | 2 | 1·7 | 0 | 15 | 1 | 8th | 201 | 462 | 285 | – |
| Old | 22·6 | 3 | 85 | 3 | | | | | 9th | 202 | 462 | 293 | – |
| Greig | 9 | 0 | 69 | 1 | | | | | 10th | 208 | 481 | 293 | – |
| Titmus | 28 | 3 | 84 | 2 | | | | | | | | | |

Umpires: T.F. Brooks and R.C. Bailhache.

Test No. 752/217

# AUSTRALIA v ENGLAND 1974–75 (3rd Test)

Played at Melbourne Cricket Ground on 26, 27, 28, 30, 31 December.
Toss: Australia.   Result: MATCH DRAWN.
Debuts: Nil.

Australia, needing to score 246 runs to win, were 4 for no wicket when the last day began. Amiss took his aggregate of runs in Test cricket in 1974 to 1,379 – just two runs short of the record for a calendar year which R.B. Simpson had set in 1964. Hendrick damaged a hamstring muscle and was unable to complete his third over.

### ENGLAND

| | | | | |
|---|---|---|---|---|
| D.L. Amiss | c Walters b Lillee | 4 | c I.M. Chappell b Mallett | 90 |
| D. Lloyd | c Mallett b Thomson | 14 | c and b Mallett | 44 |
| M.C. Cowdrey | lbw b Thomson | 35 | c G.S. Chappell b Lillee | 8 |
| J.H. Edrich | c Marsh b Mallett | 49 | c Marsh b Thomson | 4 |
| M.H. Denness* | c Marsh b Mallett | 8 | c I.M. Chappell b Thomson | 2 |
| A.W. Greig | run out | 28 | c G.S. Chappell b Lillee | 60 |
| A.P.E. Knott† | b Thomson | 52 | c Marsh b Thomson | 4 |
| F.J. Titmus | c Mallett b Lillee | 10 | b Mallett | 0 |
| D.L. Underwood | c Marsh b Walker | 9 | c I.M. Chappell b Mallett | 4 |
| R.G.D. Willis | c Walters b Thomson | 13 | b Thomson | 15 |
| M. Hendrick | not out | 8 | not out | 0 |
| Extras | (LB 2, W 1, NB 9) | 12 | (B 2, LB 9, W 2) | 13 |
| **Total** | | **242** | | **244** |

### AUSTRALIA

| | | | | |
|---|---|---|---|---|
| I.R. Redpath | c Knott b Greig | 55 | run out | 39 |
| W.J. Edwards | c Denness b Willis | 29 | lbw b Greig | 0 |
| G.S. Chappell | c Greig b Willis | 2 | (4) lbw b Titmus | 61 |
| R. Edwards | c Cowdrey b Titmus | 1 | (5) c Lloyd b Titmus | 10 |
| K.D. Walters | c Lloyd b Greig | 36 | (6) c Denness b Greig | 32 |
| I.M. Chappell* | lbw b Willis | 36 | (3) lbw b Willis | 0 |
| R.W. Marsh† | c Knott b Titmus | 44 | c Knott b Greig | 40 |
| M.H.N. Walker | c Knott b Willis | 30 | not out | 23 |
| D.K. Lillee | not out | 2 | c Denness b Greig | 14 |
| A.A. Mallett | run out | 0 | not out | 0 |
| J.R. Thomson | b Willis | 2 | | |
| Extras | (B 2, LB 2) | 4 | (B 6, LB 9, NB 4) | 19 |
| **Total** | | **241** | (8 wickets) | **238** |

| AUSTRALIA | O | M | R | W | O | M | R | W | | FALL OF WICKETS | | | |
|---|---|---|---|---|---|---|---|---|---|---|---|---|---|
| | | | | | | | | | | E | A | E | A |
| Lillee | 20 | 2 | 70 | 2 | 17 | 3 | 55 | 2 | Wkt | 1st | 1st | 2nd | 2nd |
| Thomson | 22·4 | 4 | 72 | 4 | 17 | 1 | 71 | 4 | 1st | 4 | 65 | 115 | 4 |
| Walker | 24 | 10 | 36 | 1 | 11 | 0 | 45 | 0 | 2nd | 34 | 67 | 134 | 5 |
| Walters | 7 | 2 | 15 | 0 | | | | | 3rd | 110 | 68 | 152 | 106 |
| Mallett | 15 | 3 | 37 | 2 | 24 | 6 | 60 | 4 | 4th | 110 | 121 | 156 | 120 |
| ENGLAND | | | | | | | | | 5th | 141 | 126 | 158 | 121 |
| Willis | 21·7 | 4 | 61 | 5 | 14 | 2 | 56 | 1 | 6th | 157 | 173 | 165 | 171 |
| Hendrick | 2·6 | 1 | 8 | 0 | | | | | 7th | 176 | 237 | 178 | 208 |
| Underwood | 22 | 6 | 62 | 0 | 19 | 7 | 43 | 0 | 8th | 213 | 237 | 182 | 235 |
| Greig | 24 | 2 | 63 | 2 | 18 | 2 | 56 | 4 | 9th | 232 | 238 | 238 | – |
| Titmus | 22 | 11 | 43 | 2 | 29 | 10 | 64 | 2 | 10th | 242 | 241 | 244 | – |

Umpires: T.F. Brooks and R.C. Bailhache.

Test No. 753/218

# AUSTRALIA v ENGLAND 1974–75 (4th Test)

Played at Sydney Cricket Ground on 4, 5, 6, 8, 9 January.
Toss: Australia. Result: AUSTRALIA won by 171 runs.
Debuts: Australia – R.B. McCosker.

With 4·3 of the mandatory last 15 overs to spare, Mallett had Arnold caught at short-leg to regain the Ashes which had been lost three years and 326 days previously. It was Mallett's 100th wicket in 23 Tests. Arnold took his 100th wicket in 29 Tests when he dismissed G.S. Chappell. The partnership of 220 between Redpath and G.S. Chappell is a record for the second wicket against England in Australia. In the second innings Edrich retired at 70 for 2 after being hit in the ribs by his first ball (from Lillee) and he resumed at 156 for 6.

## AUSTRALIA

| | | | | |
|---|---|---|---|---|
| I.R. Redpath | hit wkt b Titmus | 33 | c sub (C.M. Old) b Underwood | 105 |
| R.B. McCosker | c Knott b Greig | 80 | | |
| I.M. Chappell* | c Knott b Arnold | 53 | (2) c Lloyd b Willis | 5 |
| G.S. Chappell | c Greig b Arnold | 84 | (3) c Lloyd b Arnold | 144 |
| R. Edwards | b Greig | 15 | not out | 17 |
| K.D. Walters | lbw b Arnold | 1 | (4) b Underwood | 5 |
| R.W. Marsh† | b Greig | 30 | (6) not out | 7 |
| M.H.N. Walker | c Greig b Arnold | 30 | | |
| D.K. Lillee | b Arnold | 8 | | |
| A.A. Mallett | lbw b Greig | 31 | | |
| J.R. Thomson | not out | 24 | | |
| Extras | (LB 4, W 1, NB 11) | 16 | (LB 2, W 1, NB 3) | 6 |
| **Total** | | **405** | (4 wickets declared) | **289** |

## ENGLAND

| | | | | |
|---|---|---|---|---|
| D.L. Amiss | c Mallett b Walker | 12 | c Marsh b Lillee | 37 |
| D. Lloyd | c Thomson b Lillee | 19 | c G.S. Chappell b Thomson | 26 |
| M.C. Cowdrey | c McCosker b Thomson | 22 | c I.M. Chappell b Walker | 1 |
| J.H. Edrich* | c Marsh b Walters | 50 | not out | 33 |
| K.W.R. Fletcher | c Redpath b Walker | 24 | c Redpath b Thomson | 11 |
| A.W. Greig | c G.S. Chappell b Thomson | 9 | st Marsh b Mallett | 54 |
| A.P.E. Knott† | b Thomson | 82 | c Redpath b Mallett | 10 |
| F.J. Titmus | c Marsh b Walters | 22 | c Thomson b Mallett | 4 |
| D.L. Underwood | c Walker b Lillee | 27 | c and b Walker | 5 |
| R.G.D. Willis | b Thomson | 2 | b Lillee | 12 |
| G.G. Arnold | not out | 3 | c G.S. Chappell b Mallett | 14 |
| Extras | (B 15, LB 7, W 1) | 23 | (B 13, LB 3, NB 5) | 21 |
| **Total** | | **295** | | **228** |

| ENGLAND | O | M | R | W | O | M | R | W | | FALL OF WICKETS | | | |
|---|---|---|---|---|---|---|---|---|---|---|---|---|---|
| Willis | 18 | 2 | 80 | 0 | 11 | 1 | 52 | 1 | | A | E | A | E |
| Arnold | 29 | 7 | 86 | 5 | 22 | 3 | 78 | 1 | Wkt | 1st | 1st | 2nd | 2nd |
| Greig | 22·7 | 2 | 104 | 4 | 12 | 1 | 64 | 0 | 1st | 96 | 36 | 15 | 68 |
| Underwood | 13 | 3 | 54 | 0 | 12 | 1 | 65 | 2 | 2nd | 142 | 46 | 235 | 70 |
| Titmus | 16 | 2 | 65 | 1 | 7·3 | 2 | 24 | 0 | 3rd | 199 | 69 | 242 | 74 |
| | | | | | | | | | 4th | 251 | 108 | 280 | 103 |
| AUSTRALIA | | | | | | | | | 5th | 255 | 123 | – | 136 |
| Lillee | 19·1 | 2 | 66 | 2 | 21 | 5 | 65 | 2 | 6th | 305 | 180 | – | 156 |
| Thomson | 19 | 3 | 74 | 4 | 23 | 7 | 74 | 2 | 7th | 310 | 240 | – | 158 |
| Walker | 23 | 2 | 77 | 2 | 16 | 5 | 46 | 2 | 8th | 332 | 273 | – | 175 |
| Mallett | 1 | 0 | 8 | 0 | 16·5 | 9 | 21 | 4 | 9th | 368 | 285 | – | 201 |
| Walters | 7 | 2 | 26 | 2 | | | | | 10th | 405 | 295 | – | 228 |
| I.M. Chappell | 4 | 0 | 21 | 0 | 3 | 2 | 1 | 0 | | | | | |

Umpires: T.F. Brooks and R.C. Bailhache.

Test No. 754/219

## AUSTRALIA v ENGLAND 1974–75 (5th Test)

Played at Adelaide Oval on 25 (*no play*), 26, 27, 29, 30 January.
Toss: England.   Result: AUSTRALIA won by 163 runs.
Debuts: Nil.

Australia's fourth victory in the rubber was gained with two hours and 40 minutes to spare, despite the loss of the first day after overnight rain had seeped under the covers. Knott became the second wicket-keeper after T.G. Evans to make 200 dismissals in Test cricket, when he caught I.M. Chappell in the first innings. Later Knott scored the second hundred by a wicket-keeper in this series, L.E.G. Ames having scored the first in 1934 (*Test No. 234*). Underwood's match analysis of 11 for 215 was England's best in Australia since 1928–29. Thomson tore fibres in his right shoulder when playing tennis on the rest day and was unable to bowl in the second innings. His total of 33 wickets in the rubber was Australia's third-highest in this series (A.A. Mailey 36 in 1920-21, G. Giffen 34 in 1894-95). Cowdrey's 42nd appearance against Australia beat the record previously held jointly by W. Rhodes and J.B. Hobbs.

### AUSTRALIA

| | | | | | |
|---|---|---|---|---|---|
| I.R. Redpath | c Greig b Underwood | 21 | b Underwood | | 52 |
| R.B. McCosker | c Cowdrey b Underwood | 35 | c Knott b Arnold | | 11 |
| I.M. Chappell* | c Knott b Underwood | 0 | c Knott b Underwood | | 41 |
| G.S. Chappell | lbw b Underwood | 5 | c Greig b Underwood | | 18 |
| K.D. Walters | c Willis b Underwood | 55 | not out | | 71 |
| R.W. Marsh† | c Greig b Underwood | 6 | c Greig b Underwood | | 55 |
| T.J. Jenner | b Underwood | 74 | not out | | 14 |
| M.H.N. Walker | run out | 41 | | | |
| D.K. Lillee | b Willis | 26 | | | |
| A.A. Mallett | not out | 23 | | | |
| J.R. Thomson | b Arnold | 5 | | | |
| Extras | (B 4, LB 4, NB 5) | 13 | (LB 4, NB 6) | | 10 |
| **Total** | | **304** | (5 wickets declared) | | **272** |

### ENGLAND

| | | | | | |
|---|---|---|---|---|---|
| D.L. Amiss | c I.M. Chappell b Lillee | 0 | c Marsh b Lillee | | 0 |
| D. Lloyd | c Marsh b Lillee | 4 | c Walters b Walker | | 5 |
| M.C. Cowdrey | c Walker b Thomson | 26 | c Mallett b Lillee | | 3 |
| M.H. Denness* | c Marsh b Thomson | 51 | c Jenner b Lillee | | 14 |
| K.W.R. Fletcher | c I.M. Chappell b Thomson | 40 | lbw b Lillee | | 63 |
| A.W. Greig | c Marsh b Lille | 19 | lbw b Walker | | 20 |
| A.P.E. Knott† | c Lillee b Mallett | 5 | not out | | 106 |
| F.J. Titmus | c G.S. Chappell b Mallett | 11 | lbw b Jenner | | 20 |
| D.L. Underwood | c Lillee b Mallett | 0 | c I.M. Chappell b Mallett | | 0 |
| G.G. Arnold | b Lillee | 0 | b Mallett | | 0 |
| R.G.D. Willis | not out | 11 | b Walker | | 3 |
| Extras | (LB 2, NB 3) | 5 | (B 3, LB 3, NB 1) | | 7 |
| **Total** | | **172** | | | **241** |

| ENGLAND | O | M | R | W | O | M | R | W |
|---|---|---|---|---|---|---|---|---|
| Willis | 10 | 0 | 46 | 1 | 5 | 0 | 27 | 0 |
| Arnold | 12·2 | 3 | 42 | 1 | 20 | 1 | 71 | 1 |
| Underwood | 29 | 3 | 113 | 7 | 26 | 5 | 102 | 4 |
| Greig | 10 | 0 | 63 | 0 | 2 | 0 | 9 | 0 |
| Titmus | 7 | 1 | 27 | 0 | 13 | 1 | 53 | 0 |
| AUSTRALIA | | | | | | | | |
| Lillee | 12·5 | 2 | 49 | 4 | 14 | 3 | 69 | 4 |
| Thomson | 15 | 1 | 58 | 3 | | | | |
| Walker | 5 | 1 | 18 | 0 | 20 | 3 | 89 | 3 |
| Jenner | 5 | 0 | 28 | 0 | 15 | 4 | 39 | 1 |
| Mallett | 9 | 4 | 14 | 3 | 25 | 10 | 36 | 2 |
| I.M. Chappell | | | | | 1 | 0 | 1 | 0 |

FALL OF WICKETS

| | A | E | A | E |
|---|---|---|---|---|
| Wkt | 1st | 1st | 2nd | 2nd |
| 1st | 52 | 2 | 16 | 0 |
| 2nd | 52 | 19 | 92 | 8 |
| 3rd | 58 | 66 | 128 | 10 |
| 4th | 77 | 90 | 133 | 33 |
| 5th | 84 | 130 | 245 | 76 |
| 6th | 164 | 147 | – | 144 |
| 7th | 241 | 155 | – | 212 |
| 8th | 259 | 156 | – | 213 |
| 9th | 295 | 161 | – | 217 |
| 10th | 304 | 172 | – | 241 |

Umpires: T.F. Brooks and R.C. Bailhache.

Test No. 755/220

## AUSTRALIA v ENGLAND 1974–75 (6th Test)

Played at Melbourne Cricket Ground on 8, 9, 10, 12, 13 February.
Toss: Australia.   Result: ENGLAND won by an innings and 4 runs.
Debuts: Nil.

England gained their solitary success in this rubber 35 minutes after lunch on the the fifth day. Denness made the highest score by an England captain in Australia, his 188 improving upon A.E. Stoddart's 173 in 1894–95 (*Test No. 43*). Lillee bruised his right foot and left the field after bowling six overs. In the last of his record 114 Test appearances, Cowdrey extended his aggregate to 7,624; only G. St A. Sobers (8,032) has scored more runs in official Tests. His total of 22 hundreds has been exceeded by D.G. Bradman (29) and Sobers (26), and equalled by W.R. Hammond. Cowdrey's total of 120 catches remains the record by a fielder in Test cricket.

### AUSTRALIA

| | | | | | |
|---|---|---|---|---|---|
| I.R. Redpath | c Greig b Lever | 1 | c Amiss b Greig | | 83 |
| R.B. McCosker | c Greig b Lever | 0 | c Cowdrey b Arnold | | 76 |
| I.M. Chappell* | c Knott b Old | 65 | c Knott b Greig | | 50 |
| G.S. Chappell | c Denness b Lever | 1 | b Lever | | 102 |
| R. Edwards | c Amiss b Lever | 0 | c Knott b Arnold | | 18 |
| K.D. Walters | c Edrich b Old | 12 | b Arnold | | 3 |
| R.W. Marsh† | b Old | 29 | c Denness b Lever | | 1 |
| M.H.N. Walker | not out | 20 | c and b Greig | | 17 |
| D.K. Lillee | c Knott b Lever | 12 | (11) not out | | 0 |
| A.A. Mallett | b Lever | 7 | (9) c Edrich b Greig | | 0 |
| G. Dymock | c Knott b Greig | 0 | (10) c Knott b Lever | | 0 |
| Extras | (B 2, LB 1, NB 2) | 5 | (B 9, LB 5, W 4, NB 5) | | 23 |
| **Total** | | **152** | | | **373** |

### ENGLAND

| | | |
|---|---|---|
| D.L. Amiss | lbw b Lillee | 0 |
| M.C. Cowdrey | c Marsh b Walker | 7 |
| J.H. Edrich | c I.M. Chappell b Walker | 70 |
| M.H. Denness* | c and b Walker | 188 |
| K.W.R. Fletcher | c Redpath b Walker | 146 |
| A.W. Greig | c sub (T.J. Jenner) b Walker | 89 |
| A.P.E. Knott† | c Marsh b Walker | 5 |
| C.M. Old | b Dymock | 0 |
| D.L. Underwood | b Walker | 11 |
| G.G. Arnold | c Marsh b Walker | 0 |
| P. Lever | not out | 6 |
| Extras | (B 4, LB 2, NB 1) | 7 |
| **Total** | | **529** |

| ENGLAND | O | M | R | W | O | M | R | W | FALL OF WICKETS | | | |
|---|---|---|---|---|---|---|---|---|---|---|---|---|
| Arnold | 6 | 2 | 24 | 0 | 23 | 6 | 83 | 3 | | A | E | A |
| Lever | 11 | 2 | 38 | 6 | 16 | 1 | 65 | 3 | Wkt | 1st | 1st | 2nd |
| Old | 11 | 0 | 50 | 3 | 18 | 1 | 75 | 0 | 1st | 0 | 4 | 111 |
| Greig | 8.7 | 1 | 35 | 1 | 31.7 | 7 | 88 | 4 | 2nd | 5 | 18 | 215 |
| Underwood | | | | | 18 | 5 | 39 | 0 | 3rd | 19 | 167 | 248 |
| | | | | | | | | | 4th | 23 | 359 | 289 |
| AUSTRALIA | | | | | | | | | 5th | 50 | 507 | 297 |
| Lillee | 6 | 2 | 17 | 1 | | | | | 6th | 104 | 507 | 306 |
| Walker | 42.2 | 7 | 143 | 8 | | | | | 7th | 115 | 508 | 367 |
| Dymock | 39 | 6 | 130 | 1 | | | | | 8th | 141 | 514 | 373 |
| Walters | 23 | 3 | 86 | 0 | | | | | 9th | 149 | 514 | 373 |
| Mallett | 29 | 8 | 96 | 0 | | | | | 10th | 152 | 529 | 373 |
| I.M. Chappell | 12 | 1 | 50 | 0 | | | | | | | | |

Umpires: T.F. Brooks and R.C. Bailhache.

# STATISTICAL SUMMARY

| Year | | Versus | M | I | NO |
|---|---|---|---|---|---|
| 1954/55 | | Australia | 5 | 9 | 0 |
| 1955 | | New Zealand | 2 | 3 | 1 |
| | | | **7** | **12** | **1** |
| 1955 | H | South Africa | 1 | 2 | 0 |
| | | | **8** | **14** | **1** |
| 1956 | H | Australia | 5 | 8 | 0 |
| | | | **13** | **22** | **1** |
| 1956/57 | | South Africa | 5 | 10 | 0 |
| | | | **18** | **32** | **1** |
| 1957 | H | West Indies | 5 | 6 | 0 |
| | | | **23** | **38** | **1** |
| 1958 | H | New Zealand | 4 | 4 | 0 |
| | | | **27** | **42** | **1** |
| 1958/59 | | Australia | 5 | 10 | 1 |
| | | | **32** | **52** | **2** |
| 1959 | | New Zealand | 2 | 2 | 0 |
| | | | **34** | **54** | **2** |
| 1959 | H | India | 5 | 7 | 1 |
| | | | **39** | **61** | **3** |
| 1959/60 | | West Indies | 5 | 10 | 1 |
| | | | **44** | **71** | **4** |
| 1960 | H | South Africa | 5 | 9 | 0 |
| | | | **49** | **80** | **4** |
| 1961 | H | Australia | 4 | 8 | 0 |
| | | | **53** | **88** | **4** |
| 1962 | H | Pakistan | 4 | 5 | 0 |
| | | | **57** | **93** | **4** |

| Runs | HS | Av'ge | 100 | 50 | Ct |
|---|---|---|---|---|---|
| 319 | 102 | 35.44 | 1 | 2 | 4 |
| 64 | 42 | 32.00 | 0 | 0 | 1 |
| **383** | **102** | **34.82** | **1** | **2** | **5** |
| 51 | 50 | 25.50 | 0 | 1 | 0 |
| **434** | **102** | **33.38** | **1** | **3** | **5** |
| 244 | 81 | 30.50 | 0 | 2 | 3 |
| **678** | **102** | **32.29** | **1** | **5** | **8** |
| 331 | 101 | 33.10 | 1 | 3 | 10 |
| **1009** | **102** | **32.55** | **2** | **8** | **18** |
| 435 | 154 | 72.50 | 2 | 2 | 8 |
| **1444** | **154** | **39.01** | **4** | **10** | **26** |
| 241 | 81 | 60.25 | 0 | 3 | 7 |
| **1685** | **154** | **41.10** | **4** | **13** | **33** |
| 391 | 100* | 43.44 | 1 | 1 | 6 |
| **2076** | **154** | **41.52** | **5** | **14** | **39** |
| 20 | 15 | 10.00 | 0 | 0 | 2 |
| **2096** | **154** | **40.31** | **5** | **14** | **41** |
| 344 | 160 | 57.33 | 1 | 2 | 7 |
| **2440** | **160** | **42.07** | **6** | **16** | **48** |
| 491 | 119 | 54.55 | 2 | 2 | 1 |
| **2931** | **160** | **43.75** | **8** | **18** | **49** |
| 312 | 155 | 34.66 | 1 | 1 | 7 |
| **3243** | **160** | **42.67** | **9** | **19** | **56** |
| 168 | 93 | 21.00 | 0 | 1 | 4 |
| **3411** | **160** | **40.61** | **9** | **20** | **60** |
| 409 | 182 | 81.80 | 2 | 0 | 9 |
| **3820** | **182** | **42.92** | **11** | **20** | **69** |

| Year | | Versus | M | I | NO |
|---|---|---|---|---|---|
| 1962/63 | | Australia | 5 | 10 | 1 |
| | | | **62** | **103** | **5** |
| 1963 | | New Zealand | 3 | 4 | 2 |
| | | | **65** | **107** | **7** |
| 1963 | H | West Indies | 2 | 4 | 1 |
| | | | **67** | **111** | **8** |
| 1963/64 | | India | 3 | 4 | 1 |
| | | | **70** | **115** | **9** |
| 1964 | H | Australia | 3 | 5 | 1 |
| | | | **73** | **120** | **10** |
| 1965 | H | New Zealand | 3 | 4 | 1 |
| | | | **76** | **124** | **11** |
| 1965 | H | South Africa | 3 | 6 | 1 |
| | | | **79** | **130** | **12** |
| 1965/66 | | Australia | 4 | 6 | 1 |
| | | | **83** | **136** | **13** |
| 1966 | | New Zealand | 3 | 5 | 1 |
| | | | **86** | **141** | **14** |
| 1966 | H | West Indies | 4 | 8 | 0 |
| | | | **90** | **149** | **14** |
| 1967 | H | Pakistan | 2 | 4 | 1 |
| | | | **92** | **153** | **15** |
| 1967/68 | | West Indies | 5 | 8 | 0 |
| | | | **97** | **161** | **15** |
| 1968 | H | Australia | 4 | 6 | 0 |
| | | | **101** | **167** | **15** |
| 1968/69 | | Pakistan | 3 | 4 | 0 |
| | | | **104** | **171** | **15** |
| 1970/71 | | Australia | 3 | 4 | 0 |
| | | | **107** | **175** | **15** |
| 1971 | | New Zealand | 1 | 2 | 0 |
| | | | **108** | **177** | **15** |
| 1971 | H | Pakistan | 1 | 2 | 0 |
| | | | **109** | **179** | **15** |
| 1974/75 | | Australia | 5 | 9 | 0 |
| | | | **114** | **188** | **15** |

| Runs | HS | Av'ge | 100 | 50 | Ct |
|---|---|---|---|---|---|
| 394 | 113 | 43.77 | 1 | 3 | 6 |
| **4214** | **182** | **43.00** | **12** | **23** | **75** |
| 292 | 128* | 146.00 | 1 | 1 | 1 |
| **4506** | **182** | **45.06** | **13** | **24** | **76** |
| 39 | 19* | 13.00 | 0 | 0 | 6 |
| **4545** | **182** | **44.13** | **13** | **24** | **82** |
| 309 | 151 | 103.00 | 2 | 0 | 4 |
| **4854** | **182** | **45.79** | **15** | **24** | **86** |
| 188 | 93* | 47.00 | 0 | 1 | 2 |
| **5042** | **182** | **45.87** | **15** | **25** | **88** |
| 221 | 119 | 73.66 | 1 | 1 | 2 |
| **5263** | **182** | **46.58** | **16** | **26** | **90** |
| 327 | 105 | 65.40 | 1 | 2 | 5 |
| **5590** | **182** | **47.37** | **17** | **28** | **95** |
| 267 | 104 | 53.40 | 1 | 1 | 5 |
| **5857** | **182** | **47.62** | **18** | **29** | **100** |
| 196 | 89* | 49.00 | 0 | 2 | 2 |
| **6053** | **182** | **47.66** | **18** | **31** | **102** |
| 252 | 96 | 31.50 | 0 | 2 | 3 |
| **6305** | **182** | **46.70** | **18** | **33** | **105** |
| 41 | 16 | 13.66 | 0 | 0 | 1 |
| **6346** | **182** | **45.99** | **18** | **33** | **106** |
| 534 | 148 | 66.75 | 2 | 4 | 3 |
| **6880** | **182** | **47.12** | **20** | **37** | **109** |
| 215 | 104 | 35.83 | 1 | 0 | 4 |
| **7095** | **182** | **46.68** | **21** | **37** | **113** |
| 133 | 100 | 33.25 | 1 | 0 | 0 |
| **7228** | **182** | **46.33** | **22** | **37** | **113** |
| 82 | 40 | 20.50 | 0 | 0 | 3 |
| **7310** | **182** | **45.69** | **22** | **37** | **116** |
| 99 | 54 | 49.50 | 0 | 1 | 0 |
| **7409** | **182** | **45.73** | **22** | **38** | **116** |
| 50 | 34 | 25.00 | 0 | 0 | 1 |
| **7459** | **182** | **45.48** | **22** | **38** | **117** |
| 165 | 41 | 18.33 | 0 | 0 | 3 |
| **7624** | **182** | **44.06** | **22** | **38** | **120** |

# EPILOGUE

Colin Cowdrey died on Tuesday 5 December 2000.

The former Prime Minister John Major disclosed that Cowdrey had been a key figure in the return of South Africa to Test cricket after 22 years in the wilderness. Major described him as 'the great enabler'. Cowdrey was the incoming Chairman of the International Cricket Council (ICC) the world governing body, when Nelson Mandela was released in February 1990. When Major succeeded Margaret Thatcher in November 1990 Cowdrey seized the chance when visiting the Prime Minister in the following year. The first Test match was symbolically against the West Indies at Bridgetown in April 1992. The game was a triumph for Cowdrey in his penultimate year as ICC President.

Cowdrey had retired in 1975.

He was President of the MCC in 1987 the bi-centenary of the club. Sadly it was not a happy year. The Secretary, J A Bailey, the foremost paid official in world cricket, retired early. A packed AGM ended without the accounts having been approved necessitating a special general meeting some weeks later. Cowdrey's good intentions were never in doubt but by the end of August he was in hospital for a heart bypass operation.

He had travelled many thousands of miles as a mediator and endangered what had never been a strong constitution. In 1992 he was knighted in the New Year Honours. In 1997 Prime Minister Major sent him to the House of Lords as a spokesman on sporting matters.

He was President of Lord's Taverners from 1995 to 1997, President of the Association of Cricket Umpires and Scorers, and President of Kent CCC.

In 2000 Colin was a member of Jeremy Cowdrey's XI v. Leatherhead at their Fetcham Grove Ground on 23rd July. Chris and Graham were also in the team. The great man's innings was a painstaking four singles in a partnership of 57 with his son Graham which lasted for thirty-six minutes. During the time that the Cowdrey XI were on the field, Colin made a short visit to the slips cordon for about four overs before he thought it was too cold and took to the warmth of the pavilion. Several of his grandsons were present and all lined up to shake his hand as he walked from the field of play for the last time. As Derek Baker, the Club's Secretary, said: "Quite moving."

The highlight of that year, the start of Canterbury Week, was marred by Cowdrey suffering a stroke from which he was making a slow but steady recovery when he died at home of a heart attack. May he rest in peace.

# INDEX

Adcock, N    92, 93
Allen, D    129, 130
Allen, Gubby    77
Ames, L E G    185, 201, 222
Amiss, D    174, 221
Appleyard, R    17
Archer, R    15, 36
Asgarali, N R    50
Asif Iqbal    124

Baker, Derek    235
Bailey, J A    234
Bailey, Trevor    14, 43, 64
Ballistic Missile Early Warning System    130
Barber, Bob    162, 174
Barrington, K    77, 84, 118, 124, 136, 144, 152, 157, 162
'Bat & Ball' Ground, Gravesend    14
BBC Television    130
BBC's *The 60s Video*    130
Benaud, R    15, 34, 36, 65, 104, 117, 143
Black, Michael    145
Bland, Colin    157
Bob    193
Booth, B    117
Boycott, G    143, 145, 173, 181, 186, 192
Bradman, Don    12, 35, 75, 94, 95
Brearley, M    146, 173

Brown, D    201
Burge, P    118, 144
Burgess, M    214
Butcher, B    129, 185

Carlstein, P    93
Cartwright, T    194
Chappell, Greg    222
Chappell, Ian    222
Chapple, M E    169
Close, B    104, 174, 181
Compton, D C S    36, 43, 146
Contractor, N    75
Corling, G    144
Cowdrey, Chris    234
Cowdrey, Ernest    13
Cowdrey, Graham    235
Cowdrey, Jeremy    234
Cowper, Bob    162
Crystal Palace    185
Cunis, R    214

*Daily Telegraph*    200, 223
Davidson, A    34, 46, 104, 117
Denness, Mike    221, 222
Dexter, E R    72, 84, 86, 93, 102, 104, 110, 117, 118, 129, 136, 144
D'Oliveira, B    185, 193, 194
D'Souza, A    110
Durani, S    136

236

# INDEX

Edrich, John  143, 153, 192, 200, 221, 222
Edrich, W J  17
Elliott, C  92
Endean, W R  43, 44
Evans, T G  43, 50, 58, 77, 222

Favell, L  14
Fazal Mahmood  111
Fellows-Smith, J P  93
Fletcher, Keith  206
Fyson, Miss Marjory E  200

Ghulam Ilahi  201
Gibbs, L  129, 173
Goddard, T  43, 93, 95
Graveney, T  50, 110, 173, 174, 192, 200, 201
Greenhough, T  77
Griffin, G  92, 93
Griffith, C  129, 174
Grout, W  143, 144, 162
Gupte, S  77

Hall, W  84, 86, 129, 130, 174
Hammond, W R  145, 169, 192
Hanumant Singh  136
Harvey Neil  36, 64, 118, 143, 145
Hawke, N  144, 145
Heine, P  43
Hennessy, Professor Peter  130
Higgs, K  174
Hobbs, Jack  145, 222
Holford, D  174
Howard, Geoffrey  77
Humphreys, John  104
Hunte, Conrad  85
Hutton, Len  14, 17, 24, 35, 44, 145

Illingworth, Ray  193, 206
Imtiaz Ahmed  111

Insole, D  44
Intikhab Alam  124

Jarman, B  193
Johnson, Ian  14, 17, 34, 36
Johnston, Brian  201

Kanhai, R  85, 86
Kingston, Gayner  27
Kline, L  64
Knight, B  124, 136
Knott, Alan  186, 201, 214, 222

Laker, J C  35, 43, 50
Langley, G  34
Larter, J  111
Lawry, Bill  102, 162, 192
Leatherhead Cricket Club  234
Lillee, D  221
Lindwall, R  65
Lloyd, D  222
Loader, P  65
Lock, G A R  35, 72

Mackay, K  35, 102
Macmillan, Harold  75
Mainwaring, Brian  200
Major, John  234
Mallett, A  194
Mandela, Nelson  234
May, P B H  15, 35, 50, 51, 57, 64, 72, 75, 77, 84, 85, 92, 102
McCosker, R  222
McGlew, J  92, 93
McKenzie, G  102, 117, 144
McLean, R  95
Milburn, C  173, 174, 192, 201
Miller, Keith  34, 36
Milton, A  57
Misson, F  102
Moir, A  72

Morris, Arthur  14, 17
Moss, A  92, 93
Motz, R  153
Murray, J  174, 200
Mushtaq Mohammad  110

Nadkarni, R  136
National Service  27
Nawab of Pataudi Jnr.  136
Northend Cricket Club  17

Oakman, Alan  35
O'Brien, E R  222
O'Linn, S  92
O'Neill, N  104, 117, 118

Parfitt, P  124, 136
Parks, J  86, 95, 137, 157, 185
Peebles, Ian  14
Petrie, E  72
Pollock, Graeme  157
Pollock, Peter  157
Pothecary, J  95
Pullar, G  84, 85, 95, 102, 110, 117, 118

Ramadhin, S  50, 51
Redpath, Ian  144, 192, 222
Reid, John  72, 124, 152
Rhodes, Wilf  222
Richardson, Peter  34, 35, 43, 44, 50, 51, 57, 66
Robins, Walter  84
Rorke, G  64, 65
Russell, Eric  162

Schweppes  50
Sharpe, P  143
Sheppard, Rev David  35, 50, 110, 117
Simpson, Bobby  117, 144, 162
Singh, C K  85

Smith, A C  124
Smith, Collie  50
Smith, M J K  84, 86, 136, 146, 162, 173
Snow, J  201
Sobers, G  84, 85, 86, 129, 173, 174, 186, 201
Statham, B  43, 65, 75, 92, 93, 95
St Nicholas Hospital, Plumstead  201
Stocks, Mary  27
Subba Row, R  86, 93, 102
Sunrise School for the Blind, Lahore  200
Swanton, E W  162
Swetman, Roy  64, 84
*Sydney Morning Herald*  222

Tayfield, H  27, 43, 44
Thatcher, Margaret  234
Thomson, Jeff  221, 222
Titmus, F  117, 143, 153
Trueman, Fred  50, 58, 72, 85, 102, 104, 117, 124, 144, 145, 153
Tyson, Frank  15, 17

Underwood, D  193

Van der Merwe, Peter  157
Vievers, T  144
Virgin, R  34
Vorster, B J  194

Walcott, C  50
Wardle, J  17
Washbrook, Cyril  35
Watson, C  84
Weekes, E  50
Wilmington Cricket Club  14
Wilson, J V  17
Woodcock, John  222
Woolley, F  118
Worrell, Frank  50, 84, 129